ADDING
TO A
HOUSE

Planning, Design & Construction

ADDING TO A HOUSE

Philip S. Wenz

The Taunton Press

COVER PHOTOGRAPH: BOB SWANSON

Taunton
BOOKS & VIDEOS
for fellow enthusiasts

©1995 by The Taunton Press, Inc.
All rights reserved.

First printing: 1995
Second printing: 1998

Printed in the United States of America

The Taunton Press, 63 South Main Street, PO Box 5506,
Newtown, CT 06470-5506
e-mail: tp@taunton.com

Distributed by Publishers Group West

Library of Congress Cataloging-in-Publication Data

Wenz, Philip S.
    Adding to a house : planning, design & construction /
Philip S. Wenz.
        p.   cm.
    Includes bibliographical references and index.
    ISBN 1-56158-072-4
    1. Buildings — Additions — Design and construction.   I. Title.
TH4816.2.W46   1995   95-22406
690'.837 — dc20   CIP

To my folks,
who got me started,

Martin, Katherine, Carolyn, Bea, Jim, Bill Skinkis and Bill Lowe,
who helped me learn,

and Sally and Baily,
whose love sustained me as I put this together.

CONTENTS

DESIGNING AND BUILDING 173

ACKNOWLEDGMENTS

Before thanking those people who helped me with the critical task of making the technical portions of this book as accurate as possible, I must write a brief disclaimer on their behalf. Although most of the structural and technical information was reviewed by others, the final responsibility for its accuracy is mine. (The reader is advised throughout the book to consult the appropriate experts on technical matters.)

If I have inadvertently misinterpreted the technical input of those professionals who have been kind enough to share their time and thoughts with me, it should not be taken as a reflection on their high level of expertise, dedication and enthusiasm. Their intent was to make this a better book and freely allow their knowledge, which in some cases can save lives and property, to become widely available. For this we may all thank them.

Special thanks go to the structural engineer, Joshua Kardon, who read and re-read my many drafts of chapters 7 and 8 and, with patience and humor, corrected my facts and assumptions along with a little of my grammar. Thanks also to the geotechnical engineer, Larry Karp, who reviewed the material on soils and foundations. Useful information about the history of balloon and platform framing and plywood sheathing was provided by John Rose, Senior Engineer with the American Plywood Association, Seattle, Washington, and representatives of the Western Wood Products Association, Portland, Oregon. I also want to acknowledge John Reed, the contractor, electrician, writer and teacher who read the electrical section; plumbing contractor Abe Bromberg for reading and making many useful suggestions on the plumbing section; Jeff Brown, the chief field inspector and estimator for Ceridono Engineered Heating of Berkeley, California, and Chris Ferre, a private energy consultant, for reviewing and contributing to the heating section. Finally, I wish to thank Bob Steel, the Chief of Codes and Inspections for the City of Berkeley, for reviewing all of Chapter 10.

INTRODUCTION

In recent years, the amount of money spent on remodeling houses has surpassed that spent on building them from scratch. Because of the high price of land, utility development and materials, the trend is likely to continue—especially since existing houses come with land, are already equipped with utilities and require far fewer materials to upgrade them than are needed to build a new house.

Exactly what percentage of remodels is addition work is not clear, but it is undoubtedly significant since a concurrent trend is that of population growth. Families are expanding at the same time that relatively fewer new houses are being built: Adding on has become big business.

Curiously, there are few books about adding on, or remodeling in general for that matter. Nor, to my knowledge, are these subjects systematically taught—if, indeed they are even mentioned—in architectural programs or construction technology schools. No doubt the reasons vary from the educators' bias toward new construction as an artistic medium to their ignorance of remodeling and adding on—particularly their lack of hands-on experience in the field.

For in building additions, as in no other aspect of construction, a thorough understanding of the way in which houses are put together is essential to designing competently. On the other hand, to discuss construction techniques without discussing the design and engineering theories that underlie them is to mislead the reader into believing that there are set ways of doing things and that construction methods are best learned by rote, not through an understanding of the processes that gave rise to them. Both ways of thinking are traps that limit the capabilities of design and construction professionals, no matter what their preferred field of endeavor. In keeping with the trend of separating the two fields, books that explain how a building is built and then show how to formulate an aesthetic and coherent design based on that information remain rare.

My purpose in writing this book, then, is twofold. First, I hope to consolidate in one volume some of the missing or scattered information and theory needed by architects, designer/builders, contractors, home owners or anyone else who is seriously interested in adding onto a house. Second, by covering both design and construction as a single, integrated field of knowledge, I want to help bridge the artificial chasm that has been allowed to develop between designers and builders to the detriment of both.

In my 16 years of teaching construction technology and design—and in this book—I have focused on discussing concepts or principles, rather than describing specific, step-by-step operations in detail. My reasoning is that every one of the thousands of projects built each year is different and each individual project, in turn, requires literally hundreds of operations, many of which are significantly modified versions of so-called "standard" procedures. Frequently, in fact, operations are invented on the spur of the moment to solve special, one-of-a-kind problems. It is impossible, then—particularly in remodeling—to cover even a small fraction of the special cases in a single volume.

What I have tried to do in this book is introduce some of the many design issues and technical problems encountered when designing and building additions and offer approaches to their solutions that you can apply as the individual situation demands. For example, instead of explaining how to install a header in detail, I have taken the approach that every installation will be different and discussed what a header is, why it is needed, various loading conditions under which it might have to perform and how to make sure those conditions are addressed.

Specific examples of construction techniques are given, of course, and procedures are outlined in a general way. But the underlying thrust is to try to get you to approach the problems the way a professional designer/builder might.

THE SCOPE OF THE BOOK

This book covers light-wood-frame houses only—specifically, balloon and platform frames. It does not discuss timber framing, geodesic domes, masonry construction or any of the many other types of houses that someone might wish to add onto.

The reasons are primarily quantitative. First, to attempt an educated guess, I would say that at least 85% of all homes in the United States and Canada are of light-wood construction—most of them the more recently built platform frames. Builders of additions are much more likely to encounter them as potential projects. Second, there is simply not enough room in a single volume to cover all of the structural and technical information needed to do justice to more than one type of building.

However, the book does provide a great deal of useful information for designers, builders and owners who wish to add onto houses that are not of "standard" construction. The designing and planning fundamentals, along with the financial and legal parameters presented here, apply to all projects; only the specific structural and technical information varies with each type of building. Used in conjunction with references on those particular matters, this book should be helpful to anyone building any type of addition.

This book will be most useful to readers who have a knowledge of basic carpentry terms, techniques and tools, as well as some familiarity with design and working drawings, at least to the extent of being able to read blueprints. I do not explain, for example, what tools or methods should be used to measure and cut 2x4s and then nail them together to build a wall. Nor are the basics of drafting explained. If you lack such knowledge, I recommend that you get a book on construction or drafting fundamentals to read as a supplement to this text. The bibliography (on pp. 255-258) provides references for readers who need carpentry and drafting fundamentals and find that their level of technical knowledge is below that assumed by this text.

This is not to say that this book is of no benefit to a home owner or novice designer or builder. On the contrary, those sections that discuss design, planning, financing and so on provide information that anyone who contemplates building an addition or having one built should know. Much of the information will also prove useful to those involved in new construction and ordinary remodeling.

Finally, the user of this book should be aware that at no point do I suggest simple formulas, rigid methods or any other "right" ways of doing things. Situations vary, and design and construction that are appropriate for one site or project might not be for another. Ultimately, you must decide how to solve the problem at hand—it is my hope that I have provided you with some of the necessary tools.

THE
ARCHITECTURE
OF ADDITIONS

1
TO ADD OR NOT TO ADD?

For a variety of emotional, ecological, practical and financial reasons, adding on, rather than buying up or building anew, can be the best way to acquire a bigger and better house. Of all the reasons for adding on, perhaps the most important one is also the most subjective—the emotional attachment of the owners to their home and community. Most people bought their house because something about it spoke to them in a special way. Chances are, by the time they are ready to consider an addition it says even more.

THE CASE FOR ADDING ON

If the members of a family—particularly one with kids—like their neighborhood and have been there for a while, they probably have more connections to it than they'll ever realize unless they move. Staying put allows the kids to grow up with their friends and schoolmates, and the family as a whole to remain rooted in the neighborhood. It keeps us near our favorite gardens and trees, and lets us keep track of the new baby down the block, the old woman who occasionally needs help getting her groceries in and that pair of nesting birds that returns each spring. To many, this means life—particularly in today's hurried and transient world. It means that love of hearth and home, which grows year by year, is not discarded but preserved and strengthened.

Also, there is the consideration of contributing something back to the community in the larger sense. Adding on, it turns out, is much friendlier to the environment than building a new house, even an "ecologically sensitive" house. No matter how well designed a new structure is from an ecological standpoint, building it still requires the placement of infrastructure—roads, power, septic and water systems—and uses significantly more energy and materials than building an addition. At a time when the economical use of resources is critical, immediately, to the survival of the building trades and, in the frighteningly near future, to the survival of the human and biotic communities,

it makes sense to take a new look at creating new space. Additions give us the most space and value for the least cost and impact.

Practical considerations

From a pragmatic standpoint, the hassles and inconveniences of remodeling are probably at least matched by those of moving. Though remodeling can be stressful, in most cases the actual work is done by someone other than the owners, who can go on with their normal activities and jobs. Also, additions can often be built alongside the existing house, making only a small impact on the living conditions within.

To move—out of the neighborhood at least—owners not only have to pack and unpack, but also take on all the expenses and burdens of relocating, from paying movers and buying new drapes to reestablishing themselves with merchants, bankers, librarians and neighbors.

Financial considerations

To understand the potential financial advantages of building an addition, think of owning a house of, say, 1,500 sq. ft. and expanding it by 1,000 sq. ft. Compared to building a new 2,500-sq.-ft. house, the addition is much cheaper. Not only is its overall cost less, but, in many cases, the price per square foot is lower if the price of the land, utility hookups and other developmental expenses are included.

While it is true that once the owners build a new house they can sell their present house and apply that money to the new mortgage, the process is costly for several rea-

sons. First, banks normally charge a variety of fees for taking out new loans, and it may also be hard to get a loan at the old interest rate. Second, the old house is usually assessed at a lower rate than the new one. Third, the combined value of the existing house's mortgage and the loan for the addition is likely to be less than the total cost of building the larger house with today's labor and material costs, so a larger debt might be assumed by starting from scratch.

Added together, these figures represent a significant amount of money. Over a reasonable amortization period, say 10 years, they could total one-third to one-half the cost of the addition!

When building the 1,000-sq.-ft. addition is compared to buying an existing 2,500-sq.-ft. house, the advantages might be somewhat diminished but they are still significant. Let's suppose that the addition loan plus the existing house mortgage is identical to the mortgage assumed for the larger house. When a house changes hands, it is usually reassessed at a higher value and the property taxes go up. There is still a tax advantage in most cases, however, because the assessment for the existing portion of a remodeled house remains at its original rate. The addition is normally the only portion of the completed house assessed at the new rates. In the example above, the added portion is less than half the size of the overall house, so the tax hike would be minimized.

Another financial advantage of building an addition over building or buying a different house is that it is fairly easy to leverage a home-improvement loan based on a reasonable amount of existing equity, and loan fees are often waived or minimized if the money is borrowed from the current mortgage holder. Also, because of the relatively small amount involved, it may be possible to borrow some or all of the funds from family or other private sources, and pay below-market interest rates. Finally, addition projects can often be broken up into phases, making each discrete phase more affordable.

The design-control advantage

Building an addition also offers the advantage of design control. When you look for a house, you choose from what is available. Chances are, nothing will be exactly right, and sooner or later most people settle for a compromise just to get the search over with. Of course, the new house can be remodeled, but, unless the neighborhood is much better, how is that an improvement over remodeling the house you are already living in? Most people have all kinds of ideas about fixing their homes. They are usually expressed in some phrase like, "This place would be just great if...." Building an addition allows you to turn that "if" into a reality.

Of course, building a new house offers design control too, but, as we have seen above, it may be at a prohibitive cost. Which brings us to the last and one of the most important advantages of adding on. Through careful designing, we can usually create an addition that increases the value of the finished

house over and above the addition's cost, so the owners' equity position is greater than ever.

THE CASE FOR MOVING

While the advantages outlined above make many proposals attractive on the surface, it is still important to take some time at the beginning of the project to question whether building an addition is the best way to solve the problems that it is intended to solve. This analysis, in turn, requires that the problems be stated clearly and comprehensively, which is the first task in the design process.

If a house feels dark and cramped, for example, it might not really need to be bigger. Perhaps just removing a couple of internal walls and ceilings or adding French doors onto a deck would give it the open, spacious feeling the owners want. Greater privacy can be provided by converting a garage or an attic into usable space, or by adding on a relatively inexpensive, adjunct space like a bolt-on greenhouse that sits on an existing patio or even a separate prefab studio in the backyard. A more impressive look can be achieved with some work on the facade—perhaps adding a bay window and repainting—and by landscaping. Clutter can be dealt with in a variety of ways, such as building more cabinets, putting a plywood floor in the attic or getting a small metal storage shed, all of which take considerably less time, effort and money than adding rooms.

Even if it is ultimately decided that there just isn't enough space, exploring these options is still time well spent. If it is discovered that just some of the owners' needs can be met within the present configuration, the addition can be scaled down commensurately and will cost less.

If, on the other hand, more space really is needed, the option of moving should be considered carefully before deciding to add on. For one thing, comparing moving to building brings up a variety of complex considerations that go to the heart of the addition's feasibility assessment: the owners' real attachment to the neighborhood, the size and value of other houses on the block, commuting distances, existing equity, market realities and dozens of other factors.

One benefit of exploring the moving option is that it helps size and shape the addition, if indeed an addition is built. The features that the owners desire in a new house closely correlate with what they see as lacking in their present home. Many owners have a problem seeing the possibilities hidden within their own house, but can talk uninhibitedly about their fantasy home. From this, the designer or builder can learn what it is that the owners want, and perhaps show them how they can have it in their present house.

So when should the decision to build an addition be made? Only after conducting a thorough feasibility investigation. This book, of course, assumes that the conclusion to all the questioning is, "Yes, it makes sense to build an addition." But first, all the pros and cons must be considered systematically.

THE FEASIBILITY CONSULTATION

Although the professional designer or builder may have talked about the addition casually with the owners, a formal feasibility consultation should always be the first step in an addition project. (For an outline of the major phases in designing and building an addition, see the table on pp. 177-178.) The purpose of the consultation is to determine whether the owners should or should not undertake their proposed project—or whether they should significantly modify or postpone it.

While it may seem obvious, it is important for the professional to keep in mind that the purpose of the meeting is not to get a job, or "push" the project—even if the project was the owners' idea. For a number of reasons, building an addition might be a bad idea. During the feasibility phase, the professional's task is to use his or her knowledge of design and construction to evaluate the owners' proposal objectively.

For an addition, this evaluation can usually be made after a two- to three-hour meeting with the owners at the site, some research and number-crunching back at the office, and a follow-up meeting to review the findings and reach a conclusion.

To work efficiently, the designer or builder must have an agenda for the initial consultation, which entails focusing and structuring the meeting, finding out who the owners are and what they need, and evaluating the project according to the five aspects of feasibility discussed below.

Focusing the meeting

The owners' focus is usually on architecture. They've thought about how many additional rooms they need, where to put them and what they should look like: Now they want to know what the professional thinks. Typically they begin the meeting by marching through the house and, with a flourish of hands, indicating where the addition will be, and perhaps walking off its perimeter.

The experienced professional's initial focus is wider. The designer or builder needs to help the owners determine whether it makes sense to build an addition at all, and, if

---

Design Parameters:
Program Requirements and Design Determiners

In architecture, the term *program* normally means "the client's list of requirements." A typical program for an addition includes elements such as the number of rooms, their function and perhaps a list of special features like a fireplace or a certain type of countertop in the kitchen.

In this book, the concept of program is expanded to include the designer's requirements and objectives for the project. The designer's program typically requires compatibility of the project with financial and career goals, a good relationship with the owners and the opportunity to try new ideas and design to personal architectural and aesthetic standards.

Along with the program requirements, numerous preexisting physical conditions, architectural features, legal restrictions and budgetary realities influence the design of an addition. In this book, these factors are called *design determiners*. Design determiners are of two types: generic determiners, which pertain to any building, and project determiners, which apply to a specific building.

Generic determiners require that the building provide basic shelter and climate control in a safe, healthy and secure structure. Also, the building should be appropriate for its immediate and neighborhood context, uncomplicated to build and affordable. Project determiners are the conditions and characteristics of the specific site and existing building, the local jurisdiction's construction laws and the budget.

Design determiners can be considered to be both constraints and opportunities. Building codes, for example, restrict design possibilities but also set a minimum standard of safety. (The codes, based on the collective experience of thousands of builders and designers, include safety measures that could easily be overlooked by even the most conscientious designer working alone.)

Together, the program requirements and design determiners comprise the *design parameters* within which the project must be conceived, designed and ultimately built. In a sense, the first two sections of this book discuss the parameters of typical addition projects, while the third section shows how they are systematically accounted for in the creation of the new space.

For additional information on design parameters, see Chapter 11 and the "Master Design-Parameters Checklist" (Appendix III).

so, exactly what they see it doing for them. Since a trained designer normally prefers to generate solutions from the *program,* or list of the project's requirements and goals, instead of conceiving of a space and then trying to cram the various functional requirements into it, it is important to shift the focus to the owners' program early in the meeting (see the sidebar on p. 7).

Of course, there is a good chance that some, if not all, of the owners' architectural concepts will be incorporated into the final design. Even if their ideas are ultimately abandoned or modified beyond recognition, a great deal can be learned about the owners—their tastes, knowledge, fears, aspirations and how they try to solve their problems—by paying careful attention to their design concepts. If their design is weak, it should not simply be discarded but treated as valuable program information couched in visual, rather than written or spoken form.

Once everyone's focus has shifted from specific solutions to general questions, the professional should propose the agenda so that the time is well used. The first part of the discussion centers on the needs and desires of the owners themselves. Typical questions asked of the owners are presented in the sidebar below. Once the designer has a clear idea of who the owners are and what they need, it's time to guide the discussion to the five aspects of feasibility.

THE FIVE ASPECTS OF FEASIBILITY

In terms of adding on, feasibility has two meanings: one, whether an addition of a certain size and complexity can be built for a specific budget; and two, whether it is appropriate to build it.

It might be determined, for example, that a large addition can be placed on a small house for a price that the owners can afford. Even so, questions about the project's appropriateness—whether it is overbuilt for the neighborhood, whether it truly meets the family's needs or whether the money would be better spent elsewhere—must be answered before deciding to proceed.

Learning about the Owners

Early in the feasibility discussion, the designer or builder must question the owners to gain a general understanding of their needs and how they see the proposed addition addressing them. The questions are intended to stimulate discussion, and the owners should be encouraged to talk freely.

This "research" into the owners' ideas and fantasies often yields insights into their sources of inspiration, concepts of hearth and home, and attitudes toward limitations and compromises. It can bring out hopes for the project that even the owners were unaware of or afraid to articulate. It is often surprising what we can give them when we know what they (sometimes secretly) want.

The following list of questions, like all such lists in this book, should be adapted to suit the particular clients and situation:

1. How do the owners live, and how would they like to live? How does their proposed remodel relate to their lifestyle?

2. What do they see their addition or improved space doing for them? Is it a functional improvement, an aesthetic one, or both? If it is a functional improvement, just how do they see themselves functioning better with it?

3. Why did they buy their house, and what is it that they like about it? What do they dislike?

4. What are they absolutely attached to in their present environment? What can they live without?

5. Does the house reflect their sense of style, or did they buy it because of its location or their budget? What parts of the house speak to their sense of style or aesthetics? How important are aesthetics to them? What's their favorite look or style?

6. Are they very specific or particular about what they want, or are they open to a variety of possible designs?

7. Have they remodeled before, or will this be their first time?

8. What do they believe the actual construction will entail? How long will it take and how disruptive will it be?

9. What are their fears and anxieties about the design and construction of the project?

10. If they could have everything they wanted in an ideal house, what would they have?

A major factor in the feasibility of an addition project is the layout and condition of the existing house. In new construction, the budget determines how much can be built. In remodeling, the existing architectural and structural possibilities are an additional factor, because they greatly influence the budget. That factor can be a plus or a minus, depending on how well the designer works with the givens.

The feasibility test

To pass the feasibility test—and qualify to enter the preliminary design phase—a project must look as if it will work on all levels. If a second-story addition is proposed, for example, the existing structure should be able to carry it without major, expensive modifications; it must conform to height restrictions and other zoning ordinances; there should be enough money to build the minimum square footage needed to make the project worth doing; the owners must have sufficient emotional stamina and commitment to see it through; and the final product must offer them satisfaction.

In the rest of this chapter, I'll present an overview of the five aspects of feasibility that should be considered before the design work begins: architectural, structural/technical, legal, financial and emotional feasibility. Each subject is covered in depth in later chapters. Keep in mind that these five aspects could be presented in any order, because they are all of equal importance.

Architectural feasibility

Architectural issues are functional and aesthetic. Functional success is measured by the extent to which the design allows the owners to perform daily tasks efficiently and to live in comfort. Aesthetic success is more subjective, though addition projects that follow or improve upon the shapes, proportions and artistic themes of the existing building are usually judged well.

What is feasible is usually suggested and sometimes mandated by the house's size, shape, floor plan and position on the site. Some floor plans have so little extra space that an entire room would have to be sacrificed to accommodate stairs leading to a new second story. In other cases, building an addition on the side or back of the house can create yards no larger than postage stamps and in some communities will exceed lot-coverage restrictions. Some large, rambling houses may not need an addition at all, but simply need to have their corridors and rooms reorganized.

Ideally, there will not be a design at the beginning—the design will grow organically from the existing conditions and the program requirements. In this ideal world, the owners would simply state their problem, as clearly as they could, and the designer or builder together with the owners would develop solutions. As mentioned above, however, the owners usually have a design or at least a concept in mind before they have fully explored the program and before they bring a professional to the site. Architectural feasibility most often begins with an evaluation of that concept.

Evaluating the owners' proposal

People who lack design experience frequently make one of two types of mistakes. They either "under-design," meaning they include less than they really want because of perceived cost or other limitations, or they "over-design," meaning they want the addition to be too big for the neighborhood or do too much within the allotted space or budget.

Evaluating the owners' proposal, then, begins with matching it against their own program. If they say they need or want three bedrooms but designed only two because of perceived limitations, a reevaluation is called for. Perhaps the problem is not with the building or the budget but with the owners' basic approach to the project. In a misguided attempt to save money, for example, they may have considered building only a second story on their existing house, while a combination of a second story and a room addition built out into the yard could provide enough space for the third bedroom. Since some of the second-story space can be built over the relatively inexpensive room addition (building from the ground up is usually cheaper than modifying an existing structure), the cost of the extra space needed for the third bedroom may be much less than the owners realize. (See Chapter 2 for a discussion of the basic types of additions.)

By bringing greater knowledge and a broader approach to the problem, the professional may uncover new solutions. In another example, an existing overhang might become the roof over a transition area to an

This major addition/remodeling project dramatically transformed a rather plain-looking, lakeside home in suburban Minneapolis. The existing house was dressed up with new siding and windows to conform to the addition, endowing the building with an overall sense of architectural unity. (For an interior view of the remodeled house, see the photo on p. 59.)

addition originally proposed by the owners for the opposite side of the house. Such discoveries can save thousands of dollars, and perhaps even make a seemingly unafford-able project feasible.

As well as making sure that the owners' proposal substantially matches their preliminary program, the professional should critique it (gently) as architecture. The floor plan should flow, light and views must be carefully shaped, and in-terior and exterior continuity and a final sense of wholeness should be achieved. Novices are unlikely to have developed the design this far, but the professional should see a workable skeleton in place before committing to develop the owners' ideas further.

If the owners' basic concept is sound—they know what they want and it seems they can best get it by adding on—but their architecture is unsound, a new preliminary design will have to be generated. Rather than stating that their concept just won't work, it is probably better to say that it is something to work with. Then the designer can go back to the drawing board, integrate all the relevant information and come up with a plan.

The feasibility consultation is not the best time to generate new de-signs. Serious attempts to pull the design concepts together into a co-herent plan should wait until feasi-bility is established and the program is written. (See Chapters 11 and 12 for more on the design process.)

Also, owners tend to latch onto concepts easily, and let go of them reluctantly. Until they learn the basic approach to preliminary de-sign, which is that numerous ideas should be generated but not evaluated until a later time, they are likely to hear anything the professional says as a promise and be disappointed if it is not delivered.

What should come out of a feasibility conference is a feasibility assessment: "Yes, two bedrooms, a family room and one-and-a-half baths can be added to this house for a budget ranging from *x* to *y*."

Structural and technical feasibility

The detailed structural and subsystem investigation used for the design and working drawings (mechanical drawings used by the builder) is made when the "as-built" measurements are taken (see Chapters 6, 7 and 9). A general survey of the type of construction and potential problems suffices for the feasibility assessment.

A probe in the sub-area (basement or crawl space) with a flashlight, a couple of knocks on the foundation with a hammer, a quick check of walls and floors with a level and a brief survey of the site conditions show how the house is built and reveal most important structural, foundation or soil problems. Looking at the major components and subsystems—the roof and exterior walls, gutters and drainage, electrical service box, plumbing and heater—will usually indicate the need for repairs or upgrades that are significant enough to affect the design or budget.

Like architectural feasibility, structural feasibility is flexible and depends on the design. If the existing structure and foundation cannot be easily modified to take a second story, for example, the house could possibly be "bridged" by an essentially independent structure (as described in Chapter 8).

Legal feasibility

Before arriving at the site, the designer or builder should call city hall and inquire about the *design envelope,* or the maximum allowable size limits for the building, and other applicable zoning regulations. Then simple measurements will show whether the proposed addition will violate property-line setback or height restrictions, or, indeed, whether there is enough space on the lot to accommodate any design that is large enough to meet the program requirements. Programs that will not work can be eliminated at the outset so that other options can be explored. (See Chapter 10 for more on the legal aspects of building an addition.)

Financial feasibility

An addition is financially feasible if it is affordable, the money to build it is available, it does not overbuild the house for the neighborhood, it does not significantly exceed the cost of either buying or building elsewhere, and its finished value is at least equal to its cost, preferably greater. Establishing financial feasibility at the beginning of the project can be somewhat difficult, partly because the figures are rough and partly because owners may at first be reluctant to discuss their finances openly.

Many people believe that they should seek estimates for their proposed project without discussing how much money they have available. That way, they feel, they will get a price that reflects the actual value, rather than the maximum amount of money they could potentially spend. If there is a complete set of plans for the builder to work with and all the decisions about materials and fixtures have been made, this approach might prove advantageous. That is not the case in the feasibility phase of the project, however; nor does it make sense to develop a set of plans without regular reference to the budget. The scenario whereby plans are drawn and then put out to bid can open a real can of worms when it comes to getting the project built for what it "should cost," or getting it built at all for that matter.

Part of a professional's duty is to tell the owners at the outset if their budget is realistic, and, if it's not, about how much more money they'll need to build some or all of what they want. That's when the owners should begin to make informed choices about costs—not after they've paid for plans.

To do so, of course, the designer or builder must know how much money the owners can spend. It may take a little talking to get people to open up about finances to a stranger, but, in most cases, if it is calmly explained that it is to their benefit, they will. It is a matter of trust, and professionals have the advantage that they are usually asked to come to the house for some good reason—reputation, references or personal connections. In any event, establishing trust is necessary for the relationship and the project to go forward, and a frank discussion about money is a good test of good faith.

The wing addition on the left side of this California house increases its overall size by about 40%, and probably increases its market value by at least that much. Because of its small size, such an addition would have a high cost per square foot, but a low total cost, making the project financially feasible for the owners of a modest home.

As well as learning about the overall budget parameters, it is important to find out what percentage of the money is actually available and what needs to be raised. If funds for the entire project are not "in the bank" (and they seldom are), ask about the source of the additional money and how realistic the chances are that it will be obtained. Secured loans from lending institutions—household equity loans, for example—are a good bet. If the owners need to "talk to Mom" about a large sum of money, the project is not feasible, and it would be ethically dubious to proceed with the design until the funds are actually in hand.

Size and cost Because there is a certain minimum amount of work that goes into planning and building any addition, small additions tend to have high per-square-foot costs. Large additions are cheaper per square foot, but have a higher overall cost. In both directions, there is a point of diminishing return where you have either built too little to be cost-effective or more than the budget or resale value will allow.

It is usually a bad idea, for example, to add just a bathroom. Every phase of construction, from the foundations through the roof (including the installation of wiring, plumbing and numerous fixtures) would be required to produce about 50 sq. ft. of very expensive space. On the other hand, adding too much space can be both an economic and archi-

tectural mistake: On resale, the house might be overpriced for its market or neighborhood, and a huge addition might look awkward from the outside, driving the value down even more.

Controlling scale is also important for maintaining quality. A grand old house with fine woodworking throughout may be devalued by an overly ambitious expansion that hasn't a hope of matching or even successfully mimicking the original charm. Here a smaller addition, which leaves room in the budget for finer details, would fill the bill.

A good rule of thumb is that an addition should increase the floor space by at least 25% but by no more than 75%, with 30% to 60% as an ideal. In other words, assuming the neighborhood isn't going to hell and the owners have enough money to do the job, converting a two-bedroom, one-bath house to a three-bedroom, two-bath house, with perhaps a larger kitchen thrown in, makes sense. A proposal to make it a four-bedroom, three-bath house, however, should definitely raise the issue of moving, while a five-bedroom, three-and-a-half-bath monster with a recreation room should immediately raise red flags.

It is also important to keep a handle on the amount of interior remodeling included in the project. Adding two bedrooms and a bath *and* completely remodeling the kitchen costs approximately as much as adding four bedrooms and two baths. Depending on the owners' situation, this scenario could be a strong argument for buying a new house. Make sure to include the area of the original house to be remodeled in all cost calculations.

Square Footage of Typical Rooms

ROOM	CONFIGURATION/NOTES	DIMENSIONS (FT.)[1]	SQUARE FOOTAGE[2]
Living room	Standard to large	18x22 – 22x26	396 – 572
Family room	Small	13x16	208
	Comfortable to large	18x24 – 22x26	432 – 572
TV room	With couch	12x14 – 16x18	168 – 288
Bedroom	Minimum	7x10 (with 2x3 closet)	76
	Standard	10x12 (with 2x5 closet) – 11x14 (with 2x8 closet)	130 – 170
	Master-bedroom suite	Standard + bath + 20 to 40 sq. ft. of closet + 20 to 40 sq. ft. dressing area	200 (with ¾ bath) – 335 (with large bath)
Bathroom	Half	4x5 min. (toilet and sink)	20
	Three-quarter	5x5 or 4x7 (toilet, sink, shower)	25 – 28
	Standard or full	5x8 (toilet, double sink, tub with shower)	40
	Luxury	Dimensions vary (add separate shower, vanity, sauna, whirlpool, dressing area, linen storage, etc.)	50 – 125
Kitchen (food-preparation area only)	Kitchenette	5x7 (2x7 counter + 3x7 standing room)	35
	Standard	9x11 (U-shaped with 6-0 side counters, 5-0 between counters and 3-0 for passage at end of U)	99
	Large	13-6 x 15-0 (U-shaped with 8-0 side counters, 3x5 island with 4-0 clearance on sides and 3-6 passage at end)	202.5
Eating areas	Breakfast counter (seats 3)	4-6 x 5-6 (1-6 [min.] x 5-6 counter + 3-0 x 5-6 seating area)	24.75
	Small breakfast nook (seats 5)[3]	8x8 (2-6 dia. table + 2-9 seating all around)	64
	Large breakfast nook (seats 6)	10x10 (3-0 dia. table + 3-6 seating all around)	100
	Dining room	9-6 x 12-6 (2-6 x 5-6 table + 3-6 seating all around)	118.75
	Large dining room	11-6 x 17-6 (3-6 x 7-6 table + 4-0 seating all around and 2-0 wide buffet at end)	201.25
Other spaces	Halls	3-0 wide (min.) x length	(varies)
	Entry	5x5 (min.) + 2x3 closet	31
		7x9 (comfortable) + 2x6 closet	75
	Stairs	3-0 x 17-6 (3-0 min. code width; approx. 11-6 for actual stairs for standard 8-0 ceiling + second-floor joist; 3-0 min. clearance for landing at top and bottom of stairs)	52.5
	Washer/dryer	2-6 x 2-6 (stacked) or 3x5 (side by side)	6.25 – 15
	Laundry room	5x8	40
	Home office	Average bedroom size usually works for one person.	(varies)
	Work station	4-6 x 5-6 min. (2-4 x 4-6 desk with 2-8 seating in front)	25.75
	Galleries, studios, other	Custom designed	(varies)

[1] Interior dimensions given. Square footage off walls, pipe chases, etc., should be added. All dimensions are approximate, except minimums determined by code.

[2] Some municipalities require rooms to be larger than the minimum areas given here.

[3] Although nooks often have rounded or angular walls, figure dimensions as if the room were square. The cost of additional footage will compensate approximately for the cost of building the nonstandard walls.

Sample Feasibility Cost Estimate

I. BASE COST (MINIMUM ANTICIPATED COST)

Space requirements	Square footage[1]		Cost per sq. ft.[2]		Total
First story					
Modest to comfortable family room (base price)	350	x	$93.50	=	$32,725.00
Laundry in closet (base price + some plumbing)	15	x	115.00	=	1,725.00
Second story *(over existing first story—add 10% to base price)*					
1 small guest bedroom or sewing room @ 10x10 with 2x6 closet	112	x	102.85	=	11,519.20
1 standard bedroom @ 11x14 with 2x8 closet	170	x	102.85	=	17,484.50
1 standard full bath with double sink @ 5x8 (+ factor extra plumbing)	40	x	135.00	=	5,400.00
Hallway (3x12)	36	x	102.85	=	3,702.60
Other					
Standard stairwell (base price + 10%)	52.5	x	102.85	=	5,399.60
Square footage subtotal	775.5				
Walls and miscellaneous @ 5% of sq. ft. (base price)	38.78	x	93.50	=	3,625.90
Total square footage	**815 sq. ft.** (rounded off)				
			Subtotal	**=**	**$81,581.80**

Special Items

Tile-top wet bar in family room ($1,350 to 1,950 range)		1,650.00
Fireplace with tile hearth and surround in family room ($2,700 to 3,500 range)		3,100.00
Base construction cost	**=**	**$86,331.80**
Design, engineering and permit fees (approx 11%)	=	9,496.50
Total base cost (excluding taxes and interest on construction loans)	**=**	**$95,828.30**

[1] *Based on table on p. 13.*

[2] *Average cost per sq. ft. of building additions in local area is $93.50 (based on figures from bank home equity loan department, contractor's association and local builders).*

Determining costs Costs are naturally difficult to determine without a design, yet it is necessary to come up with ball-park figures when discussing feasibility. Calculations based on the cost per square foot are probably the best way to produce estimates during the feasibility phase. The table on p. 13 gives the square footage of typical rooms. Adding the rooms in the proposed addition together then factoring in 5% to 10% extra for walls, halls, and so on, will produce a reasonable working total.

Banks recognize three grades of new residential construction: A, B and C. "C" is the least expensive—low-cost housing, often multi-unit; "B" is standard—basic private homes without special features like built-in saunas or fancy tilework; "A" houses have special features and may also have custom construction like open-beam ceilings.

II. MAXIMUM ANTICIPATED COST

Average cost per square foot = $81,581.80 ÷ 815 sq. ft. = $100.10 (round to $100)

Anticipated maximum increase in overall size (factoring setback and budget restrictions) = 15%, or 122.25 sq. ft. (round to 125 sq. ft.)

Anticipated additional maximum construction expense = 125 sq. ft. x $100	=	$12,500.00
Maximum allowance for additional features, high-grade fixtures, etc., as per discussion with clients	=	3,500.00
Subtotal	=	16,000.00
Total base cost of job (from p. 14)	=	95,828.30
Cost with additional space and features	=	111,828.30
Additional design and permit fees (based on 11% of $111,828.30 minus original design fees)	=	2,804.70
		114,633.00
Plus 10% safety factor for unanticipated costs	=	11,463.30
Maximum anticipated cost (excluding taxes and interest on construction loans)	=	**$126,096.30**

III. COST COMPARISON

Value of existing house plus addition

Median anticipated cost of project = $126,096 (max.) minus $95,828 (base) = 30,268 ÷ 2 = 15,134 + 95,828 (base) = $110,962

Appraised value of existing 1,440-sq.-ft., 2-bedroom, 1-bath house = $176,500

Value of house plus median cost of addition = 176,500 + 110,962 = **$287,462**

Combined sq. ft. = 1,440 (house) + 815 (addition) = 2,255 sq. ft.

Comparable houses

Average price of 2,000–2,550-sq.-ft. house sold in same neighborhood = **$293,443**

(nearest directly comparable house = 2,420-sq.-ft. house sold for $314,500)

IV. CONCLUSION

The owners' initial suggested budget ($80,000) falls short of anticipated costs. However, the combined value of the house and addition is less than the selling price of comparable houses in the neighborhood by several thousand dollars. If the owners wish to seek the additional funds needed for the project, they are likely to increase their equity position by building the addition. They may also wish to consider making the rooms somewhat smaller, or temporarily omitting the wet bar and/or fireplace.

One way to figure the cost of a new "A" house is to base it on the square-footage cost of a "B" house, since most "A" houses are just standard construction with added features. Special features can then be listed as separate line items on the cost sheet. Listing them separately allows them to be eliminated, scaled down or included as "extras," depending on how well the project stays within budget.

A variant of this formula works well for additions. The cost of the new space can be estimated on a square-footage basis, using the "B" price for the region, then the cost of special features and the technical problems involved in remodeling the existing building can be added as separate items.

A room addition, for example, would cost roughly the same as new construction, with a small percentage added for connecting to the main building, the logistical difficulties of working in backyards, and other factors. Second stories also use new construction techniques once the new subfloor platform is built, but usually require structural upgrades on the existing house. They typically cost 10% to 30% more than room additions of the same size. Combination second-story and room additions vary, depending on what percentage of the upper floor sits on the existing building and the nature of the connections between spaces. Finally, remodeling in the area where the old house makes the transition to the addition will probably run at least 40% and perhaps 60% higher per square foot than new construction, depending on the nature of the space: Halls, storage areas and bedrooms are the least expensive, kitchens and baths the most expensive.

Part of the feasibility research is to determine costs for the locale in question. Such information can be obtained from banks, real-estate and contractors' associations and by talking to builders.

Accuracy Obviously, the initial estimates and final costs can vary enormously, and therein lies the danger of the feasibility cost determination. The only sensible strategy is to give a range of possible costs (see the table on pp. 14-15). The lowest estimate should be based on the square-footage calculations, costs of "extras" and the design and permit fees—the addition will not cost less. The highest estimate should be 25% to 50% higher than the lowest, because the square footage may go up 10% to 30%, fixtures and finished materials are as yet unspecified and the need for further improvements may be recognized before the design is complete.

Feasibility and value Once the two estimates are made, the median price (halfway between the highest and lowest estimates) should be calculated and added to the value of the existing house. If this figure is higher than the highest priced houses of similar size and quality in the neighborhood, the addition is likely to be a bad investment and the project should be scaled down or possibly abandoned in favor of moving.

If the median price is considerably lower than that of comparable houses, not only does it make sense to add on, it might also be wise to expand the project somewhat, assuming the actual cash is available. Since such calculations must include the amortized costs of loans, prices of local real estate and so on, it might be a good idea to hire a realtor or banker as a consultant when pricing the entire package.

The budget, like the design, evolves and becomes more refined as the project goes along. When a preliminary design is adopted, the preliminary budget assumptions can be reexamined, and more precise decisions about the size of the addition and the extra features can be made.

Emotional feasibility

For a designer or builder, it is a blessing to meet owners who are thoughtful and well enough organized to have integrated their project with their life's goals. If they want to add space because they are planning to have a child or need a home office, if they are reasonably certain they will be in the house long enough to amortize the cost, or if they have their own ideas but are open to suggestions, they will probably be a pleasure to design and build for.

Some owners, however, haven't really thought about the purpose of the new space, or how the project will relate to their long-term or, worse, short-term financing. They know only that they are unhappy with their house, and they want the designer or builder to fix it. In fact, the house itself might not even be an issue; fantasizing about their remodeled home might turn out to be a means of forestalling difficult decisions about their lives, trying to patch together a shaky marriage or curing boredom. Adding space as a means of dealing with emotional problems seldom works. Few things are more stressful than living through a remodeling job, and owners who are not prepared for the stresses are likely to have trouble making timely and sensible decisions.

Designers or builders should also pay attention to their own emotional response to the clients, and to the desirability of the project. They cannot expect to bring their best to a project where there is not a good connection with the owners or proper enthusiasm for the work.

Professionals and their clients by definition have an intimate relationship. During the course of the job they will discuss food and garbage, money and aesthetic preferences, bathrooms and bedrooms. They will exchange money, ideas, support, jokes and possibly insults. They must be able to rely on each other for a candid exchange, and one in which there is enough trust so that when the going gets rough the show goes on. Designers who do not bring their emotional wits to the feasibility consultation will have left home a tool of much greater importance than a tape measure.

FEASIBILITY ASSESSMENT

After the five aspects of feasibility have been explored, the owners and the designer or builder must decide whether the initial project, or some variant, should be built. Sometimes the answer is a straightforward "yes" or "no." If the program is matched to a sound general design concept and the money is in the bank, the project can go forward. If, on the other hand, it turns out that the owners don't have nearly enough money to get even a scaled-down version of what they'd hoped for, the project is clearly not feasible. Other situations meriting a "no" answer might be the discovery that the real problem lay in the organization of the kitchen, not in its size, or that adding the minimum requirement of two bedrooms, a home office, a family room and two baths would grossly overbuild the house for the neighborhood.

While owners might not like to hear "no," it's clearly better hearing it during the feasibility consultation or follow-up meeting than halfway through the design or, worse, construction phase of the job.

Often the answer isn't a simple "yes" or "no," but a conditional "yes." Something can be done, but perhaps not what was initially planned. The need is clear, the program is reasonable and enough money to make it worth developing a plan is on hand or available. Further exploration in the form of preliminary design work is merited.

Creating feasibility

There are two ways to make projects with marginal budgets work—scale them down or build them in stages. The problem with scaled-down projects is that they can be a waste of money, since they will end up costing a significant portion of the full-scale job and deliver much less satisfaction.

Alternatively, a *master plan* can be drawn for the entire project, which is then built in stages, some now, some later when the owners have more money. In fact, a master plan should be drawn for all remodeling projects so that plumbing for the future bath can be stubbed in while the walls are open and today's improvement will not have to be torn out to make way for tomorrow's. (For more on master planning, see Chapter 12.)

THE NEXT STEPS

If the feasibility assessment is positive, it is time to move to the program and preliminary design phases of the project. Though a great deal of program information has already been gathered through discussing feasibility and the preliminary evaluation of the building, it is necessary to consolidate and organize that information and fill in the missing pieces. Thorough, in-depth programming and design-parameter evaluation usually reveal the answers to the design problems, since questions that are carefully enough framed contain their own answers.

In the normal course of events, the shift from feasibility determination to program writing and preliminary design calls for a formal agreement recorded in a written design contract. The nature of that agreement and a systematic approach to writing the program are covered in Chapter 11. Before discussing program and design, however, we will take a good look at just what it is that we are trying to design in the remainder of the first section of the book. In the second section, we'll learn more about the structural and technical conditions and the legal restrictions that influence the design. Once this background information has been covered, we'll put it all together as a design and, ultimately, as a project in the final section of the book.

2
THREE WAYS OF ADDING ON

A house can be enlarged in three directions: by building above it, on one or more of its sides, or below it. *Room additions,* built alongside the house, and *second-story additions* are the focus of this book. Many designs combine room and second-story additions, adding space onto the back or side and above the house at the same time. These *combination additions* offer certain architectural and structural advantages, which will be considered as I discuss each type in order.

BASIC ADDITION TYPES

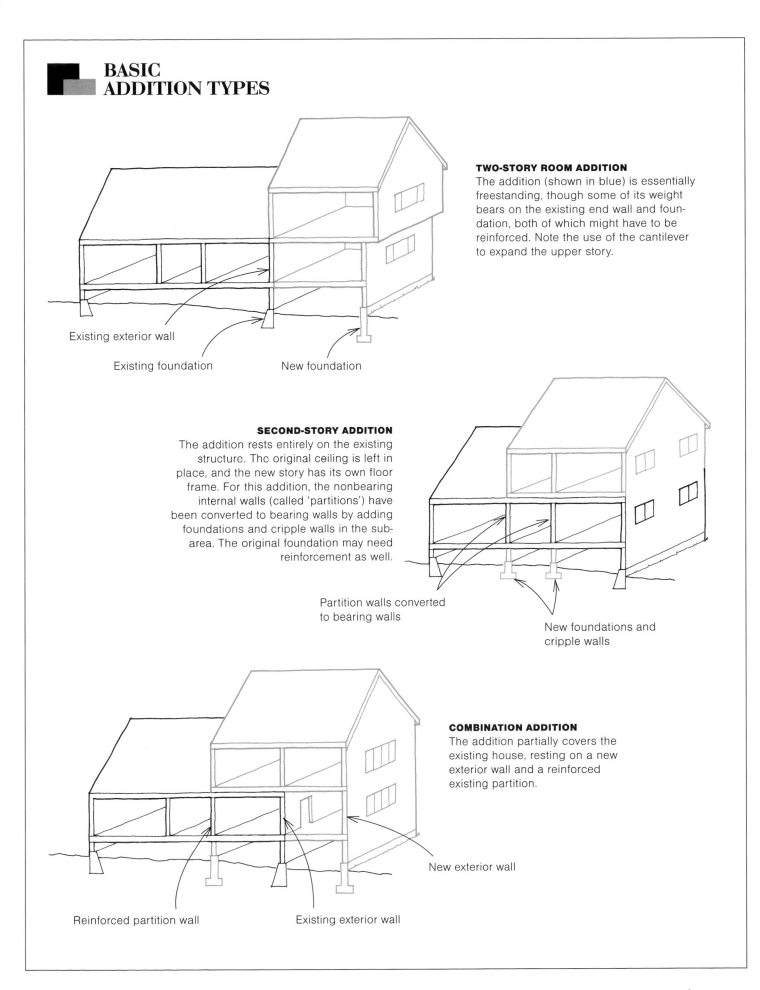

TWO-STORY ROOM ADDITION
The addition (shown in blue) is essentially freestanding, though some of its weight bears on the existing end wall and foundation, both of which might have to be reinforced. Note the use of the cantilever to expand the upper story.

Existing exterior wall

Existing foundation   New foundation

SECOND-STORY ADDITION
The addition rests entirely on the existing structure. The original ceiling is left in place, and the new story has its own floor frame. For this addition, the nonbearing internal walls (called 'partitions') have been converted to bearing walls by adding foundations and cripple walls in the sub-area. The original foundation may need reinforcement as well.

Partition walls converted to bearing walls

New foundations and cripple walls

COMBINATION ADDITION
The addition partially covers the existing house, resting on a new exterior wall and a reinforced existing partition.

New exterior wall

Reinforced partition wall   Existing exterior wall

ROOM ADDITIONS

In most cases, building out into the yard is the best way to expand a house. Room additions are essentially new construction, and are thus much easier to build than second stories, which often require extensive structural remodeling.

In addition to being technically more straightforward than second stories, room additions also provide greater opportunity to vary the design. Most second stories are simple upward extensions of the existing superstructure. Their *massing*, or general shape, conforms to the walls below, though some variation may be expressed with cantilevers and other devices. The massing of a room addition is for the most part structurally independent of the original house. This independence gives the designer much more freedom in dealing with problems of solar orientation, weather control, indoor/outdoor spatial relationships, private vs. public spaces in the yard and the house, circulation and even the appropriate scale and style for the addition—all at a cost per square foot that is usually significantly lower than that of a second story.

Although a room addition needs its own foundation (whereas a second story can sometimes be supported by the existing foundation), the "extra" expense is offset by two factors. First, second stories always need stairs, which eat up space and money. Two-story room additions also need stairs, of course, but they are much simpler to build than stairs in the house that cut through existing walls and ceilings. Second, it is the exception rather than the rule that new second stories can be supported by the existing foundation—most require significant improvements to both the foundation and superstructure. Also, it is almost always easier to build forms and cast new concrete in the yard than to work under a house. In short, the cost of additional materials and labor needed to get a room addition to the first-floor platform stage is usually considerably less than that of getting to the equivalent stage for a second-story addition.

Finally, most of a room addition's construction takes place in the yard, minimizing disruption of the owners' lives. In most cases, cutting openings into the main house can be postponed until the end of the project.

This family-room/kitchen addition opens to the side yard of a 1910 Adirondack-style home in New York State. The addition's massing, details, materials and color conform to the original house.

This two-story wing-style room addition in Connecticut helps enclose the backyard pool for privacy and protection against the wind while capturing the light and warmth of the sun.

One of the drawbacks of room additions is that they eat up yard space, and bigger yards are usually considered to be more desirable. On large lots, the problem diminishes in importance. In fact, a room addition can help shape an amorphous exterior space, making it more functional and comfortable (see the photo above and the top drawing on p. 22). The addition can be designed as a new wing, and integration with outdoor features like pools, large rocks or gardens might be as important to its plan and massing as the shape of the existing house.

In small yards, the addition naturally hugs the house more closely, and grows vertically if more floor space is needed. At the point where legal restrictions and practical considerations prohibit further climbing, it can grow over the main house and become a combination addition (see the bottom drawing on p. 22).

Other potential problems lie in the position, size and shape of the new structure. Adding on might force hard choices in floor planning because some portion of an existing room must be sacrificed to create access to the new space. Also, room additions cover exterior walls, which means blocked windows and the darkening of formerly well-lit rooms. Then there is the danger of designing so large a structure that it overwhelms the yard or adjacent yards, interferes with the neighbors' view, casts offensive shadows or inadvertently creates wind tunnels between buildings.

Solutions for these problems will be considered later, but for now suffice it to say that most of them can be handled with various design devices. The darkening of rooms, for example, can usually be resolved by joining the addition to the plumbing wall of a bathroom that has no windows, by providing openings or light wells between the addition and the house, by adding skylights, or by some other means.

All in all, it is difficult to overemphasize the advantages of building room additions over all other types. Where they are feasible, they should be the designer or builder's first choice.

LOTS AND ADDITION TYPES

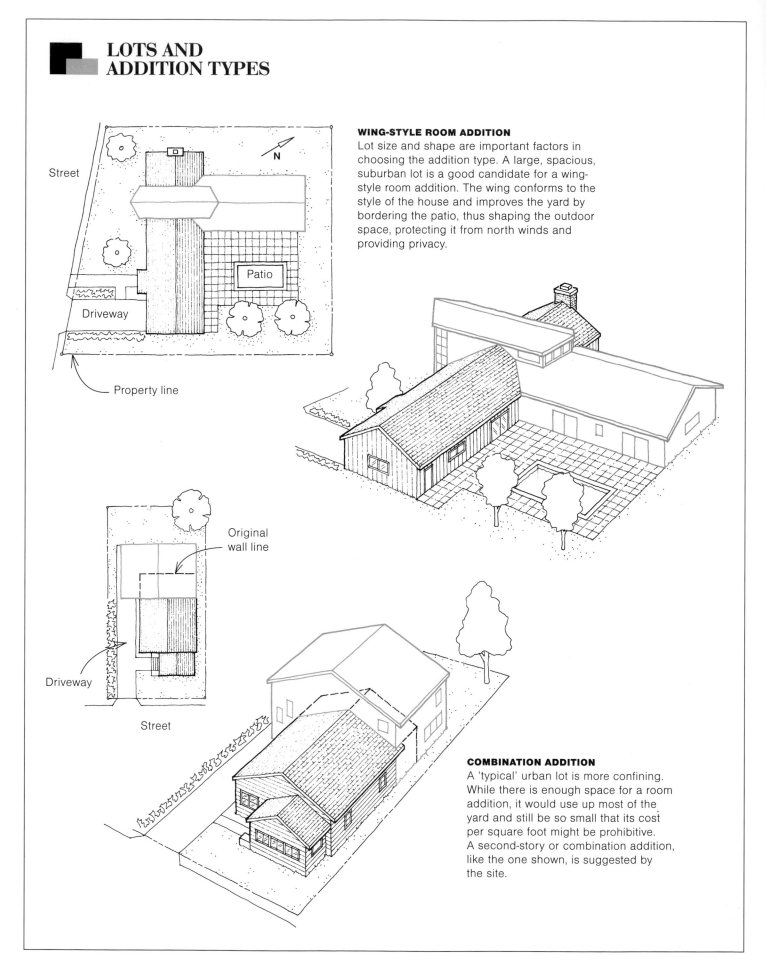

WING-STYLE ROOM ADDITION
Lot size and shape are important factors in choosing the addition type. A large, spacious, suburban lot is a good candidate for a wing-style room addition. The wing conforms to the style of the house and improves the yard by bordering the patio, thus shaping the outdoor space, protecting it from north winds and providing privacy.

Street

Patio

Driveway

Property line

N

Original wall line

Driveway

Street

COMBINATION ADDITION
A 'typical' urban lot is more confining. While there is enough space for a room addition, it would use up most of the yard and still be so small that its cost per square foot might be prohibitive. A second-story or combination addition, like the one shown, is suggested by the site.

SECOND-STORY ADDITIONS

Building a second story provides an opportunity to enlarge a house without eating up precious yard space. Second stories are a particularly attractive option in urban settings, where space is at a premium and adjacent buildings can limit views and access to light and air. Depending on the structural integrity of the existing building, second-story additions can also offer the advantage of inexpensive construction, since the foundations and lower walls are already in place.

The drawbacks of second-story additions should be considered carefully, however. They are more like remodeling and less like new construction—both slower and more expensive to build than room additions. The problem is that relatively few single-story houses are built to take the structural loads imposed by a second story. The structure can be modified, of course—it's done all the time—but the modifications come at a cost that can blow a significant portion of the budget before 1 sq. ft. of the new floor is added. Along with this major struc-

tural limitation, there are architectural difficulties, including the necessity of finding room for a staircase without disrupting the lower-floor plan, the constraints placed on the upper-floor plan by the need for vertical alignment of windows in the two stories, and a host of other considerations.

Municipal height restrictions and, in some cases, property-line setbacks also affect the design (see pp. 161-164). These restrictions can generate architectural problems like the imposition of uncomfortably low ceilings in upper-story rooms.

A second-story addition (photo at right) greatly increased the size and visual impact of this northern California home without increasing its footprint. The addition's divided windows with double-hung panes match those of the original house, and the new white trim unites the facade.

This second-story addition and stylistic makeover (right) added a master-bedroom suite and a study over a small 950-sq.-ft. house on a small lot (above). The grid-window structure at the front allows light into the new stairwell and second-story hall. (For an interior view, see the bottom photo on p. 74.)

The second-story addition (below) in the middle of this low, rambling California ranch house adds a visual center to the massing. Note how the addition's gable roof and clerestory windows reflect the refurbished facade of the wing on the right. (For an interior view of this addition, see the photo on p. 49.)

Setback regulations might require that a second story be built inboard of the existing exterior walls, forcing expensive structural adaptations. Variances can be obtained in many cases, but only after paying high fees and enduring long delays.

Finally, the relative difficulty of construction must also be considered. Added to the need to remove the roof is the difficulty of getting materials up to the second story, the need for scaffolding for the sheathing, siding, windows and trim, and the extra time required to waterproof the joints between stories. Banging about for weeks on top of a house generates noise and dust within. There is danger of cracking the existing ceilings, or slipping off a joist and stepping right through to the room below. The electrical wiring is underfoot until the new floor platform is built, and in most parts of the country the threat of rain damage exists as long as the roof is off.

The list of potential problems goes on, but the point is clear: Commit to a second-story design only when the possibilities of remodeling within the shell or building a room addition have been eliminated. Then proceed cautiously.

For the reasons discussed in Chapter 1, however, adding a second story, particularly in urban settings, is still usually a better solution than building or buying another house. The trick is to design and build the second story efficiently. The formula for success is to work with the givens—the contours and scale of the house, the structural limitations, the increased cost per square foot—and to fulfill the program's top priorities first.

COMBINATION ADDITIONS

Combination additions offer many of the advantages of room additions and second stories. They are spacious enough to fulfill most reasonable program requirements, yet compact enough to save yard space and tall enough to catch the view. Their potential advantages should be considered on any site. By connecting to the house on both the vertical and horizontal plane, they create more possibilities for locating stairs and hallways between the house and the addition. The appropriate massing, too, is resolved, since the addition usually conforms to the outlines of the existing structure, fitting over it like a helmet. The second-story portion can enhance an otherwise ordinary house by increasing its size and bearing, but the fact that a typical combination addition extends over just the rear of the building helps keep the street facade from becoming overwhelming (see the bottom drawing on p. 22).

A hidden structural advantage of a combination addition is that the new first story can provide some of the support for that portion of the second story that sits over the existing house. At least part of the second-story floor platform can be cantilevered from the new structure, reducing the downward load. Horizontal forces can be handled entirely by the addition, saving the expense of retrofitting shear wall in the sub-area (see Chapter 8).

Locating the stairs

Another potential advantage of combination additions is that the normally problematic stairs can be placed in the addition, simplifying both floor planning and construction. Stair placement depends on the use of the new space, particularly the upper story. Most city lots are rectangles, with their long axis perpendicular to the street—they are suited for backyard additions. Such additions tend to fulfill the functions normally associated with the back of the house, with kitchens and family rooms on the lower floor and bedrooms and baths above. Stairs leading to bedrooms can be placed in the new space, where they are easy to build and where they make a direct connection between the bedroom and the kitchen/family room—the areas the occupants use most.

If the design calls for a public gathering space upstairs, however, the stairs will need to be closer to the front of the house, and something must be sacrificed: Either the stairs are pushed laboriously through the old house, or the addition must expand farther into the yard to give the stairs a more central location. In this example, the configuration of the existing building suggests the addition's best design—hold the parties downstairs in the kitchen/family-room/rear-patio complex, and reserve the second story for the bedroom.

Drawbacks

While their virtues are many, combination additions are not the answer to every design problem. The advantage of cantilevering the top story is quickly lost as spans increase, requiring heavier and more expensive joists and girders to transfer the loads. There are also potential problems in the connections between the old and the new buildings. If two essentially independent structures are joined only by their

The combination addition to the main wing of the Minnesota house at left not only added to its size but also transformed its style. The street view (below) is greatly enhanced by the overall increased mass and the use of the dormers as rhythmical elements that also repeat, in miniature, the massing of the existing garage wing on the right.

Continuity is also provided by the use of windows with divided panes, shingle siding and a consistent color scheme. The themes are continued in the rear (shown at right), where the addition vaults up and over the original structure. (For interior views of this house, see the photos on p. 50 [bottom] and p. 58.)

The screened-in porch on the left of this Connecticut home (above) was replaced by a two-story room addition, which was then extended over the rest of the house (right). The exterior was completely transformed to refer to the graceful architecture of an earlier period, but with some clearly modern detailing.

siding or roof membranes, winds, earth movement or even people walking about can open caulk seams and tear flashing.

When cantilevering reaches its limit, you are forced to rely on the main house for support, and lose some of the structural advantages of the combination design, leaving you once again with the technical and budgetary headaches of a true second story.

Also, there are cases where there is no architectural fit. Tiny lots, of course, do not tolerate any increased *footprint* (the area of ground covered by the building). In spacious yards, a combination addition might seem like a strange beast hulking over a house that should be expanded horizontally. Like the room and second-story additions that are their basic components, combinations are the ideal design for *some* houses. It is the designer's task to determine which of the basic configurations will best suit a particular site.

OTHER TYPES OF ADDITIONS

There are several other ways to add space to a house aside from the three basic addition types described above. First, it is always worthwhile to explore the relatively inexpensive route of adding small bump-out spaces like dormers or cantilevered bays. Adding just a few square feet to a room can have a significant effect on its use and free up space throughout the rest of the house.

I do not consider dormers and cantilevered bays to be true additions, however, because they are small in scale and seldom require their own foundations or modifications to existing foundations. Basic carpentry references in the bibliography at the back of the book explain how they are built. The other major way to add space to a house is to build an addition below it.

Building below

While adding space below a house is appropriate in some circumstances, the specialized techniques of excavating and building properly sealed subterranean rooms or raising the building and framing a first story below it are beyond the scope of this book. References on underground architecture appear in the bibliography, and information on the feasibility of a specific project can be obtained from contractors who perform this type of work.

Certain technical drawbacks to building basements, compared to above-ground additions, should be considered. First, excavating is fairly expensive. It requires renting and operating or subcontracting for a small bulldozer or similar machine, some inevitable hand digging and usually a lot of off-site dumping. Second, waterproofing can be expensive, since drainpipes must be well below grade and must travel some distance to return to daylight. Optionally, ground water can be pumped upward, but this, too, is expensive compared to draining an

Raising this northern California house enabled the designer to add space, replace a foundation that was inadequate to support a second story and easily add shear walls.

The new lower floor adds a garage and storage area in the front and an office and family room in the back, while the living area, kitchen and bedrooms remain above.

The advantages and disadvantages of this approach must be weighed carefully, however. The disadvantage, from an architectural standpoint, is that what was presumably a sensible first-floor plan is now pushed up a full story. While an upstairs living room works in some designs, a dining room and kitchen are less appealing. If the expense of adding a new downstairs kitchen then converting the original to some other use is considered, the entire project becomes questionable.

The lower story can, of course, be used as a garage, laundry, utility room, rumpus room or sleeping quarters, but the price of these improvements should be checked carefully against other options. A laundry can fit in a closet, a heater can go just about anywhere, and a converted attic makes a great place for the kids to romp. Raising a house might be a lot of trouble just to gain a garage.

On the plus side, there are a couple of good reasons to raise a house, particularly if setbacks or other considerations make tearing off the roof and building a second story the only other logical option. The first is to preserve exceptional architecture. Many older houses have turret-roofed towers, filigreed fascias and other marvelous features that should be thrust upward for all to see. The lower portions of such houses are often comparatively plain, and it is easy enough to match or mimic them with new construction. Thus the best features of the building can be displayed, while the needed space can be provided at a competitive cost.

The second good reason to raise a house is that it may actually prove

ordinary foundation. Third, and similarly, sewage from downstairs fixtures must be removed by a somewhat costly and technologically dependent pump, rather than by the natural flow of gravity. If a basement is added, it's a good idea to consult an engineer who understands the local soil conditions.

There are some architectural problems with basements, too. It is hard to provide full basements—where the floor is 7 ft. 6 in. or more below grade—with sufficient natural light or ventilation, not to mention views. If there is a bedroom, it must have an exterior door or a window with

its sill not more than 44 in. above the floor for fire egress (1994 Uniform Building Code). Although exterior stair or window wells can solve these problems, they require more digging, building, drainage and maintenance.

Raising a house There are fewer technical problems in raising a house and building ordinary stud walls below it than in digging downward. Contractors involved in this type of work normally hire house raisers as subcontractors, then use standard construction techniques to build the addition. Special equipment and techniques are used, once again, to lower the house onto its new first story.

ADDITIONS ON SLOPES

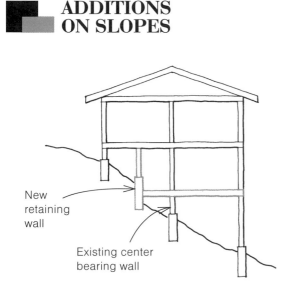

Raised ceiling in added portion increases light and feeling of space.

New retaining wall

Existing center bearing wall

Closet in cantilever

Existing exterior wall

Posts support new exterior wall.

DIGGING INTO THE HILLSIDE
Houses built on steep slopes can be expanded in their sub-area. It is expensive, however, to add a downstairs room by digging back into the hillside, building forms and pouring a concrete retaining wall. Also, the new space is dark and cave-like.

BUILDING DOWN THE SLOPE
Building down the slope is a better solution. The exterior foundation is much easier to build, and the new space has better access to natural light and a greater potential to be architecturally dynamic.

more economical than building a second story, particularly if the foundation is in bad condition. Once the house is up on blocks, it is a straightforward matter to replace the foundation, install shear walls and address other structural issues with new construction techniques, rather than laboriously retrofitting.

Additions on slopes

Houses built on slopes invite basement additions since they normally enclose a large volume of space between the grade and the main floor. Given the choice, it is better to build the addition out and step the house down the hill than to dig back into the slope (see the drawing above).

Building out saves the cost of excavating and then constructing and waterproofing a concrete retaining wall, and allows deeper penetration of natural light into the new space.

Although this type of addition—and the raised-house addition discussed above—is not specifically covered in this book, the methods of assessing feasibility and the design and engineering principles explained here apply to them as well as to room, second-story and combination additions. With a little creative adapting, the designer or builder can make good use of the information given here to plan a workable raised house or stepped-down addition.

MAKING A DECISION

Many factors influence the choice of addition type. Though a design may suggest itself, it is a mistake to commit to an addition type too early in the process only to discover a hidden flaw when the plans are half finished. Only after carefully analyzing each option should you choose and develop the addition type that best meets the requirements of the program.

3
DESIGNING FOR CONTINUITY

Additions confront their designers with a peculiar paradox. In some ways, they are harder to design than new houses because of the constraints imposed upon them by the existing building. In other ways, they're easier to design because the options are limited and the potential for confusion is minimized. While designers are sometimes at a loss for a place to begin a new building, following the patterns established by the existing house can serve as a guide to a successful design.

The designer or builder's task is to see the house for what it is and try to understand how it got that way. When you can duplicate its growth pattern, you will also know how to take advantage of its givens. Then you can integrate the addition so that the completed building looks and functions like a single entity.

REMODELED OR REMUDDLED?

There is no right or wrong way to design, just better and worse ways. Some projects go smoothly: They are completed on time and on budget, make the owners happy and enhance the original building. Others require all sorts of extra work: They call for elaborate, rather than simple and elegant, technical solutions and drive the poor owners and carpenters crazy while making the building look worse than it did to begin with.

What's the difference? How can you be sure you're improving a building with a remodel, rather than throwing away the owners' money on a "remuddle" (to use a word coined by the *Old-House Journal*)? Simply stated, continuity with the shape, style and spirit of the existing house is the key to successful addition design. Conversely, the extent to which you try to impose preconceived notions on a project is the extent to which you fail. The secret of designing a successful remodel lies in keeping out of the way and letting the building do the talking. When the work is finished, someone walking by the house should barely realize it has been added to.

This turn-of-the-century, rural home in Minnesota had been re-modeled several times before it was given a sun-porch addition (at left in the photo above) and a complete stylistic transforma-tion to match. The design objec-tive was to impart a timeless quality to the building through the blending of contemporary and historical elements.

The steep roof massing and details like the double-hung, divided windows—characteristic of other homes built in the same era and region—helped the designer capture the building's original spirit. Contemporary detailing on traditional elements like the transom windows and front-porch columns added the modern touch.

Strong historical details and modern massing combine elegantly in this two-story, wing-style room addition to a modern home with neocolonial references. (For an interior view of this house, see the photo on p. 73.)

This approach may seem anathema to young architects striving to create their own means of expression and build their reputations. However, I am not suggesting that you copy the existing building, but creatively blend the addition with it, just as you might try to fit a new, "organic" house into its landscape. Achieving continuity is the challenge, and there is plenty of room for art of a refined nature.

In fact, it is difficult, if not prohibitively expensive, to copy the stylistic features of most older and even many newer buildings. Reproducing leaded glass, antique moldings and other finishes requires specialized skills. Since such touches come at the end of a project when funds are dwindling, it might be wise to designate them as optional in the specifications. To avoid ending up with a remuddle, design for success through simplification, and avoid overrunning the budget and com-

ing up short by striving for exact replication.

Furthermore, it is not always desirable to copy the existing building exactly. Many older houses have beautiful decor yet suffer from poor basic design by today's standards. Cramped floor plans, poor natural lighting, insufficient storage and badly laid out kitchens are common deficiencies that should not be duplicated.

Classic Remuddles

There is an interesting tale behind the additions to each of these unique homes. Rumor has it, for example, that the second-story addition to the northern California house (top left) was built

instantly when an earthquake pitched a small neighboring house so high into the air that it landed on the roof of the house in the photo.

Neighbors claim that the two-story, backyard addition to the house at right was actually designed as a

drive-up taco place for an unnamed site in New Mexico, but the plans were sold to the owners of this California Mission-style house when financing for the restaurant fell through.

Finally, it is told that the owner of the house at

bottom left went to great pains to make the color of his house compatible with that of his car.

What is the essential spirit of this house? What feelings does it evoke? What type of addition would blend with its style and spirit?

The first task, then, is to determine what it is about the house that should be kept or eliminated and what it lacks that should be added. Begin with the basics, by grasping the essential spirit of the house so you can tell how to bring out the best in it.

THE ESSENTIAL SPIRIT

To capture the house's essential spirit, notice how it makes you feel. What are the subjective impressions you get as you approach it, walk through it, relax within its walls? Once you've felt your way around,

try to come up with a word or two that accurately describe the house's intrinsic qualities or the feelings it produces. Is the house "noble," "grand," "ethereal," "tidy"? What makes it so?

Perhaps your impression arises from a combination of things, like a white picket fence and a flower-lined, winding brick path leading to an arched, heavy plank door with a wrought-iron handle. Cream-colored walls are offset by dark clinker-brick veneers and small casement windows with plain, dark trim and diamond-shaped mullions. Ivy abounds. A stout shake roof holds out the December drizzle as puffs of smoke rise slowly from the chimney.

The essence is…cozy? charming? Perhaps there isn't a word for it, but there is an image, and it evokes an emotional response. This response is what should be recaptured, re-animated by whatever means are appropriate for the addition.

Would it make sense to dominate this cozy, provincial cottage's low roof line with a bulky, stark white, three-story stucco structure that has flat roofs and chrome pipe rails wrapped around curved balconies? We could laugh, if such travesties were not committed every day.

The cottage is red, textured, earthy, small, old, irregular, perhaps overgrown. Its interior is woody, dark, cool, cozy and quiet. It evokes a romantic sense of the rural life, a return to the earth, escape and peace. A stark, modern building evokes...something else.

The addition's budget may have no room for bricks, shakes or even cute little multi-paned windows, but the designer must still strive to create something that refers not only visually to the rest of the building, but also spiritually to those bygone times when life was simpler, quieter, and we were better connected to the earth. If the main house were somehow destroyed and only the addition survived, it should, ideally, arouse those same sentiments.

Unadorned and awkward houses

Certainly not all homes possess the richness of form and texture of our country cottage. A chief complaint about many, if not most, American houses of recent vintage, particularly those built by the millions in the fifties, is that they lack character. Yet even these mass-produced units were designed according to some principle, if nothing more than that of an open floor plan, which was marketed as "contemporary" but actually saved the developer the cost of building interior walls. Every house, even if it is a degenerated copy of a copy, has some original essence or spirit that can be recaptured. What is offered should be acknowledged, gratefully, and built upon.

In fact, a plain house can offer more opportunity for artistic expression— from the basic shape of the building to details as small as sink faucets. There are times, too, when a small house will have a huge addition, possibly larger than the existing structure. Unless the house has outstanding features, the addition can dictate the overall appearance.

Some houses send mixed messages. If the original designer was confused, obsequious toward an erratic client or just plain crazy, you may be confronted by a hybrid of Colonial columns, a Prairie-style roof with Spanish tiles, aluminum sliding doors and Art Nouveau wrought-iron banisters. There may be similar confusion in the relative scale and orientation of the rooms, the relation of the house to the lot or view, and so on. Here, the designer's job is to sort out what goes and what stays, choose a theme based on a major element or the owners' preference, and make it stick throughout the house and the addition.

Somewhere in the midst of the feasibility consultations, structural assessments, estimating and many other tasks needed to get the design started, it is important to spend a little time alone with the house and seek its essential spirit by taking a quiet, solitary walk through it, by sketching it or even by dreaming about it. While this book outlines numerous procedures and techniques for transforming the house as a physical object, you will have to determine how to transmit its intangible essence to the addition. After all, it is your personal reaction to the building that allows you to capture its spirit in the first place.

EXTERIOR CONTINUITY

Once you have identified the house's essence, you can survey it as a work of architecture. Look at every aspect, from its roof line and internal consistency to details as small as doorknobs. The goal is to find a practical means of recreating the ambiance in the addition.

Continuity between the house and the addition can be achieved through many design strategies and devices, and on many levels. Here, I will present some of the most important, namely the compatibility of overall massing, subassemblies, components, details, elements, materials and color.

Massing

A building's *massing* is its gross form or overall shape as defined by the shapes, sizes and relationships of its various component masses. A massing study is a rough sketch or model of a building (see pp. 194-195 for more on massing studies).

Massing is influenced by many factors, including the climate (available sunlight, dominant winds, mean temperatures), the context (the character of the neighborhood and the form, style, size and location of adjacent buildings), the site (slope, configuration, soil stability), the existing house (shape, floor plan, style, etc.) and the program. The climate, context, site and program are examined in detail in later chapters. This chapter focuses on those aspects of massing that help the addition conform to the existing house: scale, proportion, placement, articulation, symmetry and rhythm.

An Arts and Crafts Addition

This two-story combination addition (bottom photo and cover), winner of the 1995 "sympathetic addition" award from the National Trust for Historic Preservation, replaced a previous addition (top photo) built on the back of the turn-of-the-century, Arts and Crafts style home. The earlier addition was not only inconsistent with the style of the house, but was also cramped. It restricted the view into the backyard as well.

Notice how the visual composition of the two-story facade, which is essentially square in its overall proportions, is unified through the repetition of strong horizontal lines on several primary massing elements—the lower roof edge, the balcony railing and the tie rafter at the bottom of the gable-wall grille. The repetition of vertical components like the two sets of doors, balcony fencing, gable-wall grille slats and knee braces balances the strong horizontal statements and imparts a harmonious, restful feeling to the composition.

The equilibrium remains dynamic rather than static, however, because of the dynamic nature of individual components—the angled roofs, balcony walls and knee braces, and the positive/negative visual effect created by the grilles and open expanses of glass in each window. Dynamic interplay between the components, which vary in their size and relative position to the building's vertical and horizontal center lines, strengthens the effect. (Compare the static symmetry of the house in the top photo on p. 40.)

The American Arts and Crafts style, with its simple, elegant lines, lends itself both to replication and historical reference as well as to graceful composition. The Arts and Crafts motif can also be a good choice for dressing up a house that has no particular style of its own and must be tied in stylistically with an addition. (For an interior view of this house, see the top photo on p. 50.)

Scale, proportion and the relationship between masses are the crux of massing. An addition's scale is its size relative to the house. If it appears too big, it is out of scale. Its mass can be articulated, or broken up, to reduce its apparent size. If the addition seems small, using a design device like increasing the thickness of its roof edge can increase its relative scale.

The proportions of the addition, too, should reflect those of the house. Long, low masses usually work best with other long, low masses; tall with tall. Also, the relative proportions of features like chimneys and roof overhangs should be followed in the addition. Although the relationship between masses is a complex subject, learning about the principles of massing discussed here will help keep the design out of trouble.

Placement is the location or concentration of masses. In most cases, for example, the building should appear grounded and stable, not top heavy. The larger masses, then, should be kept near the ground, and oversized roofs should be avoided.

Articulation is the three-dimensional breaking up, or varying, of a surface or mass. While a degree of articulation relieves monotony, it is also possible to confuse or tire the eye with too many masses, especially if they are not arranged in a rhythmical, symmetrical fashion. Masses should appear harmonious, not jumbled. On a small-scale building, the best guideline is to keep the masses simple and relatively few in number, featuring those that say the most about the intent of the design.

Two Approaches to Massing

Although these two houses with second-story additions show different approaches to massing, the designs clearly use some of the same principles. Both buildings are good examples of articulation, or the breaking up of masses, and dynamic symmetry, or balance created with offset elements.

Notice how the masses are arranged so that they appear to flow into one another in a rhythmic succession of retreating, peaked roofs that leads the eye upward and creates a mountain-range effect. Also note how the placement of the largest masses on the first story keeps the buildings visually grounded.

The house in the photo at left is on a rectangular lot, and the massing is viewed primarily from the front. The front-porch mass is dynamically counterbalanced by the mass of the chimney on the upper left, making a subtle diagonal connection that ties the building together visually.

The house in the photo at right is seen from three sides on its corner lot (the entrance faces the corner). The entrance is flanked with wings and invitingly set back to draw in viewers or guests.

Symmetry signifies balance, or off-setting one visual element against another. If a house features a large chimney, for example, it can look lopsided. *Static symmetry,* or an exact balance, calls for a nearly identical compensating feature, like a chimney on the opposite side (see the top photo on p. 40 for an example of static symmetry). *Dynamic symmetry* calls for a visual counter force, perhaps a front porch with strong columns, to balance the mass of the chimney without replicating it.

Rhythm is the regular repetition of forms or elements—the extra beat, so to speak, that the addition might provide to clarify an otherwise weak line. Rhythm can be established by replicating bays, dormers or any number of substructures that already project from or are even added to the original house in a continuous series. Rhythm can also be developed with components, details or elements rather than masses.

The roof line The most visible characteristic of a house, especially when seen from a distance, is its roof line. To achieve unity in massing, begin by making the addition's roof fit that of the house (see the photos on p. 38). As a rule, avoid mixing shapes and styles, and keep the relationship between roofs simple. If a house has an honest, unpretentious gable, introduce a second gable of the same pitch. If further articulation is desired, consider adding a third roof or dormers. A gambrel can be crossed by other gambrels, or even have a shed extension off its lower pitch. Gambrels and other roof types, however, will often clash.

After determining the shape and style of the roof, make sure that the rest of the building's masses are proportional to it and keep to the basic design statement. If you wish to create a dramatic, reaching-to-the-sky effect, for example, a steep pitch will lead the eye upward. But a wide building below the gable will appear squat and weaken the statement.

Massing, roof lines and style A house's style and details should relate to its massing. Roofs, for example, not only shape the house, but they frequently identify its type as well. While simple gables and hips may be associated with any number of house types, flat roofs finish off severe modern massings, Queen Anne Victorians are crowned with many gables, and gambrels cover barns.

The gambrel's strong lines and humble origins as a barn roof can be left behind to some extent when it shows up in the city on a house covered with horizontal lap siding, adorned with a few columns on the porch and outfitted with shutters and heavy moldings. But overdressing the building can cause downright embarrassment. Lap siding is reminiscent of the serviceable board-and-batten barns down on the farm. Cover a gambrel house with stucco, add fancy wrought-iron filigree and Corinthian porch columns, and our wholesome country style appears pretentious, awkward and out of place.

Subassemblies

Subassemblies are units such as stairs, porches or decks that are attached to the outside of the house. Their architectural significance varies greatly. For example, some stairs simply get us from the yard to the front door, while others are major features of the entry.

Modifying existing subassemblies can help pull the house and addition together. Enlarging a porch, for example, by wrapping it around the house so it becomes a veranda connecting to an addition can serve several functions (see the drawing on p. 39). These functions might include pulling together the front and rear masses; visually increasing the lower mass to help ground a house with a tall addition; making the house seem more prominent by increasing its overall mass and enhancing its entry; improving circulation by providing a path between two exterior doors; making easier access to the side yard; and adding an enjoyable, relaxing space for the summer (and by adding removable windows, a sun room for the winter).

If cost, setbacks or other considerations prevent you from building a veranda, you can still take advantage of the existing porch—perhaps by extending its roof line to tie the new and old portions of the house together, or by building a small porch on the addition that mirrors the main porch.

In other cases it might be appropriate to eliminate a marginal subassembly altogether, stripping the building so you can redecorate it at will. If, for example, the budget allows for only simple, unadorned masses and an elaborate, dilapidated wood staircase needs rebuilding, it might make sense to scrap the original staircase and replace it with a simpler version.

Subassemblies should be consistent with the basic style of the house. It would be an aesthetic mistake, for example, to add a plain, California-style redwood deck onto a Victorian or Spanish-style house. Before designing a subassembly for a vernacular home, study the idiom and devise an affordable means of adapting to its style. Photos of houses where subassemblies play an important part in the design are shown on pgs. 10, 31 (bottom) and 36 (left).

Components

Components are doors, windows and other individual items like chimneys that both serve a function and help identify a building's style. Since components stand in relation to the rest of the building and to one another, their type, style, scale, shape, alignment, arrangement and rhythm should be considered carefully.

The roof line of this 1930s addition blends well with that of the original 1918 northern California Tudor-style house. Note how lowering the addition's roof, rather than simply continuing the massive roof on the right, provides articulation and keeps the eye moving, while the chimney helps counter the peaked-roof facade.

Consistent and inconsistent roof lines are contrasted on these gable-roofed houses with gambrel styling. The roof of the small bump-out room to the rear of the house at left blends nicely with the main roof, as does the garage in the foreground. By contrast, the addition in the photo at right stands out because of its nonconforming roof line (even though its siding and trim are consistent with the main house).

Doors and entries Front doors are special components in that they are associated with the approach to the building and entry subassemblies (porches and stairs), some of which are quite elaborate. As discussed in the example of the wraparound veranda, giving the entry special treatment can help tie the house and the addition together.

Naturally, the style of the door should be compatible with that of the entry assembly and with the other components and detailing on the house; yet it is not necessary that there be a perfect match. In the photo at left on p. 36, for example, the door that is recessed in a visually significant entry assembly is actually quite different in style and appearance from the windows. The effect is not jarring, however, in part because the door goes along with the general neotraditional motif of the house and also because the door relates more directly to the porch than to the windows and details like the knee braces that tie the rest of the composition together.

Many front and side doors, however, are more visible in relation to the rest of the components and details. It is critical that these doors match up well with the other components. Good examples of the relation of doors to other components are shown in the photos on pgs. 33, 35 (bottom) and 40 (bottom).

Windows and fenestration In most houses, the aggregate of the windows is the third largest visual feature after the roof and the walls. Windows vary from tiny wood casements that freshen the air in closets to entire walls of high-tech glass and aluminum. Since duplicating the originals in the addition may not be feasible, the designer

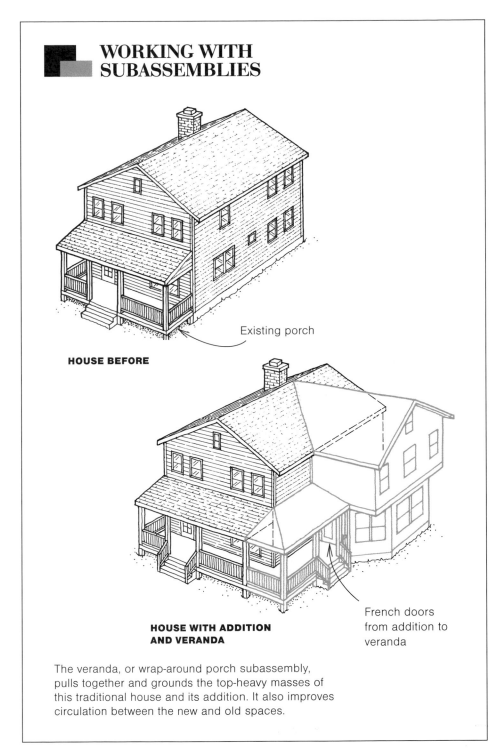

WORKING WITH SUBASSEMBLIES

Existing porch

HOUSE BEFORE

HOUSE WITH ADDITION AND VERANDA

French doors from addition to veranda

The veranda, or wrap-around porch subassembly, pulls together and grounds the top-heavy masses of this traditional house and its addition. It also improves circulation between the new and old spaces.

must frequently search for a compatible alternative.

Ideally the addition's windows will be the same size, proportions, color and shape as the house's, even if their materials and type (e.g., aluminum casement vs. wood double-hung) vary. Things are seldom

ideal, however. For example, you might find that a house's existing bedrooms have tall, narrow, double-hung units, while the new art studio along the same wall needs a wide picture window. Furthermore, the wide-trim, wood double-hung windows are painted blue, while an affordable picture window comes in narrow-trimmed white aluminum, which will usually not take paint.

One answer to such a dilemma might be to minimize the differences by combining features. Paint the blue windows white, and add a decorative sill and wide wood trim to the aluminum unit. The resem-

blance can be further improved by dividing the picture window into three sections, with two opening wings and a fixed center pane. This solution will be particularly helpful if the wings have the same tall, narrow proportions as the old windows. The similarity will be strengthened, too, if the new and old windows are the same height and their headers are at the same level.

If the differences are simply too pronounced, windows that match more closely must be chosen, even if they cost more. In such cases, you'll have to decide whether the house or addition should set the tone. Although it is usually the house, there are situations where the best choice is to preempt the existing windows and replace them

Orderly fenestration and static symmetry characterize the traditional home at left. An addition would have to be designed carefully to build on the symmetry without monotonously repeating the elements.

Orderly and disorderly fenestration are used effectively on the addition to the front of the rural Connecticut home below. While the top and bottom window groups are not directly related, rhythm and symmetry govern the relationships between each group's components. Also, the high color contrast between the windows and their background makes them stand out as a major design feature. (For interior shots of the lower windows, see pgs. 53 [bottom] and 75.)

with the type that's been selected for the addition. This approach might be appropriate if the originals are worn and dry-rotted or have already been replaced with cheap substitutes that don't fit the house, or if the addition is large compared to the house (see the bottom photo on the facing page).

While there are many approaches to matching windows visually, there are serious deterrents to moving them. Because of the expense of cutting into walls, installing headers and resealing walls, existing windows and doors should be repositioned only when absolutely necessary—to accommodate an important change in the existing floor plan, for example.

Avoid the temptation to resize or rearrange *all* of the house's windows because that can consume a large portion of the budget for the addition. Although you can change their appearance, the grouping and alignment of the windows in the main house will usually dictate the arrangement in the addition.

The arrangement of windows is called *fenestration* (from the Latin *fenestra*, meaning window). Fenestration is of two types, orderly and disorderly; the windows either line up with each other or are placed somewhat randomly, depending on factors like their position in the room and the available view. "Orderly" does not necessarily mean symmetrical. It just means arranged in a definable and repeatable pattern.

Orderly fenestration usually reflects the structure within, because the posts supporting vertically stacked

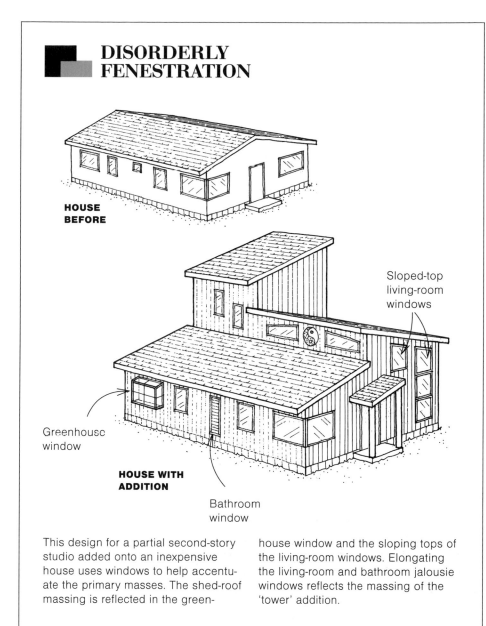

DISORDERLY FENESTRATION

HOUSE BEFORE

HOUSE WITH ADDITION

Greenhouse window

Sloped-top living-room windows

Bathroom window

This design for a partial second-story studio added onto an inexpensive house uses windows to help accentuate the primary masses. The shed-roof massing is reflected in the green- house window and the sloping tops of the living-room windows. Elongating the living-room and bathroom jalousie windows reflects the massing of the 'tower' addition.

window headers are aligned to carry their loads straight to the foundation (see the top photo on the facing page). Since the superstructure is revealed by the windows, the appearance of overall unity is reinforced and the designer's "statement" is strengthened. For this reason, as well as for greater efficiency of construction, most buildings have orderly fenestration.

Another advantage of orderly fenestration is that it can impart rhythm

to the wall surfaces. If the windows are arranged in a rhythmical pattern, such as two large/one small/two large across the main facade of a big house, these major components will help bring focus and logic to what would otherwise be an amorphous surface.

Disorderly fenestration, on the other hand, can be used to move

The diamond-shaped element introduced in the starter course of this house's new shingles refers directly to the motif of the existing diamond-patterned mullions in the windows.

the eye about the composition or provide unique and refreshing elements (see the drawing on p. 41). Disorderly fenestration must be handled carefully, however, so as not to lapse into chaos through the introduction of too many unbalanced elements.

After analyzing the existing window pattern, strive to reproduce or simulate it in the addition. Consistent vertical or horizontal alignment is a good start. A new second story will usually look best if its windows are set directly above those on the lower floor. Also, they should be the same width, or smaller. If one window is wider (unless it spans the exact width of two windows below), the structure might seem top heavy. When building out horizontally, keep the header bottoms at a consistent height (usually 6 ft. 10½ in. off the floor to match the door headers), even though the windows themselves may vary in height. Finally, observe groupings and rhythms and try to continue them. If windows come in pairs, pair them in the addition; if a pair is followed by a single window, adding another pair to the extended wall will set up a two/one/two rhythm.

Other components Other components such as dormers, bays and chimneys should follow the principles of continuity discussed above. The massing, scale and style of dormers and bays should be compatible with the overall composition, and they should be placed and arranged carefully. Incorporating dormers and bays into the addition and then introducing them onto a house where they did not previously exist can help make strong visual connections that unify the building.

Chimneys, like front doors, are an unusual component in that there is normally just one per house and they are relatively large in scale. It is important, then, to balance the rest of the composition with an existing chimney when designing the addition. Because they are large and somewhat difficult to modify or cover, existing chimneys might be a good starting point for choosing the style of an otherwise unadorned building. A smooth, brick chimney might suggest a neocolonial approach, whereas rough clinker bricks or stone could inspire a rustic cottage or an Arts and Crafts design.

Details and elements

A detail is a small part of a building, subassembly or component. It is usually both functional and aesthetic. The principles of consistency that apply to massing and components should be followed in the details. For example, exposed plumb-cut rafters on the house should be repeated on the addition; knee braces, newel posts, porch columns, railings, and so on, should also conform.

Detailing should be consistent with the overall theme adopted for the building. Rustic, hand-hewn beams clash with Victorian moldings; scalloped valances fit with cabinets from the forties, not the nineties.

Elements are purely decorative items like relief carvings on walls and painted stripes. If the house has a decorative motif, repeat it or put a reasonable facsimile in the addition. If there is no motif, you can introduce one just to reinforce continuity.

Materials

Whatever the building's styling, material consistency is critical to continuity. A brick addition, for example, stands out like a sore thumb on a house with wood siding.

Match materials whenever possible. One of the virtues of a durable material like stucco is that it shows few signs of aging compared, say, to wood shingles. When stucco is applied to the addition by a good craftsman who can duplicate the original texture, simply painting both surfaces is enough to produce a virtual match.

However, many of yesterday's siding profiles, moldings, masonry, glass blocks and so on are virtually unavailable, and might be too expensive even if they could be found. Along with the price at the store, today's builder must consider the labor of installation. Four-by-eight sheets of paneling and siding were created as part of a construction revolution stimulated by the need for efficient production of military buildings during the World War II. Houses built before the war did not have sheet materials, and were slower to build. Using sheet materials makes sense, but the problem remains that they invariably look different from earlier materials.

Compatibility of materials In cases where exact matches are not feasible, strive to achieve compatibility. The characteristics that identify a material are form, hardness, pattern, texture and color. The forms of the materials should work together. Round river stones in the fireplace do not suggest jagged flagstones in the planter by the entrance. Square, sharp-edged moldings are incompatible with round trim. Some materials need to

be hard to do their job—oak for a floor, marble for a counter. If its function is not an issue, however, a less expensive, softer material of similar appearance can be used. If the house has oak window and door trim, for example, pine or fir with an oak stain can be substituted.

Follow existing patterns. If the main roof has three-tab shingles, so should the addition's. If the interior doors and cabinets are straight-grained mahogany, birch doors with their lively grain pattern will clash. Similarly, textures should be compatible. If the house has rustic, vertical, solid-wood siding, plywood siding with a rough-hewn surface and vertical grooves could work for the addition, particularly if the transition is not highly visible from the front.

Also be aware of a material's color, and stick to certain basic principles like grouping colors in families—earth tones with other earth tones, for example—and limiting the number of colors to minimize visual confusion. Natural materials and painted surfaces should also be coordinated. The designer who places bright pink marble in a sea-foam-green bathroom has shown an exceptional capacity to take risks.

Align materials consistently. If the house's siding has horizontal lines, so should the addition's, even if the materials differ. This is not to say that you should scratch lines into a stucco addition on a brick house, but if the main theme is horizontal, some horizontal element, perhaps an embedded row of half bricks, can carry it over.

Although they have different shapes, colors and textures, the many materials that exist side by side on this house work well together. There are visual clues—like the lack of crisp edges and variants in color within each material—but the main reason they work is because of the intrinsic, rustic quality of each material. (For another view of this house, see the photo on p. 33.)

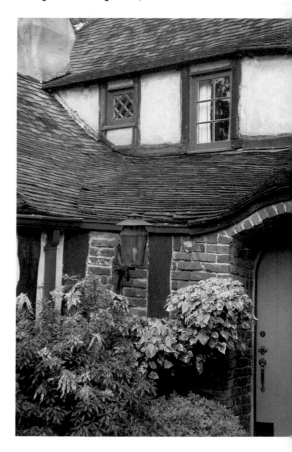

Color can be used in numerous ways to enhance a building. Here, the roof and a number of components and details, along with the otherwise undistinguished walls, are united by the pronounced, powder-blue strip with its crisp, dark edge.

Though the walls of the small, round addition on the left end of the house above have no shingles, the inconsistency is minimized because the stepped-down massing, window style and, most important in this case, roof and wall colors are consistent.

The massing and detailing of this second-story addition to a northern California home work well, but contrasting materials and colors—natural shingle and painted stucco—keep it from blending in with the original building.

Materials in the addition should be grouped in the same way that they are found in the house. If there is a 3-ft. high band of shingles at the bottom of a lap-siding wall, keep it going. If the front gable wall of a brick house is covered with vertical white boards, repeat the theme on the gable wall of the addition.

Finally, give the materials the same priority on the addition that they have on the house. If the house is predominantly stucco, with brick or wood for accents, feature stucco on the addition. If the main house does not have a clearly dominant material, choose one that best expresses the theme of the design. Featuring it in the addition will strengthen its showing on the house.

Intrinsic qualities Materials like stone and wood occur naturally and have an intrinsic appeal because they connect us with our roots. Milled aluminum and extruded plastic have a certain high-tech aesthetic appeal.

In those instances when it is simply impractical to incorporate the existing materials in the addition and you are at a loss to select an equivalent, you can once again appeal to your sixth sense and seek materials that convey the same message. The addition to a rustic stone house, for example, could combine ordinary drywall with exposed, heavy timber rafters to carry the theme. The effect could be reinforced by exposing heavy lintels and using stones selectively, say in the hearth.

Color

Designers and builders are responsible for so many aspects of a project that they often treat color as an afterthought. Overlooking color is a mistake. Paint or stain can make

or break a design, bring a house together or blow it apart. From the beginning, a coordinated color scheme for the house and addition should be given the same weight as other concerns.

Start with an evaluation of the existing paint job. Is it in good condition, or should it be redone? Do the colors work, or would the house look better with a different combination? If a loud color like bright yellow works on a small house, will it be overwhelming when the mass is doubled by the addition? Do the owners like the present color scheme, hate it or have no strong feelings either way? Does the color scheme fit its immediate context or clash with the landscape or neighboring houses?

Next, ask what statement should be made, or reinforced, with the color scheme. Will the combination of wall and trim colors seem formal, relaxed, bold, earthy or airy? Ask the same question even for a brick or stone house where the wall color is fixed and only the doors, windows and trim will be painted. Imagine a red brick house with white trim, then with dark forest green trim. The first says cheerful, bright, Colonial; the second says quiet, reclusive, a retreat.

Generally, bright colors (yellow, orange, pink, royal blue) make a house pop out from its background; dark colors (blood red, navy, violet, dark greens and greys) and rich earth tones (dark browns, burgundy, ocher) make it recede and blend in; whites, tans, pastels and neutrals can go either way, depending on the context.

Trim and wall colors The relationship between the trim and wall colors has various effects on the overall appearance. If the trim is the same color as the walls, only a slight shade darker or lighter, the overall effect will be one of simplicity and ease on the eye (see the top photo on p. 31). This color scheme might be chosen for simplicity's sake, or because the house already has a lot going on in terms of its massing, texture and details.

If the trim is not the same color as the walls, the degree of difference becomes a critical choice. A medium degree of contrast on a house with an average number of doors and windows will make the walls and the trim read as balanced (see the bottom photo on p. 35).

High contrast, achieved by intense shade differences or by using an entirely different color for the trim, will usually make the trim stand out and the walls recede. (The exception is when the walls are bright and the trim is very light or white, e.g., yellow walls with white doors and windows.) An average-size house will seem busier and usually somewhat smaller. An exceptionally stark facade with minimal trim, however, may actually seem larger, or at least be more noticeable, because of the highlighted trim. Finally, contrasting trim can enliven facades, pull the eye to recessed volumes that might otherwise fade into obscurity, and make a statement about the overall architectural intent that may not be clear from the massing alone (see the photo at left on p. 36).

A high-contrast paint job must be handled with care. The walls and trim must be truly complementary, because contrast accentuates clashes. Be sure that both the wall color and the trim color reinforce the intended message. If the walls are a serviceable, unassuming grey, bright lavender trim will go, but it will not say "modest."

This modern Tudor facade reflects a long tradition of housebuilding. Notice how the white panels between the contrasting, dark 'timbers' are used to establish patterns and rhythms. Also note the compatibility of the stucco and stained wood, which refer to earlier, more natural materials, with the fieldstone facade below. The stone and overall massing of the facade serve to counterbalance the steep, upward thrust of the roof line.

Color in context Paint can refer to natural materials and blend with outdoor surroundings. Earth tones and neutrals impart some of the feeling of a woodsy interior, and the classic dark green will never lose its appeal for trimming log cabins nestled in the forest. Phosphorescent colors and metallic greys fit into some urban settings.

On the other hand, colors that intentionally clash with their surroundings can liberate us from the traditional or mundane. Fanciful or even wild color schemes can shake off lethargy and give our spirits a quick, if not always lasting, lift. Avoid trends, however. Today's fads can rapidly degenerate into tomorrow's jokes. A designer's work is strongest when it augments what is enduring in the home.

Color and style Colors should be compatible with the style of the house. Tudor houses started as humble, two-story, "half-timbered" English farm houses. Rather than cover the frame with siding, as we do today, the builders filled the voids between the massive wood members with wattle, or woven sticks, then plastered the wattle with a layer of mud, which was given a coat of whitewash to preserve it. Over the years, the exposed wood darkened and needed oiling. The mud had to be resurfaced and whitewashed again. Thus developed the high contrast between the dark, natural wood and the stark white walls that later became a common theme in the plush country homes of the English gentry. The style is still admired and built today with false timbers embedded in ordinary stucco walls (see the photo at left).

The look is intrinsically beautiful, but part of what makes us love it is our associations with its history.

You should think seriously before staining the timbers of a Tudor anything but a rich, dark wood color, or painting the stucco anything other than white.

One advantage of adding onto a vernacular house like a Tudor is that if you are willing to yield to tradition, potentially difficult decisions are made for you. Just match the colors of the pigments that the Colonial English, Spanish or French found in their locale and get on with the work.

Many homes built since World War II, however, can be best described as modifications of the California ranch style. They are simple, gable-roofed, single-story rectangular buildings without much trim—basic houses. When taking the major step of building an addition, you can use distinctive color schemes to give personalities to these John Does of houses. But even though the functions and sizes of the addition may be clear, the potential number of color choices on these blank slates can seem overwhelming.

So far, I have discussed only two-tone paint jobs. Imagine the complexities that arise when a third, fourth or even fifth color is introduced, especially on a house like a Victorian that has highly articulated massing and fancy trim.

All designers must be aware of their limitations. It may be unduly burdensome to expect to master color theory as well as meet all the other challenges of designing an addition. Design normally requires the input of several experts, and color specialists are among those you can turn to without any feelings of inadequacy.

Contrast

Although most of this chapter has been devoted to means of achieving continuity in design, there is a place for intentional contrast in the architecture of additions. But the key word is *intentional*. There's a distinction between contrast as a design device and inconsistency as a design flaw.

Carefully designed contrast can bring out the best in a building, highlight an effect or make a statement about changing times. Employed consciously and with discretion, it can be as vital a part of the designer's repertoire as any other.

Intentional contrast (top) and strict continuity (bottom) are shown in these two New England additions. In the house in the top photo, a variety of spaces have been added onto the original barn (the white building in the background) over a period of time. A more traditional approach, and one more consistent with most of the ideas discussed in this chapter, has been taken with the addition (on the left) in the bottom photo.

4
INTERIOR STYLE AND FUNCTION

It's one thing to look at the comparatively simple shapes and surfaces of a building's exterior, but quite another to consider the complex, interacting volumes of the interior. While the exterior wall that is common, say, to a bedroom, bath and family room gives a house a sense of unity, the interior spaces it connects vary in their shapes and details. Also, as houses are upgraded over time, new materials, fixtures and appliances replace the originals, especially in kitchens and bathrooms.

Though their individual rooms vary, some houses feel unified while others feel like a collection of disjointed spaces. As designers, we should train ourselves to see the differences between the two. Some of the differences are fairly obvious, like consistent trim and color—the sorts of things discussed in the last chapter. But others are more subtle, hidden in the relative proportions of the interior spaces and their relationship with one another. It is essential to understand these subtle differences to design well.

INTERIOR STYLE

Ideally the interior styles of the house and addition will match or at least be compatible. Two problems commonly arise, however. First, the owners may want to introduce a style or theme into the addition other than that which dominates most of the house's interior. Second, the house itself may have internal inconsistencies that confuse the choice of style.

The owners may be dissatisfied because the existing rooms are poorly designed, with bad lighting or cramped spaces, or may desire to use the addition to express a particular theme. A collector of Asian art, for example, might want a Japanese-style room added as a gallery to an otherwise modern American house. Again, the ideal scenario would involve a complete transformation of the interior, as shown in the photo at right, but the budget, or the owners' program, may not always allow this option.

The interior of this ranch-style, suburban California home was transformed throughout to conform to the style of the dining-room addition shown in the background. The home belongs to a collector of Asian art, and the woodworking refers to that found in traditional Japanese domestic architecture. (For a view of the exterior transformation, see the bottom photo on p. 24.)

If a complete makeover of the interior is out of the question, two approaches might be taken to integrate the new Japanese room with the existing Western interior. One would be to segregate the space, perhaps giving it its own hallway and making some sort of visual statement at its entrance. Another approach would be to create a gradient of increasingly Japanese motifs—using Japanese art and artifacts—from the front entrance of the house to the gallery.

The challenge for the designer is to integrate the two styles and avoid creating a jarring effect. Notice that I said two styles. If you picture an Arts and Crafts style house with classical columns supporting the fireplace mantle, a Tiki room den and a powder-blue bathroom with Colonial wallpaper, you'll understand why. There is great difficulty in combining more than two styles or themes in a building as small as a house. If the existing house already has two or more styles and the owners want to introduce yet another style, something will have to go to avoid creating a chaotic patchwork effect.

The second common obstacle to continuity is that many older houses have wide stylistic gaps between various rooms—particularly upgraded kitchens and bathrooms—as a result of prior remodeling and the introduction of updated materials and equipment.

This modern version of an Arts and Crafts family room was designed to blend seamlessly with the rest of the original turn-of-the-century house. (For exterior photos of the addition, see the cover and p. 35.)

The make-over of this existing living room (for compatibility with the kitchen/dining-room addition beyond) features a fireplace mantel and white, sculpted cabinet doors that refer to traditional designs. The angled archway separating the new and old spaces is an effective simplification of the more traditional, rounded arches between living and dining rooms found in many older homes. (For another interior view of the addition, see p. 58; for exterior views, see p. 26.)

Existing (white) and new (natural wood) cabinets of similar style stand side by side in this remodeled kitchen, which was part of an addition project. The style of the new hanging lamps refers to classic lamp designs of an earlier period, while exposing the brick-fireplace back adds an element of texture and a rustic effect to the room.

In fact, the problem is not limited to what are usually thought of as "old" houses. We are getting to the point where so-called modern times can be divided into periods, each dated by their characteristic interior styling. During the 1950s, for example, hollow-core mahogany interior doors were very much in vogue with architects and decorators. In the early 1960s, ash-plywood cabinets were common in kitchens. The pinkish color and pronounced grain, respectively, of those once-popular woods are unfashionable today. Because of the fast pace of modern society, we must be aware that "historical" styles might go back just a couple of decades.

Historical reference

Exactly duplicating the features of older houses is not only expensive, but often impossible. How do you make a dishwasher look like a flour bin, and, indeed, why should you?

The designer or builder must decide whether to modernize or attempt to replicate the existing decor. While cost is certainly a factor, don't automatically assume that it is more economical to modernize than to

reproduce existing details faithfully. It's often cheaper, for example, to save and refurbish an existing kitchen than to gut and rebuild it. If the goals of continuity and economy can be served by simply duplicating a few of the old cabinet doors, why do more?

In the addition, though, building by today's methods and in today's styles almost always represents savings. How can modern methods and materials be used to achieve some sense of historical continuity? Where strict duplication is impractical, selective historical reference can achieve the desired effect.

You've probably been in houses with 100-year-old woodwork in the living room and upgraded, modern kitchens. Microwave ovens, laminate counters and modular kitchen cabinets were not yet conceived of when the turn-of-the-century journeyman fitted the finial on the newel. Yet even the most contemporary of kitchen designs can refer to their surroundings in creative and pleasing ways. The cabinets can be of natural wood, the handles "antique" ceramic, and the countertops edged with sculpted oak trim that is reminiscent of grandmother's house.

Whether the house's history resonates in some grand component, like a fireplace winged with built-in cabinets, or only in details like the moldings, paneled doors or plank floors, there is usually a simple way to make a clear reference. If paneled wood doors are too expensive for the addition, tack rectangles of mitered half-round or another appropriate molding on flat, plywood-skinned doors. If the budget calls for a plywood subfloor with carpet in the new bedrooms, run wide, plank flooring in the halls.

One pitfall to be avoided, however, is producing cheap imitations of historical originals. You must remain aware of the differences between duplicating, or copying exactly, imitating, or copying poorly, and referring. Leaded-glass windows, for example, were originally created at a time when small pieces of glass needed to be linked together to build window panels big enough to illuminate the interior. As we learned to produce sheet glass, the need for leading disappeared, but the charming old windows still had enough appeal to become collector's items.

Recently, manufacturers have begun producing dubious copies of the crisscrossed diagonal leading patterns by stamping out plastic mullions and fixing them to the front of a full pane of glass. Why bother, since the mullions do not divide the glass but only busy up the surface and interfere with the view? A visitor's first thought, rather than "charming" or "cottage," is more likely to be "phony" or "plastic."

While imitation is weak design, reference works well by bringing the observer into the process of historical transition. The observer has to make the link between the present and the past to which the reference alludes. The satisfaction is in the act of discovery.

Changing styles Sometimes it is appropriate to convert the style of the house to that of the addition. Victorian interiors, for example, are problematic for modern designers. The rooms are small, with too many entrances, too few windows and high ceilings that can almost double the heating bill. Also, period moldings are elaborate and expensive, and can seem busy or cluttered. It would be unwise to make the same design decisions in the addition, and while some historical reference is needed for unity, just a little will effectively remind the visitor of the overstated original.

Though it might seem heresy to Victorian aficionados, a better overall design can be achieved by lowering some of the original ceilings and walling off some of the doors. Assuming that the original natural woodwork has already been violated

by paint, "painting out" the trim to match the walls will minimize its sometimes overwhelming impact. More ambitious strategies, like removing partition walls so the existing tall ceilings are in proportion to the floor plans, can also be considered. These strategies may be the most practical way to make a Victorian house and its addition work as one complete building.

Historical continuity is strengthened by keeping approximately the same degree of replication or reference on the inside of the house as on the outside. If you go to the trouble to find recycled antique trim that precisely matches the frieze and porch moldings but forget the house's existing style inside the addition, guests will feel that a promise has been broken. If you are going to break with tradition, it will be regarded as more honest if you signal your intention in advance.

Color and style

The fundamentals of exterior color selection discussed in Chapter 3 work for the interior, but the choices are more critical. Houses are seen for moments at a time from the outside, but we are exposed to the interior color for hours on end. Feelings of claustrophobia or expansiveness, our ability to sustain a relaxed state and numerous other psychological factors are all influenced by room color. Also, while the house is seen from the outside as a visual attraction in itself, the interior walls usually act as mere backgrounds for furnishings and art objects.

These factors suggest the choice of light, neutral colors. Bright, intense colors overwhelm us, and dark walls

absorb so much light that rooms seem dingy and depressing.

Rooms seem bigger when the doors and trim are painted the same color or close to the same color as the walls (see the photos on the facing page). Highly contrasting trim makes the room seem cluttered and smaller, and competes with the artwork. Some contrast is desirable, however, or the paint job can look cheap. If, as it should be, the woodwork is painted with durable latex enamel, which is glossier than the flat latex on the walls, there will be sufficient contrast to highlight the trim subtly.

There are exceptions to the uniform paint job, of course. Decorators have done wonders by painting discreet stripes on dull walls, or by simply making a color statement—usually intense—at one end of a large room (see the photo on p. 57). The possibilities are infinite, but remember that fads in color and stripes come and go, while the walls will be around for quite some time.

Analyzing the existing color scheme for its effectiveness and unity will help the designer decide whether to keep it or change it, and then how to make the addition relate. Part of this process depends on the purpose of the addition. An ordinary bedroom and bath wing addition may need no special consideration if the main paint job is acceptable. A glass solarium that forms a transition to a private garden might need greygreen window mullions to bring the outdoors in. This, in turn, could lead to repainting the existing room that opens into the solarium, per-

The light-colored walls and trim of this added sitting room and refurbished kitchen/dining area complement each other and are relaxing to the eye. In spite of the many lines, the blend of the door, window and trim color with that of the walls makes the space seem larger and less busy. The cabinets, columns and divided doors are also good examples of historical reference.

haps with a light grey tint. While all this coolness might be pleasant in spring, summer and early autumn, the owners might want to bring in some warm, colorful plants and prints to offset the stark light of winter.

INTERACTING FUNCTIONS AND SPACES

When beginning a design, it is more helpful to view a house as an area in which a variety of functions interact than as a collection of rooms. This approach frees you to take an overview of several spaces at once rather than focusing on the design of particular rooms. The individual spaces are then shaped in part by their functions and in part by their relationship to adjacent spaces, including the exterior environment.

For example, think of a house as needing a better food-preparation, eating and cleanup area that also doubles as one of the family gathering places, rather than starting out by saying that it needs a new kitchen and breakfast nook. The "kitchen/breakfast nook" scenario has already locked you into a design to some extent. You think of two separate spaces, each with its own functions, facilities and possibly

This continuous space houses food-preparation, eating and sitting areas. In a more traditional house, a separate, walled-off kitchen, living room and dining room would have housed the same functions. Since the sitting area is in an addition on the front of the house, having walls separate the spaces would have made it difficult to get light into the kitchen. (For an exterior view of this space, see the bottom photo on p. 40; for another interior view, see p. 75.)

predetermined shape. While this arrangement could turn out to be the best solution, it is important to explore a variety of possibilities before deciding.

Alternatively, consider food preparation in all its aspects, from bringing in groceries to teamwork in making meals, and consider all the places where food might be eaten. These could include the existing formal dining room, an as-yet-undefined space in or near the kitchen, the family room and even the patio. This scenario suggests a continuity of space and function, as opposed to a rigid division into discrete cells or units (see the bottom photo on p. 53). One result might be a more open and flowing floor plan, half-height rather than full-height walls between some spaces, and improved access to natural light and the outdoors.

Bubble diagrams

Designers frequently use "bubble" diagrams like those shown below to represent graphically the relationship between spaces that house particular functions. (The diagrams correspond to the site/floor plans in the drawings on pp. 60-63.) Each program requirement is assigned a function or space, as shown on the hand-written list. Each function is given its own bubble, with a code letter referring to the list.

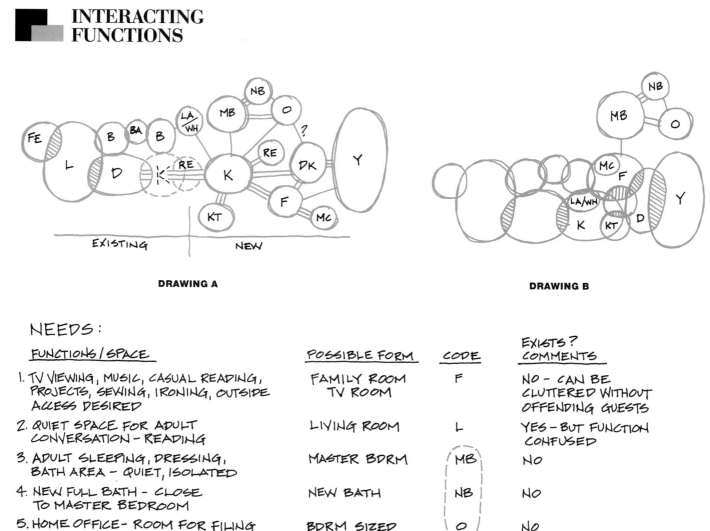

INTERACTING FUNCTIONS

DRAWING A

DRAWING B

NEEDS:

FUNCTIONS/SPACE

1. TV VIEWING, MUSIC, CASUAL READING, PROJECTS, SEWING, IRONING, OUTSIDE ACCESS DESIRED

2. QUIET SPACE FOR ADULT CONVERSATION - READING

3. ADULT SLEEPING, DRESSING, BATH AREA - QUIET, ISOLATED

4. NEW FULL BATH - CLOSE TO MASTER BEDROOM

5. HOME OFFICE- ROOM FOR FILING CABINETS, PAPER STORAGE, COMPUTER, FAX, COPY MACHINE, BOOKSHELVES, PHONE - QUIET ISOLATED ~ IDEALLY NEAR DECK

POSSIBLE FORM	CODE	EXISTS? COMMENTS
FAMILY ROOM TV ROOM	F	NO - CAN BE CLUTTERED WITHOUT OFFENDING GUESTS
LIVING ROOM	L	YES - BUT FUNCTION CONFUSED
MASTER BDRM	MB	NO
NEW BATH	NB	NO
BDRM SIZED SPACE WITH CLOSET	O	NO CAN BE SOLD AS 4TH BDRM

Two types of diagrams, the relationship diagram and the cluster diagram, are shown in the drawing. In relationship diagrams, like the one on the right side of Drawing A, the number of lines between the bubbles represents the strength of the connection between the functions. Note, for example, that bubble "KT" (kitchen table) has a direct, strong relationship to "K" (kitchen). The relation between K and O (office), however, is weak, and there is no direct relationship between K and NB (new master-bedroom bath). In the relationship diagram, the position, orientation and size of the bubbles are not important. The same strong relationship would exist between K and KT no matter where KT was on the page.

In the cluster diagrams—the existing part (left) of Drawing **A** and the lower part of Drawing B—the bubbles roughly represent the relative size, position and orientation of the various functions or the spaces that house them. Overlapping areas represent strong connections between functions or a physical flow between spaces.

Typically, new building design begins with relationship diagrams and progresses to cluster diagrams before the actual shapes are sketched. In Drawing A, however, the configuration of the existing building is

6. FOOD PREP/STORAGE CLEAN UP AREA - FRIDGE WITH FREEZER - VIEW OF OUTDOORS - CLOSE TO BREAKFAST AREA - DOUBLE SINK - SUFFICIENT COUNTERS - LOTS OF STORAGE - BROOM CLOSET	KITCHEN	K	YES - BUT INADEQUATE - OLD - REMODEL
7. FAMILY EATING, GATHERING AREA, GAMES, HOMEWORK, HELP WITH FOOD PREP	KITCHEN TABLE OR BREAKFAST NOOK	KT	YES - MAKE BETTER VIEW, YARD ACCESS
8. FORMAL DINING ROOM		D	YES - MODIFY TO ACCOMMODATE LARGER KITCHEN
9. WASHER/DRYER SPACE - ROOM FOR SOAP, SUPPLIES	LAUNDRY - CLOSET IN GARAGE	LA	YES - ON PORCH RE-ARRANGE
10. WATER HEATER HOUSING	CLOSET? OUTDOORS?	WH	" " "
11. KIDS' BEDROOMS		B	YES - MODIFY CLOSETS
12. 'PUBLIC' BATHROOM		BA	YES
13. FRONT/REAR ENTRY - EXIT	PORCH, STAIRS, DECK	FE, RE	FRONT OK, MODIFY OR REBUILD REAR
14. OUTDOOR SPACE FOR PLAY, ETC.	YARD	Y	YES

DREAMS

1. REAR PATIO OR DECK - ENTERTAINMENT - PLAY AREA FOR KIDS - OUTDOOR RELAXING	DECK, PATIO, REAR PORCH - SIMPLE STAIRS TO YARD	DK	NO
2. ORGANIZATIONAL STORAGE FOR STEREO, RECORD/CD COLLECTION COMPUTER GAMES, MULTI-MEDIA	'MEDIA CENTER' - CLOSET, SHELVING PUT WITH TV ?	MC	NO

Note. Dotted lines indicate probable groupings.

known, so the left side can be represented with a reasonable degree of accuracy. For the addition, only the program is known, so it is represented at first as a relationship diagram. Since it is fairly certain that the new kitchen will be in the same position as the old, it is shown as tentatively occupying that space, though it is temporarily kept apart from the other existing spaces so its relationship with the new spaces is not entirely predetermined.

In Drawing B on p. 54, most of the functions represented in Drawing A are assigned tentative sizes, shapes and positions. The configuration is still different from the finished house, however (see the floor plan on pp. 62-63). The finished deck, for instance, does not extend across most of the back of the house, and the laundry ends up in the center of the kitchen, not against the bath. Bubble diagrams are not sketches of buildings but graphic representations of spaces that house functions and the relationship between those spaces.

Considering the constraints of the site (see the plan on pp. 60-61), it is clear in this example that there is not enough room for all the functions to be fulfilled in spaces that are contiguous to the existing house. Thus bubbles MB, NB and O are still in the relationship stage and will need a separate space—it could be a wing or even another building, but in this case it will be on a second story.

SITE/FLOOR PLANNING FOR ADDITIONS

In this book, the first-story floor plan is seldom considered in isolation. Rather, it is combined with the site plan, the two forming a single drawing called the *site/floor plan*. Using site/floor plans reminds the designer of the relationship between the house and its surroundings. Potentially useful features of the yard—a patio alongside the house that could be part of the addition or a garden that could be its focus—become apparent. The site/floor plan also allows you to remain aware of neighboring houses and see where to make openings out to the yard, fence off a noisy street and take care of important business like planning an outdoor space for garbage cans and recycling bins (see the drawings on pp. 60-63).

Site/floor plans also help with the arrangement of internal features like kitchen and bath fixtures and furniture groupings. When locating a sofa, for example, the exterior view can be just as important as the traffic flow through the room. (Instructions for making a site/floor plan are given in Chapter 12.)

Keys to effective site/floor planning include identifying and developing the building's transition zone and focal area. Good planning also employs a variety of methods for designing for efficiency, from the systematic development of furniture groups and circulation paths to using spaces well by assigning them multiple functions and providing a lot of storage.

Schematics and Graphic Thinking

Schematics are abstract diagrams that represent written or verbal concepts in graphic form. In designing additions, they are generally used to translate program information onto the "as-built" site/floor-plan template (see pp. 190-191) and serve as an intermediate step between writing the program and designing the addition.

Three types of schematics—bubble diagrams, arrow diagrams and essence drawings—are all that are needed for most additions.

Bubble diagrams are used to assemble graphic representations of program requirements into compatible groups, which can then be translated into rough preliminary designs (see the drawings on p. 54).

Arrow diagrams, or, more correctly, arrows drawn over the as-built template, are used to analyze the site/floor plan and identify circulation paths, views and other relevant features (see the drawing on pp. 60-61).

Essence diagrams are used to give graphic form to a program require-ment (see the drawings on pp. 66-67).

There are many other schematic and graphic tools that can be used to organize ideas and clarify relationships between spaces and functions that may also be useful for designing additions. For references on schematics and graphic thinking, see the bibliography. For additional information on the role of schematics in addition design, see Chapter 12.

An Effective Transition Zone

The precise transition between the added kitchen/dining area and the original house (foreground) is marked by the truss supporting the end of the original roof. Notice the subtle repetition of a triangular theme in the truss, the shapes of the ceiling beyond the truss, the furniture grouping, the tile hearth that leads the eye to the kitchen, and the angled wall beyond the fireplace that also flows into the kitchen.

The circulation path (foreground) flows around the sofa furniture group and past the table for easy access to the kitchen and deck beyond. The work area in the kitchen is isolated from the traffic flow yet visually connected with the rest of the space.

Natural light enters from several sources, blending to minimize glare and shadows and creating different light patterns as the sun (or moon) moves. The fireplace and adjacent cabinets create primary and secondary visual focuses. Finally, the decorative color scheme, which is dynamic in its shape but restful in its hues and intensities, guides the eye through the space and ties the various visual elements together. (For a closer view of the kitchen, see the photo on p. 65.)

The transition zone

The *transition zone* is the area where the house and addition connect. It overlaps the line between the old and new structures by the width of one or more rooms. Most houses have wasted space, or functions that can be consolidated or moved without undue expense. The wasted space is frequently found toward the back of the house, where additions and the transition zones that lead to them are also often located. By remodeling in the transition zone, you can eliminate the house's worst features at the same time that you add on.

Back-porch laundry areas are a good example of transition zones (see the drawing on pp. 60-61). Most are awkwardly designed and take up too much space. The washer and dryer can easily enough fit into a closet, either side by side or stacked. The same closet can be expanded to accommodate a clothes hamper and even double as a broom closet and water-heater housing. Consolidating these functions unclogs the transition zone, opening views and freeing critical space for circulation and other important functions.

The focal area

A good way to think of the site/floor plan is as if it were for one complete building rather than a house and its addition. This approach helps you see where things line up: where the traffic paths through the house can continue smoothly into the addition, bearing walls can be extended, and small dark spaces like closets can be set back to back.

Viewing the building as a single piece of work also enables you to select a *focal area* for the finished building, from which both the house's and the addition's floor plans radiate. Since this focal area often falls in the transition zone between the old and new structures, it will probably be remodeled in a manner that blends the styles of the house and the addition. This centrally located transitional styling contributes significantly to unifying the old and new interiors.

Since the kitchen is the functional center of the modern home, it can often serve as the focal area for the overall plan (see the photo below). The existing floor plan may suggest this role: Kitchens are commonly located in or near the

The island in this expanded kitchen acts as the focal area for this Minnesota home. It is near the principal circulation hub just to the right of the dining-room table and easily accessed from the rest of the house, yet the inner kitchen work area remains out of the traffic flow. (For a photo of the living room of this house, see p. 50 [bottom]; for exterior views, see p. 26.)

Sectional sofas are grouped around a coffee table with the fireplace as the visual focal point in this living room, which was refurbished to be consistent with the style of the addition shown in the background (far right). The principal circulation path to the addition bypasses the furniture group. (For an exterior view of this house, see the bottom photo on p. 10.)

transition zone because they are close to the back or on one end of the house. Also, many kitchens need to be modernized.

Because our attitudes toward formal dining have changed, small kitchens are often enlarged to include an area for eating. Many people, as well, plan to eat occasionally in their family room. But for resale, most realtors will advise that the house's formal dining room be kept intact, not remodeled into a breakfast nook. Chances are, the older the house, the nicer the dining room's woodwork, fireplace, built-in buffets, leaded windows and other adornments.

All of this suggests that the existing kitchen should be expanded into the addition to serve as the place to eat and gather and as the "traffic central" switching yard for the house's various flow paths.

Of course, you shouldn't make the mistake of reducing the expanded kitchen design to a formula for planning additions. You can store the information—that there should usually be one focal point, it might be best located in the transition zone, and for a variety of reasons the kitchen might fit the description—but to design well you must take a fresh approach to each project.

Designing for efficiency

If possible, every design decision should be made not for just one reason but for many, and every feature of the house should serve multiple functions. The location of a breakfast nook, for example, should be determined not just by its proximity to the kitchen, but also by its access to the morning sun, its view to the outdoors and its isolation from the traffic flow through the house. Keeping these basic design principles in mind is a great aid in arranging furniture groups, providing for a variety of functions, planning circulation and accounting for space.

Furniture grouping and circulation
We have all been in houses that have an odd-sized or odd-shaped "extra" room that has no discernible use other than to collect junk. Then there are those large, nebulous rooms—oversized dens or living rooms—in which, after the furniture is assembled, there is still a great deal of emptiness. The owners must actually find a way to fill them that doesn't look too contrived. Rooms are also chopped up in funny ways, sometimes to accommodate closets or baths, and they end up with small, unusable portions sticking out like peninsulas from their main area. Since your purpose in adding on is to improve the house, you should eliminate these spaces from the transition zone if they already exist, and avoid creating them if they weren't there to begin with.

When a floor plan is a mess, it is usually because not enough attention has been paid to circulation, or the way people move from one space or activity to another, and to furniture grouping, or the arrangement of furnishings and equipment within a space.

(text continues on p. 64)

The Problem:

This small house in a mild climate was built at a time (about 70 years ago) when more attention was given than today to appearances and formalities and less to comfort and amenities. Thus the front porch, living room and formal dining room are disproportionately large compared to the rest of the house.

The back-porch laundry area was added on when washers and dryers became common. Unfortunately, it blocked the view from the kitchen table, where the family ate most of its meals, and its southern exposure caused it to become extremely hot in summer. It was in poor shape, as was the seldom-used driveway and garage.

The expanding family had one small child and one on the way. There was a need for a new master bedroom with a bath, a family room, an expanded, serviceable kitchen with a nearby dining area and a home office to be built on a modest budget.

The graphic analysis of the site/floor plan at right shows the probable transition zone and focal area, the existing and planned circulation, views and blocked views, unused or wasted space, the focus conflict in the living room between the television and fireplace, and other features. Since the brick flue between the dining room and kitchen is no longer needed for modern, efficient stoves, it could be eliminated and the built-in buffet next to it could be moved to create more space for the kitchen.

Setbac

NOTES
1. BACK PORCH
   • blocks view from kitchen
   • lots of space, little function
   • blocks access to yard
   • hot as hell in summer

2. WEST SIDE
   • ugly views
   • too much sun

3. BACK YARD
   • southern exposure - need more trees
   • open patio/deck to expand space.

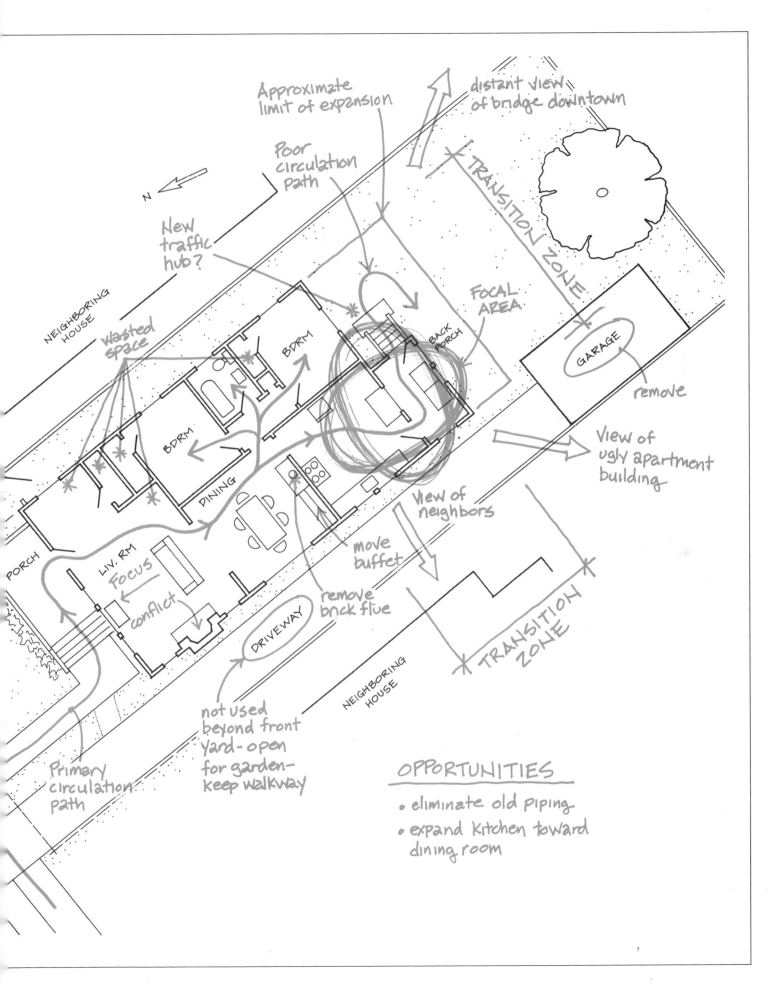

distant view of bridge downtown

Approximate limit of expansion

Poor circulation Path

New traffic hub?

N

NEIGHBORING HOUSE

Wasted space

BDRM

BDRM

TRANSITION ZONE

FOCAL AREA

BACK PORCH

GARAGE

remove

View of ugly apartment building

DINING

View of neighbors

move buffet

PORCH

LIV. RM

FOCUS

conflict

remove brick flue

DRIVEWAY

NEIGHBORING HOUSE

TRANSITION ZONE

not used beyond front yard - open for garden - keep walkway

Primary circulation path

OPPORTUNITIES
- eliminate old piping
- expand kitchen toward dining room

SITE/FLOOR PLAN: ADDITION ON A SMALL HOUSE

23 One passage is walled off and another opened to block view from dining room to bathroom. New opening is wider and enhances circulation.

24 Bedroom-closet fronts are opened and provided with sliding doors for better access.

The Solution:

In the remodeled house the furniture is arranged into "cul-de-sacs" and the circulation is smoothed out. The primary circulation hub (where the deck/yard, family room and path to the upstairs, kitchen, laundry, breakfast nook and the rest of the house are joined) is directly adjacent to the kitchen-table focal point. The door onto the deck is protected from weather in a concavity beneath the second-floor frame, thus saving the cost of building a roof over it. Throughout the building, wasted and inaccessible space is used or opened.

Good views are emphasized, and afforded from most spaces, while unattractive ones are screened off. The deck brings in the outdoors and takes advantage of the climate without trapping too much heat in the summer.

1 Desk fills empty space

2 Closet door is widened to allow better access to storage.

3 Shelves use wasted space.

4 Living-room furniture is regrouped around fireplace. Extending dining-room wall has isolated the group in what is essentially a cul-de-sac.

5 New location for buffet. Existing table has been rotated to allow for better circulation.

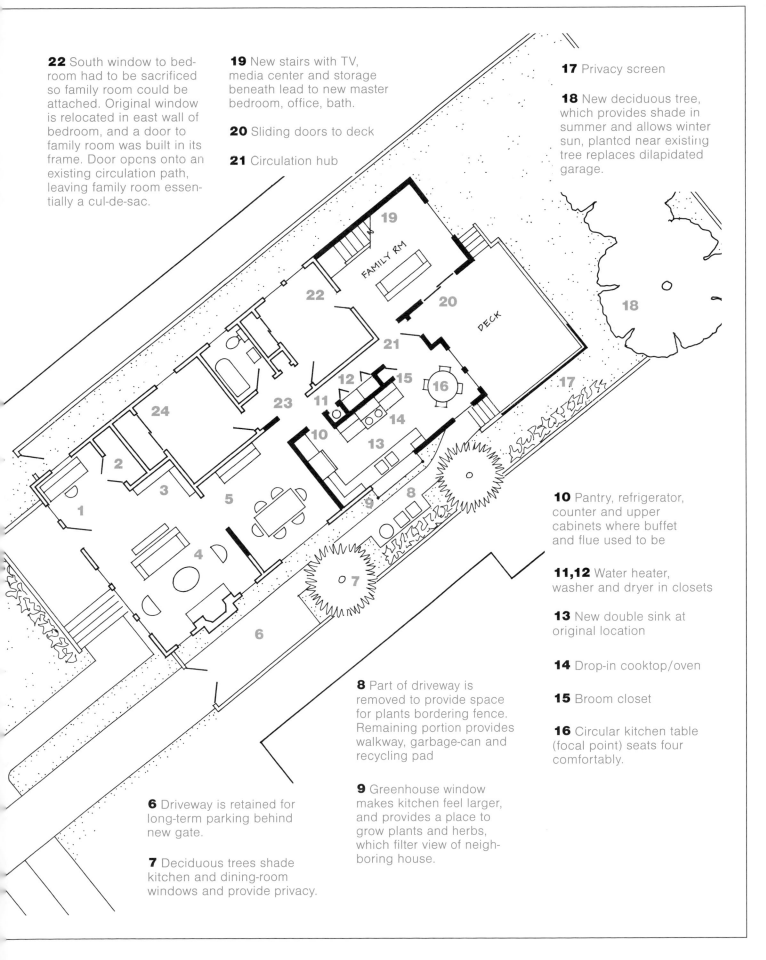

22 South window to bedroom had to be sacrificed so family room could be attached. Original window is relocated in east wall of bedroom, and a door to family room was built in its frame. Door opens onto an existing circulation path, leaving family room essentially a cul-de-sac.

19 New stairs with TV, media center and storage beneath lead to new master bedroom, office, bath.

20 Sliding doors to deck

21 Circulation hub

17 Privacy screen

18 New deciduous tree, which provides shade in summer and allows winter sun, planted near existing tree replaces dilapidated garage.

10 Pantry, refrigerator, counter and upper cabinets where buffet and flue used to be

11,12 Water heater, washer and dryer in closets

13 New double sink at original location

14 Drop-in cooktop/oven

15 Broom closet

16 Circular kitchen table (focal point) seats four comfortably.

8 Part of driveway is removed to provide space for plants bordering fence. Remaining portion provides walkway, garbage-can and recycling pad

9 Greenhouse window makes kitchen feel larger, and provides a place to grow plants and herbs, which filter view of neighboring house.

6 Driveway is retained for long-term parking behind new gate.

7 Deciduous trees shade kitchen and dining-room windows and provide privacy.

The drawings on pp. 66-67 show the relationship between furniture groups and overall circulation. Stated simply, planning is a matter of, first, designing furniture or equipment groups to serve particular functions, second, building spaces around the groups and, third, arranging for smooth circulation between those spaces. The relative location of the spaces depends primarily on their relationship with each other, and secondarily on their relationship to the building's context—the street, site access, views and adjacent buildings. In the case of an addition and its remodeled transition zone, the existing house should be viewed as part of that context.

Furniture groups, then, can be considered the basic building blocks of a house. Rather than designing rooms and trying to fit furniture into them, you should, ideally, reduce each program requirement to its essence and give it a graphic form as an essence diagram. That essential form is then developed into scaled drawings of real, dimensioned furnishings and equipment.

Attention must be given to the internal relationships of each furniture group. Make sure there's enough space between furnishings so people can actually sit at them, walk between them and talk at a comfortable distance. Information about these relationships for common furnishings can be found in numerous texts, some of which are listed in the bibliography. A problem with these sources, however, is that there are more possible configurations than they can ever show, and they sometimes call for more space than is truly necessary. This last point is a particular hindrance

for designers of additions who rely on the data for remodeling. The real dimensions of the existing house's spaces are often tighter than those shown in the books, but somehow, because of the almost infinite adaptability of human beings, they work just fine anyway. The designer who tries to stick with the books' recommendations as if they were some kind of code requirement might eliminate a number of workable possibilities.

A more convenient source for dimensions is a tape measure kept at the designer's desk. What is the minimum amount of room needed to pass between a coffee table and a couch, then turn and sit down? Surprisingly little, measurements of real spaces show. While compact designs do not always make the most gracious rooms, they get the job done. Given all the constraints of the existing building, setbacks, the budget and the numerous expectations most people have for their additions, squeezing a few inches here and there can make the difference between success and failure.

Be aware, however, that it's important either to follow established guidelines or to test each of your assumptions. While delivering an incomplete program by leaving out some of the functions in a tight space is one form of failure, cramming people into an uncomfortable space is perhaps worse. If the room isn't there, the program should be modified.

Overlapping and separated functions Some spaces have more than one function, and therefore more than one essence diagram. In that case the designer will have to decide whether the functions can be mixed, the space should be

expanded or an entirely new space should be designed to serve the second function.

The essence diagram for sleeping, for example, is quite static, while the diagram for all the activities associated with sleeping—getting undressed, putting away clothes, various bathroom activities, reading in bed, grabbing a tissue, getting dressed the next morning—is quite dynamic. All told, the activities break down into three major groups: those centering around dressing, bathing and resting. While the activities overlap, they could be separated, as they are when the bathroom is outside the bedroom and serves the whole house, or integrated, as they are when the master-bedroom suite includes a bath and distinct dressing area.

Kitchens are special cases in that they house the basic functions of preparing food and cleaning up after meals, but they have many more subfunctions than other rooms. Separating those functions would waste space and money.

Here, the designer must make essence sketches for each activity, and integrate them as smoothly as possible. The more that each activity is broken down into its subactivities, the easier it will be to eliminate contradictions and make each of the limited number of available flow paths serve as many functions as possible.

Cleaning up after a meal, for example, can be broken down into clearing the table, putting away food, washing dishes, putting away dishes and cleaning the counter. Washing dishes, in turn, involves gathering them from the table, stove and other places, stacking, scraping or rinsing, washing or loading the dishwasher, drying and finally putting them away. By listing each of these functions we can see which facilities are used the most and begin to arrange them accordingly. (While this type of detailed analysis may seem excessive, briefly pondering the number of poorly designed kitchens in the world should make it obvious that the time is indeed well spent.)

The sink, for example, is used during both cooking and cleanup many more times than the stove or refrigerator. For this reason, it should be given the central position, with workspace on both sides and easy, multi-user access. In keeping with the principle of having several reasons for each design decision, the designer should make sure that the sink's position is determined not simply by its proximity, say, to an existing window or the existing plumbing (a standard setup for almost all houses). It should also be near the dishwasher, if there is one, near a place to store the dishes, and easily accessible from the refrigerator, stove and general circulation path. If these features are not already in place, they can be moved so that the arrangement functions on all the levels it needs to.

If meals are served in the kitchen, it soon becomes clear that the sheer number of trips back and forth between the sink, stove and refrigerator, and the activities like cutting and stirring that happen along the way, pushes the dining facility out of the food-preparation area. To include it would overload the paths and hinder cooking. A sub-area with its own essence sketch and a primary relationship to the preparation center is called for.

The existing sink, then, becomes the center for the expanded preparation/cleanup area, at least in the preliminary design phase. This is a limitation only if the sink is so awkwardly placed in relation to the rest of the house or the potential areas of expansion that smooth circulation to and from it cannot be arranged.

Otherwise, the design for the preparation/cleanup area can grow from the given location of the sink. First, the essential pieces of equipment—stove, refrigerator and others—and their supporting countertops and storage are roughed in near the sink. Distances are determined by minimizing the number of steps between facilities while allowing room for the anticipated number of users and adequate counter space.

Once the preparation/cleanup area takes shape, those groupings immediately dependent on it—the formal and informal dining areas—and the more outlying spaces where food is served—patios and family rooms—can be organized around the eating and socializing core. Thus, if the kitchen is indeed the focal point for the house and its new addition, the entire plan grows outward from a single sink "work station" (which should of course be attractive and well lit).

Cul-de-sacs The principle of cul-de-sacs—dead-end streets that branch off a main thoroughfare and terminate in a quiet circle for turning around—can be applied effectively to household circulation.

A simple example is that of a bedroom with a single door coming off a hall. The room is a pure cul-de-sac:

(text continues on p. 68)

The two sinks in this kitchen separate its food-preparation and cleanup functions, making them both easier to perform and allowing more than one person to work at the same time. Someone taking food from the refrigerator can simply turn around and wash it in the 'vegetable' sink (foreground). The separate vegetable sink also allows for a generous countertop from the refrigerator to the 'cleanup' sink (background) without requiring too many extra steps between the two.

The brightly lit clean-up sink, with a convenient dishwasher on the right, is more deeply recessed in the kitchen cul-de-sac, and dirty pots and pans that pile up during cooking are less noticeable to guests seated in the adjacent living room. (For another photo of this kitchen and its surroundings, see p. 57.)

BUILDING ROOMS AROUND FURNITURE GROUPS

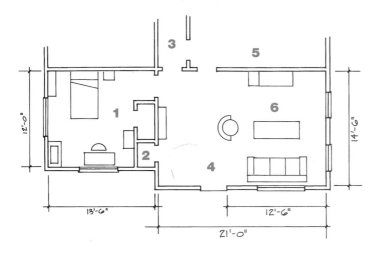

AS-BUILT FLOOR PLAN

1 Bedroom
2 Entry closet
3 Hall
4 Front entry
5 Kitchen
6 Living room

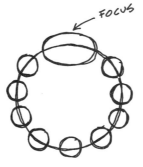

ESSENCE DIAGRAM

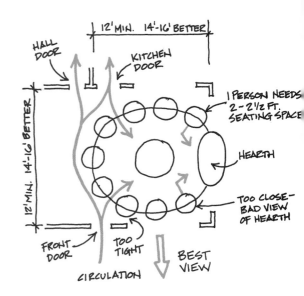

ESSENCE IN CONTEXT

The program for this addition was to modify the small, existing living room so it would incorporate comfortable, semi-formal seating for eight to ten people in a conversation group with a focus on a hearth. There would be room for shelves displaying a modest collection of antique ceramics and fine books. The space was to be contiguous with a semi-formal dining area normally seating six but able to accommodate eight. The child's bedroom (to the left in the floor plan above) would be moved to another part of the house, freeing space for the dining room.

The essence diagram above shows people gathered around a focal point that does not interfere with their view of each other. Since it was originally thought that the existing living room would serve as the gathering place, with the bedroom serving as the dining area, the essence diagram was oriented as it might be in that situation (see the context drawing above). This sketch is only approximately scaled—its dimensions are derived from the amount of space it takes to seat each person. It is not superimposed on the floor plan, but the walls, circulation, and so forth, are sketched around it.

Because of the amount of space needed for the function, it soon became obvious that it could not take place in the existing living room. Also, the bedroom is a poor location for the dining area, because it is separated from the kitchen. It was decided to reverse the locations.

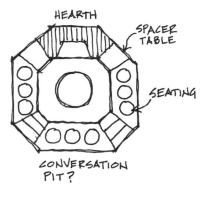

ESSENCE REFINED

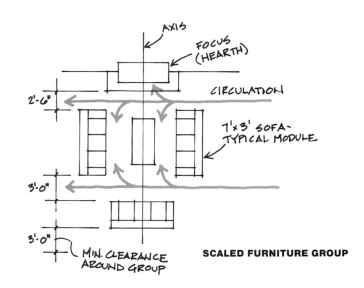

SCALED FURNITURE GROUP

Meanwhile, the essence is refined in a sketch more closely representing its final form (see the drawing above). Spacers, which could be side tables, give those seated next to the fireplace a better view. The actual seating is given form, as are the entrances to the circle. One possible design is to make them step down into a "conversation pit."

The conversation-pit idea is ultimately rejected because the program calls for a semi-formal room, and because conversation pits lack flexibility. It is decided to use matching sofas, arranged as shown in the top drawing at right. Note that the dimensions show the clearances between the hearth and furnishings and around the entire group. The dimensions could be expressed as tolerances (±) but here they are shown precisely.

The group is then placed in its new location, and the existing bedroom is rebuilt around it (see the floor plan at right). The same procedure is followed for the dining area (former

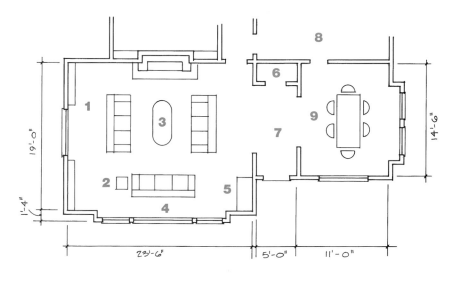

FINISHED FLOOR PLAN

living room). The remaining task is to arrange circulation so it bypasses the groups but takes people to their destinations with a minimum number of steps. Note that although the entry hall is small, it feels large because it is open on both sides. Also, the new entry closet is larger than the original closet.

1 Shelves for ceramics, books
2 Lamp table
3 Elliptical table eliminates sharp corners, facilitates seating.
4 Bay window makes room feel bigger and allows circulation around furniture group.
5 Side table for ceramics
6 Entry closet
7 Hall
8 Kitchen
9 Dining room

The circulation path in the foreground completely bypasses this cheerful added sunroom, creating a pure cul-de-sac.

There is no passage through the room, just into it and back out into the traffic flow. Many rooms, however, are part hallway. They house one or more furniture groups and are also passages to one or more other spaces (see the drawing on the facing page). In this case, the entrances should be lined up so the flow paths bypass the furniture groups, leaving them in a cul-de-sac. The furniture is then out of the paths, and people passing through the room do not disturb the people using it.

Linear and radial circulation

The primary traffic flow path shown in the drawing on pp. 60-61 is *lineal*, traveling through the house from one end to the other and branching out into the various rooms. Note, however, that when it enters the bedroom/bath area it becomes *radial*, branching out in several directions from one point.

Clearly, the radial path is a much more efficient use of space, since a minimum amount of circulation space is allocated for reaching a maximum number of destinations.

The drawing on the facing page shows how much space is saved when a house with a floor plan that is almost identical to that of the house on pp. 60-61 is provided with radial rather than lineal circulation for its primary flow path. Placing the entrance on the side of the house allows for a radial circulation from the main entryway. The living room and dining room are expanded slightly to make room for the new entry hall. Enough circulation space is saved, compared to the house with lineal circulation, to provide for a new bedroom/office where the old entry was and new central stairs.

This example is not to suggest that a radical circulation rearrangement should accompany each addition, though it should be considered where it might work. The shape of a house is largely determined by the shape of its lot, and, unfortunately, most lots are rectangles, about three times as deep as they are wide. Houses tend to fill the available space, and side setbacks usually preclude the addition of side porches like the one shown in the drawing.

What we can learn, however, is to switch to a radial plan wherever possible, such as at the circulation hub. When the principal circulation paths are found meandering through the house, they should be concentrated at the circulation hub near the transition zone, and then made to radiate out, up and sideways from that convergence (see the drawings on pp. 62-63 and the facing page).

Accounting for space

Building an addition usually means that some of the existing space in the transition zone has to be sacrificed for circulation. The owners' program helps the designer decide what to give up and what to save. If the kids are going to college at the same time the mother is starting a home office, it might make sense to cut a hallway to the addition through a bedroom and use what remains of the bedroom as a work station. If one kid is in first grade, another is in kindergarten and twins are on the way, Dad's photographic darkroom, which, by the way, hasn't seen much use lately, might have to be cannibalized for use as a nursery.

In general, alter no more of the house than is necessary to accommodate the addition. The decision to build an addition in the first place implies that the option of remodeling the existing house to meet the owners' needs has been eliminated. Of course, addition projects frequently entail upgrading portions of the house, but this should be done only when the same need cannot be better met in the addition. Since the new construction in the addition is usually cheaper and easier than remodeling within the house, try to pack as many improvements as possible into it. Limit renovations to the transition zone.

In a good design, all the space on the site—especially in the addition and transition area—is accounted for. If a space doesn't have one or more clear functions, it may not be needed. If it is too large for its function, it can probably be smaller.

Multiple functions Another way to reduce square footage is to design spaces and equipment for multiple functions. The kitchen table is a classic example. With the rearrangement of just a few items, its function changes from dining to studying to hobbies and games.

Other spaces and equipment can also serve multiple purposes. Family rooms, for example, are often expected to fulfill at least four broad groups of functions: relaxing, including resting, reading and casual conversation; projects, including hobbies and household tasks like ironing and folding clothes; television viewing; and fun, including table games and roughhousing.

For a space to be truly multifunctional, changing from one use to the next must be easy. The solution

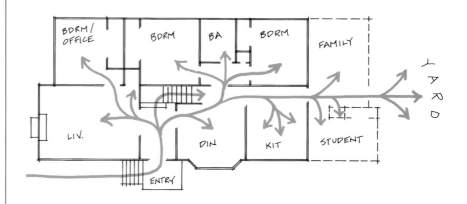

PRINCIPLES OF CIRCULATION

LINEAL AND RADIAL CIRCULATION
Lineal circulation becomes radial at nodes along the path. Each room is essentially a cul-de-sac—the circulation goes through one end while the room's furniture group is undisturbed by the traffic flow.

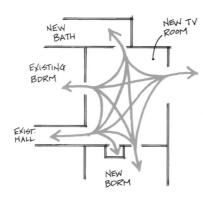

POORLY PLANNED CIRCULATION
The arrangement of the entrances chops up the room, making it difficult to place furniture out of natural traffic paths.

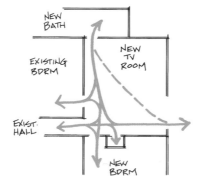

BETTER-PLANNED CIRCULATION
The entrances are placed closer together and located along 'corridors' at the edge of the room; most traffic flow follows these paths. The dashed diagonal line shows a less-traveled path, which is likely to be partially blocked when the room is furnished.

In all three drawings, note that the changes in direction are shown as curves. People do not naturally turn at right angles as they walk, and circulation should be planned with curved lines.

Storage units occupy the recess created for the woodstove in this family/dining room, converted from a garage as part of an addition project. The room was designed to be used for table games and recreational activities as well as for formal dining.

for the family room should begin with an analysis of the requirements of each function, the design of its essential shape and the design of the equipment that facilitates it. When each function is considered separately, it could become clear that they are not all compatible.

Television viewing, for example, doesn't work with much else, except eating. The noise of the television breaks up conversation and concentration, and the appropriate viewing height and seating arrangements will not work for activities like building a model or playing cards. Ideally, the television will be isolated in another room or in its own cul-de-sac within the family room.

As far as merging the other, more compatible functions goes, flexibility begins with simplicity. The more semi-permanent paraphernalia (toaster ovens, salt shakers, napkin holders, lazy Susans) that sit on the kitchen table, the harder it is to clear it off and spread out the monthly bills.

Also, the less specialized a space's layout, the easier it is to change its function. Because of its small size and linear arrangement, a typical laundry room, for example, cannot be readily converted to much else, except perhaps a photographic darkroom. A somewhat larger, more evenly proportioned bedroom, on the other hand, can be turned into a home office by simply changing the furniture. (Room proportions are discussed in the next chapter.)

Aggressive storage design Another critical component in designing for efficiency and multiple functions is providing handy storage. How many times have we all heard, or said, "Please get your books (toys, newspapers) off the kitchen table so we can have dinner—and please set the table"?

While the kitchen table is not a good place for a long-term project like a giant jigsaw puzzle, the family-room table can be, if nearby storage makes it easy to change to the next activity. The more storage, and the more varied or adjustable its individual pigeonholes, the better. Without these facilities the family-room table, which should take the pressure off the kitchen table, can itself become a mess and the focus of controversy.

The average American family has a lot more stuff than it did 50 years ago, and most older houses lack sufficient storage for today's needs. The designer should look for every opportunity to provide simple, inexpensive, out-of-the-way storage facilities.

If a door between two rooms must be closed off, for example, the remaining void—which is already equipped with a header—can be easily turned into a set of built-in shelves. Odd corners, spaces under stairs and rafters, offset walls and other normally unused spaces can similarly dress up the house while making it much less cluttered and more efficient. In the addition, storage should be considered equal to all other functions. In rooms like home offices, workshops and kitchens, the importance of storage cannot be overestimated because it enables the space to perform its function.

Freebies Most houses offer something for practically nothing—if the designer knows how to look for it. Stripping the wall off the back of an existing chimney, for example, can expose beautiful brickwork, which could help carry a rustic theme in a remodeled, country-style kitchen (see the photo on p. 51).

Since windows have headers, converting them to doorways is a snap. As long as the rough opening for the door is the same size or smaller than that of the window, the framing is as easy as cutting a hole below the window and perhaps adding a couple of studs to reduce the opening.

As a designer, you should begin each project by scanning the house for such opportunities. Each time

you take advantage of them to create a passageway or a built-in storage unit with a minimum amount of work, the budget for the rest of the project is increased.

FOCUS AND RESTRAINT

Few budgets allow for first-rate materials and highly detailed design throughout the building: Even architectural landmarks built to glorify emperors have their facades. The designer will need to choose areas or features in which to emphasize artistry and craftsmanship, leaving others plainer, at least for the time being.

Rather than diluting the effect, and the budget, by specifying crown molding all over the house, for example, it is usually better to concentrate on a couple of areas that really show. A nice front door is a good start, as is a beautiful fireplace. Decorative kitchen tiles replacing plastic-laminate counters and wood floors replacing wall-to-wall carpets are also wise investments.

Finally, designers should remember that home owners have their own decorating ideas. Too many touches can distract from the owners' paintings, furnishings and personal items. Just as designers should let the building do the talking when massing and styling the exterior, so should they serve as an instrument for the owners' expression, providing a fresh, clean palette with the walls and the proper light with skylights and windows.

5
UNIFYING THE BUILDING

A good design integrates a building's interior volumes and style with those of the exterior, unifying the entire building. We can think of the growth and development of a building as analogous to that of a living organism. Organic growth is determined by three factors: the size, shape and organization of the preexisting body, external influences and preset patterns of growth. For the purposes of designing an addition, these can be translated into the massing and plan of the existing house, the building's climate and context and the use of proportioning systems to extend the existing spaces.

The relationship of the addition to the massing and plan of the existing house was discussed in Chapter 3. The influence of the climate and context and the use of proportioning systems will be considered here, but first we must turn our attention to the interface between the building's interior and the outdoors—and those components that allow access to both while admitting the primary energizer, light, into the inner spaces and recesses.

THE INTERFACE

The interface between the site and the house happens at two locations. First, there are buffer spaces like decks, patios, courtyards, greenhouses and verandas that make the transition between the house proper and its natural environment or neighborhood context. Next come the house walls themselves, with their solid areas and openings.

Buffer spaces

Buffer spaces can serve as relatively inexpensive extensions of the basic house. Many are intended for seasonal use, and should be designed carefully to take maximum advantage of the local climate. As a rule, for example, buffer spaces should get as much sun as possible, so they can be used on at least some winter days. Decks and patios in windy areas should also have solid railings

or walls to protect their users. Attached greenhouses work well in many climates, providing extra space during the day throughout most of the year. In cold areas, however, the owners should be able to close off the greenhouse from the main house at night to save energy.

Aesthetic considerations are also important, since buffers must sensitively incorporate features of both the yard and/or the neighborhood context and the house. Some of the ways in which one type of buffer space, the veranda, can be used to unify a house and its addition are discussed in Chapter 3. Other buffers can be designed with the same goals in mind—changing and unifying the appearance of the house as well as enhancing circulation and providing usable space.

The shape of the large central window refers to the sloping ceiling of this sitting room and the mountains beyond. The glazing serves as a visual interface with the outdoors, inviting the viewer to step out onto the balcony. Light from the left side of the room balances that from the windows shown, creating a pleasing, uniform illumination. (For an exterior view of this wing-style room addition, see the bottom photo on p. 31.)

Windows as Design Elements

Windows play complex roles as interfacing components that admit and control light and outside air, visually connect the building's interior with its environment and serve as important decorative elements.

The unique bedroom gable-wall window group (top right) acts as a major design element. Note that light is admitted from a second source to avoid creating a tunnel effect in the room.

The large first-story window bank in the same house (facing page) sets up a rhythm of repeated elements with minor variations to break up potential monotony. The strong horizontal line of headers below the transoms and the vertical row of window jambs, which seem to march away from the viewer, lead the eye down the length of the room, making the space seem larger. The effect is strengthened by the smaller size of the distant windows and the "perspective" lent by the receding lines of the stairs. (For an exterior view of this building, see the bottom photo on p. 40; for another interior view, see the bottom photo on p. 53.)

The window assembly in the photo at bottom right serves as a decorative element and lights an added stairway and upstairs hall. (For an exterior view, see the top right photo on p. 24.)

The building's skin

The building's walls, windows, doors and roof act in much the same way as an organism's cell membranes: By selectively admitting or excluding energy and materials, they control their inward and outward flow. Light and heat are the two types of energy exchanged through the building's skin. Thermal exchange will be considered shortly, but first let's look at the glazing components—windows, skylights and, sometimes, doors—that control the flow of light, frame the external views and also serve as design elements themselves.

Glazing components If they are well designed, walls and their openings create a visual connection to the outdoors and a feeling of balance between the security and comfort of the home and the freedom and beauty that surround it. The degree to which security or freedom prevails—the degree to which a house is open or closed to the outdoors—depends on the site and the context. A combination of walled or fenced buffer zones and small windows may be used to segregate the home from a busy street or an aesthetically offensive urban environment. Broad expanses of glass patio doors and picture windows can be used to open onto a private garden or a distant view.

As design elements, walls and glazing form combinations of solids and voids, or negative and positive spaces. One of the critical differences between interior and exterior design is that the appearance of the glazing is reversed as the observer passes from one viewpoint to the other. That is, glazing components usually read as dark, negative spaces from the outside (unless the sun just happens to hit them to reflect a temporary glare). Viewed from the inside, glazing components become the bright, positive spaces and the walls fade into the background around them.

Two common interior-design mistakes are to isolate a window in a wall, so that its glare prevents the viewer from seeing the rest of the wall, and to admit light from one side or end of a room only, creating glare and deep shadows. When light from two or more sources is mixed, the overall light is brighter because there is more of it, wider areas of the room are lit, glare is reduced and shadows are minimized.

Additions often create deep, unlit recesses at the transition zone or in rooms that once had windows but are now buried in the interior. The designer must be sure that there is enough light, and light from enough sources, to avoid creating a cave-like effect (see the top photo on p. 76).

The positioning of the glazing components and the angles of the light are important, too. Direct sunlight creates glare where it strikes a surface, so skylights and windows should be designed carefully so that the incoming sunlight, with its ever-changing angle of incidence, does not fall directly on counters or desks, or into the eyes of television viewers. (Media rooms, in fact, should be fairly dark overall since even subtle, indirect glare can be reflected on screens.) Direct sunlight can also fade pictures and carpets and, in sufficient quantity, actually warp wood floors, so it must be controlled. Where it is not possible to shade or position glazing components for protection against intrusive sunlight, make sure to allow space around the windows for curtains or blinds.

Light penetrates this room through a second internal set of windows opening onto the illuminated stairway beyond. The room, part of a second-story addition project, is used primarily for chamber-music rehearsals and must be isolated sonically from the rest of the house.

This extended skylight system was used to illuminate the interior of an existing space that would have become too dark when additions on both sides (left and right, out of photo) darkened the hallway. The flow of light from the hallway into the side spaces acts as a unifying element that pulls together the various interior spaces.

Finally, doors and windows must be treated as design elements apart from their light-admitting function. When it is dark outside, their size, arrangement, style and trim color become major factors in the look and feel of a room. If a continuous space is created by adding a room and opening up a transition zone, the new windows and doors should match the existing ones, or at least blend with them. The principles of designing for continuity discussed in previous chapters apply to the interior appearance of glazing components just as they do to every other aspect of the building.

Thermal exchange through the building's skin Glazing components are poor thermal barriers, and the more glazing a house has, the harder it is to maintain even temperatures. Also, windows let in sunlight and trap heat (the greenhouse effect), so their size and orientation are critical to solar design. Large north windows lose a lot of heat in cold climates, whereas south-facing windows gain it.

Accordingly, in cold regions like Maine, minimize the glazing on the north wall, maximize it on the south. In Arizona, south glazing helps in the cold winters, but the building must be protected from too much solar gain in the blazing hot summers. Protection is normally afforded by carefully designed roof overhangs, thoughtful placement of windows, and auxiliary devices like shutters and insulated, reflective curtains.

Passive solar-heating systems that use glazing to trap sunlight and a thermal mass (such as a large fireplace or a thick, concrete slab floor) to store the light as heat can be easily integrated into an addition's design. These systems can provide most of the heat for the addition and often supply some heat for the rest of the house as well. Though incorporating a thermal mass for heat storage offers the greatest benefit, it is not absolutely necessary—just getting the sunlight into the house will heat the air on winter days, saving some fuel and making life more cheerful. It is strongly recommended that passive solar systems be incorporated in addition projects wherever possible. (For more on passive solar design, see the bibliography.)

Insulation reduces the thermal exchange through walls, roofs and floors. Additions should be insulated to the optimum level for the local climate, and as part of the addition project it's a good idea to insulate or upgrade the insulation of the existing house as well.

In general, since heat rises, insulating the attic returns the greatest cost/benefit value. Depending on the climate, wall or floor insulation offers more or less value. The appropriate amount of insulation is site- and area-specific, and is discussed in the references described in the bibliography (see also pp. 156-157).

In all regions, the basic principle of energy efficiency is conservation: keeping what has already been produced rather than seeking more energy. Appropriate site orientation and massing of the building, discussed below, along with the careful design of glazing and optimization of insulation help achieve this goal.

EXTERNAL INFLUENCES ON DESIGN

In Chapter 3, I explained how the existing house influences the addition's massing. Here, I'll explore the relationship of massing and glazing design to the local climate. Then I'll show how massing, style and material and color choices are influenced by the building's context.

Climate, massing and orientation

Many houses are poorly designed for their climate. Building an addition provides an opportunity to change the building's overall energy efficiency, solar orientation, natural lighting and comfort level (see the sidebar on pp. 78-79). Improvements begin with a study of the house's solar and wind orientation (as shown on the site/floor plan in the last chapter) and application of some of the principles of climate design to the addition.

A sphere is the most energy-efficient solid, because it has the least surface area enclosing the greatest volume—the area for thermal exchange between the interior and the environment is minimized. Few houses are spherical, but cubical buildings also have a pretty good surface-to-volume ratio. The more a house is stretched out, and the more its surfaces are articulated, or varied in shape, the greater its potential for heat loss in winter and heat gain in summer.

In extreme climates, then, it makes sense to design houses that are cubical or spherical. The early American saltboxes in chilly New England and the Native American adobes of the Southwestern desert are good examples. In milder climates, open designs become practical. Houses with highly articulated surfaces, breezeways, decks, balconies and unglazed verandas make living in areas like Florida and southern California more comfortable.

In recent decades, however, numerous open, southern-California-style homes have been built throughout the country, some as far north as Montana and even Canada. They are comfortable in winter only by virtue of high energy consumption, as reflected in their heating bills.

A well-designed addition will pull such a building's extended wings together, minimizing the ratio of the finished building's overall surface area to its volume. Second stories or combinations, which are compact, are appropriate addition types for such a building.

Conversely, many houses in mild climates are built like small forts,

(text continues on p. 80)

DESIGNING FOR CLIMATE

The open plan of this house, centered around a south-facing patio, is suitable for a climate like southern California's, but the design is for a site in Montana.

The overall mass-to-surface ratio makes the house difficult to heat. Also, the designer oriented the entrances toward the road on the north—the direction of the prevailing winter winds. The unprotected front wall catches the wind in its concavities. The garage and front entrance open directly into the blowing, drifting snow. Finally, the central patio can be used only a few months out of the year.

A two-bedroom, one-and-a-half-bath, family-room and front-porch addition project provided an opportunity to make the overall design more compact. The patio is enclosed and turned into a passive solar greenhouse/family room, usable all year round. Light from the low winter sun penetrates all the way into the kitchen on the darkest days of the year.

The bedrooms and baths are in a compact second story, minimizing the overall surface-to-volume ratio. The roofs on the north side are stacked, so much of the north wind is deflected up and over the building. Solar collectors for hot water are hidden from the road on the south roof.

Ideally, the garage and main entrance doors would be placed on the southeast end of the house, but this is not practical as a remodeling project. However, the new, centralized front porch reverses the wind- and snow-catching north-wall concavity, placing an unheated, glassed-in buffer zone between the entrance and the elements.

EXISTING HOUSE

REMODELED HOUSE

1 Front porch with small overhang (dashed line)

2 Main entrance is far from the driveway and in the worst location for the climate (on the northwest corner of the house, facing the prevailing winds).

3 Dining area, with large north window looking onto road

4 Living room, with large south-facing window

5 Utility/laundry room

6 Long front walk vulnerable to icing in winter

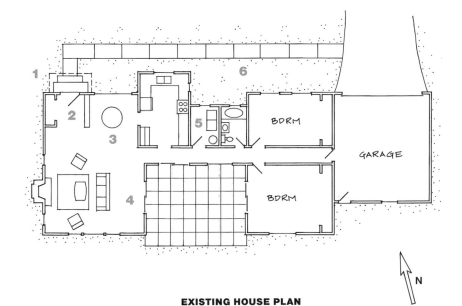

EXISTING HOUSE PLAN

1 Pine trees shield house from wind, provide isolation from road.

2 Extension of existing porch overhang helps to direct wind over house and protect dining-area window from blasts.

3 Glassed-in front-porch entryway is built on slab with flagstone floor. In summer, glass is removed and window openings are screened for cooling.

4 Shorter walkway from driveway to new entrance; extension of roof overhang protects walkway, bedroom windows.

5 New central entry

6 Living area with original south-facing window intact. The fireplace has been equipped with an EPA-approved, fuel-efficient insert.

7 Original patio doors are replaced by insulated folding doors.

8 Family room (glassed-in former patio) acts as a passive solar greenhouse.

9 New, high-tech glazing reduces glare and screens harmful UV radiation while trapping maximum amount of warming, infrared rays.

10 Thermal-mass trombe walls flank bedroom window.

11 Laundry and new solar hot-water heater

12 Extended patio

13 Deciduous trees provide shade in summer, allow sun into house in winter.

REMODELED HOUSE PLAN

with no real indoor/outdoor interplay. While opening them up and extending them with room additions makes them less energy-efficient on the coldest days of the year, it enables them to be comfortable without heating and air conditioning throughout most months—especially if attention is given to solar design and wind patterns.

Though these generalizations hold true for most buildings, their implementation is site-specific, since the temperatures, sunlight, winds and other local conditions vary not just from region to region, but also from microclimate to microclimate. Houses just a few blocks apart can have very different requirements. The intricacies of climate design are beyond the scope of this book, but several excellent references in the bibliography will provide designers and builders with the tools needed for this aspect of designing.

Context

A house's immediate context is its site and the other houses on its block. The neighborhood, town and even the region comprise its broader context. A well-designed addition helps a house blend sensitively with its context. This means making sure the finished building conforms to the masses, shapes, angles, textures and materials of the surrounding buildings.

Sometimes the building can even help fill in a void or gap, as when most of the houses on the block are two stories high but the house to be remodeled is only one story. Here, adding height can smooth out an abrupt break in the visual landscape.

Historical context should also be considered. An addition can be particularly useful in making a house that is out of context—a small, modern home built late on a block of graceful, spacious classics—join the spirit of its surroundings.

There are times when it is appropriate to juxtapose the house against its context. If the surrounding buildings are too much alike and each one is monotonous in its form and articulation, a departure that releases the potential in the building and shows how the rest of the neighborhood could be upgraded—without jarring or shaming—will definitely benefit the owners, and might influence others to follow suit.

PRESET PATTERNS OF GROWTH

In Chapter 4, I presented a method for "growing" a room around its furnishings. It must also be recognized, however, that buildings, like organisms, are often developed according to predetermined patterns. Their various nodes, or sub-units, can grow in strict mathematical relationship to one another.

Throughout history, designers and builders have been trying to understand these patterns, discover how and where they appear in nature, and learn how they can be applied to buildings. It has also been recognized that, consciously or unconsciously, the patterns are in our blood and find ways into our designs, whether we intend them to or not. The meaning attributed to them has varied from sacred to coincidental, depending on the period of history and the predilections of their advocates.

Whatever they are, nature's patterns cannot be dismissed by a designer who seeks to create pleasing spaces and arrange them harmoniously.

The walls have been all but eliminated in this second-story addition, which was specifically designed to maintain a low profile in keeping with neighboring houses. The addition is housed entirely in the attic space created by the new, higher-pitched roof.

For without using a proportioning system, the designer is always confronted with a fundamental question: "Is this building inherently attractive and harmonious or do its shapes appear out of sync with each other and its details look like afterthoughts?"

Proportioning systems in general are discussed below, but there isn't space here to cover the many systems used to design much of the world's great architecture—the Golden Section, Fibonacci series, Greek and Roman orders, Le Corbusier's Modulor, Japanese Ken and others. Designers and builders should be aware of these proportioning systems, however, and look for opportunities to employ them in harmonizing the plans, massing and details of the house and addition. (For a reference on proportioning systems, see the bibliography.)

Proportioning systems

What are the right proportions for a room? Most rooms are rectangles. Their width-to-length ratios fall between two extremes—the square, on the one hand, and a two-to-one rectangle on the other. Rooms look, feel and function better if their proportions stay within limits prescribed by convention and utility and avoid extremes. Although square rooms can work, they lack graceful proportion and compress furniture groupings. Overly elongated rooms are taxing to the eye, and also hard to furnish.

It is usually unwise to design a room with atypical proportions to serve a specific function. Functions change, and the more generic a room's shape, the greater its adaptability. If shapes approaching the extremes appear in the transition zone as the preliminary floor plan is developed, keep working toward a better solution.

Modules Modules are the basic building blocks of proportioning systems. A unit of measurement—the length of a human arm, perhaps, or the distance between two points on the site—is used as the basis for generating the individual modules. Most modules are rectangles based on extensions of the lineal measurement.

The basic rectangle is used to create a grid upon which the major design elements are laid out. In plan, the length and width of each room, position of each door and window, size of the fireplace and distance between the kitchen counters are determined by their location on the grid. In elevation, the size and position of windows, heights of doors, proportions of the fascia and amount of roof overhang are similarly governed.

If a house has an identifiable module, designing its addition can be greatly simplified. The module is simply extended, and things begin to fall into place (see the sidebar on p. 82). The elevations can grow out of the plan, often by applying the same module vertically.

The older a house is, the more likely that it is laid out on a module, since most architects trained before World War I learned proportioning systems. In newer houses, finding a consciously employed module is more difficult, though systems inadvertently used by the designer may govern the proportions of some rooms and features of the elevations.

Start by searching the plan for repeated measurements, comparing the width of the fireplace wings to the width of the windows in the same room, for example. Perhaps the width of the fireplace opening also matches that of the front door. These are clues that there may be a proportioning system.

Next, create grids of rectangles using the basic measurement and superimpose them on the plan. Since the square is the simplest module, try it first. Perhaps the distance across the width of the living room is five times the width of the front door. Perhaps the room's length comes out to a multiple of door widths, too, or is in some other way consistently proportioned to the basic lineal measurement.

Even if there is no obvious proportioning system, the exercise is not wasted, because it familiarizes you with the existing conditions. Are the internal proportions of rooms and their subcomponents consistent or erratic? Do the rooms harmonize with one another, or do some seem to have been stuck into the space that was left over?

If there are problems with the existing layout (or just to simplify designing the addition), you may want to devise your own proportioning system. Start by basing a module on an outstanding feature, such as the width of the fireplace. This module can be used in the addition and transition zone at least, and incorporated into changes made in other parts of the house. Along with furniture groupings, a proportioning system can be a great aid in swiftly laying out rooms and unifying the building.

ADDITION PLAN BASED ON MODULE

The major design elements of this small house line up on a grid based on a square, 2-ft. x 2-ft. module. The addition was designed by extending the grid.

The 2x2 square is particularly useful for designing modern homes, since 2 ft. is a division of many standard building products, such as lumber, drywall and plywood. The module is close enough to the finished size of kitchen cabinets, the depth of closets and the dimensions of fireplaces to use for preliminary design. Subtle changes in wall location can be incorporated into the working drawings, and variations of an inch or two will not affect the way people perceive the proportions of the finished room.

Normally, the grid lines will fall in the centers of the walls. This way, problems of varying wall thickness (see pp. 187-189) can be avoided. It is perfectly acceptable to use half modules, or any dimension such as 3 in., 4 in. or 6 in. that rationally divides the basic measurement.

Numbers like 17 in. or 9 ft. 11 in., however, would be difficult to work with and should be avoided if possible.

Note that the grid can align with either the center or edge of any given element. No matter what its size, for example, a window that goes in the center of a wall can be easily located. If a module is employed, however, elements like windows and doors should fit the dimensions of the grid. The house shown in the plans below will prove easier to design with a 2-ft. x 4-ft. window than with a 2-ft. 3-in. x 4-ft. 9-in. window.

Square grids are the most common, but older homes may use grids based on a variety of proportioning systems, such as the ratios of the Golden Section. While the grid system is convenient, it should be remembered that the basic size and shape of rooms are determined by their function, and most functions require furnishings that in turn must fit into the space. Design a couple of different furniture groups first to ascertain the size and possible shapes of the space, and then design the room on the grid.

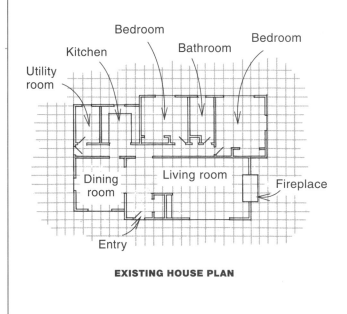

EXISTING HOUSE PLAN

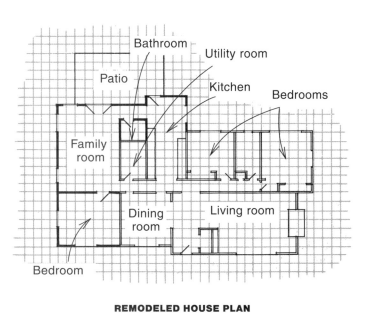

REMODELED HOUSE PLAN

***Ceilings and proportionate
volumes*** Since early times, builders
have struggled to discover the correct formula, or at least an acceptable guideline, for ceiling heights.
The situation is compounded by
the fact that many ceilings are
sloped or vaulted. Is a vault's height
defined as its base at the top of the
wall, a point halfway up its slope
or curve, or its apex? The difficulty
in establishing standards grows
when we introduce features like
mezzanines and the need to harmonize interior and exterior proportions. Although master builders of
the past have proposed various
solutions, none are definitive.

Fortunately, the existing volumetric
relationships can help with designing an addition. While measuring
the house, try to discover what
patterns, if any, are established by
the ceiling heights and the overall
proportions of the rooms. Do the
ratios of the floor plan to the ceiling
heights make sense? Do most work,
with only a couple out of place, or
do all the rooms have ceilings that
are too low or too high? Is there
any pattern to the variation in ceiling height, or does it seem purely
random?

Ideally, a house's style will indicate
the rationale behind the internal
proportioning system. Small rooms
with low ceilings would be found in
typical English or French country
homes or cottages. In Victorian
houses, parlors and living rooms
that are small and square by today's
standards had 12-ft. to 14-ft. high
ceilings to express the sense of
grandeur deemed fitting for the
home. The high rooms were consistent with tall front elevations that
were also designed to impress.

One of the problems with modern
houses is that the ceiling heights
tend to be uniform no matter what
the size of the space. This uniformity is in large part the result of building with modular materials, especially drywall. Although the 8-ft.
ceiling, arising from the most efficient application of the sheets, is
acceptably proportioned for many
rooms, it's likely to seem cramped
in larger, continuous spaces. It's
usually too low for a living/dining/
kitchen area, for example, or for a
large family room. While 10-ft. and
12-ft. sheets of drywall are available,
many houses (particularly modern
tract houses) have been designed
to avoid the extra cost of custom
framing and drywall. This problem
can be corrected while adding on.

PULLING
THE DESIGN
TOGETHER

Once the relationship between
the existing floor plans and ceiling
heights has been ascertained,
designers must make proportioning
decisions for the addition based on
the program and their own aesthetics. Let's suppose, for example, that
a simple, gable-roofed, one-story
house has no obvious module but
does have consistently small rooms
with uniform 8-ft. ceilings. If the
addition is small, say two modest
bedrooms and a bath, it's probably
appropriate to replicate the proportioning patterns for the sake of consistency by building small rooms
with 8-ft. ceilings.

If, on the other hand, you wish to
open up the house, you could knock
out an exterior wall of the existing
kitchen and build on a large family
room, creating a continuous space.
Since the family room is large, say,

18 ft. by 24 ft. minimum, it should
have a higher ceiling, at least 10 ft.
and possibly 12 ft.

One way to get a higher ceiling is
to step the family room down from
the kitchen while maintaining the
same ceiling height (see the photos
on pgs. 53 and 75). If this brings the
floor frame so close to the ground
that it's necessary to excavate to
provide sufficient clearance between
the dirt and joists, it is possible to
cast a concrete slab. If a slab is used,
be sure to cover it with sufficiently
thick carpeting or a wooden floor
on sleepers (joists laid flat) so that it
is warm and comfortable to walk on.

Another way to open up a house
and raise the ceiling in the addition
is to intersect the main gable with a
second gable and provide a vaulted
ceiling over the family room (see
the sidebar on pp. 84-86). This approach would make the kitchen the
focal point of the new floor plan,
and reflect the design of the interior
on the exterior by providing compatible massing where the roofs
come together. In the example in
the sidebar, the vaulted ceiling and
other interior volumes that directly
reflect the external massing are
highly useful for integrating the
interior and exterior aspects of the
building. Vaulting the ceiling also
keeps the addition's walls the same
height as the house's, avoiding the
need for fancy framing where the
two meet.

However, a number of considerations suggest keeping the kitchen
ceiling at its original 8-ft. height.
First, it would remain in proper proportion to the smaller floor plan of
the kitchen. Second, though the

(text continues on p. 86)

INTEGRATING PLANS, VOLUMES AND MASSES

A family room, remodeled kitchen and expanded master-bedroom addition—along with a two-bedroom, one-bath attic conversion—enables this house to accommodate a growing family with a small child, baby and third child on the way.

The existing house has some views of the large backyard with its glorious old oak trees. Limited access, however, reduces yard use and enjoyment. The addition reshapes the yard, partially dividing it into public and private areas (separate patios), and opens to it on both sides.

The main axis is now perpendicular to the street, providing a sense of flow between the front of the house and the backyard. The central

kitchen/breakfast area acts as the traffic hub and family gathering place. The formal dining room is retained, but opened onto the patio for circulation during large parties and partially opened to the kitchen for ease of access.

The living room and family room have the same shape and are almost identical in size, providing subliminal symmetry. The vaulted ceiling in the family room is consistent with its large floor area, and the tall glazing on the end wall captures the view of

the soaring trees (see the bottom drawing on p. 86). The living-room ceiling is raised to match. New glazing above the original bay-window header and the exposure of the living-room chimney to a height of 12 ft. add drama to the space.

EXISTING HOUSE PLAN
1 Street
2 Public walk
3 Driveway
4 Porch
5 Bedroom
6 Dining room
7 Kitchen
8 Living room
9 Bedroom
10 Bedroom
11 Property line

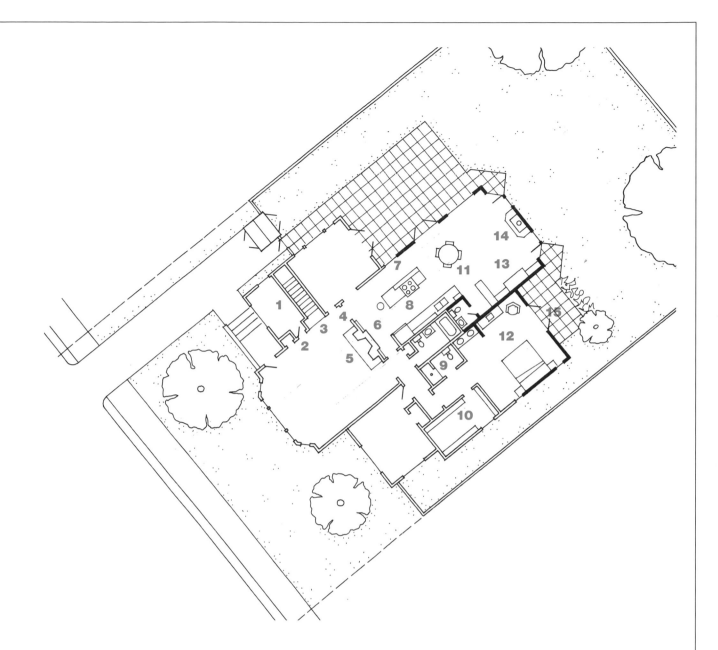

REMODELED HOUSE PLAN

1 Front bedroom is converted to small home office after installation of new stairs.

2 Closet is converted to office entrance. Existing side walls of closet are left in place to minimize work and provide appropriately scaled landing for stairs. Closet door is re-used as room door. New closet plus additional storage for office and dining room is located beneath stairs.

3 Centralized location for new stairs

4 Living room/kitchen door is removed to allow view through family room to backyard. Cooking area is hidden from living room and entrance.

5 Exposed brick chimney (in living room)

6 Exposed brick chimney (in kitchen), with shelves on sides

7 New window across from kitchen sink

8 Kitchen island with down-draft fan and stove. The design of the island, with no overhead fan or projections, is important to the overall sense of spaciousness and flow of the building and the kitchen/family-room area. Note that there is a passage behind the island so people going through the kitchen do not have to go through the cooking area.

9 Half-bath with skylight above in master-bedroom suite

10 Walk-in closet

11 Breakfast table

12 Master-bedroom suite. Space is easily gained by building two more walls during backyard expansion. Bedroom is completely isolated from family room and main part of the house, but there is potential for future indoor connection by cutting door into hall between new half-bath and media center in family room. Circulation through small passages toward ample bed area and glass patio doors makes suite seem even more spacious.

13 Media center

14 EPA-rated wood-burning stove

15 Private patio with walk-way reconnecting to family room through a glass door

INTEGRATING PLANS, VOLUMES AND MASSES (continued)

As shown in the section below, the kitchen soffit is left low for good lighting and easy cleaning and to heighten the effect of entering the family and living rooms from the kitchen. A secondary element of consistency is provided by the exposed brick on the back of the living-room chimney and the brick backdrop of the new family-room wood-burning stove. Both can be seen from the kitchen.

Centered in the family-room end wall, the tall wood-burning stove and backdrop do not interfere with the view of the trees, but rather augment their effect with a rising column similar to the trunks of the trees. Tall wing windows on either side add to the vertical thrust effect.

While the public areas are open and flow together, the bedrooms and office are cloistered and cellular, with identical, low ceilings. Their isolation provides privacy and quiet, and a sense of security while sleeping.

The massing and floor plan are integrated, as shown on the roof plan. The new rear intersecting gable mimics the existing front roof. Note that the nonconforming, low-pitched roof over the expanded master bedroom is not visible from the street or most of the property.

kitchen is in one sense part of the same space as the family room, it is a separate entity with separate functions. Since the wall that divided the spaces is gone, visual clues are needed to indicate the transition from one area to the next. Common solutions are to use different color schemes, flooring materials and ceiling heights. Third, the addition will seem even more open and dramatic by the use of the old architectural trick of having people pass from a small space with a low ceiling to a larger, higher space.

Other benefits of preserving the original kitchen ceiling include maintaining the structural integrity by keeping the original ceiling joists intact, and saving the cost of tearing out and installing a new ceiling. Finally, since kitchen ceilings tend to accumulate grease, the owners will find it much easier to clean the lower ceiling. All things considered, installing an even lower "false" ceiling that hides built-in lighting, makes maintenance still easier and further dramatizes the height of the family room might be well worth its minimal cost.

One problem with this scheme, bearing in mind the original proportioning of the house with its small spaces and low, flat ceilings, is that the large family room is radically different from the rest of the house. The contrast is likely to seem awkward. Although the designer should be careful about expanding addition projects into areas beyond the transition zone, in this example it was decided to tear out the living-room ceiling, creating a large, vaulted volume in the front of the house. This relatively straightforward and inexpensive project balances the main internal spaces by making

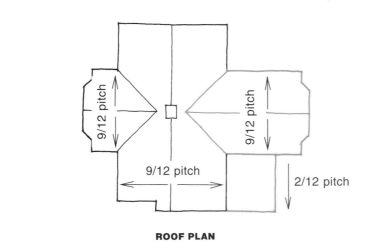

ROOF PLAN

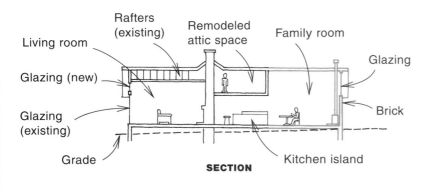

SECTION

them open at both ends while maintaining consistently small rooms in the middle and on the wings. The public gathering and entertainment spaces—living and family rooms—are similarly proportioned and flow together, while the private, quiet bedroom and office spaces remain discrete, cellular and out of the main path through the house.

COMPLETING THE HOUSE

Effective use of the architectural principles discussed so far depends on detailed knowledge of the house's structure and subsystems and the laws that regulate design and construction. We will leave the subject of design, for now, and return to it after acquiring the necessary background information.

Meanwhile, keep the types of additions and the goal of continuity in mind and observe houses with additions. Some have been expanded obviously and awkwardly. You have to look closely at others, though, to tell if their second story, rear portion or wing was added or original. Sometimes you will not know. It is as if the designer's purpose was not to add on, but simply to complete an unfinished home.

The interplay between exterior masses and interior volumes is shown in this award-winning addition to an old New England stone house. The mass of the new chimney at left reflects that of the original and brings the one-story addition into scale with the large house (top photo). In the family room, the exterior stone wall of the house is reflected by the new fireplace, developing a sense of continuity while at the same time making a gradual, downward shift in scale (bottom photo).

CONDITIONS, PROBLEMS AND SOLUTIONS

6

SITE AND SOIL CONDITIONS

Although there is already a house on the site of the proposed addition, it is not safe to assume that it was built correctly for the site and soil conditions, or, indeed, that its erection would be permitted at all under modern codes. If the soil type or condition, the slope or the drainage are causing problems, building an addition without addressing the problems will just make matters worse.

Finding and evaluating site and soil problems early in the feasibility and design phases will not only save expense and embarrassment later on, but can also give the creative designer or builder an opportunity to improve conditions that may be adversely affecting the existing house.

SITE AND SOIL PROBLEMS

The four main categories of site and soil conditions that can affect the design of an addition are steep slopes, unstable soil, water problems and vulnerability to earthquakes. Many sites have more than one problem. For example, a steep slope, which is itself a challenge, might also have loose soil and drainage problems. Acting together, these conditions can cause extensive damage—in some cases putting the building and its inhabitants in real peril—and require costly mitigation efforts.

Steep slopes

Stable, steep slopes merely present certain logistical problems. Moving materials up and down the site is arduous and time-consuming, and some allowance must be made for the cost of the extra effort. Steep slopes composed of unstable soil, on the other hand, are usually moving—technically they are landslides—and pose significant engineering challenges.

Landslides Rapid, devastating landslides, injurious to homes and lives, are unusual, newsworthy events. They do occur, however, and homes sitting at the top or bottom of steep slopes with loose soil or rubble are vulnerable to sudden destruction.

Much more common are the creeping landslides that affect millions of homes built on moderate slopes of recently upraised geological deposits, such as most of the Rocky Mountain and West Coast states and some areas of the Appalachians. Houses built on creeping ground frequently develop serious foundation problems, since the soil beneath them is always moving—in some cases, at rates of over 1 in. per year. Foundations are stretched, twisted and bent, and only the best of them remain serviceable without the need for repairs during a normal life span of 50 years or so. The house above often reflects the condition of the foundation, with cracked walls, sloping floors and jammed doors. The cost of soil investigations, engineering and beefed-up foundations on a steep, unstable slope can easily triple that of a standard foundation on a stable site.

Soil problems

Naturally loose soil and uncompacted landfill can affect the design and cost of an addition's foundation.

Loose soil Many sites have naturally loose soil that offers little compressive resistance to the weight of the house. If the soil is looser on some parts of the site and firmer on others, the house may be subject to differential settling, whereby some portions of it settle more quickly than others, causing floors to tilt, walls, foundations or chimneys to crack, and windows and doors to stick. The weight of a second-story addition will obviously exacerbate the problem, while a room addition

Cracks like those in this garage facade and retaining wall are common sights where houses are built on slowly creeping hillsides. The substantial concrete retaining wall extends into the garage, where it acts as the foundation. Its failure to hold back the moving soil affects the structure as well as the yard.

is likely to settle at a different rate than the house, causing a variety of problems at the juncture between the two structures.

Uncompacted landfill When leveling a site to build a house, it is common practice to cut and fill with a bulldozer or bring in fill dirt (see the drawing on p. 98). Though modern regulations require that the fill dirt be recompacted by machine to an engineered density, recompacting was not always required in the past. Many existing houses sit on uncompacted landfill—some of them on steep slopes or in bottomlands where water collects. Uncompacted landfill can cause many of the same settling problems as loose natural soil, but the problems are often worse because the fill is more profoundly disturbed. A large volume of fill can slide down a slope, taking structures with it or burying those in its path, and landfilled wetlands are vulnerable to liquefaction during earthquakes (see below).

Related to the problem of uncompacted landfill is that of soft areas or holes on the site, which are often the remnants of old, private water or sanitary systems that have been filled for safety reasons or to level the yard. Be on the lookout for such conditions when building a room addition, because a portion of its foundation may end up on loose, sinking soil.

Water problems

Water-related site conditions that can cause damage to the house and addition include poor drainage, underground streams or springs, flooding and expansive soils.

Poor drainage Many sites have poor natural drainage, which can be caused by the configuration of the site, the nature of the soil and other factors. Some sites that once had good drainage now have poor drainage because someone built a foundation at the point where water would normally flow off the site.

On sites with poor drainage, damage normally occurs during the wet season in rainy areas, or during the spring runoff where there is snow. Undrained or improperly channeled water may cause a variety of problems, including site erosion, or the loss of topsoil; exacerbation of landslide conditions, causing creeping soil to move faster and with more force; softening of some types of soils, resulting in subsidence, or sinking of soil under the foundations; and swelling of expansive soils, causing foundation distortion.

Underground water Some houses are built over underground water sources, such as streams or runoffs from springs that flow seasonally or year round. Depending on the site's geological structure, the flowing water may disturb the foundation or be situated well below it and have no noticeable effect for decades. Underground erosion may be occurring, however, and on sites where underground flow is suspected, a geotechnical engineer should be consulted (see p. 94).

Aquifers are strata of sand, soil or rock in which water is stored. When subsurface aquifers are drained—by wells, for example—the soil above them can collapse into the void, damaging the building above.

Flooding Some houses are built in lowlands—usually near rivers, but sometimes near lakes or marshes—that are subject to periodic flooding. Regulations against building in flood zones have been tightened in recent years, and in most states or jurisdictions it is unlikely that permission will be granted to add onto a house in a flood zone. If you suspect that the house might be built in a flood zone, check with the local authorities to determine the feasibility of building an addition.

Expansive soils Certain soils, especially those with a high plastic clay content, can expand dramatically—up to 2½ times their normal volume—when they are wet. Foundations built on expansive soils in areas of seasonal wetness are subject to a great deal of irregular heaving and subsidence, which can produce foundation cracks, separate chimneys from the house and cause other structural problems.

Expansive soils can be particularly troublesome for room additions because the old and new foundations may react differently to the swelling soil. It is possible to control expansive soils to some extent by installing a proper drainage system (see pp. 95-97).

Earthquake vulnerability

It is a myth, or perhaps a case of mass denial, that only the Pacific Coast of North America, from Baja California, to the Aleutian Islands, is vulnerable to earthquakes. While it is true that earthquakes occur more frequently in these areas than elsewhere, many parts of the continent are periodically subject to moderate or severe earthquakes. Damage to buildings in these areas will be much worse if structures are not properly engineered to resist the tremendous forces involved.

Although all houses in seismic areas are potentially vulnerable to earthquakes, some are located on more problematic sites, notably those that are near fault traces, in landslide zones or subject to liquefaction.

Faults and special studies zones
Hundreds of thousands of buildings are situated on or near fault traces, or subterranean areas indicated on seismic maps where earthquake shocks are most likely to originate. Chapters 7 and 8 describe how typical houses react to earthquakes and discuss ways to protect them. Additional measures may have to be taken for houses in "special studies zones" near fault traces, however, and the designer or builder should find out about such requirements before making a feasibility assessment. The same is true of landslide zones in seismic areas: Shaking will add to their inherent instability, and special restrictions are likely to apply both to new construction and to remodeling.

Liquefaction Liquefaction occurs in soil sitting in or at the edge of bays, lagoons and lakes or, occasionally, above aquifers. When the soil is shaken by an earthquake, it mixes with the adjacent or subterranean water and, almost instantly, turns into an ooze or soup similar to the muck found around the edges of marshes.

The fact that buildings situated on such soils normally sink and collapse dramatically during earthquakes has not deterred enthusiastic hordes of developers from scooping up every available land-

fill—from unwanted topsoil to garbage—dumping it around the edges of scenic bays and lakes, and building upon it. In response, governments have put an increasing number of controls on new or expanded construction in such areas. Even if building is permitted, there may be so much engineering required that the cost would prohibit undertaking a small-scale project like an addition.

Other hazardous site and soil conditions

A variety of other conditions may affect the site and the ability to excavate for the addition's foundation. Potential problems include the presence of dying root systems of large trees, abandoned underground fuel tanks for disconnected heating systems and the possibility that the property was once used as a dumping ground for landfill or hazardous materials. If you are unfamiliar with the means of detecting such problems, contact the appropriate local expert.

Hazards from frost and fire Before leaving the subject of site and soil conditions, it's important to say a few words about frost and fire hazards. Because frost heave can seriously damage foundations, the Uniform Building Code specifies that footings should extend below the frost line (the deepest level of the soil penetrated by frost). The depth of the frost line varies from area to area, and the designer, builder or engineer must be aware of local conditions when specifying foundation dimensions.

An increasing number of houses are built in "urban/wildlife interface zones" (UWIZ) at the edges of state parks and other natural areas where there is a hazard of wild fires. Such houses, and their additions, should be designed as compactly as possible, without wood decks or projecting overhangs that can trap the burning material that blows around during fires. Roofs and walls should be of fire-resistant materials. Siting in locations where fires naturally travel—at the tops of wooded canyons, for example—is dangerous and should be avoided. Finally, make sure that the area around the house is kept clear of potentially flammable plants and provide for drought-resistant vegetation where applicable.

The appropriate design for homes and their additions in fire-prone UWIZ is a complex subject, and designers or builders working in these areas should consult local experts in forestry and design for further information.

EVALUATING THE SITE AND SOIL

An evaluation of the site and soil for a proposed addition project should begin at state and local government offices. City halls or county offices usually have maps of flood zones, underground streams, special studies zones and other geological features of the area. If the available documents are not specific enough, a city engineer or planner can inform the designer or builder about restrictions and soil problems in the neighborhood, and perhaps on the actual site.

After learning about the general conditions and any applicable restrictions, the designer or builder should take a good look at the site, the building and the other houses and yards on the block. Some problematic conditions—extremely steep sites or low spots filled with water, for example—are obvious. If extreme conditions exist, or the site is in a special studies zone, call a geotechnical engineer to help determine the feasibility of the project.

Assuming the site is flat or only moderately sloped and not in a known problem area, look for smaller problems that, added together, might indicate the need for engineering assistance or special construction. Visual clues fall into two general categories: those that indicate soil motion or subsidence, and those that indicate the presence of excess water.

Signs of soil motion

Soil does not usually move on flat sites, though it is often washed onto them from higher ground. On many sloping sites, as discussed above, loose soil tends to creep downhill, damaging roads and foundations as it moves. The most obvious signs of soil motion, then, are cracks in retaining walls, driveways, curbs, streets, foundations, stucco walls—any rigid structure embedded in or resting on the land.

When cracks show up all over the lot, from the backyard retaining wall to the front driveway, the entire site is moving. When one or two cracks are found near each other, in a corner of the foundation and the wall above it, for example, and the rest of the site seems stable, local subsidence is indicated. Perhaps the affected corner was built over a filled-in well, or a downspout saturates the soil beneath it during the rainy season.

Signs of excess water

Signs of excess water or drainage problems on sloping sites include eroded topsoil and/or eroded channels under the foundation. On moderately sloped and flat sites, symptoms include depressions in the yard, cracks or efflorescence in the foundation (see pp. 106-107) and standing water or cracked mud from dried puddles in the sub-area.

Along with the visual investigation, it usually helps to question the owners and neighbors. They can describe the site during wet and dry seasons and provide some history that will put conditions like the rate of soil creep in perspective.

If the house is on a moderate slope or flat site, has a good foundation and shows no obvious signs of soil or water problems, it is probably safe to design and build the addition without special help from a geotechnical engineer, as long as a structural engineer is consulted along the way. (The structural engineer, who should be part of every design team, should know enough about local soil conditions to help determine whether a geotechnical engineer is needed.)

If one or more red flags are raised during the designer or builder's investigation of the site, however, it is a good idea to call the geotechnical engineer at the outset, and put doubts to rest. Keep in mind that many sites have more than one problem, that there can be more than one underlying cause of a symptom like cracks in the foundation, and that compound problems are usually subtle enough to warrant the recommendations of a specialist.

Consulting a Geotechnical Engineer

A geotechnical (or "soils and foundation") engineer should be consulted whenever there is reason to suspect that the existing site conditions may affect the design of the addition. Typically, the engineer will make a visual assessment of the site first. Then, if necessary, he or she will order investigative drillings, which produce core samples of the subsurface soil that can be tested and analyzed for their compressive strength, water permeability and other characteristics. Samples may be needed from several locations on the site, and at depths varying from 10 ft. to 50 ft., depending on conditions.

The site investigations, drillings, lab analysis, calculations and engineer's recommendations and reports may eat up so much of the budget that a small addition is not feasible. Fortunately, this decision can often be made after the engineer has conducted the preliminary, visual site investigation, which is comparatively inexpensive.

THE DRAINAGE SYSTEM

Almost all site and soil problems are exacerbated, if not actually caused, by excess water, a problem that can usually be alleviated by a good drainage system. Drainage is one of the most important and, oddly enough, least understood and attended to aspects of construction. The fact that many sites have nonexistent or poorly designed drainage systems—leading to millions of dollars worth of damage annually—is all the more lamentable because drainage design is usually straightforward, and installation is relatively inexpensive, particularly if it is done during the course of foundation construction.

Severe damage to the property from flowing water is unusual on moderate slopes and flat sites. Also, soil erosion and other damage is generally easy to repair with landfill and control with retaining walls. Usually, the most costly damage is caused by water that is standing against or running under the house foundations. Protecting the foundations is the paramount objective, if not always the first line of defense, of the drainage system.

When flowing water encounters an obstacle, it piles up until it pushes the obstacle aside, flows over or tunnels under it. When it reaches a low spot, water accumulates and begins to form a pond. The purpose of a drainage system is to channel flowing water around, or standing water away from, objects or soils that it might damage. Since water follows the path of least resistance, the drainage system simply has to give it a sufficiently large, continuous, open path to follow.

The design begins with discovering the sources of water, getting a rough idea of its quantity and seeing how it would leave the site if it were not hindered by man-made structures. Ideally, the drainage pipes will follow the same natural water course.

Sources of water

Water comes from four sources: adjacent, uphill properties; accumulation on the site itself; the roof; and subterranean sources. During wet seasons, surface runoff, and sometimes piped water from drainage systems, flows from higher properties to those below. While the surface runoff is usually about the same as it would be in a natural system (that is, if there were no houses present), the drainpipes may concentrate water that would otherwise flow elsewhere onto a particular site. If the neighbor's drainage pipes dump large quantities of water onto the addition's site, it may be necessary to hook them into an existing or new drainpipe and guide the water off the property.

Precipitation that falls onto the site itself either runs off the surface or, if there is too much of it, soaks into the soil where it is retained or moves along underground, depending on the slope and soil type. Usually, the biggest obstacle to flowing water is the foundation itself. On sloped sites, water piles up on the high side of the house, saturates the ground around the footings and eventually finds its way through or under the foundations. On flat sites or in bottomlands, water remains standing until it slowly drains through the soil to lower levels or evaporates.

Another major, often neglected source of water is the runoff from the building's roof. A typical house covers one-quarter or more of its lot, and all the water that falls on the roof is immediately shed—none of it is held in temporary suspension as it is in saturated soils. Gutters collect and concentrate this flow, and copious quantities of water are frequently dumped from downspouts right at the edge of the foundation, where they supersaturate the bearing soil.

A fourth source of water is from underground streams or channels that flow during wet seasons. A geotechnical engineer should be called to design the drainage system for houses built over subterranean water sources.

Designing a drainage system

Ideally a house, or an addition, should take advantage of the site's natural drainage. Houses are best situated on gently sloping sites. Steep sites tend to be unstable and require extensive drainage, while water ponds on flat sites—more rapidly if they are at the bottom of slopes.

Siting the foundation Whenever possible, a corner of the foundation should point into the slope, like the prow of a boat, so runoff will be effortlessly diverted along the walls (see the top drawing on p. 96). A foundation built perpendicular to the slope blocks the flow of water. A U-shaped foundation built across the slope makes the situation even

DESIGNING FOUNDATIONS
FOR DRAINAGE

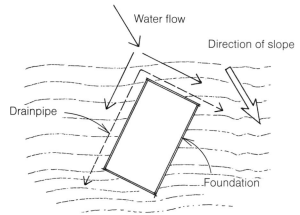

Water flow

Direction of slope

Drainpipe

Foundation

WELL-SITED FOUNDATION
A well-sited foundation meets and diverts flowing water on a slope.

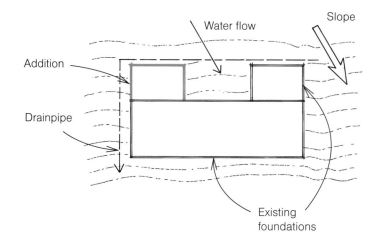

Slope

Water flow

Addition

Drainpipe

Existing foundations

POORLY SITED FOUNDATION AND ADDITION
A poorly sited foundation built across the slope acts like a dam. The addition makes the situation worse by blocking the only path the water can take along the main wall. The underground drainpipe outboard of the foundations helps, but does not stop the flow of surface runoff and will eventually clog.

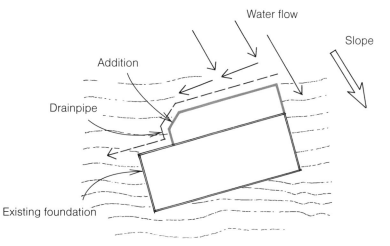

Water flow

Slope

Addition

Drainpipe

Existing foundation

WELL-SITED ADDITION
A well-sited addition allows the water to move downhill. The foundation should also be provided with subsurface drainage.

Note. These examples show a simple slope with more or less uniform water flow. Many sites have a more complex topography, and water might flow in two or three directions. Study the site's actual flow patterns before designing the foundation.

worse (see the middle drawing on the facing page). It acts like a dam, and water can only escape underneath it.

Although some of the water can temporarily be diverted by a subterranean drainpipe placed at some distance from the foundation, the overall design is a poor one. The pipe will eventually clog (see the photo on p. 100), and, even if the property is well maintained, the owners may not be aware of the situation until after the foundation is damaged. By the time water is discovered penetrating or undermining the foundation, drainpipe replacement and possibly foundation repairs will be needed.

Subterranean drainpipe should be installed along the foundation even if the foundation is well designed to divert water. The drawing on pp. 98-99 shows a typical residential drainage system. Note that there is more than one line of defense, with the drainage and potential soil motion controlled by retaining walls placed higher on the property as well as the perforated foundation drainpipe. Also, the leaders (downspouts) carrying roof water are hooked into solid subterranean pipes. (On the downhill side of some houses, leaders empty onto splash blocks that disperse their flow.) All the sources of water—from the neighbor's yard, the site itself and the roof—are controlled.

Sizing the pipe The precise sizing of drainpipes depends on a detailed analysis of the quantity of water that must be removed. Unless the site is in a region with heavy pre-

cipitation or for some other reason becomes inundated, the most practical approach is to use a pipe that is big enough to handle any reasonably anticipated quantity of water, namely, 6-in. diameter perforated pipe (see the bottom drawing on p. 98). Although 6-in. pipe is slightly more expensive than the 4-in. pipe used by many builders, the difference is minimal compared to the cost of installation and well worth the peace of mind it buys. Also, larger pipes take longer to clog, so the system will last longer. One final note: Use rigid plastic pipe, not the flexible, corrugated type, which is easily crushed by the weight of the backfill.

Draining flat sites Flat sites are more problematic to drain than moderate slopes, because gravity can become an enemy rather than an ally. Some flat sites allow water to percolate through the ground, and, after a time, are self-draining. Others are natural low areas with hardpan bottoms. Water sits in them throughout the wet season, and they do not drain but dry by evaporation.

Houses on sites with adequate natural percolation can be equipped with gravity drainage systems consisting of subterranean foundation drainpipes and sumps, or gravel-filled pits in the yard that hold excess water until it is absorbed into the ground. Normally the gravel is covered with top soil for planting.

Houses on hardpan low spots need electric sump pumps (see p. 100), usually located at the lowest point in the sub-area, to remove water from the site. Pumps are the least desirable means of drainage since they rely on outside power that can

fail during major storms. Also, disposing of pumped water can be a problem. If it is not delivered some distance from the foundations, it will simply drain back in, forcing the pump to operate constantly. In many communities it is illegal to dump sump water into the street or the house's sanitary sewer system, and neighbors don't want it in their yard. An illegally drained sump may become a major obstacle to obtaining a permit for an addition.

Sub-area ventilation Although foundation drainpipes or sumps can collect most of the water that enters the sub-area, on many sites a certain amount of moisture is trapped in the sub-area soil, causing it to become muddy. This soft soil can affect the foundations and dampen the air in the sub-area, encouraging the proliferation of structural pests (see p. 121). It is important, then, to provide adequate ventilation in the sub-area, and to avoid blocking existing vents with the addition.

The Uniform Building Code specifies that there must be a minimum of 1 sq. ft. of vent opening for each 150 sq. ft. of sub-area, and not less than 1½ sq. ft. of venting for every 25 lin. ft. of exterior wall. Vents should be placed approximately across from each other on opposite walls to encourage cross-ventilation. They should be covered with a protective mesh to keep out animals. (Standard vents that fit between kneewall studs are available at lumber and hardware stores.)

While the code specifies minimums, the optimum amount of ventilation needed depends on the region and the design, but, in general,

(text continues on p. 100)

TYPICAL DRAINAGE SYSTEM

The site for the original house on this steep slope was prepared by cutting and filling with a bulldozer. The building site was sloped gently so that surface water would drain, and the cuts were benched for stability. The original earth above the cut and the recompacted fill dirt are retained by engineered, reinforced concrete walls.

Defense against excess water flow begins with the underground perforated drainage pipe ("perf pipe") at the base of the upper retaining wall. The wall itself is bent gently into the hill, giving it better resistance to the downward pressure of soil, while at the same time cutting the length of the perf-pipe runs in half and making the yard seem somewhat larger and the wall

more visually interesting (see the drawing on the facing page). The lower retaining wall, built straight along the property line, is protected from water that falls on the building site with its own perf pipe.

The addition was placed on the uphill end of the house to avoid trapping water. Perf pipe collects water on the high side of the foundations and channels it around the house. Once the water is collected, it leaves the property in solid pipe so that it doesn't drain out into the soil beneath the yard.

The perforated pipe is installed with its holes placed downward so ground water bubbles up into them and flows away (see the bottom drawing below). The mini-

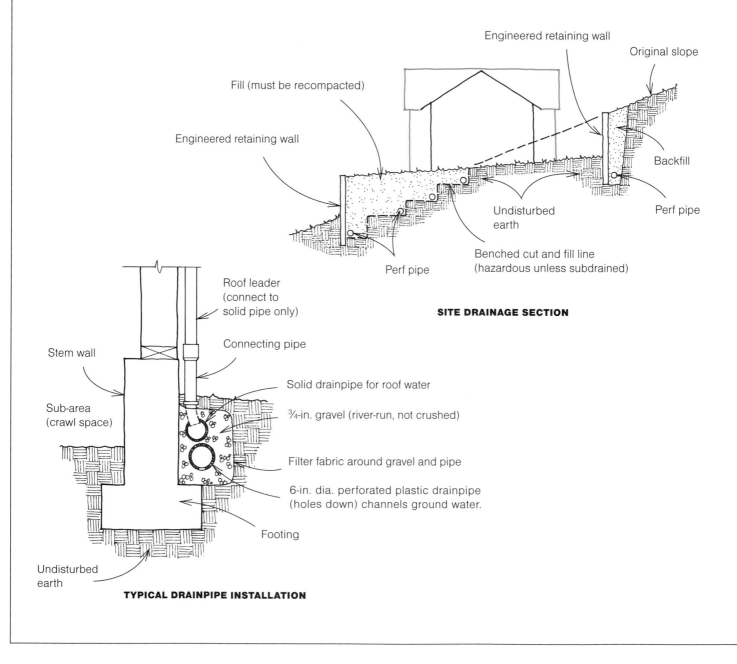

SITE DRAINAGE SECTION

TYPICAL DRAINPIPE INSTALLATION

mum allowable slope is 1:48 or ¼ in. per foot. Steeper slopes work better, but are limited by the depth of the footings, the length of the run and the cost of removing soil.

The pipe is embedded in gravel (usually ¾-in. stones) and covered with permeable fiberglass filter fabric to protect it from clogging. The top of the trench is covered with dirt and small plants with shallow root systems to keep the soil from sinking into the gravel. (Bushes or trees with large root systems shouldn't be planted near drainpipes or foundations.)

On the uphill side of the house, the roof can be drained through the same trench, but leaders should be connected to solid pipe only—roof water will leak through perforated pipe and saturate the soil around the foundations. On the downhill side of most houses, leaders can dump moderate quantities of water onto concrete splash blocks, which spread the water across the surface. In the plan shown below, however, all the roof water is carried off the site in solid pipes so it doesn't pile up behind the lower retaining wall.

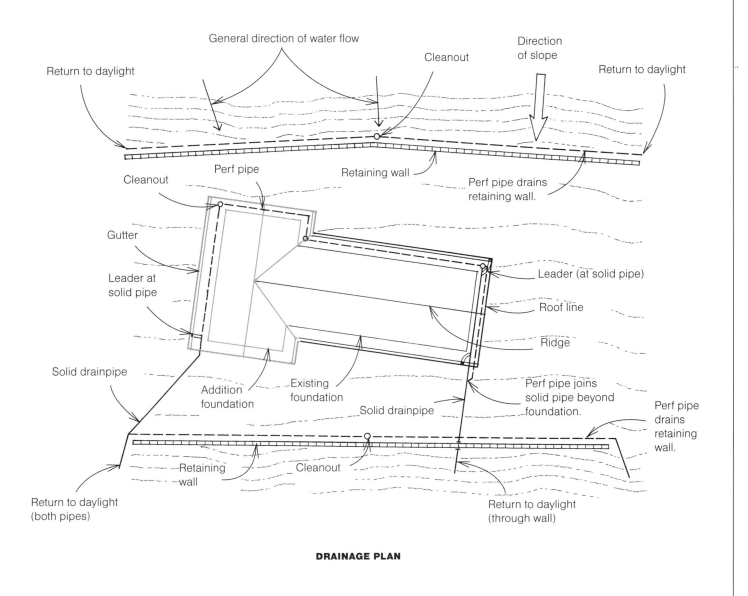

DRAINAGE PLAN

This piece of terra-cotta drain-pipe was underground for about 15 years before being unearthed in the course of installing a new drainage system. The roots from a nearby tree extended through over 30 ft. of pipeline.

the more the better. Manufacturers of vent covers and screens frequently provide information on the correct amount of ventilation for a given region.

Evaluating the existing drainage system

Begin evaluating the drainage system by looking for the symptoms of poor drainage—foundation cracks, soil erosion, cracked mud in the crawl space—that were discussed earlier in this chapter. They indicate that the system isn't working.

To understand why the drainage system has failed, look first at those components that are visible above ground. Check for runoff or drain-pipes leading from neighboring properties. Then examine the condition of the house's gutters and leaders. See if the low-side leaders discharge onto splash blocks, and the high-side leaders are hooked up

to underground pipes or just dump onto the ground. Second, look for a way to water-test the underground pipes, if there are any.

Flow test Subterranean pipes can be accessed by disconnecting a leader where it disappears under-ground, or sometimes through cleanouts or patio grates. Stick a garden hose in the opening, turn it on full blast, then go to the point where the pipe "returns to daylight" (comes to the surface). If a flow approximating that of the hose discharges quickly and cleanly from the pipe, the system is probably in pretty good shape and the addition's roof leaders and foundation can be added to it. If the flow is slow or water shows up somewhere other than the end of the drainpipe (seeping or running into the sub-area, for example), the underground pipes are clogged and must be cleaned out, replaced or bypassed with a new system.

If there are no access points for the subterranean pipes, check the low side of the house for pipes returning

to daylight. Many houses lack subterranean pipes altogether, and, if there are no visible pipes, it's safe to assume that a new drainage system will have to be installed. If there are pipes returning to daylight but no openings above, try tracing the line back and unearthing a section of pipe for the flow test.

It may also be possible to locate subterranean pipes by contacting the person who installed them. If the drainage system is not easily tested and was installed more than 15 years ago, however, it's safe to assume that it is at least partially clogged and should be replaced.

Sump pumps If the house has a sump pump, check its age and condition. Before testing the pump, make sure that it is wired safely. Pumps should draw power from electrical outlets equipped with ground-fault circuit interrupters (GFCIs); if the pump is served by a rickety old two-wire extension cord, test it with extreme caution (use a wood stick to lift the float and see if the pump operates). Do not touch the pump, pipes or water in the sump while it is operating.

There are two types of sump pumps: older models that must be switched on manually, and newer ones with devices similar to toilet-bowl floats that switch the pump on automatically when water is in the sump. Manual pumps should be replaced, because someone must be home to turn them on when it rains. If the pump has a float, fill the sump with a hose. The float should rise easily (without sticking) and turn the pump on before water overflows the sump's rim. Run the hose for several minutes to make sure that the system can handle a large quantity of water. Finally, check that the drainpipes are in good condition and discharging efficiently to a place where the water will actually run off the site, not back toward the sump.

Improving the drainage system

An addition project provides a good opportunity to improve upon an undersized or deteriorating drainage system. The first concern is to avoid making the situation worse by building foundations that trap water, grading soil or driveways so that surface runoff flows toward the building, or installing pipes that discharge in the wrong locations.

Ideally, as discussed above, the foundations can be designed so that they naturally divert water to the sides of the building where it can flow away. If the old pipes are clogged, they can be cleaned out or readily replaced when the addition's system is installed, particularly if a trenching machine is rented. Connecting to the existing system offers the opportunity to clear roots, add cleanouts and lengthen drainpipes.

Finally, gutters and leaders are normally replaced when a second story is added, and the new leaders can be hooked up to the subterranean drainage pipes at this time.

Of course, if there is no drainage system, one will have to be installed as part of the addition project, and the property will be improved overall. No matter what the situation, the designer or builder will have to add the cost of drainage improvements to feasibility considerations and the final budget.

7
EVALUATING THE EXISTING STRUCTURE

The structural knowledge needed to design an addition is neither extensive nor esoteric. Relying on the Uniform Building Code, readily available design information and common sense, any competent designer or builder can draw the plans. Standard wood-frame construction techniques have been recognized by the engineering profession as fundamentally sound. Our collective experience in building millions of homes substantiates this judgment. We *know* that walls built with 2x4s spaced 16 in. apart will support second stories and roofs, and that floor joists of a certain size and spacing will bend but not break when people crowd into a room for a party.

Nevertheless, it is a good idea to consult a structural engineer at the beginning of the project and as needed along the way. Though standard wood framing is adequate for safe construction, certain methods work better than others, and it is particularly important to be sure that the extra loads imposed by additions are handled correctly. Also, while some structural specifications such as joist sizes are available from the code book, others are not. For example, the code book does not tell you how much retrofitted shear wall is needed to stabilize a building with a new second story, or what its correct plywood thickness and nailing schedule are (see Chapter 8). These are questions an engineer is trained to answer.

The designer or builder, however, must have a general understanding of structural issues in order to produce a good basic design and to work with the engineer. An overview of the structural information needed to design an addition is given here, with a discussion of light-wood-frame houses (balloon frames and platform frames) and their problems in this chapter and some of the most common solutions to those problems in the next.

EVALUATING EXISTING FOUNDATIONS

Evaluation of a house's potential to support an addition begins with an analysis of its foundation. While the age and condition of the existing foundation are critical for building a second-story addition, it is also a good idea to check the foundation before beginning a room addition or any other substantial remodeling job. If the foundation is beginning to fail, the money that will have to be spent on it should be taken into account while developing the master plan for the house (see pp. 210-211). The foundation's condition can be the single most important cost factor in a job, dictating swings of many thousands of dollars in the overall budget.

An existing foundation can support a second story without modification only if it meets certain standards. The safe assumption is that the foundation will not work unless it meets certain criteria. If a foundation has rebar, is solid, without cracks or crumbling, and is of the right dimensions, it can probably take the load of an addition with little or no reinforcing. If it fails any of these tests, it will need reinforcement, ranging from placement of simple spread footings beneath sections where loads are concentrated (see pp. 128-129) to complete replacement.

The general condition of the foundation can be determined by visual examination, using a hammer and a flashlight. To know what to look for, you must understand a little about how residential foundation design has evolved.

Brick foundations

Today's concrete foundations became common in the 1920s, when gasoline-powered trucks for delivering the concrete were first introduced. Before that, most foundations were made of brick, or, less commonly, stone. The old brick and stone foundations were not reinforced with structural steel, and engineers call them "unreinforced masonry" foundations. These foundations have very limited capacity to support a second story.

While some brick foundations have lasted remarkably well, most are in the process of failing (see the sidebar on p. 104). The failure is due in part to the use of lime mortar between the bricks, which disintegrates gradually over time and has a normal life expectancy of less than 100 years (almost all brick foundations are more than 70 years old). Even if the mortar appears to be in good condition, its very age tells us that it is likely to have a short remaining life expectancy.

Disintegration as a result of age is not the only problem, however. Because of the basic discontinuous nature of masonry construction, differential loading or varying soil strength tends to shear or pull apart the individual bricks, and there is only the adhesion of the mortar to resist these forces. Second-story additions are commonly supported by posts that travel through the walls to the foundation (see pp. 128-130). Such concentrated loads can crack or crush bricks and shear them apart at their mortar joints.

Another problem with old, unreinforced brick foundations is that they offer little or no resistance to horizontal forces, such as those generated by earthquakes or high winds. If anchor bolts are installed, they are typically drilled into one or two bricks only. Those bricks will simply tear out when the house begins to move sideways. The result will be a displaced house with a few bricks bolted to the bottom of its mudsill.

If a brick foundation is in good condition, however, it is possible to install "screen anchors" by drilling

Brick-Foundation Failure

The brick foundation shown below has failed at the point where a post loads it with the weight of a second story. Bricks are cracked, crushed and pushed into the ground. The mudsill has deflected downward, and settling effects like stuck doors and cracked walls can result.

While some brick foundations have been replaced, designers of additions should be aware that others have been covered with a skim coat of fresh mortar to slow or hide disintegration. Still others are encased in a concrete "saddle," which raises the framing above grade and protects it from wood-destroying fungi (see the drawing at right below). The problem with such repairs is that they encapsulate a disintegrating brick foundation beneath a veneer that can look like a true battered-concrete foundation (see the drawing on the facing page).

The age of the house is a clue to the foundation type. If the house has rough-cut studs or the original permit was taken out before 1925, the house probably had bricks to begin with. Examine the foundation carefully, drilling if necessary, before concluding that the brick has been completely replaced with concrete.

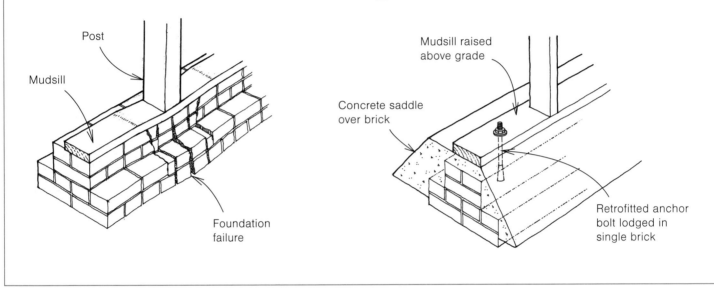

Post
Mudsill
Foundation failure

Mudsill raised above grade
Concrete saddle over brick
Retrofitted anchor bolt lodged in single brick

through several bricks, forcing resin adhesives through a screen installed in the hole, and embedding anchor bolts in the glue. Such systems should be designed by a qualified engineer.

Concrete foundations

Concrete consists of small stones ("aggregate"), portland cement (a complex, heat-treated mixture of lime, silicates and aluminum and iron oxides that glues the pieces of aggregate together) and water. Many concretes also have chemical additives that strengthen them or regulate their curing time.

When mixed with water, the powdered portland cement rapidly undergoes a chemical reaction called hydration, which transforms it into a monolithic, rocklike substance. Great strength is achieved in a few hours or days, and, unlike the lime mortar in bricks, concrete stays hard indefinitely, unless it is affected by improper additives, pollutants or poor mixing or placing.

Unfortunately, in the early days of concrete production, the technology was not as well understood as it is today. Without proper knowledge or regulation, builders added untreated lime and other pollutants, excessive water and aggregates of the wrong material or size to their mixes. They also poured during freezing or extremely hot weather, allowed parts of foundations to harden before pouring the next part and made other placement mistakes. As a result, many older concrete foundations are failing, or are at least too weak to carry additional loads.

Reinforcing concrete foundations

One of the most common failings of older, unreinforced concrete foundations is cracking caused by differential loading or varying soil strength. Unreinforced concrete is strong under compression but has

Battered-Concrete Foundation

The battered configuration shown here is typical of earlier concrete foundations. Battered foundations often don't have reinforcing steel and also tend to rotate in response to the offset downward load of the exterior wall. If the foundation is rotating, loading the wall with a second story will exacerbate the situation. If the house has stucco siding, a crack along the mudsill is a sign of rotation. The walls can also be checked with a level. If they are sloping in or out, the house may need serious foundation work before an addition can be built.

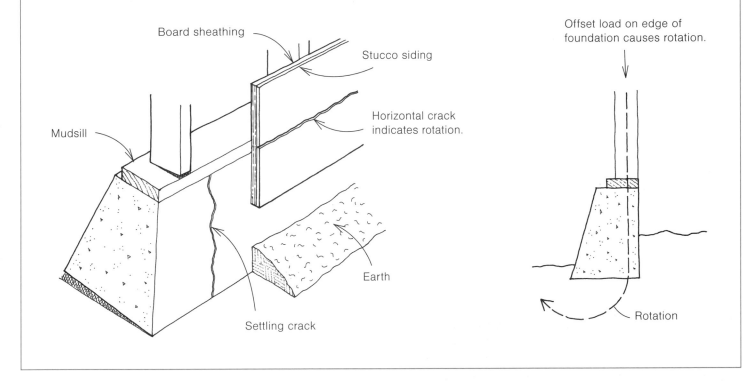

Board sheathing

Stucco siding

Horizontal crack indicates rotation.

Mudsill

Earth

Settling crack

Offset load on edge of foundation causes rotation.

Rotation

very little tensile strength. Differential loading tends to bend the foundation, placing parts of it under tension. It responds by developing major cracks where it would otherwise bend if it had tensile strength (see the sidebar above).

Adding reinforcement—usually in the form of continuous steel rods called rebar (reinforcing bar)—makes the foundation act like a wood or steel beam, which resists forces in both tension and compression. If pressure is applied at any point along the "beam," it will bend slightly and transfer the forces along its entire length. Only hairline tension cracks, which appear at the points where the foundation bends, are seen in a properly reinforced concrete foundation. They are the normal response to loading, and show that the rebar is doing its job. (Such cracks may also develop as a result of shrinkage and other factors, and do not necessarily indicate differential loading.)

Examining a foundation

To make a preliminary evaluation of a foundation's condition and capacity to support a second story look for the following four clues: its age and shape, signs of failure, the presence of rebar, and its dimensions.

Age and shape The first clue to the foundation's age is its configuration. Though designs vary, concrete foundations are of two basic types—battered (the older design, shown above) and inverted-T (shown in the drawing on p. 106). Battered foundations were built from the 1920s until the late 1940s or early 1950s, when the inverted-T began to replace them in an attempt to solve certain problems—primarily rotation caused by eccentric loading. At about the same time the inverted-T design was first employed, the use of rebar, though not required by code, became common practice.

Inverted-T Foundation

Most inverted-T foundations are reinforced and perform well under differential loading. They resist rotation because the footing extends from both sides of the stem wall, and they are less subject to disintegration because modern concrete mixtures are better controlled. Although most inverted-T foundations for one-story houses are not wide or deep enough to support a second story, they can often be beefed up easily if they have rebar and are in good condition.

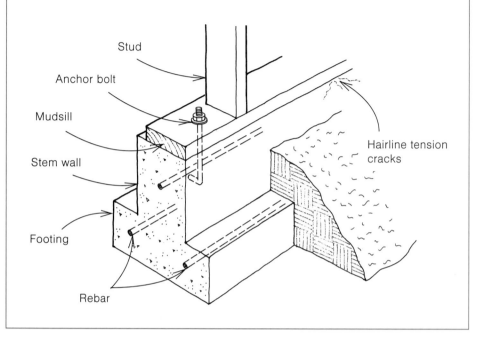

Stud
Anchor bolt
Mudsill
Stem wall
Footing
Rebar
Hairline tension cracks

may hold but the original concrete will continue to rot away. The foundation will need complete replacement in the near future.

Weakening of the cement is not always apparent through disintegration, however. If a foundation appears clean, with no signs of crumbling, some sense of its strength can be gained by giving it a sharp rap with a hammer at several strategic points. Weak concrete yields a dull thud, whereas a stronger mix causes the hammer to ring and bounce off. While this observation is hardly scientific, it can be correlated with other evidence like the presence of settling cracks, efflorescence and repairs. (More scientific tests can be made by a testing laboratory, though procedures can be expensive; consult an engineer before ordering such tests.)

Cracks, as explained above, are the result of differential settling or loading. Serious cracks are ⅛ in. wide or greater, and go all or most of the way through the foundation. One or two cracks in a 50-year-old foundation will seldom harm the existing structure. However, the foundation is already weakened, so it probably can't be loaded further without strengthening.

A foundation with numerous large cracks is failing, possibly because it was badly mixed or poured, or because there is an inherent problem with the soil. It needs replacing, whether or not an addition is built, and thus is an important factor in the budget. A failing foundation also might indicate the need for a geotechnical (soils) engineer to investigate the site before developing the design for an addition (see Chapter 6).

Another clue to a foundation's age is the age of the house itself, which can usually be found in city or county records. If the house is 70 years old, for example, and has a battered foundation, it is probably the original foundation. If the house is 100 years old and has a battered foundation, it is probably a replacement of an original brick model and could have been installed as late as the early 1950s. An inverted-T foundation in a house built before World War II is probably a replacement also.

In the case of the house with the 70-year-old battered foundation, it is reasonable to make two assumptions: The foundation may be failing, and it probably doesn't have rebar.

Signs of failure Four common signs of foundation failure are disintegration, cracks, efflorescence and evidence of repairs. Disintegration is a common sign of failure in older foundations. If the cement is beginning to powder, you can penetrate the surface with a hammer claw and dig out the aggregate stones without much effort.

Although a failing foundation is bad news for the addition project, at least it makes your choices clear. The foundation cannot simply be beefed up and loaded with an addition, since the strengthened sections

Efflorescence is the white, crystalline powder that shows up on the inner surface of the foundation as water passes through it carrying salts and minerals from within the concrete. The water evaporates on the surface of the foundation, leaving the characteristic deposits. Efflorescence can indicate a drainage problem. If the problem is confined to a small section of the foundation and not exacerbated with cracks and disintegration, there is probably no serious trouble. It would still be wise, however, to install standard drainage improvements while remodeling (see pp. 95-101).

If large portions of a foundation, particularly an older one, are covered with efflorescence, the foundation has probably been weakened by the water flowing through it. If there are other signs of poor drainage, like dampness, water-stained wood or numerous cracks in the sub-area soil, consult a geotechnical engineer before proceeding.

Repairs indicate that the foundation has failed in the past, and should be examined closely. Some of the many ways in which people attempt to repair damaged foundations include sistering on (adding a new piece of foundation alongside the original), applying skim coats of mortar, capping, and stitching with metal plates. These repairs are often non-standard and temporary—ineffective patch jobs that have outlived their usefulness. Their presence tells us that the original foundation has had problems that were addressed without complete replacement and might have been merely covered over rather than fixed. The designer or builder needs to investigate, by

probing the edges of the repaired section, and then take the age and condition of the rest of the foundation into account before concluding that it might support heavier loads.

The presence of rebar Most modern foundations are of the inverted-T type and have rebar. However, the foundation's age and style does not necessarily ensure the presence of rebar—in fact, rebar is still not required by code (1994 Uniform Building Code) in residential foundations unless specified by engineering analysis.

Along with age and type, an excellent clue to the presence of rebar is the presence of pieces of tie wire sticking out of the stem wall in horizontal rows, or, in more recent foundations, the pits left by snap-tie cones. Tie wires and snap ties have the dual functions of controlling form width and supporting the rebar in the forms before the pour: They indicate that rebar was used.

Another clue to the presence of rebar is the actual behavior of the foundation under its loads. If large cracks are present, rebar probably was not used, or something else is quite wrong with the soil or concrete. But if the foundation is free of large cracks, has tie wire and is of the right age and type, rebar is almost certainly present. If there are doubts and rebar is critical to the addition's design, a testing lab can determine whether the foundation is properly reinforced. Reinforced foundations will decrease the cost and increase the number of options in second-story design, primarily by decreasing the number of places where the foundation must be beefed up to bear loads posted down from the addition.

Dimensions A foundation must have the correct dimensions to support a second story. The 1994 Uniform Building Code requires a foundation supporting two stories to have an 8-in. thick stem wall, and a 7-in. by 15-in. footing bottoming out at a minimum of 18 in. below grade and/or beginning below the frost line. Third stories need more concrete and greater depth. These requirements are in part to ensure that the foundation will be thick enough to take its load without cracking, and in part to provide sufficient mass and depth below grade to anchor the building during earthquakes and high winds.

Unreinforced Masonry Houses

Some modern masonry houses have steel reinforcement between the courses of masonry and are good candidates for additions. Most older masonry houses, however, do not have reinforcement. Unreinforced masonry walls (of brick, stone, cinder block, etc.) are highly vulnerable to failure under added loads and horizontal forces generated by earthquakes. A second-story addition on an unreinforced masonry house is a blueprint for disaster. A room addition also can be badly damaged by the original structure, if it collapses.

Masonry houses are not covered in this book. Anyone planning an addition to a masonry house is strongly advised to consult with a structural engineer from the outset.

Single-story houses seldom have large enough foundations to support a second story. Even most newer, reinforced foundations will need some extra support.

Pier foundations

So far we have considered continuous perimeter foundations only. Many houses are built on discontinuous pier foundations. In older buildings, the piers are usually unreinforced masonry columns spaced along the perimeter walls and at intermittent points beneath the floor frame.

It is totally unsafe to build a second story on an unreinforced masonry-pier house. The piers have severely limited resistance to compression from vertical loading and insufficient holding power to anchor brackets or bolts that connect to the joists and resist horizontal shear. Also, most masonry-pier houses pre-date concrete, so their mortar has had more than enough time to deteriorate.

Concrete-pier foundations Some modern houses have reinforced concrete-pier foundations, and the existing piers may or may not support an addition. Also, many newer, engineered houses have pier and grade-beam foundations—steel-reinforced concrete piers below grade tied together with concrete "beams" (similar to stem walls) at grade. Many of these foundations can support a second story, or can be readily modified to do so. A geotechnical engineer and a structural engineer will be needed to design the modifications to existing concrete-pier foundations.

Mixing foundation types

Although an inverted-T foundation resists rotation better than a battered one, an engineer should be consulted before adding an inverted-T to an existing battered foundation. The two foundations can behave differently in soils that are prone to settlement, producing structural stresses.

Mixing a pier and grade-beam foundation with either an inverted-T or battered type can also result in distress to the building, particularly on creeping hillsides where the new piers can be dragged down the slope more quickly or in a different direction than the original foundation (see p. 91). Also, different foundation types can react differently in earthquakes.

EVALUATING FRAMING SYSTEMS

After evaluating the foundation, turn your attention next to the framing system. Approximately 85% of the homes in North America are of light-wood construction, as opposed to heavy timber or solid masonry wall. The two most common light-wood framing systems are the balloon frame and the platform frame. Because balloon frames and platform frames have different framing styles and wall finishes, different methods are used to modify each type.

The balloon frame

Balloon frames were the earliest light-wood-frame houses, first appearing in the 1830s and remaining the most common form of construction until the early 1920s (see the table on the facing page). The balloon frame is distinguished from the platform frame by its long con-

tinuous studs, which run from the mudsill to the second- or even third-story plate (see the drawings on pp. 110-111). The floors and internal walls are added after the shell is framed. Joists are typically supported near the center of the house on a girder that rests on posts and piers. At the external walls, the joists are nailed to the studs and, in most balloons, supported by a let-in ribbon.

In some of the earlier balloon frames, however, the ribbons were not let in or were even omitted. The joists were simply nailed to the studs, and the entire floor and all of the internal walls bearing on it were supported by a handful of nails! Also, in many older balloon-frame houses the joists are over-spanned (not deep enough) and the floors have sagged in the center or are pulling away from their exterior-wall supports. If you are building an addition to a balloon-frame house, examine its floor frame carefully; in most cases, you'll have to beef it up if you're planning to load it with additional walls or posts.

Rough lumber, stud spacings and wetwall Balloon-frame houses were built with rough lumber, rather than the smooth, "surfaced" lumber we use today. Rough lumber is produced by passing logs through a huge circular saw or bandsaw with 2½-in. to 3-in. deep teeth. The big teeth leave a rough, choppy surface on the wood. As the blade pushes and fights its way through the irregular logs, it sometimes bends or tilts. The cuts at each edge vary by as much as ¼ in., plus or minus, or a total of ½ in. in the thickness and width of the board.

Also, it was typical for the size, spacing and connections of the

Features of Light-Wood-Frame Houses

FRAME TYPE	DATES (APPROX.)	LUMBER	SHEATHING	INTERIOR WALL TYPE	FOUNDATION	PROBLEMS FOR ADDITION DESIGN
Balloon	1830s – 1920s	Rough to S2E[1]	Horizontal or diagonal board	Lath and plaster	Stone, brick, early concrete	Poor horizontal resistance; crumbling foundations; possible problems with floor supports/headers
Platform (early)	1910s – late 1940s	S2E to S4S[1]	Horizontal or diagonal board	Lath or backing board and plaster	Unreinforced concrete ("battered" style)	Possible poor horizontal resistance; unreinforced concrete; possible deterioration of concrete
Platform (modern)	late 1940s – present	S4S[1]	Plywood	Drywall	Reinforced concrete (inverted-T style)	Horizontal resistance may still be inadequate; foundations may be too small

[1] S2E and S4S are standard lumber-industry abbreviations meaning "surfaced (planed) on two edges" and "surfaced on four sides," respectively.

The Evolution of Framing Lumber

Balloon-frame houses were built at a time when there was a surplus of cheap, readily available lumber. Tall trees supplied the long framing members. To meet a rapidly expanding demand for housing, rough, unsurfaced lumber was rushed—often directly from temporary mills in the forests—to building sites in the cities.

The thinning of the great forests and the realization that framing members of uniform size were easier to use in the field caused the lumber industry not only to shorten framing members, but also to modify their width and thickness. Although wetwall compensated nicely for the variations in rough studs (see the drawing on p. 112), the application of less flexible exterior siding was hampered by the need for shimming and planing. Leveling floors was difficult, too. Carpenters had to plane every joist. It did not take long to discover that it was much more efficient to plane the edges of lumber in the mills.

Two-by-fours were originally intended to be 2 in. thick by 4 in. wide, give or take a little for rough cutting. When the need to plane them first arose, it was clear that it would be better to keep the rough dimensions the same and call the new product an "edge-planed 2x4," which was surfaced on two edges only (S2E). This compromise saved having to retool all the milling equipment and produce an odd-sized rough piece, say 4½ in. wide, just to allow the smooth version to net out to exactly 4 in.

Today's framing lumber is surfaced on all four sides (S4S) to make handling and accurate cutting even easier.

One result of the evolution of framing lumber is the distinction between today's *nominal* and *net*, or actual, dimensions. "Nominal" means what something is called or named. Thus today's standard piece—the one you'll get if you ask for a 2x4 at the lumber store—is only a nominal 2 in. by 4 in., while its actual, or net, dimensions are 1½ in. and 3½ in. To get a net, or "real," 2 in. by 4 in., you must specify "rough" and cope with its irregularities.

framing members of balloon houses to be determined on the site. If, in a carpenter's opinion, a section of wall needed six supports, for example, he might space the supports evenly with no concern about the actual distance between them.

One result is that many of the older houses that we remodel today have studs that are both of varying dimensions and set at random spacings. While these frames do not accommodate today's modular sheet materials, they were compatible with the standard lath and plaster interior wall finish of the time—what we now call "wetwall," as opposed to the paper and gypsum panels known as "drywall" (see the drawing on p. 112).

Addition plans must account for the variations in both the spacing and width of the balloon's studs and other framing members. Studs that are too far apart, for example, will not support a second story, and new studs will have to be be added to the wall. Similarly, if an existing wall is lengthened for a room addition, some means of compensating for the differences in width where the new studs meet the old ones will have to be devised. Compensations must also be made where joists and rafters join one another. (For means of integrating old and new framing systems, see pp. 236-238.)

Platform frames

As trees of sufficient height for the long studs of balloon frames became scarce and the price of such premium lumber rose, a new style of framing using shorter studs developed—the platform frame.

In the platform frame, the studs are discontinuous between stories. The walls are built in one-story sections,

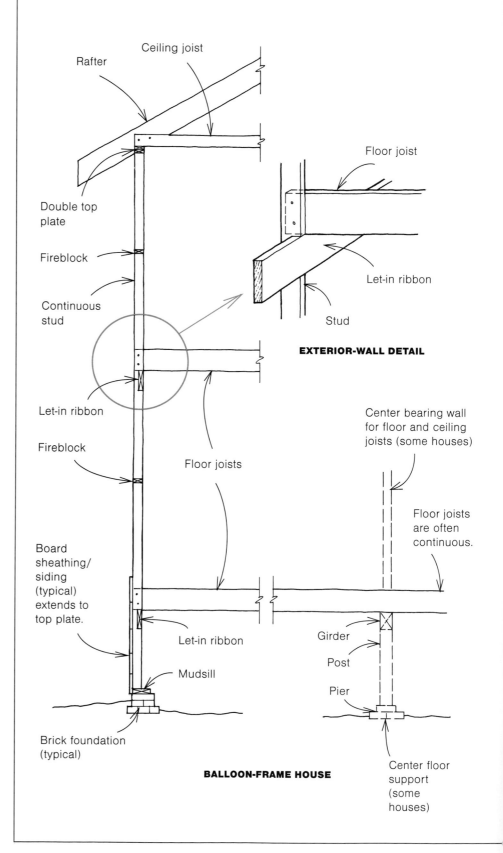

BALLOON AND PLATFORM FRAMES

Rafter

Ceiling joist

Floor joist

Double top plate

Fireblock

Continuous stud

Let-in ribbon

Stud

EXTERIOR-WALL DETAIL

Let-in ribbon

Fireblock

Floor joists

Center bearing wall for floor and ceiling joists (some houses)

Floor joists are often continuous.

Board sheathing/ siding (typical) extends to top plate.

Let-in ribbon

Girder

Post

Mudsill

Pier

Brick foundation (typical)

BALLOON-FRAME HOUSE

Center floor support (some houses)

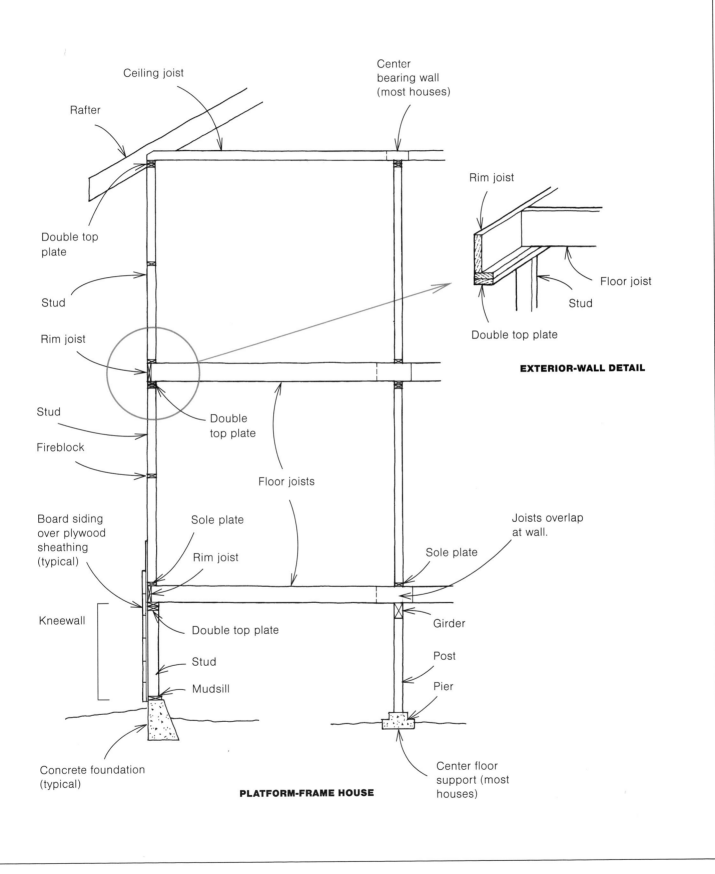

Ceiling joist

Rafter

Center bearing wall (most houses)

Rim joist

Double top plate

Floor joist

Stud

Double top plate

EXTERIOR-WALL DETAIL

Stud

Rim joist

Stud

Fireblock

Double top plate

Floor joists

Board siding over plywood sheathing (typical)

Sole plate

Joists overlap at wall.

Rim joist

Sole plate

Kneewall

Double top plate

Girder

Stud

Post

Mudsill

Pier

Concrete foundation (typical)

Center floor support (most houses)

PLATFORM-FRAME HOUSE

WETWALL AND DRYWALL

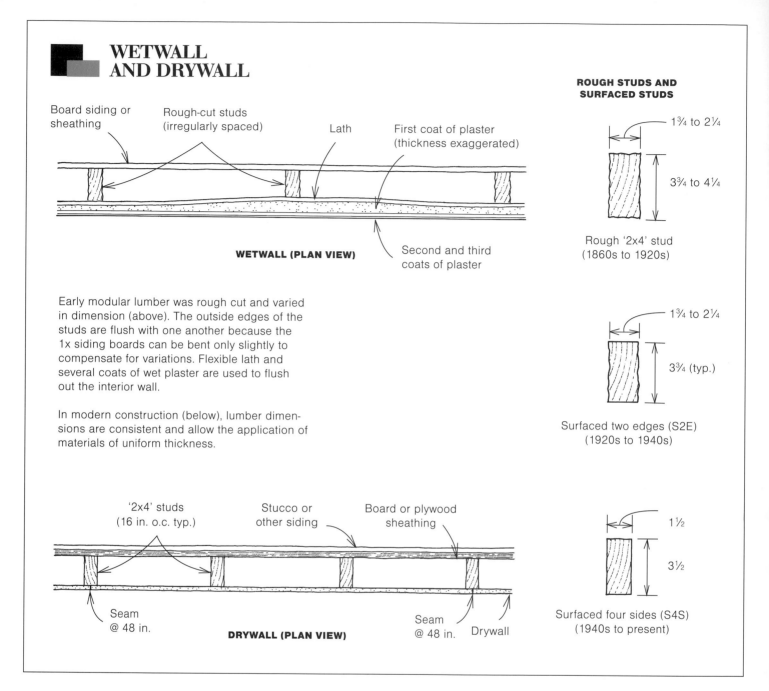

Board siding or sheathing

Rough-cut studs (irregularly spaced)

Lath

First coat of plaster (thickness exaggerated)

WETWALL (PLAN VIEW)

Second and third coats of plaster

1¾ to 2¼

3¾ to 4¼

Rough '2x4' stud (1860s to 1920s)

Early modular lumber was rough cut and varied in dimension (above). The outside edges of the studs are flush with one another because the 1x siding boards can be bent only slightly to compensate for variations. Flexible lath and several coats of wet plaster are used to flush out the interior wall.

In modern construction (below), lumber dimensions are consistent and allow the application of materials of uniform thickness.

1¾ to 2¼

3¾ (typ.)

Surfaced two edges (S2E) (1920s to 1940s)

'2x4' studs (16 in. o.c. typ.)

Stucco or other siding

Board or plywood sheathing

Seam @ 48 in.

DRYWALL (PLAN VIEW)

Seam @ 48 in.

Drywall

1½

3½

Surfaced four sides (S4S) (1940s to present)

each with its own sole plate and double top plate, and the floor joists rest directly on the external walls. The joists typically span about half the house, coming to rest on a girder, as shown in the drawing on p. 111. The floor or ceiling joists at the next level must also be supported in the middle of the house. They rest on a center bearing wall, which sits on the platform directly over the girder in the substructure.

Walls that run in the same direction as the joists do not support anything but themselves. They merely serve to partition spaces, and are called "partitions." Within reason, partitions can be removed or altered without structural implications. (Removing most or all of them would create a "soft story"—see pp. 115-116—and significantly lower the house's resistance to horizontal force.)

The drawing on the facing page shows the relationship of bearing walls to partition walls in a typical platform house. The perimeter walls bear half the load of the floors and ceilings, and all the load of the roof and gable walls. They sit on a continuous perimeter foundation. The center bearing wall, on piers, runs the length of the house and carries the other half of the weight of the floors and ceilings. Where the center bearing wall is interrupted—in the living room and elsewhere—it is replaced by an overhead beam that carries the ceiling joists.

The perimeter and bearing-wall configuration naturally influences the design of second-story additions. The easiest approach is to follow the existing pattern, using the bearing walls to support the new floor frame. Where this approach won't work, the partition walls can be modified for bearing or new bearing systems can be created (see pp. 130-133).

Determining the house's structural type

You can determine the approximate age of a house, and thus its structural type, by examining its framing. If you look in the basements or crawl spaces of the oldest light-frame houses, you'll see studs and joists that are rough on all four sides, while the framing members of the intermediate models will be planed, or surfaced on their two edges, and those of the newer homes will be surfaced on all four sides (see the drawing on the facing page and the table on p. 109).

Houses with rough studs were built from around 1865 (or earlier) to 1925 and were most likely balloon framed. Framing members with surfaced edges only were standard between 1925 and about 1945, and those that are surfaced on all four sides have been in use since World War II. For the most part, houses with surface-edged or completely surfaced framing members are of the platform-frame type, and the members have standard spacing as well as uniform dimensions—standard modern framing.

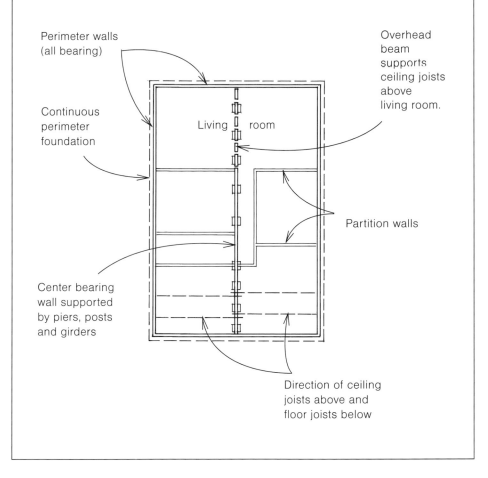

BEARING AND PARTITION WALLS

Perimeter walls (all bearing)

Overhead beam supports ceiling joists above living room.

Continuous perimeter foundation

Living room

Partition walls

Center bearing wall supported by piers, posts and girders

Direction of ceiling joists above and floor joists below

Standard framing The regular spacing of uniform framing members based on a 4-ft. module with individual members on 16-in. centers is now standard construction practice. Adding onto a house with standard framing is easier than adding onto an older house with irregular framing because fewer compensations are necessary. The new standards also simplify communications between designers, builders and various subcontractors, and have paved the way for the development of a variety of manufactured products ranging from heat ducts that fit between framing members to, most significantly, modular sheet materials like ply-

wood and drywall that conform in size to the stud spacing.

Building with studs of uniform dimensions and spacing led to the gradual realization that lath, which had to be installed a piece at a time, was unnecessary. Since bending to conform to irregular studs was no longer an issue and studs were now on even centers, flat, 4x8 modular sheets of paper-covered gypsum backing board—with holes drilled every few inches to allow the penetration of plaster—superseded lath as the substrate for plaster. Gypsum backing board was just a step away from drywall.

Plywood The development of structural plywood was perhaps the most beneficial innovation in the new system of uniform framing members covered with modular panels. By glue-laminating layers of wood veneer with their grains set in perpendicular directions, mills were able to create precisely dimensioned modular sheets of great strength and rigidity. From the point of view of builders, the new material was both cheaper and faster to apply than traditional sheathing.

From an engineering point of view, each strong panel tied together a large area of the frame—usually 4 ft. by 8 ft.—and panels could be butted together to make walls, roofs and floors that acted as single structural units. With plywood sheathing, wood frames could be stronger and stiffer than ever before. The use of plywood sheathing alone, however, does not ensure that a house is properly engineered against earthquakes and high winds or ready to support an addition. Other steps, described below and in the next chapter, must be taken to protect the structure.

Will the walls hold up?

For economic reasons, the existing bearing walls should carry the vertical loads of second-story additions whenever possible. Framing from the bearing walls' top plates is the easiest way to build a second story.

Before this design is adopted, however, it must be determined that the walls can carry new loads. Houses of any age are liable to lack sufficient

vertical support for an added second story, but especially those older homes where the spacing of the studs was left to the discretion of the carpenters. Though there were practical limits to the gaps between studs, they were sometimes placed much farther apart than today's acceptable maximum of 24 in. for one story or 16 in. for two stories (1994 Uniform Building Code). Spacings up to 48 in. or more are particularly likely if the interior walls were made of solid board rather than plaster and lath, or if the house was of cheap construction and built before the days when codes were enforced.

In houses built since World War I, the studs in the main-story walls will probably be of the correct size (i.e., 2x4s), but because the house was not designed to support a second story they may be spaced on 24-in. centers, that is, too far apart. In the substructure, the studs will probably be placed on 16-in. centers, which is sufficient, but they're likely to be 2x4s if the house is one story, while 2x6s are usually recommended for a second story. It may be possible simply to add more 2x4s to achieve adequate support, but the design should be checked by a structural engineer.

It is often difficult to see the studs or the headers above the substructure level without tearing open the house's walls. Seeing the framing is not usually a problem with balloon frames—unless the basement is finished—because the studs are continuous from the substructure up. In platform houses, however, the spacing of the studs in the substructure may not correspond to that in the wall above. Sometimes the baseboards can be removed and the

studs counted, but this is not always feasible nor does it guarantee that all of the studs are continuous to the top plate or that all of the walls in an old house were framed in the same manner. Since the stud spacing is critical, it may be necessary to open and reseal the walls. (Some other means of locating studs are discussed on p. 187.)

Headers The headers in balloon-frame houses are often not deep enough. If some of the weight of a second story bears on an undersized header, it can bend excessively, causing a variety of problems for the wall above and door or window below (see the drawing on the facing page). In some of the oldest houses, headers were simply nailed onto single studs or posts, without trimmers, and the nails can actually pull out or bend under additional loads.

If a second story is added, the existing headers may need to be replaced to accommodate the additional loads. (One good reason to incorporate orderly fenestration into an addition design is to take second-story loads off the headers and guide them directly to the foundation through the "posts," or double 2x4s, on the side of the windows—see pp. 128-130).

While there are many rules of thumb for sizing headers, none of them are actually accurate for all situations. (For a reference on ways of sizing headers and other structural members, see the bibliography.) As a practical matter, it is usually easiest to let the engineer who is reviewing the plans determine the size of the headers, beams and girders.

POORLY BUILT BALLOON-FRAME HOUSE
The window header in this poorly built balloon-frame house has two problems: At 4x4 it is undersized and, along with the double top plate above, has deflected under the load of the roof (the deflection is exaggerated in the drawing). Also, it was merely nailed to the adjacent studs and not supported with trimmers. The nails have pulled away, dropping the header below its original level.

WELL-BUILT MODERN HOUSE
The 4x6 header in this well-built modern house is properly sized for its opening and is also adequately supported with trimmers. Note that the short studs (or 'cripples') above the header do not sit directly beneath the rafters, but are spaced for nailing up plywood sheathing and drywall. This framing is acceptable, as long as the rafter lands on a double plate.

HORIZONTAL AND VERTICAL FORCES

A building must be able to support its own weight and withstand the loads that are imposed upon it. For design purposes, the forces acting on a building can be broken down into vertical and horizontal components.

Normally the building's own weight and the people and furniture within it impose vertical loads. Obviously, accounting for vertical forces is crucial when adding a second story, and the existing foundations and walls must be reinforced as needed.

Vertical loads, however, are not the only force acting on the building.

Virtually all regions of the earth are subject to occasional high winds, strong earthquakes or both. Most earthquakes and wind storms load the building horizontally (see the drawing on p. 116).

Second-story additions on houses that are not reinforced against horizontal loading can be particularly hazardous. They increase the potential horizontal instability in two ways—first, by increasing the overall mass and, second, by raising the center of mass. If the greater, higher mass gets moving, as it can in an earthquake, it increases the leverage applied at critical connections, particularly on the foundation and first-floor levels. Also,

raising the building increases the amount of surface exposed to winds, as well as the amount of leverage the wind applies.

Room additions pose problems because they can react to storms or earthquakes by moving in a different direction from the original house. The old and new structures must be sufficiently braced against horizontal motion and well connected to one another so they react as a unit.

Earthquakes and soft stories

The most common area of failure during an earthquake is a house's substructure, or lowest story. Engineers call this a "soft story" because, unlike the house above, it has

SOME EFFECTS OF EARTHQUAKES AND HIGH WINDS

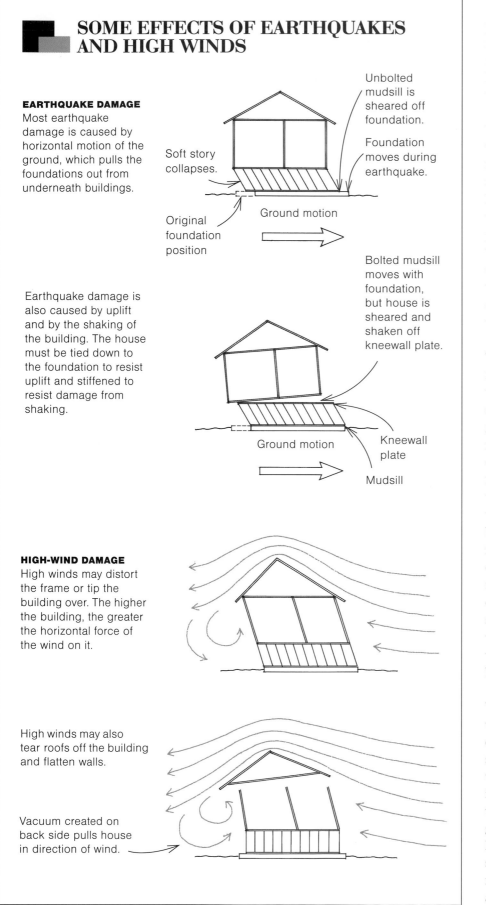

EARTHQUAKE DAMAGE
Most earthquake damage is caused by horizontal motion of the ground, which pulls the foundations out from underneath buildings.

Soft story collapses.

Original foundation position

Unbolted mudsill is sheared off foundation.

Foundation moves during earthquake.

Ground motion

Earthquake damage is also caused by uplift and by the shaking of the building. The house must be tied down to the foundation to resist uplift and stiffened to resist damage from shaking.

Bolted mudsill moves with foundation, but house is sheared and shaken off kneewall plate.

Ground motion

Kneewall plate

Mudsill

HIGH-WIND DAMAGE
High winds may distort the frame or tip the building over. The higher the building, the greater the horizontal force of the wind on it.

High winds may also tear roofs off the building and flatten walls.

Vacuum created on back side pulls house in direction of wind.

perimeter walls only, and no internal cross walls to resist lateral forces. When excessive horizontal loading occurs, something gives in the soft story.

What gives depends on what's there. In a worst-case scenario, the mudsill simply rests on top of the foundation (see the top drawing at left) and the kneewall studs are tied to it with toe nails only. The floor joists are also toe-nailed to the kneewall's top plate, and the building is sheathed with horizontal boards. To understand why this is a potentially dangerous situation, let's consider the effects of earthquakes.

The effect of horizontal ground motion is similar to that of pulling the rug out from under a couple of stacked boxes. If the lower box is glued to the rug, it will move with it. If the upper box is just sitting on the lower box, it will tend to remain in place due to inertia, and the lower box will slide out from underneath it and topple the upper box. Similarly, a foundation, which is in the ground and moves with it during an earthquake, will slide out from under a house. The house is connected to the foundation by the soft story's frame and sheathing. If the soft story is not strong enough to "pull the house along," the building collapses.

What has actually occurred is that the foundation has been sheared out from under the house. Shear results when a material or an object is trapped between two forces moving in opposite directions. In this case, the two forces are the motion of the ground and the inertial force of the house's mass above. The failure in shear can occur at the point of connection between the foundation and mudsill, or, if the kneewall framing moves with the mudsill, between the kneewall and the first-floor frame. (For methods of resisting shear forces, see pp. 123-127.)

Problems with older houses

A major problem with older houses, which has important implications for addition design, is that their builders did not always understand the effects of horizontal forces. Though most older houses have sheathing and some form of corner bracing, they are either missing critical components and connections or are just dangerously underbuilt (see the drawing on pp. 118-119).

Diagonal corner braces are typical features of older platform-frame houses. Braces serve to square the frame during construction and offer some resistance to light horizontal forces. They offer little resistance to heavy loads, however.

The basic problem with corner braces is that they depend on nails holding against "pullout" (backing out in the direction they were hammered in) to resist horizontal forces. Nails are weak in resisting pullout and strong in shear—or resisting forces across their shank. Just because a house has corner braces, then, it is not safe to assume that it has good resistance to horizontal loads. It will probably need to be strengthened in order to support an addition.

In most balloon frames, the situation is somewhat better. Long let-in braces run continuously from the mudsill to a substantial framing member, tying many studs together at once. Whatever stability the braces offer is transferred from floor to floor, and sometimes all the way to the roof line. The braces are nailed flat onto the studs so the nails resist shear forces.

Board sheathing Board sheathing strengthens the house, of course, but it is discontinuous and does a relatively poor job of connecting the disjointed members of a platform frame. The board that connects the mudsill to the studs does not normally reach the kneewall's top plate or the rim joist; few boards are wide enough to span from the kneewall plate to the first-floor sole plate, and a board of such a width is vulnerable to splitting. (Sheets of plywood easily span the joints between floors and can be retrofitted in the soft story of a house with board sheathing so it can take an addition—see pp. 126-127.)

The most common failures occur at the top and bottom of the kneewall where there is the greatest load on the joints. In the sub-area the sheathing boards split or their nailing fails, and the weak connections between the kneewall studs and mudsill or the kneewall plate and floor frame, which should be reinforced by the sheathing, also fail. Secondary failures occur wherever an upper-floor platform rests on a wall, and at the attachment of the roof to the frame.

Many of the better-built older homes had diagonal sheathing, which offers much more lateral resistance than horizontal sheathing. Diagonal sheathing makes a tie from the mudsill across the framing break at the first-floor platform. It then goes well up into the structure, terminating at a corner post or a substantial horizontal member like a window sill or wall plate.

Although houses are much safer with diagonal rather than horizontal sheathing, there is still the danger that the mudsill, which may not be bolted, will slide off the foundation during earthquakes or high winds. Bolts are easily retrofitted, however, and in many cases the problem of horizontal shear is sufficiently addressed if this step is taken. Assuming that it is correctly nailed (which can be verified by taking off some of the siding), the presence of diagonal sheathing can be taken as a good sign because it reduces the amount of horizontal-force resistance that will have to be provided, thus freeing up money for other parts of the project.

Wall openings and soft-story living areas

Door and window openings weaken a house's resistance to horizontal forces by breaking the continuity of the sheathing. Large openings like garage doors and walls with multiple windows make houses particularly vulnerable to damage or collapse.

Forces can be redirected around these openings, however, by means of headers that continue beyond them and to the ends of their respective walls. Also, metal brackets can be used to reinforce critical joints. If the house has large openings or they are planned for the addition, an engineer should be consulted during the feasibility assessment to make sure that the structure can be kept sound at a reasonable cost.

Large, open spaces like family rooms or combined living/dining rooms comprise partial soft stories. It is usually not desirable to subdivide these spaces with cross walls, so their inherent weakness must be addressed by some other means.

(text continues on p. 120)

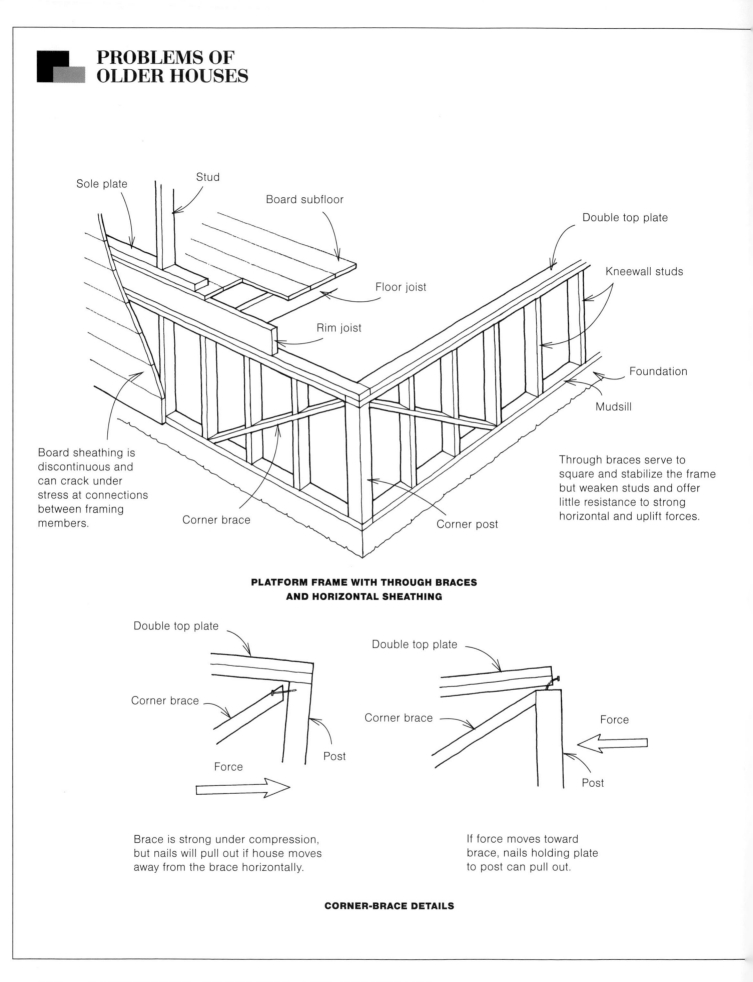

Sole plate

Stud

Board subfloor

Double top plate

Kneewall studs

Floor joist

Rim joist

Foundation

Mudsill

Board sheathing is discontinuous and can crack under stress at connections between framing members.

Corner brace

Corner post

Through braces serve to square and stabilize the frame but weaken studs and offer little resistance to strong horizontal and uplift forces.

**PLATFORM FRAME WITH THROUGH BRACES
AND HORIZONTAL SHEATHING**

Double top plate

Corner brace

Post

Force

Double top plate

Corner brace

Force

Post

Brace is strong under compression, but nails will pull out if house moves away from the brace horizontally.

If force moves toward brace, nails holding plate to post can pull out.

CORNER-BRACE DETAILS

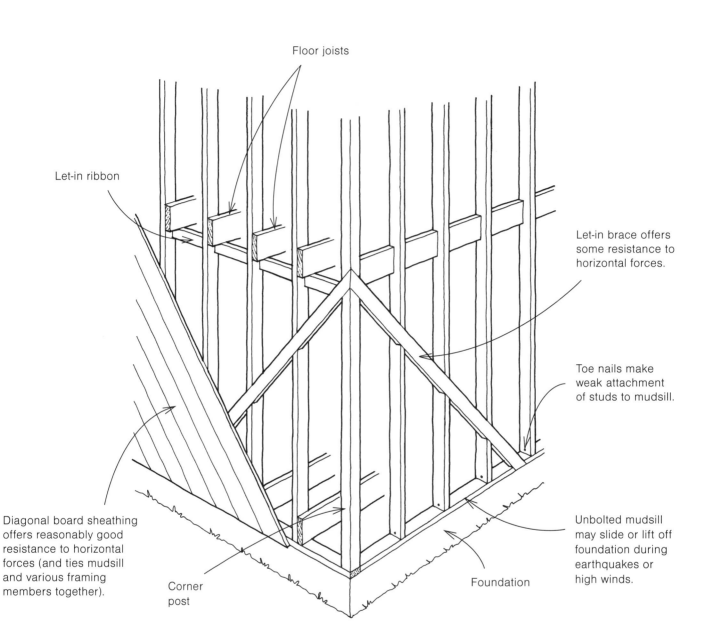

Floor joists

Let-in ribbon

Let-in brace offers some resistance to horizontal forces.

Toe nails make weak attachment of studs to mudsill.

Diagonal board sheathing offers reasonably good resistance to horizontal forces (and ties mudsill and various framing members together).

Corner post

Foundation

Unbolted mudsill may slide or lift off foundation during earthquakes or high winds.

BALLOON FRAME WITH LET-IN BRACES AND DIAGONAL SHEATHING

Note. These drawings should not be taken as representative of all balloon and platform frames. For example, some older platform houses have diagonal sheathing as well as corner braces and can accommodate additions with a minimum amount of reinforcement. Many balloon frames have horizontal sheathing and some lack bracing entirely, making them highly vulnerable to damage from horizontal forces.

The large doors and windows and open interior spaces make this house particularly vulnerable to the horizontal forces of earthquakes. Without significant reinforcement, it would not be a good candidate for a second-story addition.

Building a second-story addition over the living-room area of the house in the photo above would not be advisable unless the large openings and the garage and living-level soft stories were substantially reinforced. A reinforcement design might include installing plywood shear panels to stabilize the garage walls and replacing the garage-door header and side posts with a steel "moment frame" made up of a steel beam and posts anchored in a concrete grade beam. Similar steel connections might be required around the living-room corner window.

THE CONDITION OF WOOD STRUCTURES

The house's structural condition affects the design, or at least the cost, of building the addition. The designer or builder must know if the framing is doing its job, that is, if it is sagging or out of plumb. It is also important to determine whether the structure has deteriorated as a result of infestation by wood-destroying organisms.

Level and plumb structures

Older houses frequently have floors that aren't level. If the floors slope to the outside of the house, it is usually because the foundation has settled or rotated. If they sag in toward the center bearing wall, the center girder is probably missing or under-supported and sagging. Settlement of center-bearing-wall piers themselves is also possible, though this usually occurs only when a lot of water gets beneath the house, and excess water generally affects the perimeter foundation as well. If the joists bottom out, or sag, halfway between the perimeter and interior bearing walls, they are over-spanned and need support at the low point.

The designer or builder should examine the nails that hold the ledgers or let-in ribbons supporting the floor joists of balloon-frame houses, since they may be partly responsible for the sloping. If the nails are rusted or pulling out, the ledgers or ribbons should be firmly re-nailed or bolted to the studs, particularly if weight will be added to the floor frame.

Floor settling should be stopped, or at least slowed down. The floor can usually be corrected by placing posts and girders beneath the affected joists and improving the drainage. However, floors that slope severely indicate serious foundation settlement and the need for general rebuilding of the substructure.

Although the substructure may have to be rebuilt, it is usually not necessary or desirable to attempt to jack up or re-level the house. Jacking up a house can crack plaster and stucco, jam doors and windows that have adjusted themselves to the settling, and knock previously unaffected floors and walls out of whack. In most cases, it is better to strengthen the house in its present position rather than attempt to jack it up.

For most addition designs, the condition of the bearing walls, which is often indicated by sloping floors, is more important than the comparatively minor problem of the sloping floor itself. If a floor slopes toward a wall on which it rests, chances are the wall itself has leaned out or in, or possibly moved downward. In a platform-frame house, the walls may lean even if the floors are level.

If a wall is simply lower relative to other walls, its top plate can be shimmed to level the new framing for the addition (see the drawing on p. 138)—assuming the underlying condition that caused the wall to drop has been addressed.

If the wall is out of plumb, the problem is more serious. If the center third of the top plate is horizontally out of line with the center third of the sole plate, the wall is unstable and should be corrected (in fact, the building is legally condemnable). While there is no absolute rule of thumb, a wall that has leaned so that its top and bottom plates are even ¼ in. out of line with each other is a shaky support for an addition, and a second story should not be built on it without consulting a structural engineer.

Nor should you attach the wall of a room addition to an existing out-of-plumb wall. The out-of-plumb condition must be corrected—no easy matter in an existing house— or an addition that does not connect with the wall in question must be designed.

A sagging roof line, on the other hand, usually means nothing more than undersized rafters and ridge boards. Although correcting the condition is desirable, it is not a prerequisite for building a room addition. Building a purlin or propping up rafters at strategic locations is a simple enough matter, however, and it is probably a good idea to have the carpenters correct a sagging roof line while they are on the site.

Structural pests

Structural pests eat through the structure. Not only can termites, boring beetles, dryrot fungi and other pests cause thousands of dollars worth of damage, they can also weaken the very framing and sheathing that is counted on to support the addition. The house must be free of such organisms and their damage before an addition is built.

Some structural-pest conditions are easy to find and identify. Termite tunnels made of mud, obvious dryrot and conditions such as wet crawl spaces that foster pest growth are clues. Some organisms are difficult to spot, however, and dryrot is sometimes hidden within walls or other inaccessible spaces. If the designer or builder is unsure of the presence of structural pests, a termite inspector should be hired. For a set fee, the inspector writes a report describing the conditions, and usually includes written estimates for their correction.

Depending on the nature and location of the damage, the designer or builder might take advantage of the need for structural-pest repairs when planning the addition. In a faulty grade condition, for example, the combination of a settling foundation and rising ground level lowers the mudsill until it is level with or below grade. Dryrot fungus, always present in the soil, finds its way through the siding and attacks the sill and substructure studs. The typical solution is to cap or saddle the foundation, removing the infected wood members and adding new concrete on top of the old foundation to raise the level of the mudsill. Since this involves both foundation and sub-area structural work, it is possible for the designer or builder to stipulate that the improvements go beyond merely solving the pest problem, and sufficiently strengthen the foundation and framing to provide some of the support for the addition.

Whether or not the structural-pest work is integrated into the design, however, it must be done, because structural pests will continue to proliferate. Remediation costs, then, should be considered when planning the budget for the addition.

PRELIMINARY DESIGN DECISIONS

A general assessment of the house's structure is critical for making preliminary design decisions, such as whether a room addition or a second story is the best choice for a particular house. For example, the cost of a structural upgrade on a balloon-frame house with a poor foundation, too few studs and undersized headers could preclude building a second story. On the other hand, a platform house with standard 2x4 walls, 2x6 studs in the sub-area, and a solid one-story foundation with rebar is a good candidate for a second story, since the walls and foundation can take the vertical loads with minimal reinforcement.

The platform house may be poorly protected against horizontal shear, however, and need strengthening. Since, as is explained in the next chapter, this is a fairly straightforward and affordable modification, the preliminary design can proceed under the assumption that a second story is feasible from a structural standpoint. An engineer should verify the assumption before too much time is spent on detailed designing, however.

8
BUILDING A SAFE STRUCTURE

Structural considerations play a greater role in determining the architecture of additions than that of new construction. While it is possible to design a new building and then work out its structure, the type and shape of an addition are usually determined by the location of the existing walls and the condition of the foundations. Ignoring these givens will not only increase the cost but can also compromise the architecture, since a well-designed house should reflect its structure.

The two main objectives in the structural design of an addition are to take advantage of the existing structure wherever possible and to make the building at least as sound as it was before it was added to—preferably stronger.

The first objective follows principles basic to any good design: Use what's there and do what's easy. Only when the existing walls and foundations are insufficient or cannot be easily modified to support an addition should new supports be installed.

The second goal is required by the building codes and all professional standards of practice. Conscientious builders will make every effort to build soundly, and usually get into trouble only because of their lack of knowledge (which is why they need to use qualified engineers and the city or county's building departments as resources to verify their structural design assumptions).

This chapter explains some of the means of achieving these goals and integrating structural design with architectural objectives. Each addition is a special case, however, and the designer will find that coming up with simple and elegant structural solutions is one of the most challenging aspects of addition design.

Shear wall provides resistance against the horizontal forces of earthquakes and high winds. Here, plywood installed on the existing first-story bay and the new second-story addition serves as both shear-wall sheathing and exterior siding.

SHEAR RESISTANCE

All types of additions must address the problem of horizontal loads discussed in the last chapter. Horizontal loads from earthquakes and winds tend to shear parts of buildings away from each other or shear entire buildings off their foundations. The building's resistance to horizontal loading can be greatly increased with specially designed plywood "shear walls," which attain much greater strength than traditional sheathing or bracing.

Shear walls

The three basic components of a typical shear wall are anchors, shear panels and shear-wall-to-frame connectors (see the drawing on p. 124). Anchors are anchor bolts, steel plates or other types of metal connectors that tie the mudsill and studs to the foundation and thus anchor the structure to the ground. Another type of anchor, called a "hold-down," must also be installed to keep the shear panels from rocking up at their ends or to resist other uplift forces.

Shear panels are usually sheets of plywood or oriented strand board (OSB) that provide effective resistance to horizontal forces. For shear wall to function correctly, each piece of sheathing must be nailed along all of its edges and every few inches in the field (along all the

The hold-down was bolted to an existing stud on the same house to help resist uplift forces generated by earthquakes.

FULL-HEIGHT SHEAR WALL

A full-height shear wall is installed when a second story is added by removing the siding of the existing first story. The shear panels may be ordinary sheathing plywood, which would be covered with siding, or special siding/sheathing plywood (see the sidebar on the facing page).

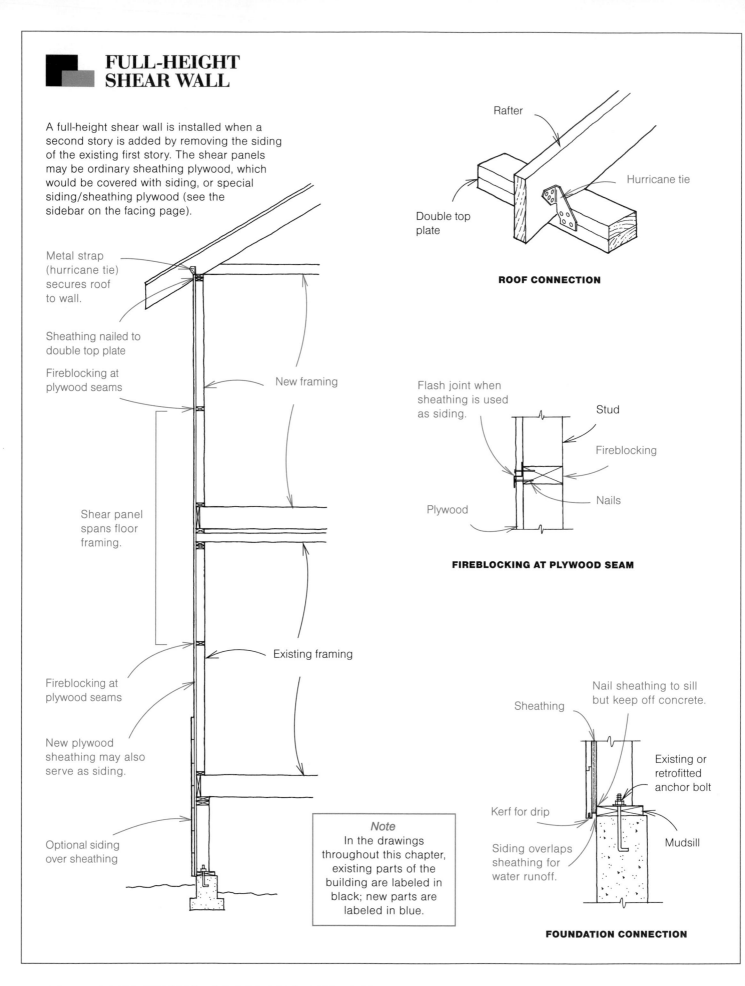

Metal strap (hurricane tie) secures roof to wall.

Sheathing nailed to double top plate

Fireblocking at plywood seams

New framing

Shear panel spans floor framing.

Fireblocking at plywood seams

New plywood sheathing may also serve as siding.

Existing framing

Optional siding over sheathing

Note
In the drawings throughout this chapter, existing parts of the building are labeled in black; new parts are labeled in blue.

Rafter

Double top plate

Hurricane tie

ROOF CONNECTION

Flash joint when sheathing is used as siding.

Stud

Fireblocking

Nails

Plywood

FIREBLOCKING AT PLYWOOD SEAM

Nail sheathing to sill but keep off concrete.

Sheathing

Existing or retrofitted anchor bolt

Kerf for drip

Siding overlaps sheathing for water runoff.

Mudsill

FOUNDATION CONNECTION

studs and other framing members it covers). Shear-wall-to-frame connectors tie the floor frames and/or roof framing to the shear wall. Frame connectors are usually sheet-metal brackets, though wood blocks may be used in some circumstances.

The size and frequency of the anchors (bolts and hold-downs), the thickness and nailing schedule of the shear panels, and the number and size of the shear-wall-to-frame connectors should be specified by a structural engineer.

The three basic components can be thought of as links in a chain—all three must be in place for the shear wall to function correctly. Without anchors, heavily sheathed walls can still slide or lift off their foundations. A roof or floor frame that is not well tied to its shear wall can bounce off, slide or twist away during a violent storm or earthquake.

As well as resisting the horizontal loads generated by earthquakes and high winds, shear walls protect against the uplift or vertical forces that are sometimes generated and also help dampen the repeated vibrations and oscillations that tend to shake houses apart. By resisting horizontal and vertical forces as well as stiffening the house, a shear wall serves multiple structural functions, and some shear-wall plywood panels can even double as exterior siding (see the sidebar below).

Continuous shear wall A state-of-the-art, modern house design calls for shear wall from the mudsill to the highest wall plate, as shown in the drawing on the facing page. If it is economical to replace the siding when a second story is added to an existing house, continuous shear wall can be installed to tie everything together, as it does for a new house.

The mudsill is bolted to the foundation, and the shear panels tie all the framing members together. Each plywood seam is blocked to prevent the sheet from failing at the loose edge and tearing out the nails one at a time (known as the "zipper effect"). Ideally, the seams are located in the vertical center of each wall section, and a single sheet of plywood spans the connections between the floors. This arrangement allows for the use of full sheets and ensures a strong, continuous connection from floor to floor. In practice, the seams may be placed anywhere, as long as they join at the center of a block or a supporting framing member. There should be a gap of about ⅛ in. to ¼ in. between sheets to accommodate shrinkage.

The roof must be firmly attached to the top plate with metal clips—called "hurricane ties"—that resist both uplift and lateral shear. It is usually not necessary to attach the floor frames to a shear wall of the design shown in the drawing with metal clips or brackets, as long as the rim and common joists are nailed frequently and firmly to the wall plate and the shear-wall plywood. Whether additional reinforcement is needed should be determined by a structural engineer, however.

Shear Wall as Siding

One way to cut costs when installing shear wall is to use an exterior plywood panel that serves as both sheathing/shear wall and siding (see the photo on p. 123). Such panels have inexpensive veneer cores, but are skinned with an acceptable siding material like pine, Douglas fir, cedar or redwood.

The plywood will not match the siding of older houses, and this is where a sort of amortized economy of materials comes into play. For example, a house may have aging wood shingles that will need replacing in a few years. The program calls for a second story to be built on a tight budget. In this case the plywood panels can be used as temporary siding, which will serve well enough if they are stained to match the shingles. When the shingles need to be replaced, they can be stripped and the wall beneath them sheathed with inexpensive plywood shear panels to flush it out to the thickness of the temporary siding. Then the whole house can be reshingled. This approach helps make the addition affordable by postponing the expense of reshingling, which usually costs several thousand dollars.

If a room addition is proposed, the same one-shot sheathing/siding may be the permanent solution, depending on the nature of the original siding.

Certainly the plywood panels are incompatible with stucco, but they may blend well enough with wood lap siding. Their main drawback is their durability, and after a few years their outer veneer may delaminate or wear thin, particularly on the sunny, south side. Again, if the plywood begins to wear, it can still serve as sheathing/shear wall and be covered with new shingles, stucco or board siding.

SOFT-STORY SHEAR WALL

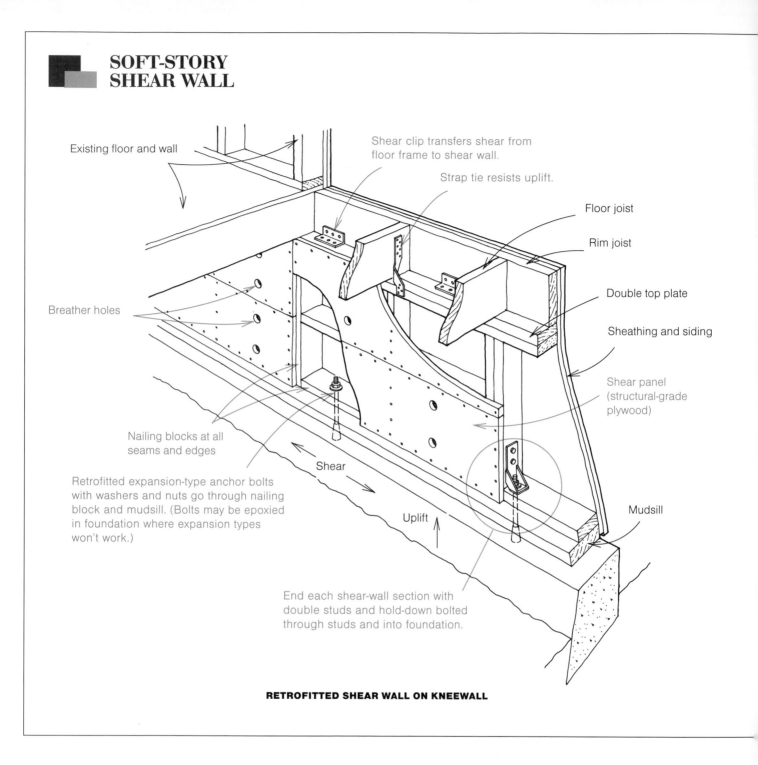

Existing floor and wall

Shear clip transfers shear from floor frame to shear wall.

Strap tie resists uplift.

Floor joist

Rim joist

Double top plate

Sheathing and siding

Breather holes

Shear panel (structural-grade plywood)

Nailing blocks at all seams and edges

Shear

Retrofitted expansion-type anchor bolts with washers and nuts go through nailing block and mudsill. (Bolts may be epoxied in foundation where expansion types won't work.)

Uplift

Mudsill

End each shear-wall section with double studs and hold-down bolted through studs and into foundation.

RETROFITTED SHEAR WALL ON KNEEWALL

For most houses, shear resistance is provided primarily by the exterior walls, and it is not usually necessary to strengthen the internal posts and girders. Consult an engineer before doing so, because over-strengthening in the wrong areas can actually weaken the structure's overall performance.

Retrofitted shear wall Removing and replacing the existing siding to nail on shear panels may be impractical on some houses. In such cases, a variety of stabilizing strategies can be devised that involve, first and foremost, stiffening the sub-area kneewall and making a good connection between the foun-

dation and the first-floor frame (see the drawing above).

Generally speaking, the more shear wall, the better the protection. However, cost may necessitate installing just enough shear wall to stabilize the house under all reason-

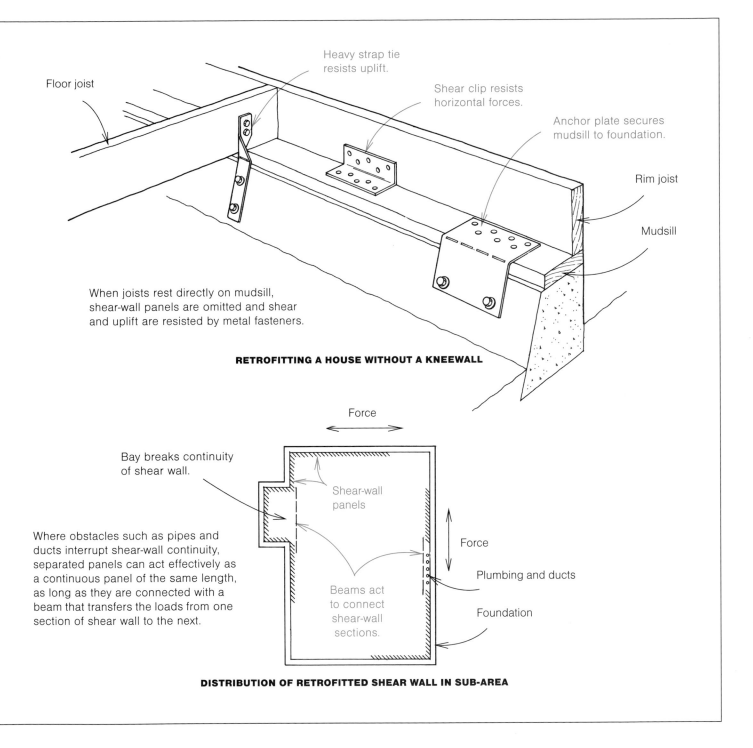

Floor joist

Heavy strap tie resists uplift.

Shear clip resists horizontal forces.

Anchor plate secures mudsill to foundation.

Rim joist

Mudsill

When joists rest directly on mudsill, shear-wall panels are omitted and shear and uplift are resisted by metal fasteners.

RETROFITTING A HOUSE WITHOUT A KNEEWALL

Force

Bay breaks continuity of shear wall.

Shear-wall panels

Force

Where obstacles such as pipes and ducts interrupt shear-wall continuity, separated panels can act effectively as a continuous panel of the same length, as long as they are connected with a beam that transfers the loads from one section of shear wall to the next.

Beams act to connect shear-wall sections.

Plumbing and ducts

Foundation

DISTRIBUTION OF RETROFITTED SHEAR WALL IN SUB-AREA

ably predictable conditions. The house can usually be stabilized by installing shear wall along one-half to two-thirds of the length of the kneewall. The shear wall should be evenly distributed on all four walls, to avoid placing excessive stress on the unreinforced walls (see the lower drawing above).

Once the kneewall is stiffened and a good connection between the foundation and first-floor frame is made, the rest of the existing structure can be strengthened. Strategies include taking advantage of the shear values of the existing external and internal walls, stiffening floor frames and using sheet-metal connectors to tie

together the roof, walls, floors and foundation. Many of these designs are integrated with the vertical support systems described below—after all, it is the new second-story load that makes horizontal reinforcement so critical.

POINT LOADING

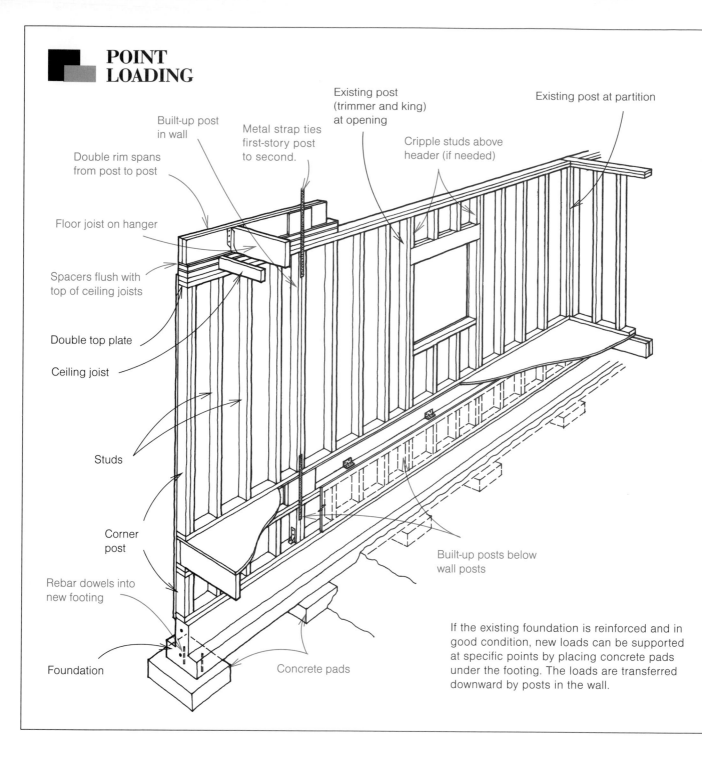

Built-up post
in wall

Double rim spans
from post to post

Floor joist on hanger

Spacers flush with
top of ceiling joists

Double top plate

Ceiling joist

Studs

Corner
post

Rebar dowels into
new footing

Foundation

Metal strap ties
first-story post
to second.

Existing post
(trimmer and king)
at opening

Cripple studs above
header (if needed)

Existing post at partition

Built-up posts below
wall posts

Concrete pads

If the existing foundation is reinforced and in good condition, new loads can be supported at specific points by placing concrete pads under the footing. The loads are transferred downward by posts in the wall.

SUPPORTING SECOND STORIES

Adding a new second story to most older houses means strengthening the entire building from the foundations up to support the vertical load. These structural improvements can eat up a significant portion of the budget, so the designer should carefully consider all of the possibilities discussed here to determine which will prove the most cost-effective.

Strengthening the foundation and transferring the load

In some cases the existing foundation and walls can support a second story without any strengthening.

More commonly, however, the structure will not take the new load, though the walls are seldom the problem. Existing 2x4 studs on 16-in. or even 24-in. centers are adequate to support most second stories. The dimensions or condition of the foundation is usually the weak link in the support system, and

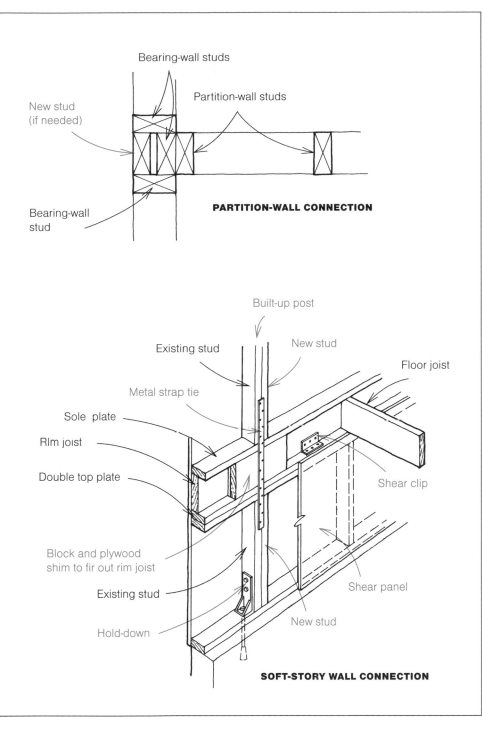

PARTITION-WALL CONNECTION

Bearing-wall studs

Partition-wall studs

New stud
(if needed)

Bearing-wall
stud

Built-up post

Existing stud

New stud

Floor joist

Metal strap tie

Sole plate

Rim joist

Double top plate

Shear clip

Block and plywood
shim to fir out rim joist

Existing stud

Hold-down

Shear panel

New stud

SOFT-STORY WALL CONNECTION

Point loading The roof and second-story load is normally distributed more or less evenly across the first-floor top plate and down all the studs until it ultimately rests on the foundation. If the foundation cannot handle this load, it must be replaced or beefed up. Replacing all of a foundation, however, is so expensive that it could make an addition unaffordable. In most cases, it is cheaper and easier to beef up or replace portions of the foundation, and carry the load to those points down posts installed in the walls.

The foundation can be strengthened in several ways, depending on its condition and dimensions. If it is reinforced and in good condition, it may be possible to underpin it by digging beneath it and casting concrete pads (or "spread footings") as shown in the drawing on the facing page (see also the drawing on p. 235). The new concrete should be reinforced with rebar and securely connected to the foundation with rebar dowels that are epoxied in place.

Alternatively, it is possible to sister a piece of concrete alongside the existing foundation, effectively widening it so that it can transfer greater loads to the soil. If the foundation is in poor condition, it may also be possible to remove and replace small sections of it, resting the posts on the new concrete.

In this context, a post is a vertical member that is at least twice as thick as a typical stud (studs are 2x4s; posts are 4x4s or 4x6s laid flat in the wall). A single post carries the load of several studs, and posts are typically installed at intervals of 4 ft. to 6 ft. or more, minimizing the number of loading points.

it is here that the design strategy for the entire structure begins.

There are three common methods of compensating for inadequate foundations: point loading, or concentrating the new load onto a series of posts that transfer it through the existing walls to points on strengthened sections of the foundation; converting existing partition walls to bearing walls and supporting the second-floor frame on them; and bridging the building with an essentially independent superstructure that both supports the second story and becomes its own architectural element.

An existing stud can be converted to a post by solidly nailing another stud onto it, creating a nominal 4x4. Building new posts in an existing wall is a somewhat expensive operation, however, since the wall must be opened and resealed. One way to reduce the number of new posts needed is to take advantage of the "posts" that already exist in the walls at fairly regular intervals. Corners are normally of three- or four-stud construction, windows and doors are usually framed with built-up posts and the intersections of bearing and partition walls are similarly reinforced (see the drawing on pp. 128-129).

Not all windows and doors are framed in such a way as to create continuous posts, however. Some are missing cripples, trimmers or other members. Since placing a cripple at the edge of the opening (directly above the trimmer) is not always necessary for even stud spacing, for example, some framers omit this piece. If the cripple was left out, a minimal wall opening will suffice to install a cripple, which can be fastened with screws to avoid trying to swing a hammer inside the wall.

Whether or not the posts are continuous, existing wall openings are the preferred location for new posts for two reasons. First, orderly fenestration requires that upper-story windows sit above first-floor windows, and that the roof load be posted around them and carried to the foundation. If the design calls for orderly fenestration, the first story will need posts to transfer the load downward. Second, older windows and doors generally have wide moldings that can be removed and replaced. New posts can be hidden behind these moldings, and re-

moval of plaster or drywall will be limited to the short sections immediately above or below them.

Bearing walls are typically connected to partitions (cross walls) by a three-stud intersection, as shown in the top drawing on p. 129. This assembly is as strong as a 4x post, and can be used as a built-in bearing point if the kneewall and foundation directly below it are reinforced.

Keep in mind that you cannot simply load the second story on the existing posts without making sure that they can take the additional weight. They are already loaded by the roof, and it is often necessary to add studs to the existing posts or add new, intermittent posts to carry the second-story floor and walls. An engineer should design the support system.

One of the factors limiting point loading is the distance that the second-story rim joist can span between posts. As the spanning capacity of the joist increases, the number of supporting posts can decrease, thus decreasing the number of openings in the walls and the points of foundation reinforcement. However, since there are fewer supporting posts, the load on each post is increased, and the foundation will have to be reinforced accordingly.

One way to increase the distance between posts is to double up the rim. The exact reduction in the number of posts depends on the loading conditions, but, assuming a constant load, the distance can be increased by approximately one-third, which might make the difference between having to open the middle of a wall or being able to use an existing post at a window or in a corner. If the rim is doubled, how-

ever, the floor joists no longer have adequate bearing on the plate, and will have to be carried by hangers, as shown in the drawing on p. 128.

While point loading can solve the vertical support problem, it does not provide horizontal shear resistance. By itself, it could create a dangerous situation by essentially propping the new second story up on a few posts. The upper and lower walls must be tied together with continuous shear panels or some other engineered means of ensuring structural continuity and resistance to horizontal forces.

If it is not practical to cover the entire exterior wall with shear panels, the soft-story wall can be sheathed and the posts at the different levels connected with metal strap ties (see the bottom drawing on p. 129). Though in new construction the strap ties are usually applied to the outside of the frame, they can be installed on the interior wall, as shown, and covered with drywall.

The floor-to-floor fasteners primarily provide protection against uplift. An engineer will be needed to determine whether the existing interior walls provide sufficient shear value and bracing to resist horizontal loads, or whether the interior finishes will need to be stripped so shear panels can be installed on the studs.

Converting partition walls Badly disintegrated concrete, inaccessible areas and other factors can make it impractical to reinforce the existing foundation. In such cases, the partition walls can be made into bearing walls by pouring foundations and building kneewalls with shear panels beneath the partitions. A floor

CONVERTING PARTITION WALLS TO BEARING WALLS

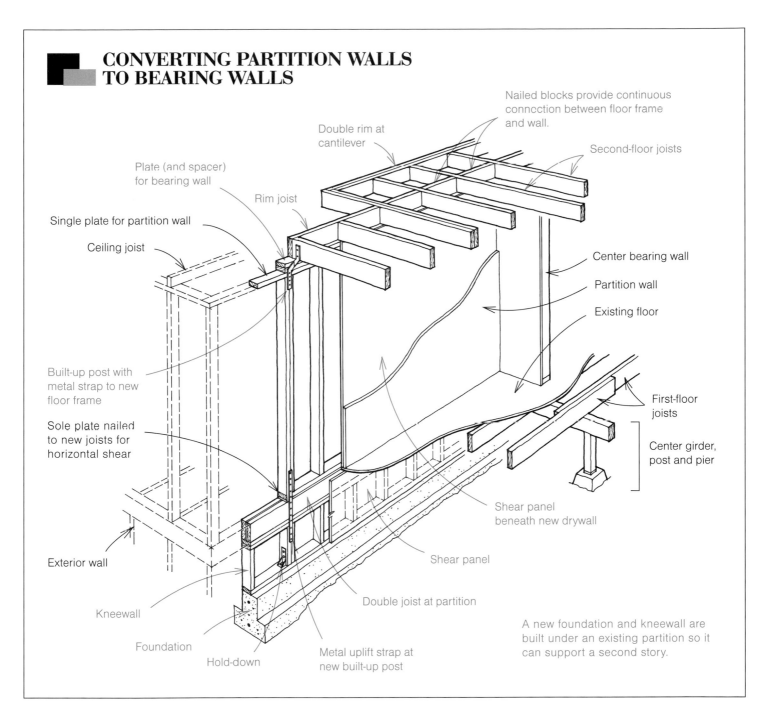

Nailed blocks provide continuous connection between floor frame and wall.

Double rim at cantilever

Second-floor joists

Plate (and spacer) for bearing wall

Rim joist

Single plate for partition wall

Ceiling joist

Center bearing wall

Partition wall

Existing floor

Built-up post with metal strap to new floor frame

First-floor joists

Sole plate nailed to new joists for horizontal shear

Center girder, post and pier

Shear panel beneath new drywall

Exterior wall

Shear panel

Double joist at partition

Kneewall

A new foundation and kneewall are built under an existing partition so it can support a second story.

Foundation

Metal uplift strap at new built-up post

Hold-down

frame with its joists running perpendicular to the first-floor joists can then be installed atop these newly created bearing walls.

The addition can sit at either end of the building or over the center. If the partitions do not provide a convenient location for the second-story walls, the new floor frame can be cantilevered to create more space (see the drawings on p. 132). In other words, the addition can be located just about anywhere over the house. This freedom of location not only offers more architectural flexibility, but also allows you to avoid variance hassles when current property-line setbacks are inboard of existing walls (see Chapter 10).

Because of the great number of possible locations for the addition, be careful of architectural gaffes, like misaligning the new second-story windows with the existing windows below. Such mistakes can be avoided by taking the unified approach to design discussed in Chapter 12.

SUPPORTING A SECOND STORY
WITH CONVERTED PARTITION WALLS

In a typical house, the perimeter and center bearing walls carry the load of the floor and ceiling joists, while the partitions merely support themselves.

The partitions are converted to bearing walls, and a second story is added. The lateral shear component is addressed by the partition walls, while longitudinal resistance is provided primarily by the center bearing wall, which will need a foundation of its own. (The unmodified perimeter walls provide some shear resistance, but not enough to stabilize most additions.)

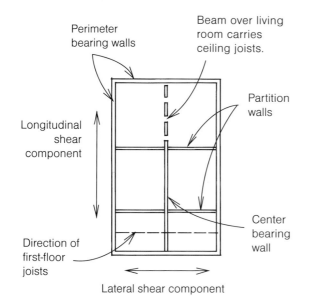

Perimeter bearing walls

Beam over living room carries ceiling joists.

Partition walls

Longitudinal shear component

Center bearing wall

Direction of first-floor joists

Lateral shear component

**FIRST-STORY PLAN
(CONTINUOUS PARTITIONS)**

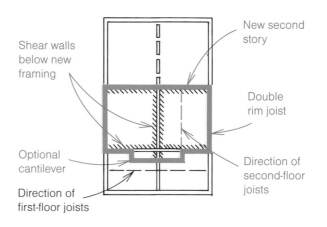

Shear walls below new framing

New second story

Double rim joist

Optional cantilever

Direction of second-floor joists

Direction of first-floor joists

SECOND-STORY ADDITION

When partitions are discontinuous, a beam can be used to provide vertical support and transfer horizontal shear to the beefed-up partition wall.

Additional shear resistance can be provided by anchoring and sheathing the nearest partition wall.

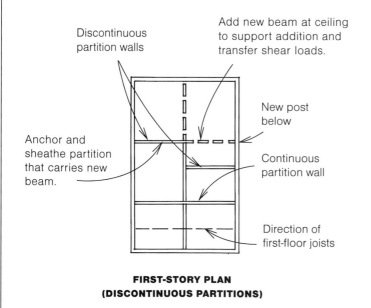

Discontinuous partition walls

Add new beam at ceiling to support addition and transfer shear loads.

New post below

Anchor and sheathe partition that carries new beam.

Continuous partition wall

Direction of first-floor joists

**FIRST-STORY PLAN
(DISCONTINUOUS PARTITIONS)**

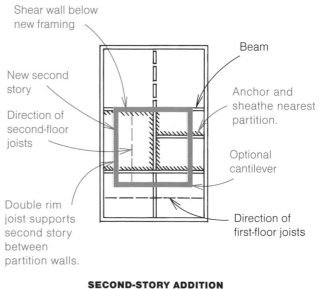

Shear wall below new framing

New second story

Direction of second-floor joists

Beam

Anchor and sheathe nearest partition.

Optional cantilever

Double rim joist supports second story between partition walls.

Direction of first-floor joists

SECOND-STORY ADDITION

Resisting horizontal forces can get tricky. The existing partition walls have some shear value and can be used to resist forces in the lateral or short direction (see the top drawings on the facing page). The partitions should be anchored to the new kneewalls with sheet-metal connectors, and the new second-story frame should be securely attached to the partitions' top plates. Longitudinal shear (long direction) can be picked up by the center bearing wall, which would then need to be anchored with a grade beam or foundation of its own. The internal walls may have to be stripped, sheathed with structural plywood and resurfaced, usually with drywall, to provide adequate shear. (You can assume that the exterior bearing walls will provide some shear resistance but not enough, since their deteriorated foundations will not hold bolts. It is probably easier to cast a new foundation beneath the center bearing wall than to remove and replace those of the exterior walls.)

Another problem is that partition walls do not always align with one another as they cross the house. For vertical support, the void can be spanned with a beam resting atop the bearing wall and over a post and pier that is installed at the exterior wall (see the bottom left drawing on the facing page).

These half-length partitions will probably not provide adequate shear resistance as they stand, and will almost certainly need to be stripped, sheathed and resurfaced. The end of the beam must be firmly attached to the top wall plate to ensure a solid connection.

Structural Do's and Don'ts

1. Don't add a second story without increasing the house's resistance to horizontal loads.

2. Don't build alongside the existing house without providing sufficient horizontal-load resistance for the addition and a connection to the house that compensates for differing horizontal motions.

3. Don't mix foundation types without consulting a structural or soils engineer.

4. Don't use the existing ceiling joists as floor joists.

5. Don't jack up a wall unless the floors around it sag so badly that they need correcting. Adjust the wall to the other walls by shimming it at the top.

6. Don't use the floor to support new bearing members or bearing walls. Make sure vertical loads are carried directly to the ground, or are at least sitting above a double floor joist. Partition walls, too, should sit over double joists.

1. Do use existing bearing walls to support second stories where possible.

2. Do check the bearing walls to make sure they are able to support the addition. Don't assume there are posts at wall intersections or openings. Find them.

3. Do convert to platform framing to simplify building the addition.

4. Do design for hazards in your bioregion—earthquakes, hurricanes, desiccation of wood siding or delamination of siding plywood in desert climates, fast growth of wood-destroying organisms as a result of excessive moisture, and so forth.

5. Do consult a structural engineer about structural design.

Even when they are anchored on their own foundations and heavily sheathed, however, the half-length partition walls may still not provide sufficient resistance to horizontal loads. Additional resistance can be provided by anchoring and sheathing the nearest partition wall, as shown in the bottom right drawing on the facing page.

Bridging the structure In some situations it is impractical to rest the addition directly on the house. In such cases, a second-story addition can be supported on a partial or complete bridge. The bridges may be supported by pilasters, columns or walls.

In this context, *pilasters* are posts that are attached to the outside of the perimeter bearing walls but sit on their own concrete pier footings (see the drawing on p. 134). They provide the vertical support, while the existing wall provides horizontal shear resistance. If there is enough shear resistance in the existing wall, the pilasters may be applied over the siding. Otherwise, the siding is stripped, the wall is sheathed with plywood and the pilasters are installed directly over the sheathing. In either case, the pilasters are usually attached to the existing wall with bolts into studs or blocks in the wall.

BRIDGING WITH PILASTERS

Since the foundation of this house could not support an additional vertical load, 4x8 posts on independent concrete footings were bolted to the wall to form special columns called pilasters. Girders are supported on the pilasters and joists hung from the girders. The original siding was stripped and replaced by plywood sheathing, which was then stuccoed over.

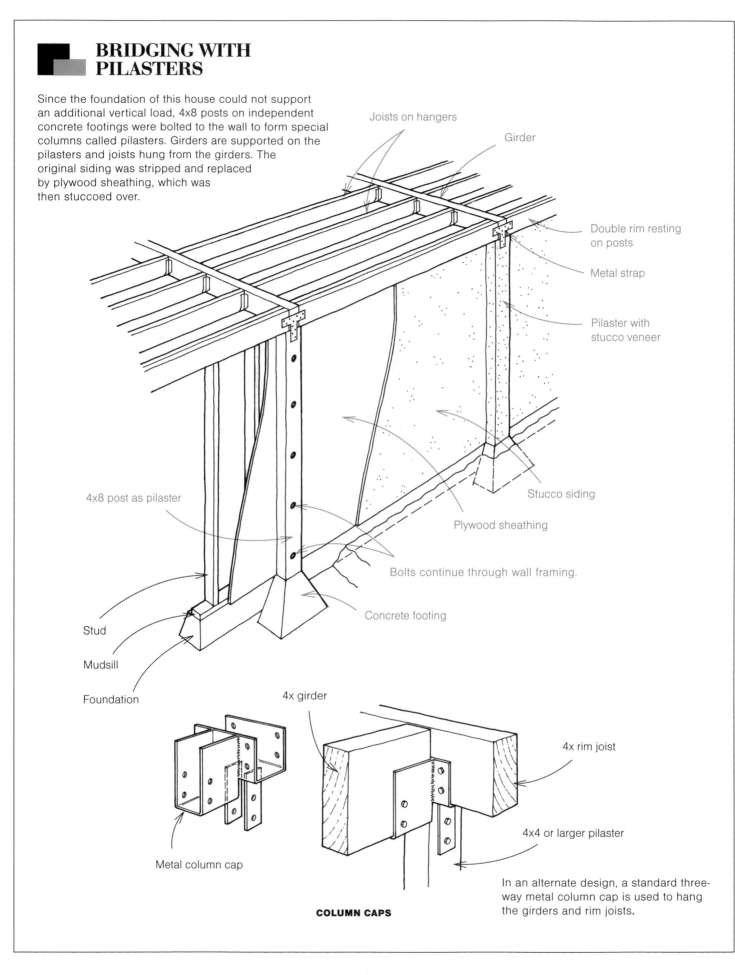

Joists on hangers

Girder

Double rim resting on posts

Metal strap

Pilaster with stucco veneer

Stucco siding

Plywood sheathing

Bolts continue through wall framing.

Concrete footing

4x8 post as pilaster

Stud

Mudsill

Foundation

4x girder

4x rim joist

4x4 or larger pilaster

Metal column cap

COLUMN CAPS

In an alternate design, a standard three-way metal column cap is used to hang the girders and rim joists.

Pilasters are normally thought of as being architecturally integral to the wall, and therefore have the same finish. The pilasters on a stucco wall, for example, are usually encased in stucco themselves. It is not always necessary to do so, however, and, in the right context, a row of rhythmically arranged pilasters of exposed rot-resistant wood can enhance an otherwise bland exterior.

Columns stand free of the wall. They may be made of wood, reinforced masonry or metal. The second story can be supported by girders and joists that rest on the columns.

The resistance of a row of columns to horizontal forces depends in part on the strength of the attachment of each column to the beam or floor frame above it. While steel columns and girders can be welded together to make a moment frame, the cost of such an assembly can be prohibitive. The weakness of wood columns, however, is that the nails attaching them to the floor frame can tear out under large horizontal loads. Horizontal shear resistance, once again, can be provided by the house walls.

In the drawing below, horizontal stability is provided by anchoring and sheathing the longitudinal bearing walls and the lateral partition walls. Note that in this design the sheathed partitions line up with the internal columns, which makes it easy to tie the joists that sit on top of the shear walls directly to the columns.

Additional column stability can be provided by building an extra-stiff floor frame—using thicker subfloor plywood and tighter nailing schedules—and/or by nailing a plywood soffit on the exposed, underside of the floor frame. The girders must be firmly attached to the columns with metal connectors. A standard column cap like the one shown in the drawing on the facing page will work in most situations.

Columns are an important architectural element, and their number and location should be considered carefully in both plan and eleva-

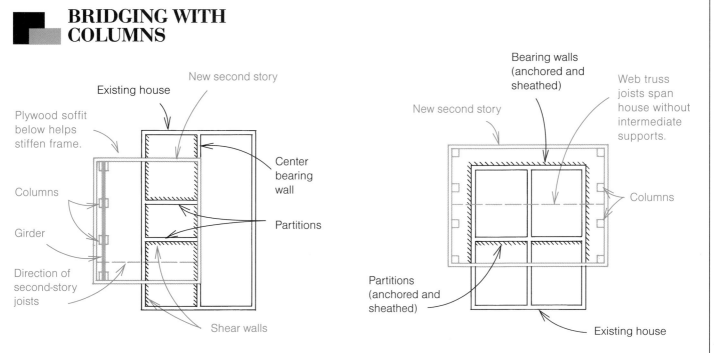

BRIDGING WITH COLUMNS

PARTIAL BRIDGING

Partial bridging of this house is accomplished by resting the second-story floor joists on a girder that spans a new row of columns and on the existing center bearing wall. The joists are cantilevered beyond the columns to protect the tops of the columns from the weather. The area between the columns and the house might be used as a breezeway or enclosed porch.

FULL BRIDGING

This small house is completely bridged by columns and web truss joists (see p. 136) that span the second-floor frame without intermediate bearing. The existing walls are anchored and sheathed to stabilize the second-story frame. The space between the columns and the house might be used as a wrap-around veranda.

tion. They should be placed and scaled so they enhance facades and do not block views.

A second story may also be supported on walls built outboard of the original walls. The basic configurations are bays, freestanding walls, and true room additions that support second stories bridging over part of the existing house, thus becoming combination additions.

Bays, like pilasters, bump out from the main wall and sit on their own foundations (see the drawing on the facing page). Girders from which joists are hung rest on the corner posts.

Freestanding walls are sometimes incorporated into porches or elaborate entryways, and are often used to support the end of a carport. If an addition sits over the carport, however, the problem of shear resistance across its open ends must be addressed. One solution is to enclose the back wall, so the structure evolves into a half garage. At the front opening, a beam can be used to transfer forces to a shear wall, while also acting as a header across the opening.

The floor frame supported on walls or bays can bridge all or a portion of the structure. Partial bridges made of ordinary framing lumber normally terminate at the center bearing wall or a converted partition wall. A partial bridge can be brought from the other side so a double partial bridge completely spans the house. Web truss joists (see below) can also span the entire building, and the cost of this approach should be weighed against that of modifying a center bearing wall to take a new load.

The floor platform

Whether the house has a balloon or a platform frame, the addition should be platform-framed. Platform framing is easier and cheaper than balloon framing, and attempting to tie into an existing balloon frame can be a technical nightmare. Once the problems of supporting the second story have been resolved, you can design the transition between the existing frame and the new floor platform.

In some cases the existing ceilings are removed, and the new floor can be framed off the top plate as it is in new construction. Usually, it is cheaper and easier to keep the ceilings, however, and the floor must be built with them in place.

A glance at the span tables in the Uniform Building Code shows that ceiling joists (which are usually 2x4s or 2x6s) cannot be used as floor joists—they are about half as deep (for information on the span tables, see Appendix IV). Undersized joists will bend and crack ceiling plaster and cause floors to squeak or pull loose with ordinary use. A large social gathering could cause complete failure of the floor.

Though ceiling joists can be built up, it's best to resist the temptation to do so. Reinforcing members must somehow be laminated or attached to the existing joists, not simply stuck on top. Because there is no assurance of proper quality control, building departments will not allow new and old framing members to be laminated by field-applied glue.

Edge-joining members by toe-nailing one piece on top of another accomplishes little because the nails loosen when people walk on the floor. Sistering one piece to the other by side-nailing or bolting could be ef-

fective, since nails and bolts have adequate shear strength to carry the load. However, there must be at least 3 in. of overlap to avoid splitting the wood. In most situations this would interfere with the existing wiring. Finally, resting new floor joists directly on the existing top plate (flush with the bottom of the ceiling joists) usually means depressing and sometimes cracking a plaster ceiling, and might mean that some of the existing ceiling and new floor joists end up trying to occupy the same space at the same time.

Experienced builders usually bypass the existing ceiling frame altogether by installing 2x spacers, as shown in the drawing on p. 138. The spacers, with a plywood shim in between, are installed to flush out to the top of the existing ceiling joists. Then an additional ¾-in. plywood "plate" is nailed across the blocking and joists to tie all the pieces together and make sure the floor joists clear the ceiling joists. The plywood plate can be leveled with shingle shims, if needed. Make sure that the leveling shims are placed directly beneath the new joists for proper bearing.

Typically, the new floor joists are supported at both the exterior and center bearing wall, which is also flushed out with spacers. One advantage of this method, if the house has settled unevenly, is that it allows the builder to use shims to level the second-floor platform without having to jack up the house.

Web truss joists With the recent introduction of web truss joists that can span up to 32 ft., it is now possible to omit the support at the center bearing wall (see the drawing on p. 139). The economy of materials is much greater than that of

BRIDGING WITH EXTERNAL WALLS

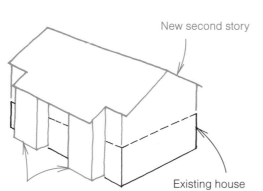

New second story

Existing house

New two-story bays outside original house support second story.

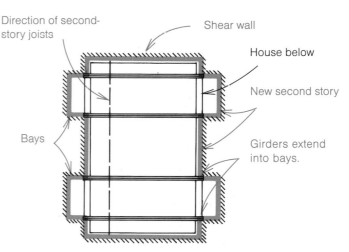

Direction of second-story joists

Shear wall

House below

New second story

Bays

Girders extend into bays.

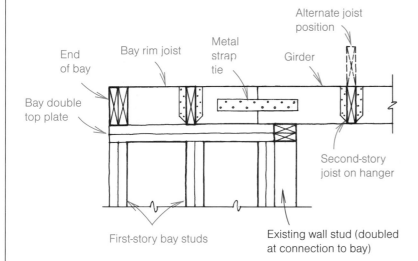

End of bay

Bay rim joist

Metal strap tie

Girder

Alternate joist position

Bay double top plate

Second-story joist on hanger

First-story bay studs

Existing wall stud (doubled at connection to bay)

BAY WALLS

To add a second story, a one-story house can be bridged by girders that rest on bays built outside the existing perimeter walls.

The girders can sit on top of the bay walls or be let into them, depending on height restrictions and architectural considerations. The joists, too, may sit on top of the girders or be hung between them. In the schematic floor plan above, the joists sit atop the girders so they can cantilever to the end walls.

If the top of the girder is at the double-top-plate level, the existing ceiling will have to be removed or opened to accommodate the girder. Depending on conditions, this could be used as an opportunity to add an attractive, exposed-beam ceiling in the first story.

FREESTANDING WALLS

This house had an existing carport with a flat roof that is a continuation of the flat main roof supported by a single wall off the left end of the structure. Though the wall could be reinforced and sheared to support a second story, the portion of the addition over the carport would be vulnerable to horizontal forces. A new rear wall was added to the carport to help resist horizontal loads.

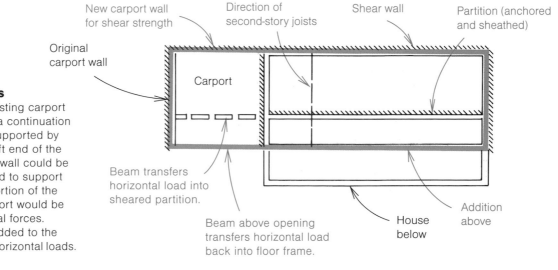

New carport wall for shear strength

Direction of second-story joists

Shear wall

Partition (anchored and sheathed)

Original carport wall

Carport

Beam transfers horizontal load into sheared partition.

Beam above opening transfers horizontal load back into floor frame.

House below

Addition above

SECOND-STORY PLATFORM

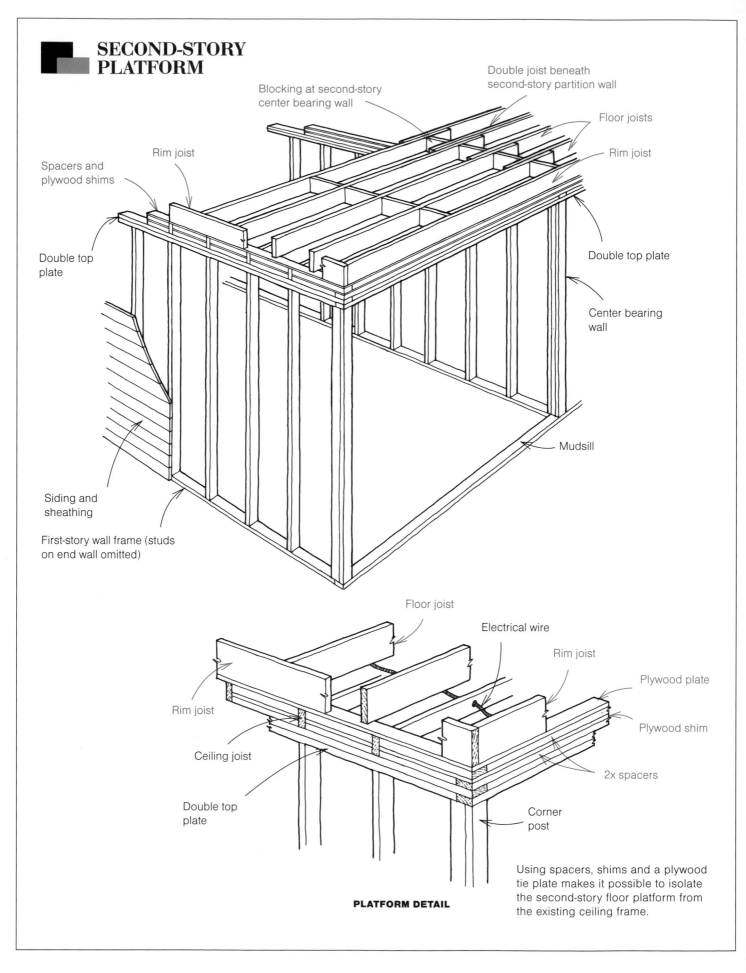

Blocking at second-story center bearing wall

Double joist beneath second-story partition wall

Floor joists

Rim joist

Rim joist

Spacers and plywood shims

Double top plate

Double top plate

Center bearing wall

Mudsill

Siding and sheathing

First-story wall frame (studs on end wall omitted)

Floor joist

Electrical wire

Rim joist

Plywood plate

Rim joist

Plywood shim

Ceiling joist

2x spacers

Double top plate

Corner post

Using spacers, shims and a plywood tie plate makes it possible to isolate the second-story floor platform from the existing ceiling frame.

PLATFORM DETAIL

solid wood, and the cost is comparable. Light weight, ease of handling and the uniformity of manufactured tolerances are among the advantages of these joists.

A disadvantage of skipping the center bearing wall is that all the load of the floor and roof is now carried by the perimeter foundations only, and they could require significantly more reinforcement. Also the required joist depth—up to 16 in. is needed to span 32 ft.—can push the overall height above the legal limit or make single stair runs too long. Because the trusses can be nailed on their top and bottom edges only, metal joist hangers or other connectors must be used wherever they intersect. Finally, the joists are sel-

dom in stock at lumber stores—they must be ordered—and many building departments require engineering calculations before granting permits to use them. (Ordinary joists can be called out by the designer or builder from the code book, see Appendix IV.)

Web truss joists are a great boon where there is no intermediate bearing wall beneath the addition or if for some other reason long distances must be spanned. Otherwise, their use is a matter of personal preference.

Whether or not the floor is built with web truss joists, it may be desirable to use roof trusses and omit the center bearing wall in the upper story. Spanning the entire width of the second floor allows complete freedom in locating walls and defining spaces. A large master bedroom or family room could be planned, for example. Large open rooms, of course, lack the bracing normally supplied by cross walls, and will need stronger shear panels on the exterior walls and perhaps stronger roof sheathing and hurricane ties as well. Still, the combined cost of installing a center bearing wall, rafters and ceiling joists is usually much greater than that of using trusses and beefing up the shear wall.

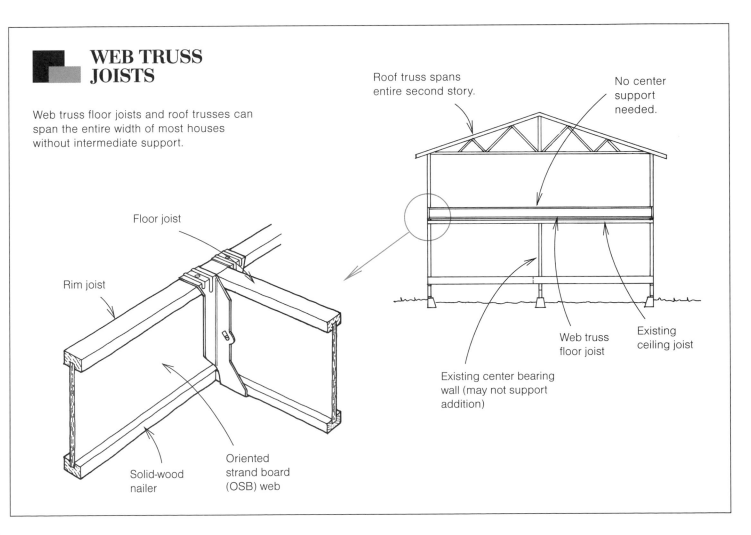

WEB TRUSS JOISTS

Web truss floor joists and roof trusses can span the entire width of most houses without intermediate support.

Roof truss spans entire second story.

No center support needed.

Floor joist

Rim joist

Solid-wood nailer

Oriented strand board (OSB) web

Web truss floor joist

Existing ceiling joist

Existing center bearing wall (may not support addition)

9
EVALUATING SUBSYSTEMS

In the previous two chapters, we looked at the critical issue of the house's structural system. The designer of an addition must also take into account the condition of the building's weatherproofing skin (roofing, siding, doors and windows) and the principal mechanical subsystems (electrical, plumbing and heating). These subsystems must be in good condition and of adequate capacity to serve the existing house and the proposed addition. Undersized or deteriorating subsystems will have to be upgraded or replaced, which can take a considerable bite out of the addition's budget.

This chapter is intended to help the designer or builder understand subsystems well enough for a preliminary evaluation of their condition and potential problems; it does not cover subsystems in detail. The information is sufficient for the feasibility assessment (see Chapter 1), but it's a good idea to seek professional help before getting too far into the final design or working drawings. Roofers, electricians, plumbers and other specialists are profitably called near the beginning of the design process and as needed along the way. These specialists tend to give more attention to a project when they are paid a reasonable consulting fee.

THE BUILDING'S SKIN

Here, "skin" means the entire outer covering of the building, including the roofing, siding, doors and windows. While these items are often considered separately, they serve the same general purpose of weatherproofing the structure and may be viewed as a single system.

The condition of the skin should be evaluated as part of the feasibility assessment for an addition. As well as affecting the budget, the need to repair damage and deterioration can create design opportunities. Replacing a deteriorated roof, for example, allows the designer to make a perfect match with the new roof on the addition.

Roofs

Roofs usually have greater solar and weather exposure than siding and degenerate much more quickly. Different grades and types of roofing materials are designed to have different life spans. If the age of the roofing is correlated with observations on its condition, you can make a reasonable estimate of how much longer it will last.

For the purpose of evaluating their condition, roofing materials can be divided into three general types: soft, petroleum-based materials such as composition shingles, roll roofing, tar and gravel, and other soft coverings such as wood shingles or shakes and fiberglass shingles; metals such as galvanized steel and copper roofing; and hard, stone-like materials such as slate, ceramic tile and lightweight concrete.

Soft roof coverings The longevity of soft roofing materials is determined both by their quality and their exposure. The sun is the primary enemy of most roofs. The south sides of composition-shingle roofs, for example, often need replacing several years before the north sides.

Composition shingles, roll roofing and tar-and-gravel roofing all work—and disintegrate—in a similar fashion. They are made of layers of tar-saturated felt or similar material with a protective layer of gravel embedded in their surface. The tar provides the actual waterproofing, and the gravel surface reflects and absorbs sunlight, which would otherwise harden and break down the tar.

The black bald spots on this tar-and-gravel roof show that the roof has been loosing its light-colored, protective gravel surface for some time. Plans for a room or partial second-story addition would probably have to include the cost of replacing the existing roof.

Over time, some sunlight gets through the gravel filter and the tar hardens and loses its adhesion, allowing some of the gravel to fall off. Then even more sunlight gets through, more tar is hardened, and still more gravel falls off. The process accelerates toward the end of the roof's life.

Petroleum-based roofs that are starting to show signs of wear have small black bald spots where the felt or tar shows through the gravel surface. Roofs that will soon need replacing have large bald areas. By simply looking at a roof from the street, then, you can usually tell if it is recently installed, in its middle years or near the end of its serviceability.

It is also possible to approximate the age of composition-shingle and roll roofing by testing the brittleness of the material. When twisted gently with the fingers, newer material is pliable, while older material is hard and brittle. Exercise caution, since pieces of brittle shingles may snap off.

Wood shingles and shakes tend to wear at the point that water runs onto them—right below the edge of the course above. If the shingles are worn more than one-third of the way through, and there are loose or split shingles or other signs of deterioration, the roof needs replacing.

Even if there is not enough rain to erode wood shingles, they will eventually dry out in the sun and crack by a process that, once again, accelerates toward the end. A 17-year-old shingle or shake roof is likely to need replacing in 3 to 5 years, even though it may presently show little sign of wear.

No matter what their material, quality or exposure, most soft roofs last for about 18 to 24 years. If a composition-shingle roof, for example, is showing small bald spots and is 14 years old, it's safe to figure on replacing it in 3 to 5 years (though it may last longer). If the age is unknown but the roof is showing small bald spots, it will probably need replacing in 5 years at the outside.

Metal roof coverings The life span of metal roofs varies greatly depending on the material. Cheap galvanized roofs exposed to adverse weather conditions can rust through in a decade, while thick copper might hold up for a century. The remaining life of a metal roof is hard to predict unless there are obvious signs of deterioration.

Stone-like roof coverings Stone-like materials can easily last for 100 years or more. If the tiles or shingles are not broken or worn through, replacement of the existing roof will not factor into the addition's budget. However, slate and tile can be difficult to cut into, replace or match, and raise a variety of practical and aesthetic issues.

The addition and the roof The addition, of course, needs its own roof, but since it is often built close to or actually joined with the existing roof the question of putting on an entirely new roof inevitably arises. The advantages of total replacement are that the roofs will match, long-range costs may be pared down because of the economy of scale (covering a larger area with one application), and the old roof will not be damaged by roofers walking on it.

The main disadvantage is that replacing the original roof cuts into the addition's budget. Also, replacement may involve more than simply applying shingles. It is common practice to apply new layers of roofing over old ones, and many existing roofs have more than one layer. The code specifies, for example, that only three layers of composition shingles may be added before total replacement is required. Removing the old roofing, as well as repairing dryrot and other damage that may have been caused by leaks, will further increase costs. If the existing roof's condition is marginal, then, it is a good idea to ask an experienced roofer for an evaluation and an estimate for both the addition and the whole house.

Siding

The condition of the siding, like that of the roof, can affect the design of the addition. If siding is damaged or deteriorated, it may allow water to penetrate to the framing beneath, causing the growth of dryrot fungus. The damage will need to be repaired before the addition project goes forward. If large areas of the original siding are damaged or deteriorated, you may want to replace all the siding so that it matches the addition's.

Houses with stucco or masonry siding built on unstable soil often develop cracks that allow water penetration. As well as pinpointing possible dryrot infections, severe cracks indicate the need for a soils analysis (see Chapter 6).

Wood siding is more flexible and seldom cracks as a result of differential settling. Wood that is unprotected by paint or stain, however, can warp and split so badly in the sun that moisture can enter through cracks and knotholes. Also, deteriorated paint exposes nails that can rust and create small water channels.

When checking the condition of the siding, pay particular attention to the point where the building meets the ground. Even stucco siding will allow dryrot fungus penetration if the mudsill is at or near grade (see p. 121).

Doors and windows

Wood moldings around doors and windows are particularly vulnerable to the weather. Differential settling, varying coefficients of expansion of the molding, siding and jambs, solar exposure and a variety of other factors can cause separation between the joints in the molding or the walls and moldings. Basement- and garage-door jambs are frequently at or near grade or in contact with moisture-absorbing concrete, thus continually exposed to moisture and possible dryrot.

Rotting wood in a door or window usually means that the unit will have to be replaced. While the condition of a single door or window will hardly affect an addition project, several deteriorated units could suggest changing the original windows to match those of the addition.

Windows and doors should also be checked for sticking. If sticking cannot be attributed to problems with lifting mechanisms or hinges, it is probably caused by settling, which might indicate the need for a soil or foundation investigation.

THE ELECTRICAL SYSTEM

The existing electrical system must be evaluated to determine whether it can safely deliver enough power to supply the house and the addition. The two major components of a household electrical system are the service entrance, where the power comes into the house, and the house's internal wiring. An evaluation that is sufficient for preliminary design and cost estimates begins with a look at the service entrance.

The service entrance

A typical service entrance has two principal components: the weatherhead assembly, where electricity enters the house, and the main distribution panel, where the power is subdivided and distributed through the smaller wires of individual circuits to the various lights, outlets and appliances.

The weatherhead assembly In a typical setup, the utility company's supply wires connect to the house's service wires at the weatherhead, as shown in the drawing on p. 144. As household electrical demands have grown over the years, the size and number of wires entering the weatherhead, and thus the capacity of services, have increased.

The amount of electrical current is measured in amperes, or "amps." The larger a wire, the more amps it can carry. From about 1900, when domestic electricity started to become common, through about 1950, the standard household service capacity was 30 amps. During a transitional period from 1950 through about 1965, services were typically increased to 60 amps

(sometimes up to 80 amps), and, in the late 1960s, to 100 amps. Today services vary, depending on the size of the house, from 100 or 125 amps for a medium-size house to as much as 200 amps for a large house (see the table on p. 145).

In pretransitional systems (before 1950), two wires enter the weatherhead. One is hot, or positively charged, and carries the electricity toward the house. The other is neutral and returns the unused electricity from the house to its source to complete the circuit. The hot wire in most of the older systems was capable of carrying 30 amps, though some larger transitional-period wires can carry 60 or 80 amps. Some services installed during the transitional period, and all post-transitional services, have three weatherhead wires, two hot and one neutral. Each post-transitional hot wire can carry 100 amps or more.

While the amount of current is measured in amps, electrical pressure (or potential difference) is measured in volts. Appliances such as wall heaters and clothes dryers that use a great deal of electricity run most efficiently on 220 (or 240) volts, as opposed to the 110 (or 120) volts supplied to ordinary lights and outlets.

The older systems with one hot wire (two wires total) supply 110 volts only. Systems with two hot wires (three wires total) can supply 220 volts, or 110 volts through each wire. When an appliance such as a stove or dryer requires 220 volts, two 110 lines are brought together to supply the circuit that serves the appliance.

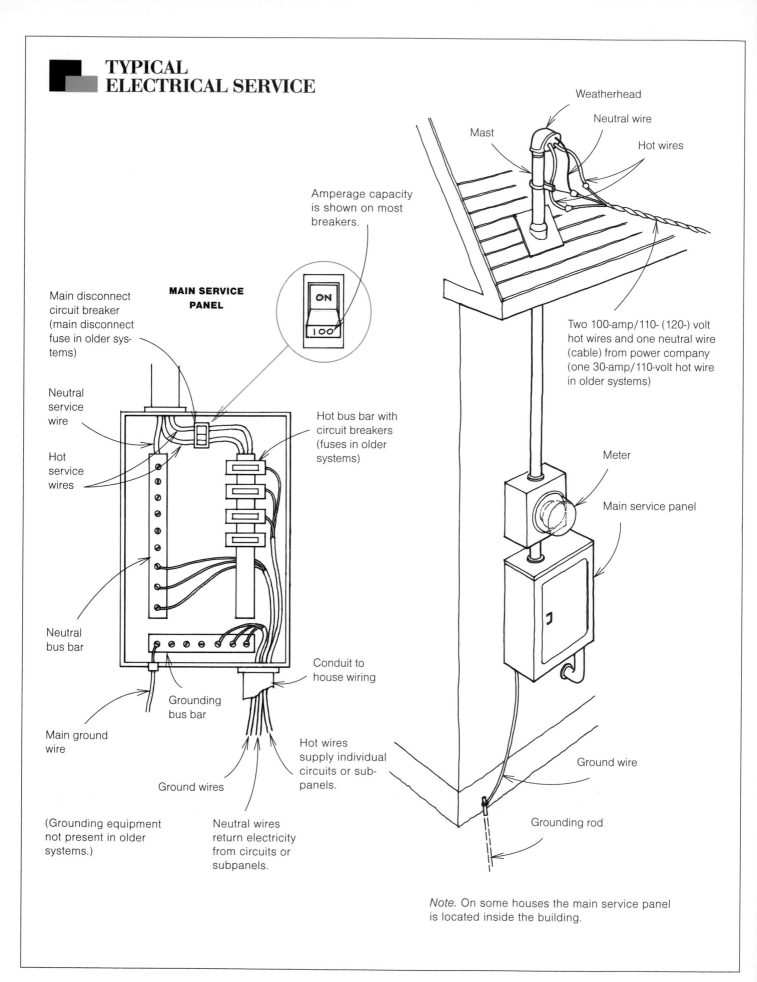

TYPICAL ELECTRICAL SERVICE

Weatherhead

Mast

Neutral wire

Hot wires

MAIN SERVICE PANEL

Amperage capacity is shown on most breakers.

ON

100

Main disconnect circuit breaker (main disconnect fuse in older systems)

Neutral service wire

Hot service wires

Hot bus bar with circuit breakers (fuses in older systems)

Two 100-amp/110- (120-) volt hot wires and one neutral wire (cable) from power company (one 30-amp/110-volt hot wire in older systems)

Meter

Main service panel

Neutral bus bar

Conduit to house wiring

Main ground wire

Grounding bus bar

Ground wires

Hot wires supply individual circuits or sub-panels.

Ground wire

(Grounding equipment not present in older systems.)

Neutral wires return electricity from circuits or subpanels.

Grounding rod

Note. On some houses the main service panel is located inside the building.

Characteristics of Electrical Systems

DATES (APPROX.)	SIZE AND TYPE OF SERVICE	MAIN PANEL CIRCUIT PROTECTION	SUBPANEL(S)	NUMBER OF CIRCUITS	GROUNDING	INTERNAL WIRING
1900–1925	15–30 amps 110 volts 2 wires	None (or toggle-switch shutoff or early wire fuses)	Rare	1 or 2 per house	None	Knob and tube (sometimes bare neutral)
1925–1950	30 amps 110 volts 2 wires	Glass screw-in fuses	Common (glass screw-in fuses)	2–8 per house	None	Knob and tube (insulated wire throughout)
1950–1965 (transitional period)	30 amps/110 volts 60 amps/110 volts 60 amps/220 volts 80 amps/220 volts 2 or 3 wires	Glass screw-in fuses, cartridge fuses, circuit breakers	Common (glass screw-in fuses or circuit breakers)	6–12 per house	In some houses	Knob and tube 2 wires in sheath (ungrounded) 3 wires in sheath (grounded)
1965–present	100 amps/220 volts 125 amps/220 volts 200 amps/220 volts 3 wires	Circuit breakers	Almost always (circuit breakers)	12–24 per house	For all circuits (GFCIs for some circuits)	3 wires in sheath (grounded)

By just glancing at the weatherhead and counting its wires, then, you can see whether the electrical system can supply a maximum of 30 or 60 amps and 110 volts (which is barely adequate to run even a small modern house) or 80 to 125 amps and 220 volts (which is sufficient to supply a modern three- or four-bedroom house). If there are just two wires, you know immediately that at least the service, if not the entire electrical system, must be upgraded as part of the addition project.

The main panel

After the service wires enter the weatherhead they travel through a "mast," or pipe, pass through the meter, and enter the main panel, which is the second part of the system that must be evaluated.

Open the panel carefully (some boxes are missing their inside cover plates and have exposed hot wires). Vegetation surrounding a box is dangerous, because plants are full of water and excellent conductors—they act like wires leading into the negatively charged ground. Touching a hot wire or a service panel that has a short and accidentally touching a plant at the same time puts you in the middle of a positive to negative flow of electricity, and can be fatal. Cut back any vegetation that is close enough to touch you or the box. Also, wear rubber-soled shoes for insulation from the ground, and avoid standing on wet soil or metal ladders or contacting other conductors when touching any part of an electrical system.

As the service wires enter the main panel, they pass through the main shutoff, which can be one or more fuses in older systems or a switch called the main disconnect circuit breaker in newer models. If the fuses are unscrewed or the main breaker is switched off, the entire electrical system within the house (beyond the switch) is shut down. The main shutoff device in the panel is usually matched to the service wires. Older systems with two weatherhead wires will have fuses, whereas post-transitional three-wire systems usually have circuit breakers.

The service's capacity is usually marked on the main shutoff device. Older 30-amp systems are protected by one or two 30-amp glass screw-in fuses, with their amperage-carrying potential printed on a label inside the glass face. Transitional fuse systems may have glass or cartridge fuses—little cardboard tubes with metal conductors at each end. Cartridge fuses typically carry 60 amps, and some have their capacity printed on their sides. Main disconnect circuit breakers usually have their amperage capacity stamped on the front of the switch. While most modern breakers are designed to "trip," or shut off, at loads of 100 amps or higher, some of the earliest breakers trip at 60 or 80 amps.

Individual circuits In transitional and newer systems, the hot service wires pass through the cartridge fuses or main disconnect breaker and connect to a metal hot bus bar that carries a number of lower-amperage fuses or breakers, each controlling a separate internal circuit. The neutral service wire is attached to the neutral bus bar (see the drawing on p. 144).

Each individual circuit consists of a hot wire, originating at the hot bus bar and protected by a fuse or breaker, one or more devices (such as lights, outlets or an appliance) that use the electricity and a neutral wire returning from the device(s) to the neutral bus bar. Depending on their size, modern houses have between 12 and 24 circuits.

Today's electrical codes require separate 110-volt circuits for the overhead lights (usually two or three circuits in a typical house), the wall outlets (two or three per house) and every major appliance. Modern kitchens alone require the installation of about half a dozen circuits—one or more for the lights and counter outlets and one for each major appliance (including the dish-

washer, trash compactor, garbage disposal, microwave and sometimes the refrigerator). Electric stoves require separate 220-volt circuits.

In the oldest fuse systems, however, the disconnect fuse and the internal circuit fuses are one and the same; that is, the internal wires are directly controlled by the main disconnect fuse. The presence of a single 30-amp fuse not only means that there isn't enough power, but also that just one circuit serves every light, outlet and major appliance in the entire building!

Circuits and the addition Before an addition is built, a 30-amp service that has just one circuit (or even two) should be replaced. More power is needed at the main panel, and new circuits will have to be installed not just for the addition but for almost all of the existing house as well. Rough estimates for the electrical work should be obtained as part of determining the project's feasibility.

Whether they have cartridge fuses or circuit breakers, transitional 60-amp and, in most circumstances, 80-amp services will not supply enough power for the house and the addition, and the service (but not necessarily the internal wiring) will have to be replaced to provide more power. However, there is a difference between the oldest systems and the more up-to-date ones. In the more modern 30-amp systems (1930s to 1950s) and most of the transitional systems there are four, six or more fuses or breakers in the main box, and often subpanels with two or more circuits. (A subpanel is a secondary circuit box located at some distance from the main panel. It redistributes some of the power to circuits in that area.)

If the system has several circuits and the wiring is in good condition, it is likely that most of the existing circuits can be used as they are. That's good news, because rewiring the existing house—feeding wires through closed walls, cutting and replacing plaster—is expensive compared to running new wires for the addition. Although a larger-capacity service will be needed and the addition will require new circuits, there will be an overall savings of between one-third and one-half of the total cost for rewiring the entire house.

Fuses and circuit breakers The increase in service capacity was not the only change made during the transitional period; there was also an advance made from fuses to circuit breakers.

The purpose of a fuse or circuit breaker is to protect the wires from becoming overloaded. If a circuit were not protected and more and more lights and appliance were added to it, its wires would continue to provide electricity up to their capacity and beyond. Eventually the wires would heat up until they literally glowed red hot, melted their insulation and started a fire inside the walls.

The fuse or breaker is gauged to the carrying capacity of the wire it protects. Fuses blow and breakers trip well before demands on the circuit overheat the wire. Fuses can be changed by anyone, however, and unknowing home owners may replace a blown fuse with one of higher capacity, mistakenly thinking that they are improving the electrical system. Using a fuse that allows a greater flow of electricity through its wire actually defeats the fuse's purpose and increases the likelihood of a fire.

Large-capacity (25- or 30-amp) fuses on internal circuits usually indicate an insufficient number of circuits or other problems with the internal wiring. Almost all older circuits have 15-amp wires and originally had 15-amp fuses; 25- or 30-amp fuses were used as replacements when overloading caused the 15-amp fuses to blow. Thirty-amp fuses should be stepped down and replaced with 15s. If they blow with normal usage, more circuits will be needed or the internal wiring may have to be completely replaced.

Changing a circuit breaker is more involved than changing a fuse, and anyone qualified to do so will know enough to install a new breaker of the correct size. If a breaker trips, the home owner, tenant or landlord cannot turn it back on until the lights or appliance that created the excess demand are turned off or disconnected. For this reason, the electrical code has required the use of breakers rather than fuses since the transitional period. (If a breaker continually trips because it is overloaded by normal use, an additional circuit must be installed to carry some of the load.)

How much power is needed? The amount of power required for an addition depends on its size and the number and types of circuits it will need. While precise load calculations for the main wires and subpanels serving the addition should be left to an electrician, it is sufficient for feasibility purposes to say that today's 100- to 125-amp standard service will comfortably supply a three- to four-bedroom, one-kitchen, 2½-bath home of 2,000 to 2,500 sq. ft.

If, for example, a two-bedroom, one-bath house has a 60-amp service, any addition to the house large enough to be worth building—say, converting it to a four-bedroom, two-bath house—will require a new service. Normally, the power should be boosted all the way to 125 amps, which is only slightly more expensive than 100 amps and anticipates future needs.

Internal wiring

After determining the system's capacity and counting the number of circuits at the service entrance (and subpanels), the designer or builder should check the type and condition of the internal wiring where it is visible in the substructure and attic.

Grounding The internal circuits of systems installed before the transitional period have hot and neutral wires only. The wires are spaced about 12 in. apart as they run through the walls and come together at the junction boxes that house light fixtures, switches or outlets. If the hot line is damaged, it cannot easily touch the neutral and cause a dangerous short circuit. The system is known as "knob and tube" wiring and is shown in the drawing on p. 148.

Since the transitional period, the electrical codes have required that a third wire, called the ground wire, be run from one junction box to the next and returned to the grounding bus bar in the main service panel. Ground wires are not intended to carry electricity under normal circumstances. They are safety features and carry a charge only when there is a short in the system caused by loose connections or damage to the hot wire. When there is a short, the ground wire redirects the power to the negatively charged earth (ground) through a steel grounding rod driven into the yard near the main panel. (A cold water pipe is used for grounding in many older houses, though this is no longer legal.)

In modern systems the hot, neutral and ground wires run together in a single, flexible plastic sheath (usually called Romex cable), which is much faster to install than the separated wires of the older knob and

KNOB AND TUBE WIRING

Circuits in most houses built between 1915 and 1950 had two single-strand wires—one hot and one neutral. The wires are spaced about 12 in. apart as they travel through walls and ceilings and come together only in enclosed metal junction boxes that house light fixtures, switches or outlets.

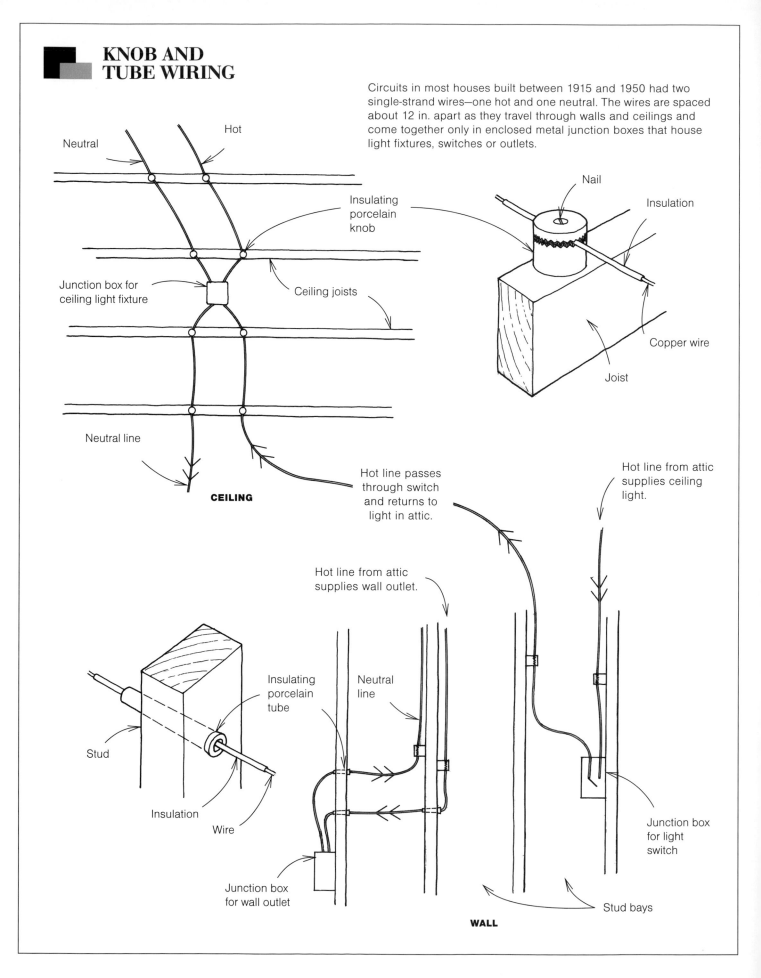

Neutral

Hot

Insulating porcelain knob

Junction box for ceiling light fixture

Ceiling joists

Neutral line

CEILING

Nail

Insulation

Copper wire

Joist

Hot line passes through switch and returns to light in attic.

Hot line from attic supplies ceiling light.

Hot line from attic supplies wall outlet.

Neutral line

Insulating porcelain tube

Stud

Insulation

Wire

Junction box for wall outlet

Junction box for light switch

Stud bays

WALL

tube system. This is known as a three-wire system, as opposed to an ungrounded, two-wire system. (This should not be confused with a system that has three wires entering the weatherhead. "Three-wire system" refers to the internal circuitry, past the fuse box. The ground wire is not directly connected to the service wires but simply runs through the junction boxes and back to the ground.)

All of the electrical work in the addition will be grounded, of course. Whether the existing work also needs to be grounded depends on the factors discussed below.

Mixed systems and safety Many houses have mixed electrical systems, with upgraded services and new circuits serving some areas and the original circuits still intact throughout the rest of the house. The electrical codes do not require the upgrading of properly wired existing circuits when a system is modified.

For example, there is nothing wrong with knob and tube wiring per se, except that it is ungrounded and, because of its age and/or improper fusing, might have failing insulation. Grounding is critical in areas where people themselves can become grounded, like kitchens, bathrooms and outdoor locations where running water and pipes that might be touched are close to electrical outlets. Living rooms, bedrooms and family rooms are less hazardous, and knob and tube circuits in good condition are frequently left in place in these rooms.

Building departments require that existing unsafe wiring be replaced during an upgrade. Wiring is unsafe when it is in bad condition or over-

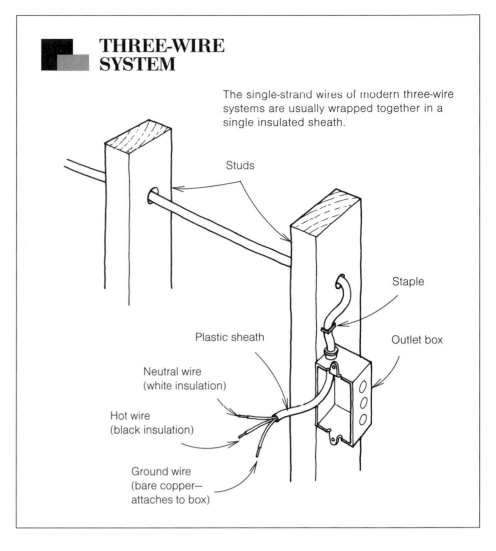

THREE-WIRE SYSTEM

The single-strand wires of modern three-wire systems are usually wrapped together in a single insulated sheath.

Studs

Staple

Plastic sheath

Outlet box

Neutral wire (white insulation)

Hot wire (black insulation)

Ground wire (bare copper— attaches to box)

loaded (specific signs of unsafe wiring are listed in the sidebar on p. 147). A licensed electrician should be called if there is any uncertainty about the system's condition.

As long as all the changes to the original wiring system were done by professional electricians (and with permits), chances are that none of these unsafe conditions exist. If there is an updated service with sufficient power and everything seems to be in good working order, it is safe to assume that electrical costs will for the most part be limited to the wiring of the addition.

THE PLUMBING SYSTEM

If the addition requires plumbing, it is critical to know the local regulations pertaining to water supply and waste-water disposal. Many cities restrict new hookups to conserve water or control density. Similar restrictions apply to increases in sewage discharge. The investigation of the plumbing system, then, should begin at the appropriate governing agency.

Assuming the project is not limited or prohibited by regulations, the designer or builder must determine the adequacy of the existing plumbing to serve the needs of the expanded house. This section covers city and county systems that are dependent on multi-user water supplies and sewers. Private systems with wells and septic tanks are not covered, though the internal plumbing of houses linked to either system is essentially the same.

Supply pipes

Water-district pipes typically join the house's plumbing system in a small, subsurface concrete box at the edge of the street. After the water passes through a water-company shutoff valve and a meter, it enters the house's water service pipe (main supply), which crosses the yard at 2 ft. to 4 ft. below the ground and surfaces inside the house. In most systems there is a house shutoff valve, which can be located just outside the house or in the sub-area (see the drawing below).

Pipe capacity and the addition

The water service pipe must have a large enough internal diameter to allow a sufficient amount of water at the correct pressure to supply the existing house and the addition. The exact sizing of pipes requires determining the number and type of fixtures (toilets, sinks, etc.) to be served and factoring in the water pressure, type of pipe (copper, galvanized or plastic), number of stories in the house and location of the particular pipe along the line—that is, whether it is the main supply, secondary supply (distribution pipe) or supply to an individual fixture.

The main supply pipes to most houses are either ½ in., ¾ in. or 1 in. in diameter; ½-in. pipes are the oldest and no longer allowed by code. For feasibility and preliminary

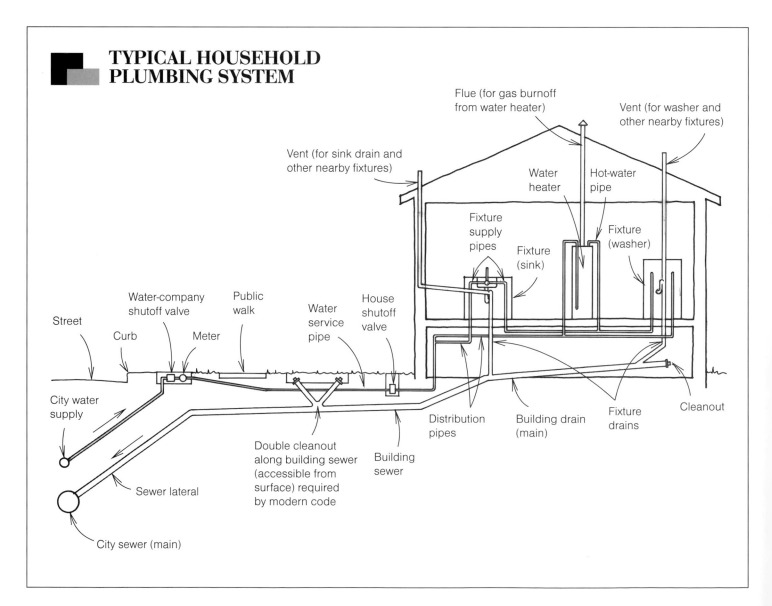

TYPICAL HOUSEHOLD PLUMBING SYSTEM

Flue (for gas burnoff from water heater)

Vent (for washer and other nearby fixtures)

Vent (for sink drain and other nearby fixtures)

Water heater

Hot-water pipe

Fixture supply pipes

Fixture (washer)

Fixture (sink)

Water-company shutoff valve

Public walk

Water service pipe

House shutoff valve

Street

Curb

Meter

City water supply

Double cleanout along building sewer (accessible from surface) required by modern code

Building sewer

Distribution pipes

Building drain (main)

Fixture drains

Cleanout

Sewer lateral

City sewer (main)

design purposes, the designer or builder of an addition can make the following assumptions:

First, if the house has a ½-in. service pipe of any type, the pipe will have to be replaced because it will not supply more than one kitchen and one bathroom, the minimum configuration for any house before it is added to. It is likely that many of the water distribution pipes down line from the main supply will also have to be replaced, since they are old, probably galvanized and likely to be partially clogged (see below).

Second, if the water pressure is adequate, a ¾-in. service pipe in good condition will supply a house with a typical kitchen, two bathrooms and a laundry. If a house with a ¾-in. service pipe has a kitchen, one bathroom and a laundry and the addition will add just one more bathroom, it's reasonable to assume that the service pipe will not have to be replaced and the addition's distribution pipe(s) can tap into it. If a house with a comparable number of fixtures is supplied by a 1-in. pipe, it will almost certainly supply another bath with water to spare.

Third, if the house has a ¾-in. service pipe that is already supplying a kitchen, bathroom, laundry and, let's say, a half bath, and the proposed addition adds another full bathroom, the water supply or pressure may be inadequate and the plumbing inspector may not pass the job. The total number, flow rate and position of the plumbing fixtures must be calculated carefully. Does the existing kitchen have a dishwasher and vegetable sink as well as the regular sink? Will the new bath have a double sink, a vanity, a separate shower or spa?

In marginal situations, even a 1-in. service pipe, especially a galvanized one, might be inadequate. Large additions with many fixtures may require a 1½-in. or 2-in. main supply.

Digging up and replacing the service pipe is a big job and should be avoided if possible. Since factors such as the system pressure and the design and choice of fixtures (flow rates vary) could affect the decision to replace the pipe, it's probably best for the designer to consult a licensed plumber in marginal situations.

The existing service pipe's hypothetical capacity as measured by its diameter is only part of the story: Its condition—whether or not it is clogged and how long it is likely to last—as well is its size determines its real capacity to meet greater demands. The designer or builder must understand something about the different types of pipe to inspect their condition.

Types of supply pipe Three kinds of pipe are used in modern household water supplies: galvanized iron, copper and plastic. (Lead pipe, found in some older houses, is no longer allowed by code and might have to be removed.)

Galvanized pipe, so called because its iron core is coated with rust-resistant zinc applied by electrogalvanic action, is by far the most common type found in older houses. Galvanized pipe is comparatively cheap and easily installed because its connections are threaded and the pipes simply screw together.

Its disadvantage, however, is that the zinc coating dissolves over time, and rust and scale accumulate inside the pipes and slowly reduce

the water flow until the pipes become unusable. While many houses operate adequately for a while on the reduced pressure, adding more plumbing can force the replacement of individual pipes or the whole system.

Copper pipe, while initially more expensive and labor-intensive to install, does not corrode. Old, clogged galvanized pipes are often replaced with copper pipes for this reason. Since the relative cost of copper versus galvanized is such a small part of the overall budget of an addition, it makes sense to choose the more durable alternative for the new plumbing.

Plastic pipe is a mixed blessing. While it is cheaper than copper and easier to install than either copper or galvanized, it hasn't been around long

---

Gas Supply

Gas, like water, must be delivered in sufficient quantity and with enough pressure for fixtures like stoves, water heaters and furnaces to operate efficiently. Factors affecting pipe size include gas pressure, the length of the various runs of pipe and the demands of the appliances. Typical modern service pipes have a 1-in. internal diameter, but the size can vary. Older houses often have smaller pipes.

To determine whether the gas service and distribution pipes are adequate, use the plumbing references in the bibliography or consult the local public utility company, which will usually check the existing system and give advice on the addition for free.

enough for its durability to be firmly established. Also, there is an ongoing debate about the possible toxicity of its petroleum base. Finally, local codes often prohibit the use of plastic pipe for a variety of reasons.

For an addition, then, the best overall choice is usually copper. A hard choice, in many cases, is whether to salvage or scrap the existing system.

Evaluating the supply system
Begin an evaluation of the existing system by inspecting the service and water-distribution pipes. First, measure the external diameter of the pipes and then calculate their internal diameter. Copper and plastic pipe are thin walled, and the internal diameter will be just slightly less than the external. Galvanized pipe has relatively thick walls, and its internal diameter will be about ¼ in. to ⅜ in. less than its external diameter.

Next, look at the joints between the pipes. Galvanized pipes frequently have accumulations of rust, scale or white salt crystals, which indicate internal corrosion. Also, check to see if some sections of the galvanized pipe have been replaced by copper pipes. Those sections were probably clogged or corroded and indicate that the rest of the galvanized system can't be far behind. Normally the only problems that turn up in a copper system are minor leaks, which are usually readily apparent.

If the pipes appear to be in good shape, make a rough check of the pressure by turning on one or two faucets then flushing a toilet. If the flow drops noticeably, the pipes are clogged. If the condition is marginal or unclear, a plumber can pressure-test the system for a modest cost and also give advice and preliminary estimates for plumbing the addition.

If a house has an adequate supply pipe, an all- or mostly copper system and good pressure, the existing system will need little modification and most of the plumbing costs will be limited to the addition. Replacement of or major repair to an existing system, however, is a significant factor in the budget.

Waste and vent pipes
Working back from the fixtures toward the public sewer there are three main types of drainpipe: fixture drains, the building drain and the building sewer.

As their name implies, fixture drains remove waste water from one or more sinks, toilets or other fixtures. The building drain, also known as the main drain, accumulates the discharge from all the fixture drains. It is usually visible in the sub-area and goes underground after all the fixture drains join it and before it crosses beneath the foundation (see the drawing on p. 150). The building sewer starts a few feet outside the foundation line and carries the discharge to the public sewer lateral beyond the property line. (The public sewer lateral drops sharply from its connection to the building sewer to the public sewer main in the street.)

It is possible for some of the addition's plumbing to be attached to existing fixture drains. For example, if a new bathroom is added back to back to an existing bathroom so they share a plumbing wall, the existing pipes can be used, as long they are in the right location and of the proper size.

Pipe capacity
The correct diameter of a waste pipe is determined by several factors, including the slope of the pipe, its orientation (horizontal or vertical), the type of waste discharged (solid, liquid or liquid with grease) and the amount of discharge of the various fixtures draining into the pipe (expressed in fixture units). A variety of specific rules also apply, such as the requirement that a building sewer must have a minimum diameter of 4 in. no matter what the total of the fixture units. The designer or builder must be careful to account for all relevant factors or consult a licensed plumber before deciding that the existing drainpipes will handle the new load.

Fixture Unit Values for Determining Drainpipe Size

TYPE OF FIXTURE	FIXTURE UNIT VALUE
Lavatory	1
Kitchen sink	2
Laundry sink	2
Bathtub (with or without shower)	2
Shower stall	2
Clothes washer	2
Dishwasher	3
Toilet	4

Most houses have a 3-in. or 4-in. diameter building drain. While a 4-in. drain is sufficient to handle almost any residential plumbing system (from 180 to 250 fixture units, depending on the slope), a 3-in. drain may not be. The difference between fixture unit values for 3-in. and 4-in. pipe is dramatic. At ¼-in. fall per foot, for example, a 4-in. pipe is rated for 216 fixture units, while a 3-in. pipe can handle only 27 units. And no matter how little discharge enters a 3-in. pipe, it can handle no more than two toilets. Thus, if a house has a 3-in. building drain, check its slope and number of fixture units to make sure it won't have to be replaced: Chances are, if a new bathroom is installed, it will.

Although visible portions of the building drain may be the code minimum 4 in. in diameter or larger, it is not safe to assume that subterranean portions of drains in older systems are that size. Ask the owners if there have been any problems with the drain clogging, and, if so, have it checked out by a plumber.

Condition of the drains Drains should be checked for their condition as well as their size. Most building drains are cast iron or, if newer, plastic. Cast-iron pipes can be checked by looking for holes in the pipe, rust at the joints or evidence of leaks on the sub-area floor. Also look in the yard above the building drain and building sewer for slumping or softness in the soil, which might indicate a subterranean leak. Check, too, for large trees growing nearby, since roots seeking water and nutrients are likely to penetrate even through cast iron (see the photo on p. 100). Make sure there are cleanouts; if not, add them when building the addition. Finally, check the water flow by turning on several fixtures for a few minutes.

Another potential problem with older plumbing systems is that the roof and yard drainage is dumped into the sewage pipes. One clue that this situation exists is a roof leader disappearing beneath the ground near the point that the main waste pipe leaves the house. This adds rainwater to the system's load in an unpredictable manner, and the field inspector might insist that it

be changed if new fixtures from the addition will be fed into the old pipe. (In most cities, it is now illegal to dump yard or rain water into the sewage system.)

Vent pipes Vent pipes allow air into the drainage system to prevent a vacuum from developing when material moves down the waste pipes. Although the waste pipes may be large enough to handle the new load from the addition, the vent pipes that serve them may not be.

Like supply and waste pipes, the required diameter of a vent is determined by the number of fixtures it serves. For economy, plumbers normally install vents that are just large enough to do the job. Added fixtures, then, might need their own vents. This requirement is particularly important to keep in mind if a new bathroom is built adjacent to an existing one. The proximity of the existing plumbing represents a savings, but most likely an additional vent pipe will have to be installed.

Plumbing and the Floor Plan

When designing an addition, try to place the new plumbing near the old to save the cost of running long supply lines and drains. Ideally, the new and old fixtures should be placed back to back along a common wall so they can share drains and supply pipes. If the back-to-

back arrangement won't work, at least group all the new bathrooms and place them as close to the existing kitchen and bathrooms as possible.

When planning a second story, make sure to provide a vertical path such as a wall, a boxed-in "pipe chase" or an out-of-the-way exterior surface

for the drainpipes. Don't place a new bathroom over the middle of an existing living room, for example, because there is no place for the drains to run.

Drains can travel laterally for a short distance at a minimum slope, usually ¼ in. per ft. Most second-story additions give you a

little extra room for lateral drainpipe travel because the new floor frame is built above the existing ceiling frame. (Supply pipes can travel horizontally through the floor or attic, and can be routed from almost anywhere.)

Water heaters

Older houses typically had 20-gal. water heaters, which are barely adequate for small houses with today's water demands. While a 30-gal. heater is the norm for a four-person household, the addition of a full bathroom will probably increase demand to the point where a 50-gal. unit is more appropriate.

If there are indications that the existing water heater has problems—corroded pipes or casing, leaks, inadequate hot water supply—plan to replace it with a larger model. The cost is reasonable, and the benefits, including more efficient energy use, protection against possible leaks and plenty of hot water, more than outweigh the expense, particularly if the existing unit's size is marginal.

If the addition has extensive plumbing, it may be more practical to provide it with its own water heater than to hook up to the existing one, particularly if the old heater is some distance away.

Trim plumbing

The condition of the trim plumbing—toilets, faucets, shower heads, and so forth—is of less significance for designing the addition than that of the pipes, but it should still be checked. Fixtures wear out over time, and individual faucets with low pressure or toilets that frequently overflow might indicate that the plumbing hidden within the adjacent walls or floors is faulty. Also, the replacement of marginal fixtures should be considered for the architectural continuity provided by matching the old fixtures to those in the addition.

THE HEATING SYSTEM

The addition can be heated in one of two ways: with a central heating system that serves the entire house, or with local area heating systems or room heaters. The choice depends on the size of the addition, the type, capacity and condition of the existing heating system, and whether the owners are looking for long-term or short-term economy.

In general, it is best to consider the house and its addition as one contiguous space and use central heating. In most situations, the cost of running new ducts to carry the hot air from the existing heater, assuming it is adequate, is cheaper than buying and installing new area heaters. Central heaters also use less energy overall. With a "zoned" system that sends heat only to those portions of the house where people are active at certain times of the day, the operating costs are even lower. There are times when expanding the existing central heating system or installing a new one is not the best choice, but before deciding it is necessary to understand something about central heaters.

Central heaters

Most household heaters are run on one of three energy sources: natural gas, the most common overall; oil, still the mainstay in New England and on much of the East Coast; and electricity, an easy-to-install but increasingly expensive-to-operate and ecologically harmful means of heating. Gas heaters are by far the cheapest to run and the kindest to the environment. Public utility companies encourage their use and often give installation rebates or other benefits to home owners who choose them over oil or electricity.

Heater capacity While central heating with gas is usually the best solution, an existing gas heater might have to be upgraded to meet the new demands of an addition. First, the heater must have an adequate capacity as measured by its output of British thermal units (Btus) per hour. The proper sizing of heaters depends on a number of variables, including the size of the house to be heated, the climate and the house's heat-retaining capacity (which depends on architectural configuration, insulation, windows, and so forth), the size and efficiency of the heater, and the length and routing details of the duct system.

The goal is to install a unit that will heat the house at least to code levels with minimal fuel output and operating expense. (The Uniform Plumbing and Heating Code requires a system that can be operated by a switchlike device and maintain a temperature of 70°F at 24 in. above the floor throughout the house.)

To get a sense of whether the heater will be large enough for the house and addition, the designer or builder can check the unit's Btu output, which is usually printed on a metal plate on the front of the outer casing. As a rule, household heaters with outputs of 60,000 to 100,000 Btu/hr. can heat a typical house of 2,000 to 2,500 sq. ft. in a temperate climate. Thus, if 750 sq. ft. of insulated space with standard ceiling heights is added to a 1,500-sq.-ft. house, an existing 80,000-Btu unit—probably the most common size installed in typical houses in recent years—should be able to maintain code comfort level without operating continuously and placing undue stress on the motor. Like all rules of thumb, this one should be followed only with its exceptions in mind: The climate and the house's style and heat-retaining capacity influence the size of heater needed. A more precise evaluation by a heating, ventilation and air-conditioning (HVAC) specialist should be made not long after the preliminary design sketches are complete to confirm that the existing heater is adequate.

Heater type and condition Along with its capacity, the heater's type and condition must also be considered. The earliest central heaters were located below the living space and were gravity operated, which means that the hot air simply rose through the ducts. Today's forced-air heaters are provided with an electric fan that drives the hot air through the ducts. Forced-air heaters are more energy efficient than gravity heaters and can be located on any floor or even in the attic (some models can be laid on their side to fit into tight spaces).

Fans are frequently added to gravity heaters, and many of the old units were oversized and are therefore capable of heating an addition. There are often problems with gravity heaters, however, including corrosion or gas leaks in the heat exchanger (the chamber that isolates the heated air we breathe from the toxic gas or oil burnoff) and the presence of highly toxic asbestos insulative lining between the heat exchanger and the outer casing. Airborne asbestos particles are a serious health hazard, and adding new ducts to an asbestos-lined unit is no longer allowed in many states. A gravity heater should be inspected by the public utility company or a licensed HVAC contractor before it is modified.

Although the more efficient forced-air heaters are usually more carefully sized than gravity heaters, they still might have enough extra capacity to heat a small addition. Like gravity heaters, their condition must be evaluated. Older units may have bad heat exchangers, asbestos insulation, failing motors or other problems.

If the existing central heater is in bad condition or its output is too low, the most practical solution might be to replace it with a new unit of adequate capacity. That way, the existing ducts and supply pipes can be used, and it will not be necessary to create space for a new heater in the addition.

However, technical problems may be encountered when adapting an existing heater or installing a new one. For one thing, the plenum (the sheet-metal box on top of the heater from which the ducts originate) might not have room to accommodate more ducts. If this is the case, it is possible to replace the plenum, usually with a custom-built box, but this would require that all the existing ducts be reconnected to the new plenum. The expense might not be worth it in light of the condition of the heater or compared to the cost of installing area heaters in the addition. A second potential problem is that the plenum and the existing ducts might be covered with asbestos, and new ducts could not be attached to the system unless the original ducts were replaced. Third, there might not be enough room to expand the plenum or route the new ducts.

If it is impractical to use or beef up the existing central heating system, there are two alternatives: to install a second, "central" heater in the addition (which is probably the cheapest and best solution for large additions, say five rooms or more), or to use area heaters.

Area heaters

There are two main types of area heaters: gas wall units, capable of heating more than one room; and permanently wired electric base-board heaters, usually installed in individual rooms. (Plug-in electric heaters and other temporary units do not meet code requirements.)

Another type of area heating system, radiant-floor heating installed in concrete slabs, can offer an excellent level of comfort for some room-addition designs. However, although radiant systems operate economically, they can be expensive to install and require the services of a specialty contractor.

Wall heaters Gas wall heaters can be the right choice for large, open spaces like kitchen/family rooms. The initial installation costs for the unit, its pipes and flues will eventually be offset by cheaper operation (compared to electric heat) if the space is heated on a regular basis. Properly located units with remote thermostats heat large volumes of air uniformly, and their vertical configuration saves wall space.

Although gas wall heaters work well in large, continuous spaces with openings to other parts of the house, most models cannot be installed legally in bedrooms because they use up the room's oxygen as they burn. Installing them in a hall, to serve several bedrooms, is a questionable proposition. Heat can be wasted in the hall while the individual rooms remain cold. Also, doors must remain ajar to allow at least some heat in, and privacy is compromised. One other drawback of wall heaters is that many people don't like their appearance, though newer units tend to have more pleasing designs.

Baseboard heaters If there is an adequate electrical supply, electric baseboard heaters can be the best choice for an addition, especially if individual rooms are to be heated, since the units are cheaper and easier to install than gas heaters. Although baseboard heaters are not energy efficient, electrical bills can be kept down if the heaters are of the radiant type supplied with 220 volts and equipped with a thermostat and timer.

Baseboard heaters are quiet and clean and do not use up the room's oxygen. Their main limitation is that they can heat only relatively small spaces, like bedrooms or studies, so several units are needed for a typical addition. Also, they take up a fair amount of wall space and should not have furniture placed directly in front of them. Ideally, they should be located beneath a window where their rising, warm air will mix with the cool air near the glass (and where furniture would not be placed anyway).

Choosing a heater

The ultimate design of the heating system should depend as much on its intended use as on the technical factors involved. Although zoned central heating is usually the best overall solution, an infrequently used guest room might be served well enough by an electric baseboard heater, especially if the electrical system must be upgraded anyway and the existing central heater has marginal capacity for expan-

sion. Also, some "additions," such as attached solar greenhouses, can be treated as unconditioned spaces, that is, spaces that by code do not require heating, as long as there is a way to separate them from the conditioned, or heated, space. A sliding glass patio door, normally used to separate conditioned space from the outdoors, is acceptable, and the unconditioned space could be equipped with a portable heater.

Alternative heating systems

The standard means of heating a house discussed thus far are mandated by law and will therefore have to be included whenever a conditioned space is added to a house. It is difficult, however, to overstate the value of alternative systems, especially the use of passive solar design, and, to a lesser extent, the use of energy-efficient wood-burning stoves and other devices. Passive solar design was considered briefly in Chapter 5. While there is not space to discuss the recent developments in wood-burning technology, a few comments are warranted since many owners want to have fireplaces in their additions.

As a heating device, the traditional fireplace is a thing of the past. Far more heat goes up the chimney than into the room, and fuel use and pollution levels are unconscionable. There are, however, many extremely attractive alternatives in the form of small, highly efficient wood-burning stoves that meet the EPA's pollution standards. They use a minimal amount of wood, and sometimes burn "pellets" of mill scraps. Wood-burning stoves are less expensive than many fireplaces and serve the same aesthetic and emotional purpose, allowing people to gather around a hearth and open flame on chilly nights.

Although people frequently use such stoves as their primary, if not only heating device, regulation heaters are still required. Owners who intend to use alternative heating can install the cheapest standard devices, usually electric baseboard heaters, and simply not use them. It's important for the designer to make sure of the owners' resolve to use the stoves, however, because baseboard heaters are among the least energy-efficient of heating devices. If the owners get in the habit of simply flipping on the switch of the baseboard heater, they will not only have to pay excessive electrical bills, but also defeat the environmental purposes of installing the stove in the first place.

INSULATION

Many states now require insulation for all new spaces, and, frequently, in existing uninsulated, heated spaces if the building or its heating system is altered. Whether it is required or not, installing insulation is a good idea, and one of the best long-term investments of the home owner's money.

An insulation's resistance to heat loss is called its R-factor. R-factors vary from one material to another and increase in direct proportion to the thickness of the insulation. Fiberglass batts (paper-backed strips), for example, are R-11 or R-13 at 3½ in. and R-19 at 5½-in. thickness (the width of 2x4 and 2x6 studs and ceiling joists). Standard 3-in. thick rigid urethane foam panels are R-22, which means they provide about twice the R-value per inch of fiberglass. Urethane is three or four times the price of fiberglass, however, and the relative energy savings may not justify the cost.

There are several other types of readily available insulation, which vary in R-value and cost. Most of them fall within the ranges given above for fiberglass and urethane foam. While the choice (panels, batts, blown-in powder or other types) depends on the application, I recommend that you avoid the blown-in powder, if possible. It's cheap and easy to install, but it settles (losing some of its R-value), gets into the light and fan fixtures in the attic and hides the ceiling joists (making it dangerous to walk about and difficult to perform electrical repairs or other work).

Many factors, including the climate, site, massing of the house, amount of solar gain, type of glazing and the projected cost of energy vs. the amortized cost of energy-saving technology, determine the appropriate amount, type and placement of the insulation. The optimum balancing of these factors is an art in itself. References on energy design are given in the bibliography for those who wish to tackle the subject. It is perhaps more practical, however, to take advantage of the services of the growing cadre of energy-calculation specialists who, for a reasonable cost, can analyze the plans and specify the amount of insulation needed to satisfy regulations or for voluntary energy-efficiency upgrades.

Insulation and architecture

Since insulation can be worked into most hollow wall structures, it is usually acceptable for standard construction in temperate climates to proceed with the design and have an energy consultant provide specifications when the working drawings are in the final stages. It is a good idea to run the preliminary design drawings by the consultant, however, because there are times when the insulation affects the architecture of the building.

In areas with extreme temperatures, for example, high R-factors must be attained in order to make insulation effective at all. While the R-value can easily be raised in typical attics by piling one layer of insulation upon the next until sufficient depth is achieved, the thickness of the walls is often determined by the most cost-effective means of insulating them. If R-19 minimum walls are recommended or required, for example, 2x4 (3½-in.) walls with fiberglass-batt insulation, valued at R-11 or R-13, will not work. The designer will have to decide whether it is cheaper to build the addition with 2x6 walls with fiberglass insulation valued at R-19—even though there is no structural reason to use 2x6s—or standard 2x4 walls with 3-in., R-22 urethane panels at four times the cost. The cost of the insulation is not the only consideration, however. Two-by-sixes themselves are more expensive than 2x4s, and doors and windows with jambs based on 2x6 framing may be expensive or hard to find.

In another example, the thickness of the roof insulation, which can vary from 5½ in. to 11 in. or more, determines the thickness, weight, appearance and cost of the roof where there is no attic (an exposed-beam ceiling, for example) and insulation is installed above the soffit. The need to insulate the addition's floor is an important cost item, too, as is the need to increase insulation in the existing house. Both of these may be required in extreme climate zones.

OVERALL EVALUATION

Making an assessment of the site and soil conditions, the house's structure and the subsystems is critical to determining both the feasibility and appropriate design of the addition. The condition of a particular system may determine the addition's type or otherwise change the design strategy. The designer must be able to assess many systems accurately and efficiently, and decide whether the proposed project should be built, modified or abandoned before too much time or money has been spent.

It helps, of course, to have the opinions of specialists, but it is often impractical, particularly during the early feasibility assessment, to bring in a consultant for every system and aspect of the project. To some extent, designers and builders are on their own; they have both the first word and the dubious honor of standing where the buck stops.

To facilitate evaluating the building's condition, I suggest that the designer or builder of an addition create an "Existing Conditions Checklist" similar to the one shown in Appendix I. Items on the checklist can be derived from this book and other sources, as well as the designer or builder's own experience. The list will grow and change over time and will have to be modified somewhat for each project. The checklist is an indispensable tool for making a quick and reasonably thorough evaluation of the major systems and how their condition and capacities will influence the addition's budget and design.

10
CITY HALL

As well as addressing the technical problems discussed in previous chapters, designers and builders must make sure that the addition complies with the laws governing construction—principally building codes and zoning ordinances. Most residential construction is regulated by local, rather than federal or state authorities. Until the publication of the first Uniform Building Code (UBC) in 1927, the various municipalities and counties had to write their own codes. Confusion resulted, because builders and designers who worked in more than one community had to change their accustomed practices, learn regulations that they might use only once, or find that a structure that was considered safe in one jurisdiction was not in another.

The UBC was created and published by committees of engineers, architects, contractors, tradesmen, suppliers and building officials to set a single standard for everyone involved in construction. The UBC and other Uniform Codes (Plumbing, Mechanical, Fire, etc.) are not laws themselves but a set of building conventions voluntarily adopted by most municipalities and counties as the basis of their own building regulations.

The UBC deals with construction and building safety only; it does not regulate the many other ways in which the creation of a new building affects the community. To control these non-construction aspects of building, most jurisdictions have created departments of planning and zoning, and also have proposed projects reviewed by their public works, fire and traffic-engineering departments. Projects that expand the footprint or shell of a building or increase its potential occupancy load (i.e., all additions) must be approved by most or all of these departments.

Planning and zoning regulations affect broad aspects of the addition project that must be accounted for before the preliminary designing begins. Plan reviews and zoning-ordinance compliance checks probably delay more addition projects than any other single set of regulations. As a designer or builder would in actual practice, we will consider the planning and zoning requirements first, then turn our attention to the building codes.

THE PLANNING AND ZONING DEPARTMENT

A planning and zoning department writes and enforces the regulations that control those aspects of the built environment that affect the quality of life in the community. Although most jurisdictions combine planning and zoning into a single department, the two branches normally have somewhat different areas of responsibility. The planning branch deals with issues such as the long-range development of the community, the allowable density and type of housing within a residential district and, sometimes, the aesthetic or architectural qualities of buildings.

Typically, city planners in the planning branch study the issues and propose general regulations or solutions to specific problems, which are then adopted by a publicly elected planning commission and made into laws (usually called "zoning ordinances"). The planning commission ultimately operates under the jurisdiction of the city council and mayor, or an equivalent group of elected representatives.

Zoning ordinances

The zoning branch may be thought of as the administrative or enforcement agency of the planning and zoning department. Zoning maintains maps, surveys and documents, checks plans for compliance to the zoning ordinances and provides information for designers and the general public. The designer of an addition should call or visit the zoning office even before the initial feasibility consultation. Then addition proposals that will not comply with the zoning ordinances can be eliminated from the outset.

Typical zoning ordinances affecting additions cover the building's use, residential density, the building's design envelope and architectural design reviews.

Use The purposes for which a building may be used depend upon its location within the town or jurisdiction. Retail commercial development, for example, is normally prohibited in residential districts. Though at one time it was fairly common to see small stores, hair salons or craft shops built onto the front of houses, such additions would be against the rules in most communities today. Exceptions are rare, since neighbors are likely to object to such projects because of increased traffic, and for aesthetic and other reasons. This use restriction may change, however, as commuting becomes increasingly difficult and the traditional walk to the corner store has renewed appeal.

One challenge to the restrictions on commercial use is the growing trend to use all or part of an addition as a home office. While the intent of the use regulations is to protect the quality of life in a residential district—thus, an office with clients coming and going and several workers needing parking would be frowned upon—rush-hour traffic jams and the availability of new telecommuting tools have greatly increased the demand for home offices. Also, the restrictions are largely unenforceable, since a space shown on the plans as a bedroom or den can easily enough be used as an office. Pressure is being put on planning commissions to make home offices legal so they will be

TYPICAL DESIGN-ENVELOPE REQUIREMENTS

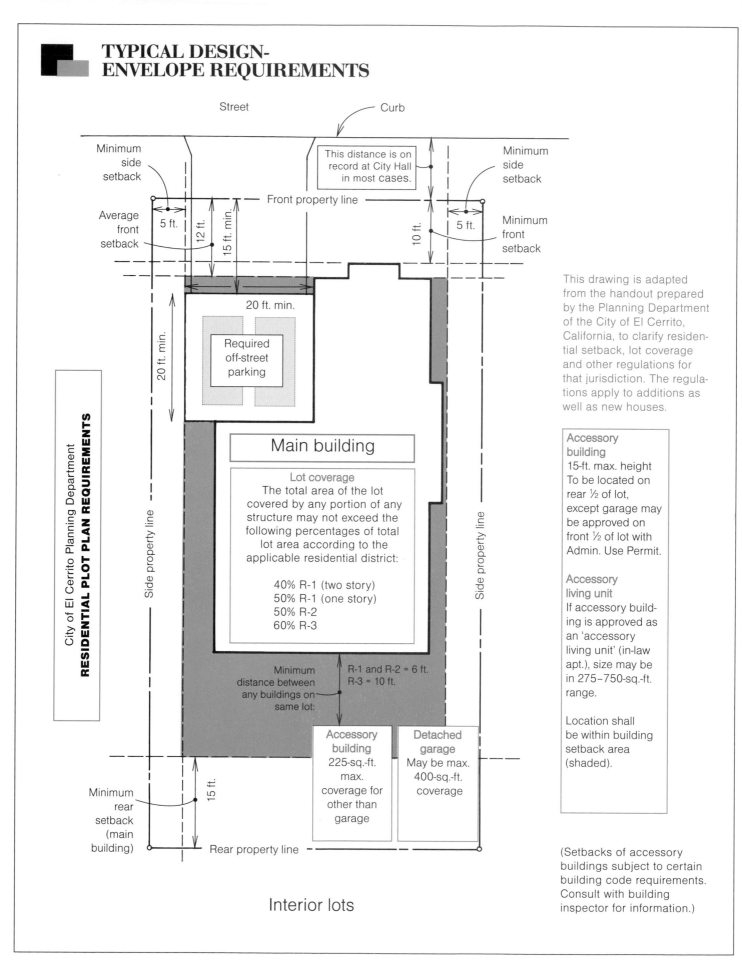

Street

Curb

Minimum side setback

This distance is on record at City Hall in most cases.

Minimum side setback

Front property line

Average front setback

5 ft.

12 ft.

15 ft. min.

10 ft.

5 ft.

Minimum front setback

20 ft. min.

20 ft. min.

Required off-street parking

City of El Cerrito Planning Department
RESIDENTIAL PLOT PLAN REQUIREMENTS

Side property line

Main building

Lot coverage
The total area of the lot covered by any portion of any structure may not exceed the following percentages of total lot area according to the applicable residential district:

40% R-1 (two story)
50% R-1 (one story)
50% R-2
60% R-3

Side property line

Minimum distance between any buildings on same lot:

R-1 and R-2 = 6 ft.
R-3 = 10 ft.

Minimum rear setback (main building)

15 ft.

Accessory building
225-sq.-ft. max. coverage for other than garage

Detached garage
May be max. 400-sq.-ft. coverage

Rear property line

Interior lots

This drawing is adapted from the handout prepared by the Planning Department of the City of El Cerrito, California, to clarify residential setback, lot coverage and other regulations for that jurisdiction. The regulations apply to additions as well as new houses.

Accessory building
15-ft. max. height
To be located on rear ½ of lot, except garage may be approved on front ½ of lot with Admin. Use Permit.

Accessory living unit
If accessory building is approved as an 'accessory living unit' (in-law apt.), size may be in 275–750-sq.-ft. range.

Location shall be within building setback area (shaded).

(Setbacks of accessory buildings subject to certain building code requirements. Consult with building inspector for information.)

fully insurable and in compliance with business regulations.

Other use restrictions may prohibit the building of rooms to house certain potentially dangerous pets or noisy rehearsal studios. Also, zoning restrictions frequently control the minimum sizes, egress, ventilation and other health and safety features of rooms (as do portions of the UBC) and should be checked carefully.

Density Density regulations restrict the number of dwelling units allowed on one lot in a given district. On most zoning maps, a capital "R" followed by a number identifies a residential district. The number tells us how many dwelling units are allowed per lot: R-1 is single family; R-2, duplexes; and R-3 and R-4 cover larger residential complexes.

An addition is usually defined as a "second unit" (separate apartment) if it has its own kitchen, that is, if it has facilities that could allow a separate, unrelated individual or family to occupy part of the house. It is against most zoning ordinances to build an addition with its own kitchen onto a house in an R-1 zone unless the original kitchen is torn out. While it is often possible to obtain a variance (see p. 165), related restrictions like a requirement to provide off-street parking for the second unit could bring the project's feasibility into question.

Design envelope The design envelope is the legal limit of the building's size as determined by *setbacks*, or the distance from the property line where the building must stand; the building's *footprint,* or the percentage of the lot covered by its base; *height restrictions*; and *easements*, or legal rights of way through

SETBACKS AND ADDITIONS

Even if existing portions of a house are within the setback zone, they cannot be extended horizontally or vertically without a variance.

**ROOM ADDITION
(PLAN VIEW)**

- Current setback line
- Original setback line
- Proposed room addition
- This portion illegal without variance
- Existing house
- Portion of existing house in current setback zone
- Property line

- Vertical projection of current setback line
- Vertical projection of original setback line
- Vertical projection of property line
- Proposed second-story addition
- This portion illegal without variance
- Portion of existing house in current setback zone

**SECOND-STORY ADDITION
(ELEVATION)**

the property. It is important to distinguish between the legal design envelope and the building's shell, which is the physical, external skin of the existing building and proposed addition.

Many jurisdictions have changed their design-envelope requirements over the years. *Setbacks,* for example, are usually greater today than they were in the past, and it is not safe to assume that just because a house is a certain distance from a property line that an addition can be built adjacent to or even above the existing walls (see the drawing on p. 161). Setbacks usually pertain to walls but may apply to any projecting portion of the building, including roof overhangs.

While variances can be obtained to relax zoning-ordinance setbacks in some cases, building-code variances are hardly ever allowed. With rare exceptions, the UBC restriction that no projecting portion or overhang of a residential building may extend closer than 3 ft. to the property line should be taken as an absolute by designers and builders.

Setback requirements can vary considerably, even within sub-areas of one residential zone. If an R-1 district includes both mid-priced and expensive properties, for example, the side setbacks could vary from 5 ft. for the less expensive lots to 10 ft. or more in plush neighborhoods with larger lots.

Property lines from which setback lines are derived can sometimes be located accurately enough for building purposes by measuring to existing fences, adjacent buildings, public walks and other landmarks,

then checking those measurements against property records. If two side fences are 49 ft. 6 in. apart, for example, and the lot is described on the deed, county assessor's records or other legal documents as 50 ft. wide, the property lines can be shown as 50 ft. apart on the proposed site plan and an addition that is the correct distance from the fence will probably be acceptable. It is not safe to assume that this approximate location of the property line will be accepted, however, and the designer or builder should check with the zoning department to see if a survey is required.

The fee for a legal survey depends on the location of the nearest benchmark—which could be anywhere from a block to a mile away—and the number of obstacles between the benchmark and the property. It is seldom necessary to have an entire property surveyed to build an addition. One side line is usually sufficient, for example, since the other dimensions can be extrapolated from it. If there are questions about front or rear setbacks, one of those lines, whichever is cheaper to survey, may also be needed.

The *footprint,* or the area used for calculating the building's lot coverage, is usually defined as the base of the building proper, not adjunct structures like decks. The lot area is the product of the length and width of the property lines as described in legal records. Figuring unusually shaped lots may take a few extra steps, but the geometry is straightforward and the formulas are readily available in construction and design manuals (see the bibliography).

Most jurisdictions regulate the heights of buildings to preserve the neighbors' views and access to

sunlight. *Height restrictions* vary depending on the jurisdiction. Some towns allow nothing over two stories, period. Others base requirements on location—hillside lots featuring premium views differ from those in the flatlands where available sunlight may be the principal consideration.

Height restrictions pertain to the ridge line, not incidental projections like chimneys. On flat sites, the height is usually measured from the grade to the ridge line. Methods for calculating heights on sloping sites vary from jurisdiction to jurisdiction (see the top drawing on the facing page); check with the zoning office to make sure the accepted method is used.

To match existing roof lines, or for other architectural reasons, it may be appropriate to design a roof with a steep pitch in an area that has height restrictions. Be aware that the steep roof can reduce the floor space, since the Uniform Building Code states that the soffit must be 7 ft. 6 in. high over at least 50% of the floor area (see the bottom drawing on the facing page). Floor area is defined as those portions of the room that have a soffit of at least 5 ft. 0 in. Areas with soffits below 5 ft. 0 in. may be used for storage or other purposes but may not be counted as part of the floor space for the ceiling-height calculation.

Easements can also impinge upon the design envelope. Generally, it is illegal to build any permanent structure over or within an easement, even if the right of way is not currently in use. For example, if a city or county holds a sewer easement through a property but does

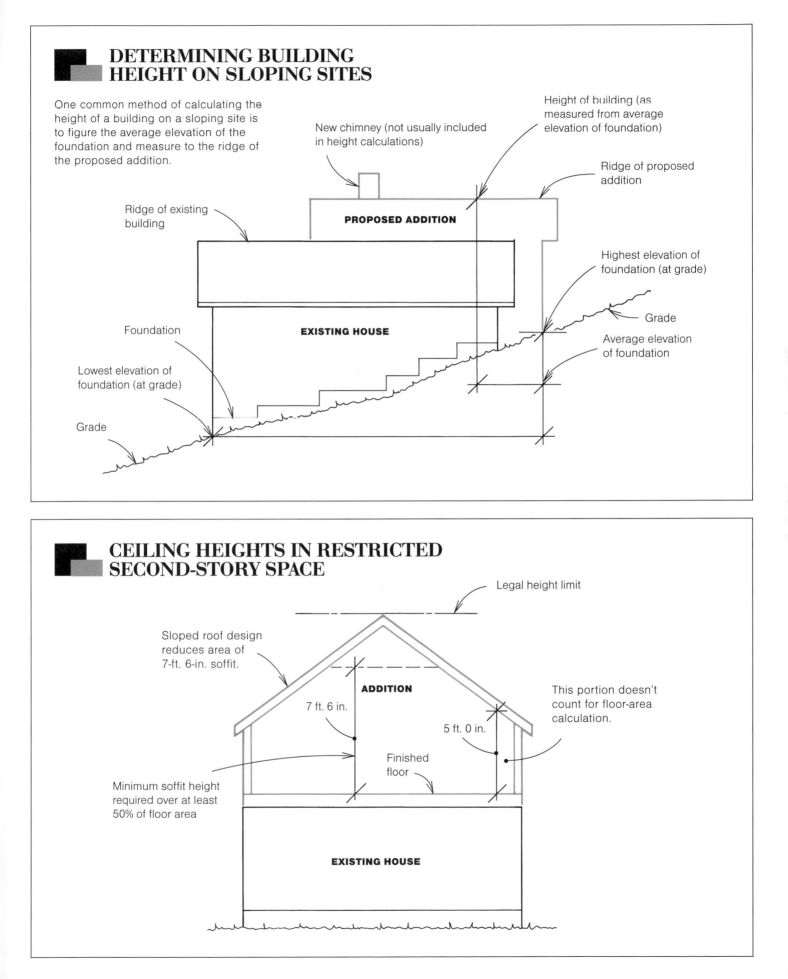

DETERMINING BUILDING HEIGHT ON SLOPING SITES

One common method of calculating the height of a building on a sloping site is to figure the average elevation of the foundation and measure to the ridge of the proposed addition.

New chimney (not usually included in height calculations)

Height of building (as measured from average elevation of foundation)

Ridge of proposed addition

Ridge of existing building

PROPOSED ADDITION

EXISTING HOUSE

Highest elevation of foundation (at grade)

Grade

Average elevation of foundation

Foundation

Lowest elevation of foundation (at grade)

Grade

CEILING HEIGHTS IN RESTRICTED SECOND-STORY SPACE

Legal height limit

Sloped roof design reduces area of 7-ft. 6-in. soffit.

ADDITION

7 ft. 6 in.

This portion doesn't count for floor-area calculation.

5 ft. 0 in.

Finished floor

Minimum soffit height required over at least 50% of floor area

EXISTING HOUSE

not have a sewer line in place, it is unlikely to give up its rights because the easement was probably originally planned as part of some future development. Fortunately, many easements are along the edges of properties, in the zone already restricted by setbacks, and will not affect the design. Still, the designer or builder should check with the zoning department to make sure that easements don't cut into the design envelope.

Architectural design reviews Many jurisdictions today require a design review, which may or may not involve a public hearing. Design restrictions can be minimal, perhaps simply ensuring that the pad for garbage cans is placed behind the building rather than in public view. They may also be quite detailed, as in the case of historic Santa Barbara, California, which requires all buildings to be in the Spanish Colonial style, complete with rounded roof tiles and white stucco exteriors that mimic the original whitewashed adobe structures of the area. Before beginning

---

Dealing with Planning and Zoning

A workable approach to dealing with planning and zoning requirements is as important to a successful addition project as, say, the correct sizing of structural members. The following strategies will be helpful:

1. Gather planning and zoning information early. Call the zoning office even before the feasibility consultation (see Chapter 1) and find out about the site's use and density requirements, design-envelope restrictions and design-review requirements. Having this information at the preliminary feasibility consultation can save a lot of time.

2. Take the preliminary design sketches to the zoning office and discuss them with a staff member. Some jurisdictions regularly schedule such pre-design conferences. In others, the designer or builder will have to find a staff member who is empowered to give tentative approval to the design before it is developed further.

3. Get on the planning-commission calendar as soon as possible. Planning commissions usually meet in the evening, once or twice a month. (Most commission members are not professional planners, but elected citizens with other jobs.) Only a certain number of cases are scheduled for each hearing, and they take more or less time to hear according to their complexity. Cases that can't be heard spill over into the next meeting. It can take months for a variance application or design review to be considered. Get on the calendar even if the need for a hearing is uncertain—the appointment can always be canceled.

If possible, sign up immediately and bring plans in later. If plans and documents are needed to get on the calendar, dash something off and get it in the file. It can be modified up until the deadline, which is usually a couple of weeks before the hearing.

4. Seek variances only when absolutely necessary. Though they are usually affordable, even minor variances are not cheap, and can cause considerable delays, if they are granted at all. Ideally, zoning ordinances should be treated like existing site conditions, structural limitations or any other given: The good designer will find creative ways to comply and still meet the program requirements.

In some cases, however, obtaining the variance will significantly reduce the construction costs or have a major impact on the addition's function or style. Then, and only then, should the designer suggest that the owners try for a variance.

5. Make friends of the neighbors. Whether or not the design requires a variance, it's a good idea to try to get the neighbors to support the project. Neighbors often know things about the area or site that the owners (especially new owners), designers or builders are unaware of. They may have good design suggestions, too. Sometimes a minor concession, like trimming a tree that blocks a view, can win their support for a critical variance.

6. Don't start on the working drawings until after the hearing. The planning and zoning office usually requires scaled design drawings for approval. This requirement is not a major inconvenience to the designer, however, because even preliminary addition designs should be drawn over a scaled template so they can be easily converted to working drawings (see Chapter 12). If the project is not approved, however, time spent on the working drawings themselves will be wasted.

7. Have a backup plan. If a height-restriction variance is sought, the planning commission may approve the project but may still insist that the height be lowered somewhat, perhaps enough to accommodate a particular neighbor's view. When developing the preliminary design, make sure the addition will work with the truncated roof. Explain the backup plan to the owners before submitting the preferred plans, which may need to be modified.

---

to design, check to see what aesthetic guidelines or restrictions, if any, apply to houses and additions in the area.

Variances

An addition's plans are initially checked for compliance to use, density, design-envelope and architectural design restrictions by the planning and zoning staff. If the design is not in compliance with zoning restrictions, the applicant may seek a variance.

Variances are exceptions to the regulations allowed for one particular project. Their existence is a recognition of the impossibility of writing an ordinance that covers every possible exigency. Variances are of two types: minor variances and major variances.

Minor variances Commonly sought minor variances involve expanding the design envelope or adding a legally zoned second unit (R-2) without meeting all the requirements—that of providing additional off-street parking, for example.

Applications for minor variances are reasonably priced, and many minor variances are granted. In many jurisdictions, in fact, some types of minor variances can be granted by the zoning staff without any public input. These are called administrative variances, and save the applicant the delays and potential traumas of a public planning commission hearing.

Most minor variances have a potential effect on the neighbors' quality of life or property values, however, and thus require a public hearing.

(In some cities, all projects require a hearing.) In a typical scenario, the zoning staff sends written notifications informing all neighbors within a certain distance—usually for two or three houses up and down the street and directly across—that an addition project has been proposed. The neighbors and general public then have a right to comment on or object to the project in writing or in person at a planning commission hearing. A hearing date is set, usually at least 30 days (and sometimes up to six months) from the date of the application.

Shortly before the hearing date, the deadline for written public input passes, and the property file is closed. The zoning staff meets to discuss its findings and the public input, if any. The staff then makes a written recommendation to grant, deny or modify the variance to the planning commissioners, who read the file before the hearing. Staff recommendations carry considerable weight since members of the staff are trained in the field, should have the benefit of the entire community in mind, and work regularly with the commissioners.

If there are written objections from neighbors, they may be commented on in the staff report. Since the neighbors also have a right to speak before the planning commission, the staff normally limits its comments to citing the applicable regulations, and lets the commission make the final decision.

Depending on its nature, public input is given greater or lesser consideration. If the neighborhood grouch who made a big stink over a minor issue in a case a few meetings ago shows up at the hearing and objects to the project on spurious grounds,

chances are his wishes will be ignored. Reasoned arguments and objections by more than one neighbor will naturally have greater influence.

While it is difficult to stop a project that is in compliance with zoning ordinances, a variance application can be turned down for the slightest reason, and neighbors' objections may be one of them.

When listening to contested applications, the planning commission weighs the staff's recommendations, public input, the applicant's arguments and its own members' opinions. Depending on the complexity of the issue, the commission may reach its decision during the hearing or postpone deciding until a future meeting, allowing more time for debate or staff research. Whether a variance is major or minor, whether it is decided administratively or through the hearing process, its success is never guaranteed until the commission decides.

Major variances Major variances are usually required to override use and density regulations. You may not turn a house into a store or build a second unit in an R-1 zone without a major variance, for example. Applications for major variances are expensive and almost always require the opportunity for public input at a planning commission hearing. They are unlikely to succeed unless some special need or severe hardship on the part of the applicant can be proven.

Commissions and staffs grant variances only when they do not defeat the intent of the law. Frequently, therefore, variances are granted

HEIGHT VARIANCE WITH CONDITIONS

Because of existing height restrictions, a variance was needed in order to build a second story on this house and provide it with a code minimum ceiling height of 7 ft. 6 in. Since the height limit had to be exceeded in order to build the addition at all, the designer proposed a steep roof under the same variance application.

Neighbors objected that the roof would block their view. The planning commission granted a variance to build the addition, but with the condition that the overall building height would be restricted to 2 ft. above the legal height limit. This allowed enough room to build the 7-ft. 6-in. ceiling and cover it with a flat roof while preserving the neighbors' view.

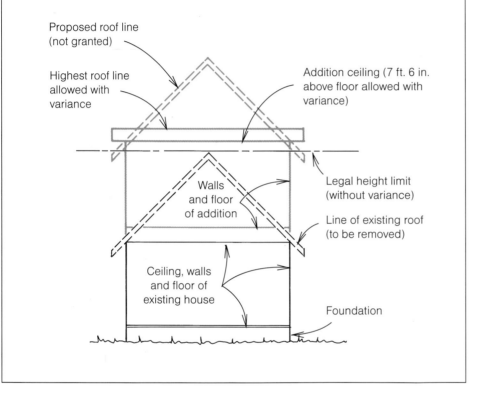

Proposed roof line (not granted)

Highest roof line allowed with variance

Addition ceiling (7 ft. 6 in. above floor allowed with variance)

Walls and floor of addition

Legal height limit (without variance)

Line of existing roof (to be removed)

Ceiling, walls and floor of existing house

Foundation

with conditions (see the drawing above). While the conditions may eliminate the designer or owners' first choice, or raise the cost of the project, they are usually not so severe as to prevent a modified version of the project from being built.

Appeals

Planning-commission decisions can be appealed. Normally, appeals are taken first to the city council or the county board of supervisors, and ultimately to the courts. These higher authorities are reluctant to overturn the commission's decisions, however. The commission is deemed to have expertise in the field, and busy councils and courts do not want to set a precedent of inviting every disappointed applicant to come their way. Also, there must be a good legal reason to override the commission's authority.

As a practical matter, designs are usually adjusted to the planning commission's requirements. If the applicant feels that it is a matter of principle, a case can be appealed more or less indefinitely. The applicant must decide how to spend his or her time and money: litigating or building.

THE BUILDING DEPARTMENT

While the planning and zoning department creates and enforces ordinances that regulate the ways in which a building project affects its neighborhood and community, the building department is concerned solely with the building itself—primarily its safety and durability as determined by its design and construction and the quality of materials used. The specific functions and responsibilities of building departments will be considered below, but first let's take a look at the nature and purpose of the building codes and their application to additions.

Building codes

Most communities have adopted verbatim the entire Uniform Building Code (UBC) and its related Uniform Codes covering plumbing, mechanical installations and fire safety as the model code on which they base their own building codes. Although the UBC is not the only model code—residential wiring, for example, is covered by the National Electrical Code (NEC)—it is by far the most commonly used.

In addition to the UBC, many jurisdictions have special building regulations of their own, known as "local codes." Local codes typically strengthen the minimum requirements of the UBC and occasionally regulate some aspect of construction not covered by it. Local jurisdictions may also be charged with enforcing state codes or federal regulations or specifications. While federal regulations seldom apply to private residential additions, state health-hazard, energy and other regulations frequently do.

The designer or builder working in an unfamiliar jurisdiction should call the building department and find out, first, if it has adopted the UBC, and, second, what other codes might apply to the project. Building departments normally sell their local code books, and may also provide extracts from relevant state regulations.

Concerns for safety It is important to understand that the primary intent of the UBC is to make buildings safe. Many of the lessons behind the regulations were learned the hard way, as lives and property were lost to structural failure or fire. It is equally important to realize that the codes do not mandate particular solutions, but allow us to build in any way we choose, as long as it is safe.

Despite popular misconceptions about needless regulations and bureaucracy, the codes are actually designed to function, and for the most part do function, as an important public safeguard without impinging on anyone's reasonable rights. Their effectiveness in protecting lives and property may be verified by the results of two major earthquakes of approximately equal strength: the first in 1989 in the densely populated San Francisco Bay Region, in which 56 people died (fewer than 20 because of building failures); the second in 1993 in an essentially unregulated rural region of India, in which more than 20,000 people died, some from cholera and starvation, but many because their homes, stores and public buildings collapsed.

Keep in mind that the codes set minimum standards only, and that they are not themselves sufficient to guarantee the safety of structures. Many code requirements —the spacing of anchor bolts, for example—must be exceeded to ensure an acceptable degree of safety in some areas. The UBC may be used as a starting point or reference for builders who, when striving to do the best job, may often surpass its standards.

The Uniform Building Code and additions The UBC states that the addition must be built according to current codes for new buildings and may not weaken or otherwise cause the existing building to become unsafe. If the existing building is below current code, it may be added to without being upgraded, provided that the addition does not make it less safe.

While some ways of reducing a building's safety, like closing existing exits without providing new ones, are obvious, others are less so. Mixing foundation types in seismic or landslide zones, for example, is not specifically against code and could easily be overlooked even by building officials, particularly in rural districts that may not have structural specialists on the building-department staff. In such cases, it is up to the designer and engineers to do as conscientious a job as possible in complying with the spirit, if not the letter, of the law.

The Code Books

The Uniform Codes are available in two forms: comprehensive volumes and shorter volumes.

Comprehensive volumes, which average almost 1,000 pages in length, cover all types of construction and contain a great deal of information that is not needed for building houses or additions. Only some of this information is organized according to building types; that is, residential requirements are frequently mixed in with, and sometimes indistinguishable from, those of other buildings and structures.

Shorter volumes, averaging about 100 pages, cover residential construction only. Published under the titles "Dwelling Construction under the Uniform Building (or Mechanical) Code," these handy booklets contain almost all of the information needed to design an addition. They are easier to use and considerably less expen

sive than the comprehensive codes from which they are derived. Each section of the shorter codes is followed by a reference to the parent edition, so more detailed regulations can be readily located. (Public libraries frequently have copies of the comprehensive Uniform Codes.)

Dealing with the building department

If all goes well, the designer of an addition will have to make just three trips to city hall: one to the zoning department (see above) and two to the building department.

Submitting the plans The first visit to the building department is to apply for a building permit (for more on permits, see p. 170). The permit application must be accompanied by a set of working drawings (which should be completed after the preliminary design has been approved by zoning). While scaled design drawings are sufficient for a planning and zoning review, the building department will accept only complete working drawings (with all the construction details), since they need to review every facet of the project before issuing a permit. (The requirements for working drawings are presented in the table on p. 206.)

The Role of the Building Department

A typical building department has four basic responsibilities:

1. Checking plans to make sure they comply with the codes.

2. Coordinating the review of the plans by the zoning, fire, public works and other departments.

3. Issuing permits, collecting fees and keeping records of transactions and inspections.

4. Inspecting the project to make sure it is built in accordance with the approved plans and specifications.

The working drawings are assigned to a "plan checker," usually an engineer or architect with specialized knowledge of the codes, who normally processes them in the order in which they are received. The plan checker typically works off a checklist like the one shown in Appendix II.

To save time and avoid mistakes, it is helpful for designers and builders to develop their own building code and zoning ordinance compliance checklist so they can review the working drawings before submitting them. The International Conference of Building Officials (ICBO) and many local building departments have checklists like the one in Appendix II that can be used as the basis for the building-code portion of the list. Planning, zoning and other departments may have similar handouts.

If the plans contain confusing information or substantially unworkable designs, they will be returned to the designer for redrawing. As a practical matter, minor mistakes (such as the failure to specify the R-value of insulation) are sometimes corrected directly on the submitted blueprints in red ink (for example, "Provide minimum R-19 insulation").

The working drawings and written specifications, if any, show the addition's design and "scope of work," or the amount and type of work the project entails. If the design or scope of work is changed during the course of the job, the plans must be modified or redrawn to show the changes and resubmitted for approval.

Delays should be expected during the plan-checking process. Reasonable and predictable delays are part of the construction business; exces-

sive and unexpected delays can create havoc for designers, builders and owners. It's wise for the designer, then, to check with the plan checker —not the staff at the counter—for information about the expected time frame and factors that might cause delays.

Normally it will not be necessary for the designer to return to the zoning office or visit any of the other departments at city hall after the permit has been applied for because the building department will circulate a copy of the plans to all the departments for review (see below). Once the plans have been reviewed, assuming there are no problems, they are returned to the building department.

Plan approval On the second visit to the building department, the designer or builder secures a building permit and an approved copy of the plans. Only the approved plans, which are stamped by the building department, or identical copies may be used for construction (earlier versions of the working drawings should be thrown away). The approved plans are usually kept in a safe place on the job site, where they must be made available to the building inspector, while copies are used by the builder.

COORDINATING DEPARTMENTAL REVIEWS

As well as checking the plans for building-code compliance, the plan checker is usually responsible for obtaining approval of the project from the other departments. In a typical jurisdiction, plans are reviewed by the fire, public works and traffic-engineering departments as well as planning, zoning and building.

Fire

The fire marshal is responsible for making sure that buildings and additions conform to the Uniform Fire Code and any other regulations the jurisdiction may impose. A building that complies with zoning ordinances and the building codes will usually comply with fire regulations as well, at least in the most important aspects of its design. For example, the Dwelling Construction booklet states that:

"Except where zoning regulations are more restrictive, any exterior wall having windows or other openings must be at least 3 ft. from the property line. Other walls may be less than 3 ft. from property lines but must be at least of one hour fire-resistive construction."

Zoning regulations are generally more restrictive than the building-code minimum, and most jurisdictions today require a minimum 5-ft. setback. One reason is that buildings are considered to be more pleasant and habitable if there is more space between them. But fire is the primary consideration: Not only will the greater distance slow the spread of flames, but it will also allow safer and faster access through corridors between buildings for firefighters. Coordination between the fire and zoning departments has already incorporated this line of thinking into the zoning ordinances. If they are followed, the fire marshal is usually satisfied.

Variances and unique situations, however, may require special measures. Walls and projections built beyond the setback lines with a

The houses in this photograph were built before modern zoning ordinances, building codes and fire codes took effect. Placing houses this close together would not be permitted by today's ordinances and codes, nor could a variance be obtained to build the small addition to the second story of the house on the left.

variance are not only required to have fire-resistant construction but may need sprinklers, too. The number, size, type and location of exits and exterior stairs are also of concern to the fire marshal, because they can affect the ability of civilians to escape from the building and firefighters to enter it.

Again, compliance with the building codes and zoning ordinances, which are integrated with the fire codes, will usually fulfill the requirements. Some additional minor measures may be needed, however, like the placements of lights over all exits. If there are questions about compliance with fire regulations,

the designer or builder should call the plan checker or fire marshal.

Public works

Public works is the department in charge of streets, sewage, water supply, the location of electrical poles and other facets of the infrastructure. Since new power lines, sewers or wider streets are not normally needed for residential additions, this department's review of the project is limited to ensuring that water or sewage moratoriums are not violated, and that the addition will not impose excessive loads on existing infrastructure systems. Compliance with the building, electrical, plumbing and mechanical codes satisfies the public works regulations in most cases.

Traffic engineering

The traffic-engineering department is concerned with traffic and pedestrian safety and parking. If an addition changes the location of a driveway, decreases visibility along a street or at an intersection, reflects blinding sunlight into the street, or in any other way affects the flow or safety of traffic, the traffic department may impose conditions or restrictions.

Other reviews

Some jurisdictions require that plans be reviewed by departments other than those mentioned above. Additions built adjacent to public lands or rights of way, for example, may require review by the parks and recreation department. Adding to existing buildings in a flood, geological-hazard or fire zone or in an environmentally sensitive area may need the approval of one or more special departments. Adding to buildings in neighborhoods protected by historical-preservation ordinances often requires special approval, too.

The designer or builder should find out if the addition is within a zone with unusual requirements as part of feasibility determination. The plan checker and planning and zoning staff member responsible for reviewing the project should know of all such restrictions.

PERMITS, FEES AND RECORDS

A building permit is issued only after the plans are approved. It is illegal to begin the project, even the demolition, before the permit is issued. (The UBC provides for a doubling of the inspection fees if the job is started early.) Also, building inspectors cannot look at the work until the permit is issued, and work that is completed without an inspection will probably have to be opened up to show compliance and may have to be torn out entirely.

The permit papers are of two types: the permit proper and the inspection record card. The permit contains a brief written description of the work and the means of executing it—that is, whether the addition will be built by a licensed contractor, owner/builder, unlicensed carpenter, or owner (see Chapter 13). Regulations governing the execution of the work vary from state to state. Since the means of building the addition and the skills of the builder must be considered in the design, the designer should know what is permissible.

The inspection record card, along with the approved set of plans, must be kept on the job site for reference and signing off by the field inspector.

Fees and taxes

Permit fees vary greatly, depending on the jurisdiction, project type and other factors. Jurisdictions use methods varying from square-footage calculations, which may or may not include higher rates for kitchens, say, over bedrooms, to charging a percentage of the overall project cost as estimated by the contractor. Some cities collect state and county fees as well. Since the fees can be as high as 2% or 3% of the total job cost, the designer or builder should get a fee estimate from the building department to include in the preliminary budget.

The house's net equity, or the increase in the property's value less the addition's amortized cost, is part of the project's long-range feasibility picture. The designer and owners should be aware that the addition will increase the house's assessed value and therefore the property tax base. One responsibility of the building department is to provide the city or county assessor's office with the square footage of the project, number of bedrooms and other information used to assess value.

Records

Building departments keep records of all permits in the property file, but most departments do not have sufficient storage facilities to keep blueprints or enough money to save plans on microfilm. This situation is unfortunate, because copies of the original plans could answer many questions and save a great deal of time in measuring the building and drawing the as-built template (see Chapter 12).

Permit records can still be useful, however. Most designers and contractors practice locally, and permits often name contractors or former owners who may have copies of the plans or know the original architect or designer. It is standard practice, and in some states a matter of law, for architects and engineers to keep plans on file indefinitely. A little calling around can often produce a ready-made set of as-built drawings.

Permits also tell you if the building has been modified and give you a general description of the changes. This information might help, for example, in determining the age of a foundation: Say a house was built in 1924 but added to in 1964 with a foundation of the same style. If the older foundation is in good condition, it may be hard to tell the two foundations apart visually, but it is useful to know the age of the concrete as a clue to its strength and the presence of rebar (see Chapter 7).

FIELD INSPECTIONS

Like plan checkers, field inspectors have a thorough knowledge of the building codes and frequently have construction experience as well. The builder, then, should expect the field inspector to be both knowledgeable and sympathetic to the difficulties encountered in actually building something, as opposed to drawing a picture of it.

Questions about what is allowable, or sensible, arise constantly, and it can't hurt to ask inspectors what they might do, or will approve. Tapping the inspector's knowledge not only gives you access to a valuable source of information, but it normally increases his or her degree of empathy as well.

Passing inspection

As each phase of the job passes inspection, the inspector signs off on the inspection record card and the builder is free to proceed with the next phase. If there are serious problems with the work, the inspector will not sign off until after the work is corrected and reinspected.

If the work does not pass inspection for minor reasons, inspectors often sign the card, although they are technically not supposed to, and ask the builder to correct the deficiencies before covering the work. This favor can be very helpful to the builder, particular in pressure

situations as when a foundation inspection is scheduled for the morning and a concrete pour for the same afternoon. Inspectors are more likely to overlook minor deficiencies if they know the builder's work to be sound.

It is unwise for the builder to count on such favors, however. Rushing seldom saves time, and a more reasonable schedule could save an ultimately more time-consuming delay as well as the cost of, say, sending away a truck load of concrete.

LIABILITY AND SAFETY

Legal liability for the structural integrity of the building ultimately rests with the designer and/or builder, not the building official. It's the responsibility of the designer and builder, then, to employ every possible means of ensuring the building's safety and performance. These means include not only hiring specialists as consultants, but also relying on the building codes and advice from building officials whenever there are unanswered questions.

No one has all the answers, and complex projects are best tackled by a team of individuals with varying perspectives and information. The building officials, with their specialized knowledge of the codes, should be considered part of that team. The wise designer or builder will solicit their opinion when there are questions of code compliance, or more important, safety.

Safety should be the primary concern of everyone in the design and building process. The designer should consider the codes as

minimum legal requirements only, and make every effort not only to comply with, but also to understand the intent of the regulations and turn that intent into reality wherever possible.

When to Get an Inspection

The rule of thumb for when to get an inspection is simple: Get something inspected before it is covered.

The UBC "Dwelling Construction" booklet calls for five inspections:

1. Foundation inspection: After the trenches, forms and reinforcing steel are complete, and before the concrete is poured.

2. Under-floor or under-slab inspection: After the plumbing, wiring, and so on, are in place, and before the concrete slab is poured or the wood-frame subfloor is installed.

3. Framing inspection: After the framing (and usually the exterior sheathing, siding and roofing) and all the pipes, vents and wires that go in the walls are in place, and before the walls are closed.

4. Stucco backing, lath and/or drywall inspection: After the stucco backing, lath and/or drywall is in place and before the exterior stucco or plaster is applied or the drywall taped.

5. Final inspection: When the building is ready for occupancy.

The UBC also provides for other inspections as deemed necessary by the local building official.

DESIGNING AND BUILDING

11
GETTING READY TO DESIGN

In the previous section we looked at how the existing site, the building and its subsystems and the laws governing construction affect the design of an addition. In this final section we will pick up where we left off at the end of Chapter 1, with the project's feasibility determined and the designing about to begin. After an overview of the phases of design and construction, this chapter describes the steps needed to prepare for designing the addition: entering into the design contract and gathering, consolidating and reviewing the design-parameter information needed to generate the preliminary design.

THE PHASES OF DESIGN

The table on pp. 177-178 shows the major phases in designing and building an addition. In reality, the design process is not divided into distinct phases but is a continuum that begins when a project is first conceived and ends only when the construction is complete. Thinking of design as divided into separate phases, however, is convenient for organizing the project, communicating with the owners, builders and others and keeping track of progress.

To some extent in design, and more so in construction, the phases are linked to the official financial and legal policies that govern building. Funds are released or permission granted to proceed only after a universally recognized step, such as finishing the rough wiring and plumbing within the walls, is complete. The phases shown in the table are the standard demarcations generally recognized by lenders, building officials and the construction industry.

The transition from one phase to the next frequently marks the time for conferences between the designer and the owners, inspections by building officials, payments for the work that has been completed or advances for the work that's about to begin, and the signing of new contracts or addenda to existing ones. The transition also calls for a shift in focus and methods on the part of the designer.

Although in theory the design work is completed at the end of the design-development phase, in practice designs are frequently modified during the working-drawing phase and even while the actual construction is underway. The further along the design and construction path you are, however, the more expensive it is to go back and take a different path, especially since a change to one element of the design usually requires changes to many others.

While minor modifications to the design are always possible, most of the major decisions must be made early in the process, when there is less information available. Since, we need to make decisions only when we have incomplete information— that is, if we had complete knowledge, the correct solution would be obvious and nothing would have to be decided—many possibilities must be evaluated and either discarded or developed on an intuitive basis. The final result rests upon our earliest "takes" of the situation. That is why it is critical to write a detailed program and make sure that all the design parameters are accounted for. Before that work begins, however, the designer and owners should have a contract.

THE DESIGN CONTRACT

Once it has been determined that the project is feasible (see p. 17), the designer and owners should enter into a formal contract for the upcoming design work, including the program writing, the detailed physical assessment of the property, various meetings, as well as the actual designing and drawing. (Note that the feasibility assessment should be paid for separately because it may not lead to more work for the designer.)

Although handshake and verbal contracts are valid in some states, written contracts provide a record that both parties have seen and presumably understood all the terms of the agreement. Written contracts not only stand up much better in court, if it comes to that, but they are also one of the best guarantees that the parties will not end up in court, at least over misunderstandings of their mutual obligations. Remember, a written contract is not valid unless it is signed and dated by both parties.

Essentially, a contract delineates the responsibilities of the signers to one another. The more detailed the description of those responsibilities, within reason, the easier it is to make sure they will be fulfilled to the mutual satisfaction of both parties.

Types of contract

Contracts can be written in a variety of formats, and the designer should contact a local attorney with experience in design and construction law to find out what is permissible or customary in a particular state or jurisdiction. The two most common formats in use are a custom-written letter of agreement and a standard-form contract.

Letters of agreement The letter of agreement is simply a letter, usually written by the designer and addressed to the owners, that describes the terms of their agreement. It should include all the elements of a design contract listed in the sidebar on p. 179. The advantage of the letter of agreement is that it can be kept brief and simple and be written in plain English so that it will be less likely to alienate or intimidate the owners than a complex legal document. The disadvantage, from a legal perspective, is that letters written by nonspecialists are often incomplete and ambiguous.

No contract is perfect, and, to some extent, all rest on two assumptions: that of mutual goodwill and the knowledge that it is impossible to write a complete description of a single task, let alone an entire project. Therefore the *intent* of the parties is given weight by the courts when a complete description of the specifics is not included in the document.

The more details and possible pitfalls that are included in a contract, however, the less likelihood there is that the parties and the courts will misunderstand the mutual intent. For that reason, and as a matter of convenience, many designers and builders use standard-form contracts that have been written by attorneys and cover most of the problems that are likely to arise. (Custom contracts written by attorneys are usually too expensive for addition budgets.)

Standard-form contracts Preeminent among the standard-form contracts for small-project design is the American Institute of Architects' (AIA) "Abbreviated Form of Agreement Between Owner and Architect for Construction Projects of Limited Scope" (AIA Document B151). The eight-page contract, written clearly enough for the attentive layperson to understand, comes with instructions and is cross-referenced to several supporting documents also published by the AIA. It can be obtained from local branches of the AIA, which are listed in most phone books.

Whether designers use the document verbatim or choose to adapt and paraphrase it for writing their own letter of agreement (be careful of copyrights!) is a matter of discretion. Although simply filling out and signing the document is the easiest thing to do, the designer should be aware of some potential pitfalls.

To begin with, the contract calls for the use of binding arbitration to settle disputes, unless the parties specifically agree to exclude the arbitration clause. What binding arbitration means is that if there is a dispute that cannot be resolved by the contracting parties, it will be resolved by a professional arbiter, usually an attorney, and that that individual's decision is "binding and mandatory."

The arbitration hearing is typically held at the arbiter's office and in many ways resembles a courtroom trial—the disputing parties are allowed to tell their stories, introduce plans and photographs as evidence and may call witnesses on their behalf. Because it bypasses lengthy pre-trial maneuvering by attorneys, courtroom protocols and possible appeals, binding arbitration is normally much less expensive, less stressful and quicker than an ordinary trial.

However, as good as it looks on paper, binding arbitration has two great drawbacks that can make it a real disaster. First, all the power of judgment is in the hands of one individual, who, for any number of reasons, may not be objective. There is no jury, no debate between attorneys, no guarantee of a systematic cross-examination of witnesses and few rules of permissible evidence to protect against innuendo, misleading arguments or lies.

Second, the judgment is final—there's no second chance. If for some reason the evidence is presented poorly, or not at all, if the arbiter is prejudiced or mistaken... tough luck. The designer or builder should consider such matters carefully, and probably get the advice of one or more business and legal professionals before entering into a contract that stipulates that binding arbitration be used to settle disputes.

Another consideration is the ethical issue raised by Article 5 of the AIA contract. Article 5 is designed to limit, if not entirely eliminate, any responsibility the architect (or designer) may have for the ultimate construction cost. Although it is a well-intended attempt to protect the architect in the real world of construction business, the AIA contract inadvertently sets a tone that could be interpreted as license to act unprofessionally or irresponsibly.

A designer has a vested interest in getting a design contract—that's how bread gets on the table. If there is a conflict between the owners' program and their budget—that is, they want more than they can afford—the designer has no financial incentive to point out the discrepancy, and in fact has an incentive to produce the design and let the final bids fall where they may.

Major Phases in Designing and Building an Addition

Feasibility assessment
Feasibility consultation (site)
Research/calculations (office)
Feasibility decision meeting

Make preliminary evaluation of architectural, structural, financial, legal and emotional aspects of proposed project. Engineers and other consultants may be needed. Usually requires research on legal and other issues and a written preliminary cost calculation (discussed in Chapter 1).

DESIGN PHASE

Design contract
Determine contract type

Design phase begins formally with writing and signing of design contract (Chapter 11).

Design parameters
Program writing
Design-parameters checklist
Design-parameters review
Design-parameters report

Make systematic checklist and written report on the project's design parameters (program requirements and design determiners); review with owners (Chapter 11).

Preliminary design
Detailed building assessment
(measurements, photographs)
As-built design template
Preliminary design drawings
(with master plan)
Preliminary design presentation
(review feasibility cost estimates)

Take detailed measurements and photos and draw scaled, as-built template. Represent program information graphically, then translate into sketches of the addition. Draw master plan for phased projects, select a design and convert sketches to drawings for formal presentation to owners (Chapter 12). Submit preliminary design to zoning department for approval, if needed (Chapter 10).

Design development
Develop design drawings
Present final design

Modify design and refine and complete drawings (Chapter 12).

Construction documents
Prepare working drawings
Attach reports and specifications

Complete design drawings with labels, measurements, etc.; draw architectural and structural details. Obtain and attach energy reports, engineering calculations, etc. Add written specifications for materials and fixtures, if needed (Chapter 12).

PERMIT PHASE

Apply for permit
Attend variance hearings (if needed)
Obtain permit

Submit construction documents to appropriate authorities; attend hearings or meet with plan checkers, if necessary. Pick up permit (Chapter 10).

CONTRACT, ESTIMATING AND PLANNING PHASE

Building contract
Choose a builder
Determine contract type
Draw up the arrangement

Decide on nature of contract, write and review draft with owners, sign all documents and collect deposit (Chapter 13).

Estimating
Materials take-offs
Labor estimate
Subcontractor bids
Assembly of estimate

Calculate material quantities from plans and obtain prices from suppliers. Estimate labor, gather bids from subcontractors, assemble estimate into presentable format as fixed bid or range of costs (Chapter 13).

(continued on p. 178)

Major Phases in Designing and Building an Addition (continued)

CONTRACT, ESTIMATING AND PLANNING PHASE

Planning
Job-site evaluation and blueprint check
Job flow chart
Work crew/subcontractors
Suppliers

Check the site for logistical problems, storage areas and features affecting job. Check blueprints for accuracy. Create flow chart. Line up crew, subcontractors, suppliers (Chapter 13).

CONSTRUCTION PHASE

Setup
Site preparation
Demolition
Shoring

Clean and organize areas needed for materials and equipment; enclose area of new work with dust, noise and weather protectors; set up safety barriers. Remove or demolish fixtures, walls, etc. Build shoring as needed (Chapter 14).

Layout

Build batter boards for foundations or establish guide strings and benchmarks for second stories.

Concrete work and drainage

Dig new trenches or undermine existing foundation, build forms, install structural metal, place concrete, install drainpipe, and backfill.

Rough construction
Framing
Sheathing
Plumbing, wiring, heat ducts

Set up scaffolding if needed. Frame from foundation or platform through roof. Apply sheathing and protective roofing felt. Run plumbing, wiring, cables and ducts.

Weatherproofing (exterior finish)
Roofing, flashing, gutters
Siding
Windows, doors and trim
Specialty work

Complete weathertight shell. Build patios, decks or other adjunct spaces. Complete walks, fences, stairs.

Interior finish
Drywall or plaster
Prime paint
Cabinets and built-ins
Trim electrical and plumbing
Moldings
Floors
Final details and touchup

Seal walls and install all fixtures. Paint or stain.

COMPLETION PHASE

Final cleanup

Final inspection
Certificate of occupancy
Conversion of construction loan (owners)

Move in.

Most designers, of course, try to avoid such practices. It is unethical and bad for their reputation to lead their clients down the primrose path. However, we are discussing contractual obligations, not personal predilections, and designers who choose to use the AIA contract without alteration should at the very least inform their clients of the risk. The owners may have to pay for a set of plans that can never be built and not have the benefit of legal recourse.

A better alternative is to keep the owners informed about the true costs, as closely as they can be calculated, from the beginning of the design process. This can be done in a variety of ways, as discussed in Chapter 13.

A final problem with the AIA contract is that it is illegal in many states for persons who are not licensed architects to use the term "architect" to describe themselves. Therefore, each time the word "architect" is used in the contract, it must be crossed out and replaced with "designer" or "architectural designer." (Note that the latter may be too close to architect to be allowed in some states.)

The decision to use or, with the help of an attorney, modify the AIA contract must be made by each designer or architect based on his or her business practices and ethics. At the very least, though, obtaining and studying the contract is a good starting place for learning about some of the legal pitfalls that may await designers who write their own letters of agreement or, worse, proceed without a written contract.

Designer/builder contracts If one person serves as both designer and builder, he or she should still keep the design and construction contracts separate. Although an experienced designer can estimate the design costs fairly well, accurate estimates of the construction costs must wait until the working drawings are complete. To enter a construction contract without complete working drawings puts both the designer/builder and the owners at risk. (Even if the construction work will be performed on a time and materials basis, few owners will sign a carte blanche contract, and some fairly close estimates of the overall cost will be needed.)

Also, the designer/builder or owners may decide not to proceed with the construction when the design is complete. Perhaps the construction funds have not materialized, or the relationship between the owners and designer/builder turns out not to be as rosy as it at first seemed.

Elements of a Design Contract

The basic elements of a design contract for an addition are:

1. An introductory clause that states the names and titles or functions of the parties (e.g., owner, designer, architect, contractor) and states that they will enter into a contract as described in the following paragraphs.

2. A brief description of the project, including its address.

3. A description of the obligations of the designer. Normally these include:

  a. Program writing, assessment of the property, research into relevant codes and ordinances, design conferences with the owners and other work related to designing.

  b. Producing design and working drawings and, if needed, written specifications.

  c. Construction supervision, if mutually agreed upon.

  d. Other services, such as representing the owners at zoning hearings, as needed.

4. A list of tasks that are needed to complete the design but are not normally performed by the designer. These include producing engineering, energy and environmental-impact reports and obtaining permits. Typically, the designer arranges for or assists the owners in obtaining such services, if so stipulated in the contract.

5. A section limiting (and explaining) the designer's liability for such items as the final cost of the project.

6. A section listing the responsibilities of the owners: primarily to pay money, and secondarily to provide documents like deeds and plot plans, meet with the designer in a timely fashion and generally cooperate with the design process.

7. A description of the means of payment and the schedule of payments.

8. A description of the means of settling disputes, either through binding arbitration or the courts.

9. Lines for signing and dating the document.

DESIGN FEES
AND PAYMENTS

Although it is more efficient to produce working drawings based on an as-built template (see pp. 190-191) than to extrapolate them from rough design sketches (the typical practice for new construction), addition designs are still a lot of work. Not only must the existing house be physically evaluated, measured and drawn to scale, but all of the connections between the existing house and the addition must also be shown in detail. In most cases additions require far more detail drawings than new houses.

Also, additions usually involve a number of considerations about the treatment of the existing building and its subsystems: Should the heating system be replaced or just added to? Is it time to replace the trim on the whole house? These concerns require the designer to spend more time consulting with specialists and more time drawing than would be needed for a new house. Overall, designing an addition usually takes more work (and costs more) than new construction of the same size and quality.

Calculating fees

The three most common ways to calculate design fees are to charge a percentage of the construction cost, a fee per hour or a fixed fee for the whole job. An alternative method is to establish minimum and maximum fees and to include an incentive clause in the contract to encourage efficiency.

Percentage of construction cost

The percentage of the construction cost method is a traditional practice in the architectural profession. Over the years, the typical design fees

have risen from an average of about 8% of the total construction cost to a current average of about 12%. Engineers' and consultants' fees and the cost of producing the construction documents are normally included in this figure; construction supervision, which is best performed on an hourly basis, is usually billed separately.

While this figure may seem high, it is a fairly accurate reflection of the cost of designing an addition for a reasonable profit. The larger the project, the greater the number of drawings and conferences, so that, on average, if the construction cost doubles, so does the amount of design work.

There are several drawbacks to the percentage of the construction cost method, however. First, while the formula works in most cases, there are many exceptions. For example, because of the amount of detailed drawing required, designing a small, complex job could take as long as designing a larger, simpler job, even though the small job may not be more expensive to build.

Second, there's the matter, once again, of ethics and business practice. If the owners are tempted to add features to the addition as the design develops, a designer who works for a percentage of the construction costs and has no incentive to keep costs down might be less likely to take command and insist on sticking to basics.

The third drawback is pragmatic. Few people are willing to write a blank check to the designer. Owners want to know what something is going to cost, and may even regard with suspicion the individual who proposes the percentage method. It's a hard sell.

Hourly fee

The same is true for the second cost-calculating method, charging by the hour. ("When does the bleeding stop?" as one owner put it.) While some designers and builders write an hourly contract with a ceiling, charging the owners only for the hours they spend and not exceeding the top figure, this practice seems rather foolish. The designer, presumably an independent business person, can then be paid for his or her time only, takes all the risk and does not stand to make a profit over and above the cost of labor and drawing materials.

Fixed fee

The third option, charging a fixed fee for the job, has the great advantage of making the owners feel secure. The obvious risk is that the designer, even one with a fair amount of experience, may not charge enough and could end up working for very low wages.

An alternative approach to calculating design fees is to base the fee on a figure that is already available; in other words, charge the industry standard 10% to 12% of the projected construction cost that was used for the feasibility assessment (see pp. 14-15). That way, the owners will be guaranteed a fixed price, and the designer will be assured of at least reasonable compensation, if not a fat profit. (The designer should use the highest construction cost estimates in case unexpected problems arise.)

Incentive clause

The designer and owners might also consider including an incentive clause in the contract. Using the 10% to 12% of the feasibility estimate as a base figure, they can agree upon a maximum cost (usually somewhat higher than

12%) and a minimum cost (possibly lower than 10%). If the designer delivers a satisfactory set of plans at the lower end of the fee scale, he or she is given a bonus and therefore gets more money for less work (greater efficiency). As the cost of the plans goes up, the amount of the bonus goes down. When the maximum cost is reached there is no bonus, of course, and the designer must complete the plans, even if they take longer than originally anticipated.

Incentive clauses work well both in design contracts and in building contracts, where there is a great deal more money involved. Incentive clauses for building contracts are discussed in Chapter 13.

DESIGN PARAMETERS

A good design does more than just look good. It addresses *all* of the project's design parameters (program requirements and design determiners—see the sidebar on p. 7). To develop a good design in a reasonable amount of time and for an affordable fee, the designer must take a systematic approach to dealing with the many parameters that affect the design.

Design-parameter information is gathered from a variety of sources, including interviews with the owners, input from engineers, subcontractors, realtors and other consultants, research on design requirements for the building type, research into the applicable building codes and ordinances, and an assessment of the property itself. For purposes of clarity and reference, this information should be organized into a written report (discussed below), which may be supplemented with site plans or other illustrations.

The "Master Design-Parameters Checklist" (see Appendix III at the back of the book) divides the design parameters for an addition into two broad groups—the program requirements of the owners and the designer, and the design determiners. The checklist is intended to be used as a master list that coordinates all the other lists in this book that contain design-parameter information. The master checklist can be used to assemble and summarize all the information about the design parameters in one convenient form.

Program writing

It is essential to have a thorough understanding of the owners' program before beginning to design. Program requirements that are not accounted for at the outset can surface as major problems or dissatisfactions after a great deal of work has been done.

For a small project like an addition, many of the program questions are asked and answered during the feasibility consultation. (The feasibility and program phases are often much more distinct on a large project.) Don't suppose, however, that the information gained during the brief feasibility investigation constitutes an adequate program. If you proceed directly from the feasibility phase to the design without a thorough and systematic inquiry, you are likely to neglect important information.

The owners' program For a project the size of an addition, it is usually sufficient to discuss the program with the owners in two sessions— the initial feasibility consultation (see pp. 7-8) and a second interview to refine the owners' initial ideas and add missing details. The program information is then written down and reviewed by the clients during the design-parameters review session described on p. 183.

It is particularly important for the designer to show the owners a written version of their own program. They are often surprised when they see their ideas in writing. "Did I say that?" the owners may well respond upon hearing their own words repeated or concepts represented. "Well, what I really meant was...." It is best to know what was really meant before spending several days drawing a version of what was not intended.

The designer's program Although it is not always acknowledged as part of the design process, the designer will also have a personal, sometimes subliminal program.

It is important to recognize that the designer has an agenda, and to make it an open and conscious part of the program—something to discuss with the owners. This way the designer's architectural preferences can take their place among other program elements, and their importance in determining priorities will be clear.

As well as architectural preferences, the designer's requirements might include the compatibility of the project with his or her skills, availability and financial needs. There should also be a good emotional connection with the owners.

Design determiners

As shown on the master checklist (see Appendix III), design determiners can be divided into two types: generic determiners and project determiners. Generic determiners, which apply to any building, include the provision of shelter, architectural appropriateness, ease of construction and affordability. Project determiners, which apply to a specific building, include the site and building's physical characteristics, the building's architecture, and the legal and budgetary factors that influence the addition's design.

Generic design determiners All buildings must provide shelter. Although "shelter" in its most rudimentary sense is included in the definition of "building," stipulations that a shelter be made healthy, safe and secure and provide a sense of hearth and home may be seen as program requirements. It cannot be taken for granted that these requirements will be considered, since owners seldom mention them and many designers are not explicit about including them in their personal goals for the projects they undertake. These most fundamental requirements, then, are included in the checklist to ensure that they are not overlooked in the design.

Architectural appropriateness is discussed in some detail in chapters 2 through 5. The basic goal, that the addition be designed appropriately for its context, is covered in the master checklist.

As far as ease of construction goes, one of the most common mistakes made by designers who are not builders is the failure to consider what it takes to get the job done. Putting a room addition behind a house with no exterior access to the backyard, for example, can take up to 20% longer than building a comparable addition on a house with a driveway along one side.

For the project to be successful, construction logistics and techniques must be integrated with other program considerations as the design is developed. It's essential for the designer who lacks experience in this area to work with an experienced builder from the beginning of the feasibility and design processes (see Chapter 13).

The requirement of affordability—a basic goal for all construction projects—can be met if the design is developed with the budget in mind. Each design decision, from determining the square footage of the building to details like choosing materials that are available at the local lumber store, affects and is affected by the budget. The project's affordability is also controlled by good financial planning and management.

Project design determiners The physical evaluation of the site and building made during the feasibility phase is inadequate for design. A thorough survey, usually conducted at the same time that the building is measured (see pp. 187-189), is outlined in the "Existing Conditions Checklist" (see Appendix I). Information from that checklist can be included in the master checklist.

A building's architectural features, such as the location of its entrance or the layout of its rooms, often provide design opportunities or impose constraints. As discussed in the first section of this book, the building's form and style must also be considered. These concepts are reviewed on the master checklist.

The legal information on the "Existing Conditions Checklist" can be transferred to the master checklist as well. The budget created for the feasibility assessment (see the table on pp. 14-15) is usually adequate to begin designing, and also can be added to the master checklist.

The design-parameters review

When all the design-parameter information has been gathered, it should be organized and put into a presentable form. The designer or builder must decide whether the master checklist itself, a written report based upon it or a combination of the two is the appropriate format (see the checklist on the facing page). Site plans, schematic drawings and other illustrations may also be included. In any case, a formal, written document should be prepared and copied for the owners. This way the designer and owners will know that they are working from the same list.

The designer should meet with the owners and review the design-parameters document thoroughly. The review serves three purposes: first, to make sure that the master list is complete; second, to provide an opportunity for the designer and owners to agree upon ground rules for design decisions and to set clear goals for the project; and, third, to determine the project's priorities. Once there is a complete list of the program's minimum requirements and additional desirable features, their order of importance can be established.

Goals and priorities The goals for the project can be written as a checklist and attached to the design-parameters document. They should include the minimum design requirements; the design objectives listed by priority; the scope of the design work and its limits— that is, what will not be done by the designer, such as developing detailed drawings for some future component of the master plan; the schedule for the design; and as accurate an estimate of the construction budget as has thus far been developed.

The design-parameters document will usually be modified somewhat during the course of the review. As a final step in the design-parameters phase, the designer should make a revised copy of the document, attach the new list of goals and priorities and send a completed document to the owners.

Completing the design-parameters document marks the turning point between gathering essential background information and the actual design of the addition. If the work has been done thoroughly and correctly, a great deal of what should and should not be designed has already suggested itself.

12
DESIGN METHODS FOR ADDITIONS

The act of designing has both chaotic and disciplined aspects. On the one hand, to produce a good design you must access material from your subconscious and integrate it with information from the exterior world, a process over which you have limited control at best. Key design solutions that come in the form of intuitive flashes may appear at any time of the day or night—while you are at the drawing board, engaged in an entirely unrelated activity or even in the form of dreams while you sleep.

On the other hand, there is a certain logic to design. An addition, for example, is designed by exploring possible configurations on tracing paper over "as-built" templates. Through a process of elimination, the designer can more or less systematically discard those configurations that will not work and reduce the options to those that best fit the design parameters.

THE NATURE OF DESIGN

While designing, you must constantly shift focus between the many interacting factors that bear on the problem. A commanding view, for example, might lead you to consider enlarging a window. Climatic and cost factors immediately crop up as constraints, however, and you must also account for the effects of the change on the structure, design of the roof overhang for shade, internal air flow, location of heat ducts, energy-code compliance, privacy and the house's overall appearance. A change in any one of those factors, say, extending the roof overhang, might in turn engender more changes, such as widening the fascia to keep it proportional to the extension, introducing knee braces to support the extension or changing the gutters.

Designing, then, can be seen as a process of producing solutions that address many, sometimes contradictory requirements simultaneously. The solutions may either be com-

promises that partly fulfill opposing demands or, better, entirely new syntheses that eliminate the tensions between opposites.

For example, the need to enlarge the window to encompass the view conflicts with the need to make it smaller to minimize heat loss. The compromise solution would be to design a medium-sized window that addresses both problems to some extent, but doesn't quite catch the full view or hold heat loss to a minimum. By exploring the possibility that the two needs are not necessarily in conflict, however, you might produce a new design—such as converting the window to a solar collector by adding a thermal mass on the floor or wall behind it, and then making it larger so it would capture both more sunlight and more of the view.

In many such examples the synthesis is catalyzed by the introduction of a third element, in this case the thermal mass. The creative stroke of introducing the element needed to break the deadlock encountered when resolving opposing demands is the essence of designing. It requires the application of intuition to a problem that has been posed by a logical process.

Part of the struggle of keeping your creative juices flowing is to avoid becoming bogged down in the innumerable factors and constraints that must be accounted for while the design is taking shape. A systematic approach to information gathering and program writing, discussed in the last chapter, is one way of making sure that nothing of great significance has been overlooked. Design is primarily a graphic activity, however, and the written program requirements must be

translated into graphic form before they can be manipulated.

One means of graphically representing and keeping track of the various factors and their complex interaction is through the use of a design circle, as shown in the sidebar on p. 186. Although the circle is not part of the addition design per se, it can become a "design of the design," or a model of a graphic approach to solving design problems, as well as a means of organizing the particular addition's design parameters. An example of a design circle in action—the design sketchboard—is shown later in this chapter.

A system for designing an addition

The design system described in this chapter is intended to help with the demanding task of turning program requirements into working drawings in two ways. First, the system provides a means of checking and cross-checking the drawings to eliminate potential mistakes before they develop. Second, it makes it possible to eliminate or shorten several of the steps needed for designing new buildings when designing an addition. Developing the floor plans directly over the as-built template rather than on an empty site plan, for example, saves time, effort and money.

The seven major steps in my system for designing an addition are preparing the as-built templates, assembling the design sketchboard, drawing schematics over the templates, generating preliminary designs over the templates, choosing and presenting a design, developing the design, and producing the construction documents (working drawings).

It is important to proceed in a systematic fashion, completing one step, insofar as possible, before taking the next. When a sequence is established and followed, backtracking is minimized and the process of designing an addition becomes relatively straightforward.

PREPARING THE AS-BUILT TEMPLATES

After the design-parameters review (see p. 183), the designer should return to the site (without the owners) to measure, photograph and conduct a detailed physical assessment of the building. This visit also gives you a chance to sit with the house for a while, make some sketches and think through the design possibilities in a way that is difficult with

the owners present. Measuring, photographing and evaluating the building will take a number of hours, and you should allow sufficient time to do a thorough job. With the information gathered from this assessment of the building, you will be able to draft the as-built drawings and then photo-reduce these drawings for use as as-built templates on the design sketchboard.

The Design Circle

All of the factors that influence an addition design interact with one another, and designers must keep several factors in mind simultaneously as they draw each line and confront each decision. To avoid confusion, it is helpful to represent the various factors and their interactions graphically. A design circle with lines representing the relationship between factors is a convenient format that can be used for a variety of circumstances and at several levels of detail.

Any of the factors shown on the circle could become the basis for another circle that would provide a more detailed look at a set of factors. The budget, for example, could be broken down into the project's absolute cost, the amortized cost of loans, equity benefits and other interacting factors.

The designer can quickly draw as many circles as needed to represent the factors influencing each phase of the design process. The "design sketchboard," described on pp. 191-192, shows a means of putting the design-circle concept into practice when developing an addition design.

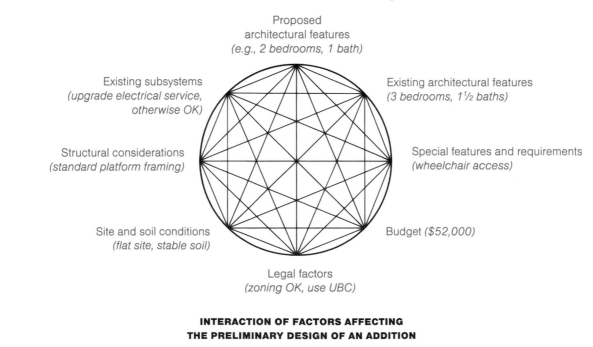

Proposed
architectural features
(e.g., 2 bedrooms, 1 bath)

Existing subsystems
(upgrade electrical service, otherwise OK)

Existing architectural features
(3 bedrooms, 1½ baths)

Structural considerations
(standard platform framing)

Special features and requirements
(wheelchair access)

Site and soil conditions
(flat site, stable soil)

Budget *($52,000)*

Legal factors
(zoning OK, use UBC)

**INTERACTION OF FACTORS AFFECTING
THE PRELIMINARY DESIGN OF AN ADDITION**

Measuring the existing building

The quick, rough measurements that were taken during the feasibility consultation (see p. 11) should be discarded, and all measurements taken from this point on should be up to working-drawing standards, that is, sufficiently accurate for construction. The tolerance for a single measurement should be plus or minus ⅛ in. (± ⅛ in.); the tolerance for the overall building should be ± 1 in. (The requirements for working drawings are given in the table on p. 206 and should be reviewed, if necessary, before time is spent in the field.)

Because the thicknesses of wall finishes and trim vary, the dimensions shown on plans for new construction are measured from *face of stud to face of stud* (F.O.S. to F.O.S.). In other words, the carpenter builds the frame to the dimensions shown, and ignores the dimensions of drywall, stucco siding and other finishes.

Ideally, remodeling dimensions would conform to the face-of-stud convention. However, it can be difficult to locate the existing studs precisely. For example, there are usually shims in the gap between the king and trimmer studs and the window jamb (see the top drawing on p. 188), and the thickness of the shims varies from installation to installation. It is also difficult to tell the precise thickness of lath and plaster interior finishes and stucco siding, because the number of coats and consistency of the material vary.

It is impractical, however, to use any convention other than that of measuring to the face of the studs for final dimensions on the working drawings. It is common practice, then, for architects and designers to include a statement like "The builder shall verify all dimensions in the field" in the general notes that appear on the plans. Thus, the builder has the ultimate responsibility to make sure, for example, that the framing of a new second story is correctly aligned with that of the existing first story. If there is a significant variation, a mistake has been made and the builder should review the plans with the designer.

There are times when precise measurements are needed to make design decisions. The depth of a joist, for example, is determined by its span, which is measured to the inch (see Appendix IV). In such cases, it is necessary to find the exact location of the supporting studs within the walls.

The search begins with determining the width of a typical stud. It will usually be 3½ in., 3¾ in. or 4 in., depending on the age of the building (see Chapter 7). You can see the type of lumber—S2S, S4S or rough—used in the original framing in the sub-areas or attics of most houses.

Once you've determined the width of the stud, you can locate its precise position within the wall. Typical interior walls of a modern house, for example, are 4½ in. thick because they are framed with 3½-in. wide studs and covered with ½-in. drywall on both sides. The stud is ½ in. behind each surface.

In older houses, the thickness of the lath and plaster finish varies, but it is usually consistent enough on a single wall to measure to acceptable tolerances. Check the thickness of the wall surface by removing an outlet or switch cover and measuring to the stud to which the junction box is attached. The thickness

Measuring is a straightforward task, but it takes time and is subject to annoying errors. The principal mistakes are failing to check the sums of incremental measurements against overall measurements, and gathering insufficient information (necessitating another trip to the site).

It is usually easier to measure a house from the inside, standing on the floor, than from the outside, where you may have to climb over shrubbery or work off a ladder. Internal spaces are measured a room at a time, however, and the measurements must be totaled. Naturally, the length of a wall should be the sum of its incremental measurements, but it doesn't always work out that way. Incorrect addition, omission of measurements, cumulative small errors, erroneous assumptions about the thicknesses of walls and overlooking hidden pipe chases are but a few of the common mistakes that can show up when the designer attempts to draft the as-built template or, worse, when the construction is underway.

The solution—measuring the overall outside dimension and checking it against the sum of the component measurements—is simple enough in principle, though it sometimes requires a little ingenuity to get around obstacles.

As far as thoroughness is concerned, measure everything, even the parts of the building that will not be remodeled. The designer will sometimes need precise information about these other spaces to make decisions about the addition. Also, energy codes require that the total volume and surface area of the building as well as the size of all of its openings be accounted for when calculating insulation thickness and the size of the windows in the addition.

MEASURING THE EXISTING BUILDING: PLAN

For consistent horizontal measurements, measure rooms from wall surface to wall surface (not to the baseboard) and windows and door openings from jamb to jamb (see the drawing below). Finished wall thicknesses, as shown in the window-jamb detail at right, are identical to the jamb width in most situations.

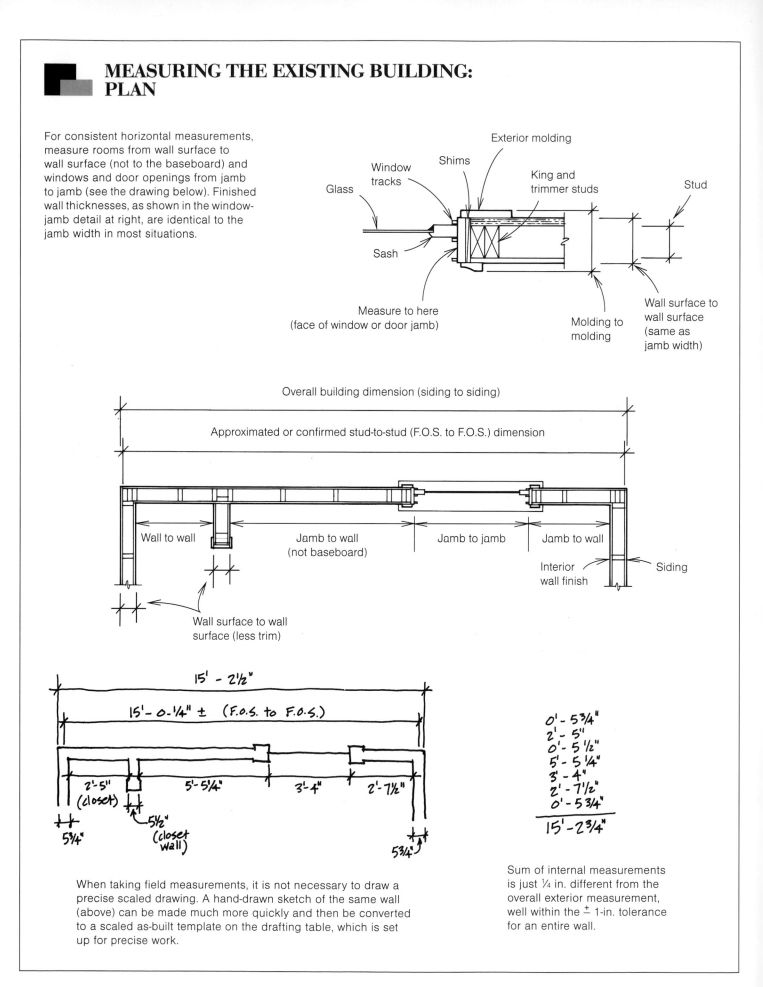

Exterior molding

Window tracks

Shims

Glass

King and trimmer studs

Stud

Sash

Measure to here
(face of window or door jamb)

Molding to molding

Wall surface to wall surface
(same as jamb width)

Overall building dimension (siding to siding)

Approximated or confirmed stud-to-stud (F.O.S. to F.O.S.) dimension

Wall to wall

Jamb to wall
(not baseboard)

Jamb to jamb

Jamb to wall

Interior wall finish

Siding

Wall surface to wall surface (less trim)

15' - 2½"

15'-0-¼" ± (F.O.S. to F.O.S.)

2'-5"
(closet)

5'-5¼"

3'-4"

2'-7½"

5½"
(closet wall)

5¾"

5¾"

0' - 5¾"
2' - 5"
0' - 5½"
5' - 5¼"
3' - 4"
2' - 7½"
0' - 5¾"
_____
15'-2¾"

When taking field measurements, it is not necessary to draw a precise scaled drawing. A hand-drawn sketch of the same wall (above) can be made much more quickly and then be converted to a scaled as-built template on the drafting table, which is set up for precise work.

Sum of internal measurements is just ¼ in. different from the overall exterior measurement, well within the ± 1-in. tolerance for an entire wall.

MEASURING THE EXISTING BUILDING: ELEVATION

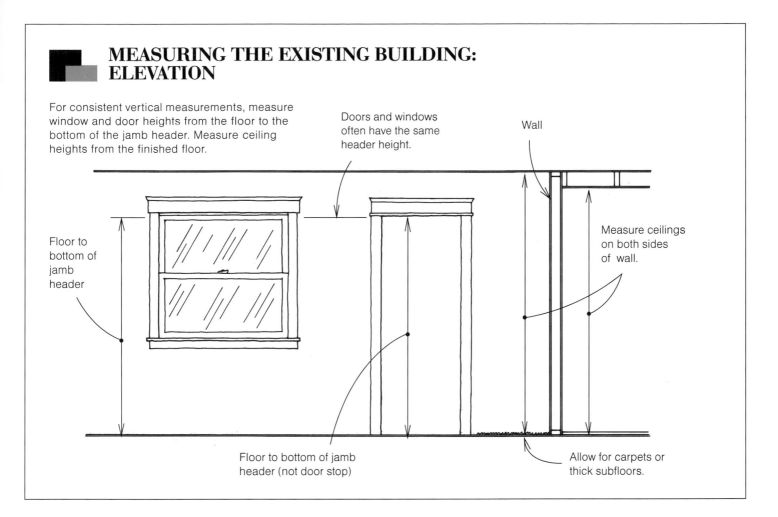

For consistent vertical measurements, measure window and door heights from the floor to the bottom of the jamb header. Measure ceiling heights from the finished floor.

Doors and windows often have the same header height.

Wall

Floor to bottom of jamb header

Measure ceilings on both sides of wall.

Floor to bottom of jamb header (not door stop)

Allow for carpets or thick subfloors.

of the exterior siding can be deduced by measuring a door or window jamb for overall wall thickness and subtracting the width of the studs and the thickness of the interior finish.

As well as measuring the rooms, measure the principal structural members (girders, joists, rafters, etc.). Their dimensions will be needed for drawing the sections and details.

Site measurements are discussed in Chapter 10. Normally, their tolerance can be significantly less than that of the building's measurements, depending on the proximity of the addition to the setback. Tolerances of 3 in. to 6 in. are acceptable in many situations, though critical setback measurements may have to conform to a tolerance of $\pm \frac{1}{2}$ in.

Photographing the building

Photographs play an important role in my system for designing an addition. Many of the design sketches are made on tracing paper over photographs of the existing house. You'll need photos of all the building's elevations and shots from approximately 45° off of each corner. Take corner shots up close, to get a sense of what the addition will look like as one approaches the building on foot, and from a distance to provide "perspectives" for massing studies (see pp. 194-195). Photos of the site and the building's immediate surroundings, and views from the building, especially from the roof for a second-story addition project,

are essential. Also photograph the entrance, trim, distinguishing interior features and anything else that could be of interest. Film is cheap; time on the site, expensive.

Standard, 3½ x 5-in. prints are adequate for elevations. Take closeups of details. Medium-fast film (ASA 200 to 400) allows shooting in shadows and still retains sufficient detail for blowups. If possible, shoot when the sun is low in the sky so that light penetrates into recesses like porches and the shadows cast by overhangs are minimized. Color gives more information. Prints that are processed by a quality lab rather than a fast-photo place are sharper, easier to trace over and look better in the designer's portfolio.

THE AS-BUILT SITE/FLOOR-PLAN TEMPLATE

The ¼-in.-scale as-built floor plan for this 540-sq.-ft. cabin in a scenic, hilly area of California was photo-reduced and carefully positioned onto an ⅛-in.-scale site survey made by an engineering firm. (Only the building-site portion of the large lot is shown.)

The development of a preliminary design for an addition to this house is featured in the drawings in the rest of the chapter.

Sketching at the site

After photographing the building, you may wish to make a few sketches to preview your design ideas in context. Site sketches are optional, but you may find that they help you generate ideas and save the need for future trips to the site.

Preparing the as-built drawings

Using the house measurement sketches as a reference, make accurate as-built drawings on your drafting board. The as-built site plan, floor plans, elevations and the principal section will eventually be incorporated into the final working drawings, and should be drafted to the correct scale on standard-sized, 24-in. by 36-in. sheets of transparent vellum, or high-quality drafting paper. (These original drawings are often called "tracings" to distinguish them from blueprints, or copies.) Typical site plans are drawn at ⅛-in. scale (⅛ in. = 1 ft.), and the floor plans and elevations are usually drawn at ¼-in. scale (see the table on p. 206).

The ¼-in. scale is large enough to show the details on a floor plan but small enough to allow the plans for two floors (or all four elevations) of most houses to be drawn on a single 24 x 36 sheet. Thus one plan (or elevation) can be aligned with the next, simplifying drafting and making it easy to compare similar views.

Preparing the as-built template

Once you have prepared the ¼-in.-scale as-built drawings, you can photo-reduce them on a copy machine (to 50% of their size) for use as templates on the design sketchboard. Reduce the floor plans to the same scale as the site plan (⅛ in. = 1 ft.). Then carefully cut out the outline of the floor plan and glue it

onto the site plan. Copies of the paste-up are used as templates on the design sketchboard (see below). The ¼-in. scale elevations and section can simply be photo-reduced to ⅛-in. scale for use as templates.

Eighth-inch-scale drawings are used for the design templates for three reasons. First, the smaller scale enables you to see the entire site/floor plan at a glance, making it easier to visualize the big picture and integrate the preliminary floor plans with the site and immediate context.

Second, ⅛-in. scale encourages you to work quickly with the building's larger components and avoid getting hung up on small details. Rough sketching on tracing paper over the site/floor plan is easy, because the whole building can be covered with one or two hand strokes (for a discussion of sketching, drafting and rendering, see the sidebar on p. 194). When it comes time to tighten up the preliminary design drawings for presentation to the owners, larger components like doors, windows, cabinets and stairs can be drawn in accurately enough.

Third, the smaller drawings fit nicely onto the design sketchboard, and there's enough room for all the principal templates—site/floor plans, elevations and photos—to be arranged in the correct relationship to one another.

ASSEMBLING THE DESIGN SKETCHBOARD

Ideally, the designer should work with several views of the building at one time. This approach helps integrate the building's masses with its floor plans and get light into the

right areas while controlling views and privacy. It also helps you avoid the common mistake of spending hours developing a floor plan only to switch to the elevations and find, for example, that the addition's well-placed windows don't line up with those of the story below.

It is difficult, however, to keep all of the views—massings from several angles, floor plans for one or more stories, four elevations, the principal section and various details—in mind. One way to address this problem is to assemble a design sketchboard with the as-built site/floor plan in the center surrounded by photographs, elevations and sketches of the building (see the photo on p. 192).

By arranging the various views of the building around the site/floor plan, you can consider them simultaneously. The effects of a change on the plan can be immediately sketched onto the corresponding elevation and section; a change in the roof line can be viewed as it will appear on all four elevations and a number of perspectives; massings can be quickly appraised in terms of the building's overall context and the close-up pedestrian view from the street.

The design sketchboard is a means of putting the design-circle concept—considering all of the factors in relationship to each other—shown on p. 186 into practice. Not only does using the design sketchboard save time and prevent mistakes, it also helps you integrate disparate views of the building and design it as a single entity.

The Design Sketchboard

This design sketchboard, a piece of 24-in. by 36-in. posterboard, is set up for preliminary design work on the addition featured in this chapter. The $1/8$-in.-scale site/floor plan templates in the center are surrounded by photos of the house.

The views are as follows:

1. The site/floor-plan analysis (see p. 193).

2. A preliminary second-story floor plan sketched on tracing paper over a photocopy of the as-built site/floor plan.

3. A photograph of the southwest corner of the existing cabin. It is aligned with the corresponding corner of the site/floor-plan analysis.

4. The west elevation, aligned with the corresponding edge of the site/floor-plan analysis.

5. A massing sketch drawn on tracing paper over a photo of the northwest corner.

6. The north elevation.

7. The northeast corner.

8. The principal view to the east. These three photos were taken in roughly the same spot, with a little overlap, then cut to fit and taped together.

9. The east elevation, which would normally be on the east side of the lower floor drawing but has been moved aside to keep the view photos in correct relation to the site/floor-plan analysis.

10, 11. Interior shots of the cabin.

12. Lined paper for calculations and notes.

The drawings and photos are taped down lightly so they can be moved easily. At some point, the designer might want to replace the photos of elevations, for example, with scaled drawings. The sketchboard can be hung on the wall for viewing or carried to the site for discussion with the owners (or to the beach for inspiration). When the preliminary design work is finished, the board can be easily rearranged for the design presentation to the owners (see pp. 198-202).

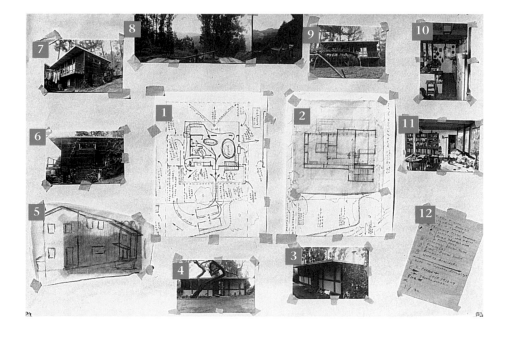

DRAWING SCHEMATICS OVER THE TEMPLATES

Once the design sketchboard has been prepared, the next step is to translate the written program information into graphic form by drawing schematic diagrams (bubble, arrow and essence diagrams) over the site/floor-plan templates where applicable. (Schematic diagrams are discussed in Chapter 4.)

Take care not to omit this step and proceed directly to the preliminary design, because schematic diagrams indicate the relationship of important design factors such as principal views and circulation paths to the building and the ideal relationship of the internal spaces to one another.

The drawing on the facing page shows a schematic analysis of the site/floor plan of the cabin on p. 190. The analysis was drawn loosely and quickly on inexpensive, "flimsy"

SITE/FLOOR-PLAN ANALYSIS

The cabin on the site/floor plan shown on p. 190 belongs to a young couple with its first child on the way. The program for the addition project included a phased expansion of the cabin to a house that was suitable for a family with up to three children. The budget was tight.

The first phase was to include building bedrooms for the couple and the first child. The long-range, or master, plan (see pp. 210-211) provided for a future family room and master bedroom with a bath.

As well as showing the views, focal areas and circulation paths, this site/floor-plan analysis identifies several unique characteristics of the property. First, the site is on a forested north slope and gets very little direct sun except early on summer mornings. Solar gain is not an important factor in the design. Insulation and extended eaves for weather protection are, however, since the area is often damp and chilly.

Also, the site above and below the house is steep enough so that only the pre-excavated garden and patio, along with the relatively flat area on the north end of the house, could be built upon easily. These areas are identified for easy expansion because the budget prohibited expensive, down-slope construction.

Finally, the existing parking area is at the end of a narrow private road, where it is difficult for cars to turn around. Any long-range plan should include a turn-around area.

tracing paper, which comes in rolls of various widths available at blueprint and art-supply stores.

GENERATING PRELIMINARY DESIGNS

Once the schematic design is complete, you can start generating the preliminary design of the actual spaces. From there, the next steps are to choose one or more designs to draw to scale and to present the design to the owners.

Generating ideas

Preliminary designs are generated by sketching on flimsy over the design sketchboard. Ideally, the designs should be generated by working up massing sketches and floor plans at the same time. The massing sketches (see the facing page) should reflect your concept of the building's appearance and the approximate volume of enclosed space

needed to fulfill the functional program requirements. The floor plans (see pp. 196-197) should reflect the interspatial relationships of the bubble diagrams as much as possible (but don't make the floor plans look like the bubble diagrams).

It is in the design-generation phase that your intuition comes into play most strongly, and it should be given free rein initially. Turn off the judging, evaluating side of your personality, as much as you can, so that ideas can flow freely. Work quickly and loosely with a soft pencil, blocking in the main areas first and worrying about details like the exact arrangement of cabinets or the number of stairs later. (Refer to the table on p. 13 for the approximate sizes of typical spaces.)

Adopt an experimental attitude and try all sorts of possibilities, withholding judgment until enough massing and floor-plan combinations have been generated to ensure that important possibilities have not been overlooked. Locking into the first design that presents itself may cause you to miss an even better solution.

Don't be afraid to draw lines where they don't "belong," and try any approach, however radical or silly it may seem. Those ideas that don't work will be naturally and almost effortlessly superseded by those that do.

In some cases, you may find it useful to make a massing model of the addition as well as drawing rough sketches. Models can be made efficiently by cutting the major shapes from sheets of cardboard or foamcore board (available at art-supply stores) and assembling them with a hot gluc gun.

Sketching, Drafting and Rendering

In design, *sketching* means drawing freehand; *drafting* means drawing to scale with tools. Schematic and preliminary design drawings are usually sketched, whereas working drawings, which must be precise, are drafted. The drawings used for presenting the design to the owners can be sketched, drafted or both, depending on the degree of formality required.

Renderings are formal drawings, usually perspectives, that are filled

in, or "rendered," as opposed to remaining in outline form. Renderings may be colored and frequently show shadows and other details that make the sketches more realistic. Although perspective drawings and renderings are time-consuming to produce, they are usually needed for new construction design presentation, since there is no existing building for the clients to visualize.

For the most part, formal renderings are not needed for presenting addition designs. The drawings

shown in this chapter—drafted versions of the site/floor plans and elevations and informal perspective sketches made over photographs—give the owners all the information they need to understand and appreciate the design.

The design-presentation drawings can be spiced up with a little color, without going to the trouble of creating a full rendering. For example, a green marking pen can be used to outline the vegetation on a perspective drawing.

If the designer is involved with choosing the paint for the building, however, it is worth taking a few minutes to render a copy of the principal elevation with colored pens that at least approximate the final color scheme. Although the owners may eventually change the color scheme of the addition, the way the job looks right after it is finished is critical to the success of the project and the reputation of the designer.

PRELIMINARY MASSING SKETCH

This massing, or rough perspective, sketch was drawn on the design sketchboard over a photo of the northwest corner of the house. It was developed concurrently with the preliminary site/floor-plan "master" sketch (pp. 196-197). However, the massing shows only the current project, while the floor plan shows both the current and future projects. The wall nearest the viewer is in the same plane as the wall of the existing house. Like the site/floor plan, the massing sketch evolved after several other solutions, including one where the staircase was at the opposite end of the building (closest to the viewer), had been tried.

The roof and porch shapes are examples of massing issues. While various roof shapes were theoretically possible, the budget demanded a simple solution, and the gable roof, with an extension over the stairwell, seemed logical. The mass of the roofed stairwell, in turn, is reflected on a smaller scale by that of the entry porch.

While many massing sketches are drawn with the side of a crayon or lead stick and show volume only, sketches for additions (where the massing is already partially determined) can be drawn with a soft pencil and use lines to show detail. The narrowness and height of this house, for example, and the fact that it is located among pine trees, suggest not only the massing of the pitched roof but also details like vertical siding and deck rails.

Pulling the design together

As the design evolves, one room or area will often be worked out to your tentative satisfaction, while the rest of the building remains unresolved. Label that drawing ("Kitchen #1," for example) and tape it down over the template. Then roll out some more flimsy and, drawing around the "solved" kitchen on the new layer, continue to develop the rest of the plan.

One advantage of working with flimsy tracing paper and soft, dark pencil is that you can stack several solutions on top of one another and see through the layers to trace over the best part of each version. The drawing on p. 196 is such a master sketch. It was traced over earlier sketches on which the rough plan for the kitchen was developed and approximate location and dimensions of the carport and stairwell were determined. It represents one possible design for the lower floor, and while others can be generated, they are unlikely to differ greatly from the master sketch because so many of the possibilities have already been tried.

As the design is coming together, it is useful to make quick sketches of the building's structure, to establish

(text continues on p. 198)

PRELIMINARY DESIGN SKETCH: SITE/FLOOR PLAN

By the time this "master" sketch was traced over several layers of other rough design drawings, a number of fundamental decisions had already been made. The first was to build a second story, since the only other means of providing enough space for the long-range program would be to cover the entire entrance patio with the building (which would be jammed against the parking lot) or to build down the slope (which was deemed too expensive). In keeping with the "try everything" philosophy, both of these solutions were sketched, but ultimately rejected.

The northwest corner is the only logical turn-around area for cars, and it was quickly decided that it would be the location for a future carport. That left the "flat" area directly north of the house as the only feasible space to develop. The flat area was simply not large enough for four future bedrooms and a family room, even if it was two stories high.

Given the space available and the requirements, it became apparent that the house needed a full second level. Since it seemed important to keep the future family room on the first floor, and the future master bedroom with a bath is about the size of a family room, it was decided to build the currently needed bedrooms above the existing house and reserve the space north of the house for future expansion.

The stairs are placed outside the house to preserve a decent-sized living room and simplify construction. The location of the stairs, in turn, allows the main entrance to be at one end of the living room, perpendicular to its long axis. Also, the wind that would blow into the living room is partially deflected by the offset doorway. By happy coincidence, there is space under the upper stair landing for an entry closet.

The principal focus areas on the site/floor-plan analysis (p. 193) have become the dining-area table and living-room furniture group. The main views and the fireplace can be seen from both.

The existing circulation path through the rear entry and kitchen, past the dining area and toward the living room and deck is preserved. If the carport and the family-room/master-bedroom addition are

built, this will probably become the most frequently used path through the house.

The new family room and all but the smallest of the bedrooms take advantage of the principal view. The house remains narrow and is stretched along the slope on the easiest ground for building, so that most rooms are separated from the forest and hills by just a window or a door.

Finally, all of the plumbing for the current and future projects is concentrated near the existing kitchen. Although the design calls for moving the existing bathroom to make space for the dining area, some of the costs of moving the bathroom will be recouped by keeping the plumbing together.

One problem is that the stairway is in one corner of the house, and far away from the family room. Earlier sketches showed that if the stairs were given a more central location, they chopped up the living room or interfered with the view. The corner location for the stairs was kept in the preliminary design presentation floor plan (p. 200), so that the pros and cons could be discussed with the owners.

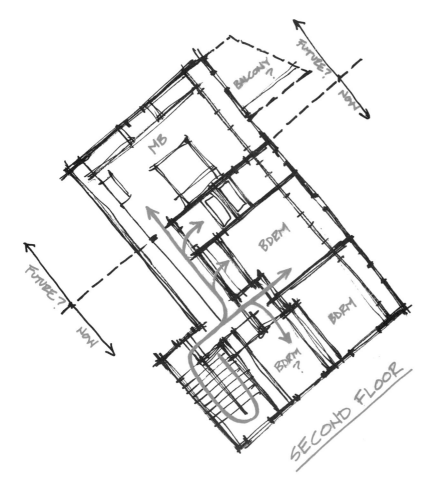

the feasibility of the drawings. This can be done by sketching a structural section over an elevation photograph or an as-built section drawing.

Evaluating the designs

Once most of the feasible ideas have been sketched and one or two designs have been developed to the master-sketch stage, it is time to stop working loosely and evaluate the plans systematically.

Refer to the "Master Design Parameters Checklist" (Appendix III) to make sure that nothing has been overlooked. Begin by evaluating how well the design fulfills the owners' and designer's program requirements. Are the requirements met in the order of their importance to the owner? Next, make sure that the generic design determiners are accounted for. Does the design provide adequate and secure shelter? Check to see that generic architectural goals are met. Is the building integrated with its surroundings?

Similarly, make sure that ease of construction and structural feasibility have been addressed. Is the addition on an accessible portion of the site? Does the design demand special construction techniques? Will engineering be required, and at what cost?

Turning to the project design determiners, do the sketches account for the conditions of the site, soil, structure and subsystems? Is there architectural continuity between the old and new masses, materials and details? To what extent do the functional interrelationships, as represented by the bubble diagrams, hold up in the real spaces? Does the plan flow well? Are all the kinky little nooks and crannies ironed out? Are the views framed well?

Finally, double-check the legal and budgetary requirements. Do the plans and elevations conform to the design envelope? Are rooms such as bedrooms close enough to the minimum allowable size so they will work on the final version of the plans? Is the square footage close to that allotted in the original budget, or has it somehow grown by 20%. Have special features been added that were not in the original budget?

You may find that the design fails to meet some program requirements or design parameters. Although it is acceptable to allow low-priority items to drop out of the program, never give up on resolving each essential portion of the design to your complete satisfaction, even though this might mean starting again at the generating-ideas phase. There are a half-dozen solutions for every problem. Through the persistent use of a combination of intuition and logic, you will find one that matches all of the design parameters.

Choosing a design

In my opinion, the responsibility for choosing a design should be the designer's, not the owners'. The owners have no more basis for making the choice than the designer, and probably less since they haven't looked at as many possibilities or spent as much time thinking about the problem. It is generally not a good idea to present the owners with two designs that are radically different and then ask them to choose. Showing them entirely different buildings based on utterly divergent concepts will probably confuse them and may weaken their confidence in the designer.

The owners should be encouraged to decide on variants of the basic design, of course, and to choose fixtures and finishes, but the scope of their choices should be circumscribed by the professional designer.

So how do you decide that your design is ready for presentation? In a sense, the design chooses itself. Many unworkable solutions will have been tried and discarded while developing the first, complete master sketch. The proposed solutions are generated intuitively and rejected logically. As this reciprocal process goes on, fewer and fewer plausible designs remain. Those that survive get better and better as their details are worked out.

When all the issues that can be resolved logically have been addressed, the question still remains: Is the design completely satisfactory? To answer, go back to basics and to the discussion of the house's essential spirit in Chapter 3. A successful design will capture and expand upon that spirit. Any design that fails to do so, no matter how well it fulfills its other requirements, should not be built. Ultimately, the designer must like the house and the plan for the addition. Only when you are enthusiastic about the work, can you make a good case for its acceptance by the owners.

PRESENTING THE PRELIMINARY DESIGN

The presentation of the long-anticipated design is an exciting event for the owners and designer alike. Since it's easy to get off track and allow a lengthy discussion of minor details, it's important that the designer set a clear agenda for the meeting.

The Design-Presentation Board

This presentation board was set up quickly and easily on a clean 24-in. by 36-in. piece of poster-board. The drawings are neatly arranged and held down with white tape that has been cut, rather than torn.

The photos and drawings are as follows:

1. Photos of the principal view (moved from the design sketchboard). The view is one of the outstanding aesthetic features of the site, and an underlying rationale for the orientation of the rooms and many other features of the design.

2, 3. The scaled site/floor plan and second-floor plan (pp. 200-201), respectively, in their correct orientation toward the view in the photos above.

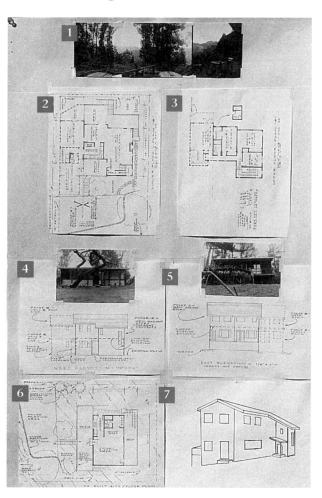

4. The west elevation (p. 204), or principal facade, with a photo of the west side of the existing house in its correct orientation to the site/floor plan.

5. The east elevation (p. 204), with a photo of the east side of the house.

6. The as-built site floor plan (p. 190), for comparison.

7. A hard-line perspective drawn over a rough perspective sketch.

The drawings can be placed on the board in any order, but there should be some logical progression from one drawing to the next. The designer may also choose to prepare a second board with more drawings, in order to show the rest of the elevations, photos of views from various windows, details or even process drawings (schematics and rough sketches).

Essentially, the first part of the meeting should be a monologue in which the designer explains the plans, with as little interruption from the owners as possible. Once the entire design has been explained, the owners are free to react and ask as many questions as they like.

Preparing for the presentation

The meeting should take place at the owners' home, so they can more easily visualize the proposed changes. The designer should come equipped with a roll of flimsy for drawing over the plans, an architect's scale, pencils, a tape measure for demonstrating actual sizes or checking the house as ideas come up, a notebook to record the discussion, and copies of all the drawings and the budget review to leave with the owners.

The preliminary design drawings, sketches and photographs should be assembled on the design-presentation board in a logical order (see the sidebar above).

Reviewing the underlying rationale

Begin the preliminary design presentation by reiterating the project goals that were written down as a summary of the design-parameters review meeting (see p. 183). Reiterating the goals will serve to refresh everyone's memory and set the stage for the design presentation. The design's success should be judged by how well it fulfills the goals, and, it is hoped, exceeds expectations.

(text continues on p. 202)

PRELIMINARY DESIGN-PRESENTATION DRAWINGS: SITE/FLOOR PLAN

These drawings were prepared at ⅛-in. scale over the as-built site/floor-plan template (p. 190), and with reference to the preliminary design sketches (pp. 196-197). They are an adequate rendition of the preliminary design for a small project such as an addition, and took considerably less time to draw than the detailed, ¼-in.-scale representations that are frequently used. The ⅛-in.-scale drawings are also sufficiently accurate to be blown up as templates for working drawings.

Note that the master plan for the addition (see pp. 210-211) has been divided into three phases: first, the current second-story addition and first-story expansion; second, the future one-story carport, laundry and family room; and third, the future master bedroom on the

second story. Phases II and III could be built at the same time, separately or not at all, depending on the owners' situation.

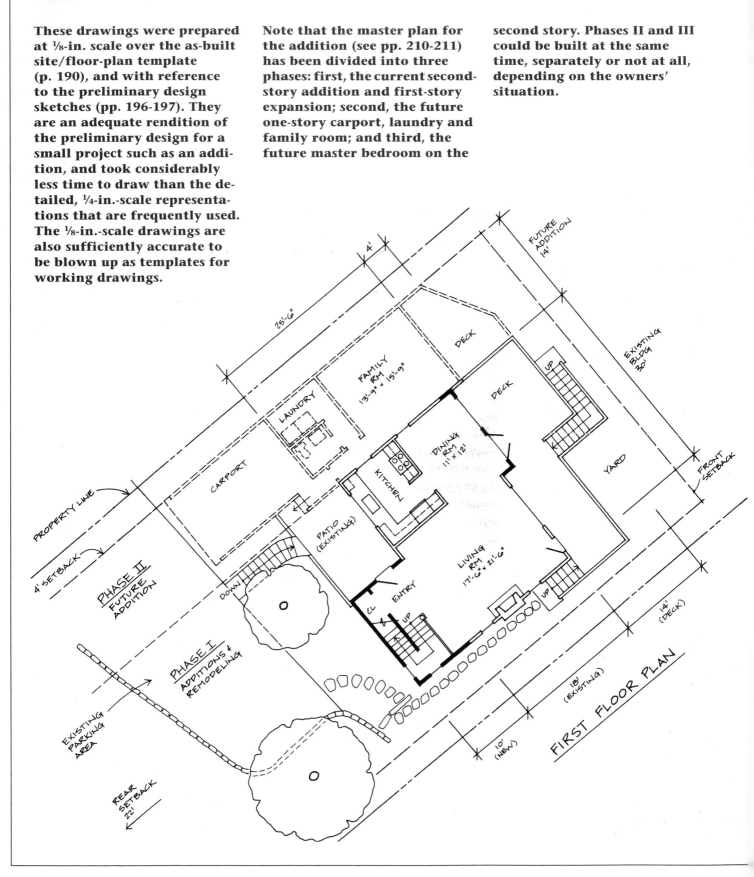

FIRST FLOOR PLAN

Two issues were discussed and resolved during the presentation of this design. First, the owners had initially thought that the current project would be built on the location of the proposed future family room, because the designer had mentioned, perhaps prematurely, some of the advantages of building a room addition. The rationale for the major decision to build a second story rather than a room addition (see p. 196) was discussed at the beginning of the presentation, and the owners eventually agreed with the designer's reasoning.

Second, the owners were concerned about the location of the stairs in a corner of the house. However, by actually pacing off the distance from the future family-room/dining-room passage (the north wall by the existing bath) to the proposed stairs, the owners were convinced that the stair location was convenient enough.

The owners also suggested some minor changes, including adding more kitchen cabinets and expanding the deck in front of the living room. Aside from that, they were delighted with the design, and the designer was able proceed to the design-development phase.

BALCONY

FUTURE MASTER BEDROOM 13'-9" × 15'-9"

CLOSET

CLST

PHASE III FUTURE ADDITION

PHASE I ADDITION

BDRM #1 8'-10" × 14'-0"

PHASE III MASTERBATH

BDRM #2 10'-8" × 14'-10"

DOWN

BDRM #3 8'-6" × 11'-8"

SECOND FLOOR PLAN

SQUARE FTGE
1ST FLOOR = 1120
2ND FLOOR = 1022
TOTAL 2142
(LESS EXISTING) <575>
TO BUILD 1567

Next, explain the underlying rationale for the major decisions—like building a combination addition instead of a second-story addition, or eliminating a bathroom to keep within budget. During the guided tour of the plans (see below), show how the design follows that rationale.

What the designer should not do is begin by walking the owners through the house from feature to feature: "Uh, this is the kitchen door, and this is the little hall going to the bedroom. These are the stairs. Here's the kitchen, and the refrigerator is that little rectangle in the corner."

There are two problems with this approach. First, the clients have no way of telling *why* the kitchen or the refrigerator is where it is. Second, the owners aren't stupid. The designer provides them with perfectly good drawings that show where everything is. The plans should be gone over in detail, of course, but only in the context of explaining the reasons for each design decision.

The guided tour

When taking the owners on a tour of the plans, start, once again, with the big picture, not by meandering through the house from detail to detail. Where are the principal views, the focal areas, the transition zone? What are the most important features of the existing house? What are the constraining factors? Some designers actually show the process drawings—the bubble diagrams and the site analysis—to help the owners follow their thinking. Others prefer to show the finished product only, filling in the owners

on the thinking behind it as they go along. Either way, have a plan, and follow it through.

In most cases, it is logical to use the site/floor plan—which contains the most information—as the map for the tour (see pp. 200-201). Begin with the approach to the house and its main entrance. From the entry, proceed to the next space, usually the living room, and on through the rest of the house systematically. Make sure that each space is described in detail before moving on.

While touring the site/floor plan, refer to auxiliary views as needed. "Notice that the main circulation path ends on the deck. Here's a sketch of the deck from the outside." Return quickly to the site/floor plan, however, and stay with it until the tour is complete. Don't get off on a tangent with another view.

Once you've covered the site/floor plan, go through perspectives, elevations and other drawings systematically, one view at a time (see the drawings on pgs. 203 and 204). Explain how each exterior view relates to the existing building, the site and the building's context.

Finally, review the presentation by returning to the discussion of the principal goals, recounting how the design addresses them. This last step should not be omitted, because it brings the owners back to the beginning and thus helps them recall the entire presentation.

Discussing the design with the owners

It is a good idea to take a break after the guided tour, which should take about an hour, so that the owners have a chance to absorb what they

have been told and to frame their responses. Once the discussion of the design begins, the designer should let the owners do all the talking at first (except for answering questions). They'll probably have a lot to say; if they don't, they can be prodded by asking what they think about specific parts of the design.

The designer's purpose in the discussion is to gather information, not deflect criticism. By this time, the owners and designer have traveled some distance together. Through discussing the program they've gotten to know each other, shared ideas and developed some trust. The rejection of some of the designer's ideas at this point, then, need not be taken personally, but as an honest expression of the owners' preferences, which were perhaps impossible for them to articulate before seeing the contrast between the preliminary design drawings and their own concepts.

A discussion of ideas that the owners dislike can lead to a better design. Or, by simply being allowed to air their views, the owners may come around to seeing things the designer's way after all. Such discussions are almost always fruitful. One way to get the best from them is for the designer to start to sketch on flimsy over the drawings. "Well, if you want more storage for canned goods, perhaps we can put shelves in the left half of this broom closet…."

Reviewing the budget

The preliminary designs, which are the first scaled drawings of the proposed project, provide a great deal of information that was lacking when the feasibility assessment was

PRELIMINARY DESIGN-PRESENTATION DRAWINGS: "PERSPECTIVE"

This drawing was traced over the massing sketch (p. 195) with a straightedge in about 45 minutes. A certain amount of fudging was needed to keep the lines "in perspective" and give the illusion that the sizes of the various components are correct in relation to one another. A true perspective, with vanishing points and horizon lines, would be more accurate, but would also take much longer to set up and draw. It was not necessary for a preliminary design presentation of this addition.

While it is quite acceptable to show the owners a fudged perspective drawing during the preliminary design review, its inaccuracies must be ex-plained. The owners should never get the impression that their building will look exactly like the drawing. In fact, when the owners sign the preliminary design drawings just before production of the working drawings begins, they should not sign any perspective drawing, since perspectives do not represent the true dimensions but only the correct proportions of objects.

Notice that the roof over the back porch, which was peaked in the rough sketch, is flat in this drawing. The peaked roof would go better with the gable above, but since it is more expensive to build than the flat roof and will be removed when the family-room addition is built, the designer decided to save the money. The owners felt differently, however, and a small peaked roof was designed so that it could be bolted to the wall for easy removal when the family room is built.

made. Using these drawings, the designer can fine-tune the original square-footage calculations (see the table on pp. 14-15) and begin to analyze the costs of major components like cabinets, plumbing fixtures, doors and windows. There will also be a better sense of the technical difficulties and other factors that affect the cost.

At this point, revising the budget need not be an elaborate, time-consuming task. In most cases, the formula used for the preliminary budget can simply be reworked and the new numbers substituted for the old. In fact, it is a good idea to staple copies of both budgets together, so the owners can see how well the design complies to the original estimates.

Reviewing and noting changes
As the final item on the meeting's agenda, go back over all the changes to the plans that have been discussed with the owners. Once you've made sure that everyone is in agreement about exactly what will change, record the changes, either in a notebook or directly on the flimsy. The notes and sketches will prove invaluable during the design-development stage.

PRELIMINARY DESIGN-PRESENTATION DRAWINGS: ELEVATIONS

These principal elevations are scaled, accurate drawings, and contain enough detail for the owners to understand the house. Note that the roof line of the future master bedroom is shown as slightly below that of the main house. The roof line is dropped down because it is easier to weatherproof the connection of a new shingle roof to a wall than to an existing roof. Also note that the edges of the second-story windows align with the first-story openings.

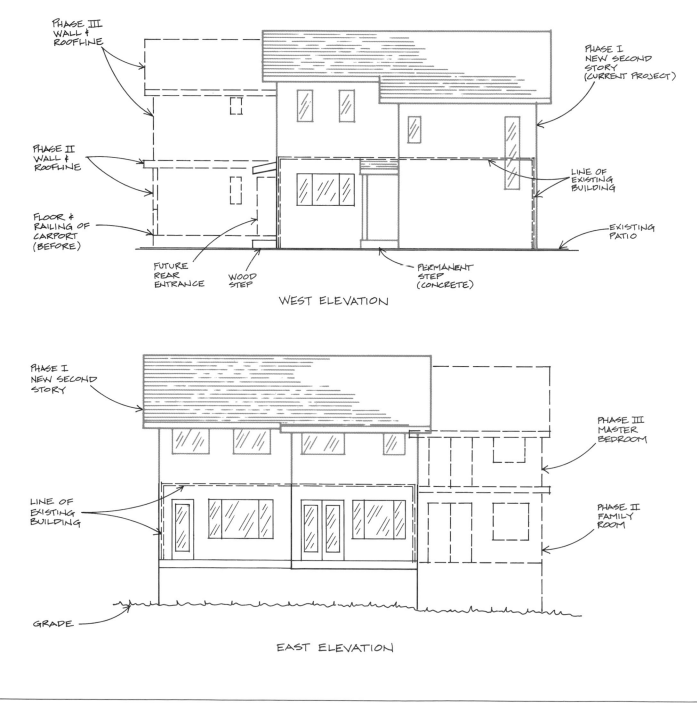

PHASE III WALL & ROOFLINE

PHASE I NEW SECOND STORY (CURRENT PROJECT)

PHASE II WALL & ROOFLINE

LINE OF EXISTING BUILDING

FLOOR & RAILING OF CARPORT (BEFORE)

EXISTING PATIO

FUTURE REAR ENTRANCE

WOOD STEP

PERMANENT STEP (CONCRETE)

WEST ELEVATION

PHASE I NEW SECOND STORY

PHASE III MASTER BEDROOM

LINE OF EXISTING BUILDING

PHASE II FAMILY ROOM

GRADE

EAST ELEVATION

DEVELOPING THE DESIGN

If the owners approve the basic design, suggesting only minor modifications, the designer can begin to work out the details. A request for major changes would necessitate generating new preliminary designs, perhaps even discarding everything but the schematic drawings. (Major changes are unlikely at this stage if the design parameters were well researched and a number of ideas were explored during the preliminary design phase.)

Aligning and tracing the design

As a first step, blow up the ⅛-in.-scale, design-presentation site/floor plans to ¼-in. scale (200% of their size) on a copy machine. The blow-ups will be somewhat inaccurate, which will have to be compensated for as the plans are drafted.

Tape the blowups on a drafting board, then tape the transparent sheets with the original ¼-in.-scale as-built drawings over them, with the original as-built plans on one side and the new design on the other. Carefully align the two drawings, so a straightedge can be used to transfer lines from one drawing to the other.

Choose a long, straight line common to both drawings and trace over it lightly. It will become the baseline from which all the new plan's measurements are derived. Using the underlying blowup of the design for reference, trace the plans at ¼-in. scale. (As soon as the outline is complete, remove the blowup because it will make the tracing hard to read.)

Keep the tracing light, and do not label it or fill in the walls since the design still needs more development. Use a similar process to transfer the design-presentation elevations to a full-sized sheet that will become part of the working drawings.

Modifying the plans

By the time the design-development stage is reached, it is no longer necessary to generate new basic concepts, and most problems can be approached logically and systematically. The owners want a linen closet in the master bath and are willing to sacrifice some of the drying-off and dressing space to get it. The skylight in the hall was a nice idea, but it's not essential since everyone agrees that enough light comes in through the windows. How about tucking a built-in bookcase into that empty corner?

To incorporate the minor changes resulting from the design-review discussion, sketch carefully and to scale on flimsy directly over the plans. Once the modification is designed, draft it onto the tracing.

The "final" design

Once the design is complete, the outline should be darkened so it can be blueprinted, or reproduced. Most of the labels can be added, but it is still too early to "poché," or fill in, the walls since any remaining changes to the walls would require a great deal of messy erasing.

Make two or three copies of each tracing. The final design drawings should include, at a minimum, the ⅛-in.-scale site plan, the ¼-in.-scale floor plans, and all four elevations. From this point on, mark each blueprint "Preliminary, not for construction" with a red pen so that there is

no chance that the builder will use any drawings except those approved by the building department. (Some designers have rubber stamps made up for marking multiple copies of plans.)

Before beginning the working drawings, have the clients review the final design and sign and date a small note on each sheet that states that they have seen and approved the drawings. Revising the working drawings, with all of their details, labels and dimensions, is costly, time-consuming and frustrating. It will seem less so if they have to be revised because the owners have changed their minds and are willing to pay for the revisions rather than because the designer neglected to show them the plans.

No design is truly final until the construction is complete. The signed note on the blueprints should include a statement to the effect that the drawings may be modified in minor ways by the designer as the working drawings evolve and opportunities for improving the plans present themselves. Major changes, however, should be approved by both parties.

PRODUCING THE CONSTRUCTION DOCUMENTS

Construction documents are plans and written reports that are approved by the building authorities and followed by the builder. Three main types of documents suffice for most additions: working drawings, engineer's reports and energy reports. Occasionally miscellaneous

Requirements for Working Drawings

SHEET #	DRAWING TYPE	DESCRIPTION AND COMMENTS
1.	Site plan (⅛-in. scale typical)	Site plan shows all property boundaries, setbacks, easements, etc., the existing house and the "area of new work," which includes the addition and remodeled portions of the house. The proposed addition and other new work can be shaded to stand out. Show other important site features like slope contours, walks and driveways, retaining walls and trees. Show north arrow, direction and pitch of roof slopes, drainage lines. Show footprint as dashed line within roof line.
	General notes	General notes include contents of drawing set; table of abbreviations; nailing, shear-wall, header, door and window schedules, lumber grades, energy specifications and other information.
2.	First-floor plans (¼-in. scale typical)	As-built and proposed first-floor plans. Show all walls, doors with swings, windows and permanent fixtures such as stairs and cabinets. Label all rooms. Show all dimensions (frame to frame). Locate skylights above. Show permanent electric lights, switches and outlets with dashed lines to indicate connections. Show location of shear wall, with references to schedules. Label doors and windows and refer to schedules in general notes. Show location and direction of principal sections. Show structural features as needed (such as post in wall or beam over). Show special features as needed.
3.	Second-floor plans (¼-in. scale typical)	Same as first-floor plans.
4.	Elevations (¼-in. scale typical)	Usually four to a sheet, aligned for easy drafting. Elevations show the building from grade, not floor level. Show conformity to height regulations and other critical dimensions. Show existing building in outline.
5.	Principal section (¼-in. scale typical)	Show size and position of principal structural members, including studs, joists, rafters, girders and beams. Show foundations in section. Show as many structural details as possible on the same sheet. Refer to details on other sheets.
6.	Foundation and floor-framing plan (¼-in. scale typical)	Show foundation and first-floor framing in plan, with sections and details.
7.	Roof-framing plan (¼-in. scale typical)	Show roof framing in plan, with sections and details.
8.	Stair sections and details (½-in. scale typical)	Show stairs in section, with supports, railings and details. (Can be consolidated with other drawings below.)
9.	Cabinet elevations and miscellaneous details (scale varies—½ in. typical)	Specify cabinet sizes, number of drawers, doors, countertops, etc. Show installation details as needed.
10.	Deck elevations and structure (½-in. scale typical)	Show elevations and structural details of deck; compliance of railings and stairs with code.
11.	Miscellaneous internal and external elevations and details (scale varies)	Elevations could include fireplace, entry or other special features. Show also remaining details of structural connections that will not fit on earlier sheets.

Note: A detailed list of requirements, used by a city plan checker, is shown in Appendix II.

documents such as surveys, zoning applications and environmental-impact reports must be attached to the plans as well. In addition to these legally required documents, optional specifications for materials and fixtures may be attached to the plans if the owners hire the designer to select these items.

Working drawings

The main difference between working drawings for an addition and working drawings for a new house is that the former need to show the existing conditions as well as the new work. There are also some differences of organization (see the table on the facing page).

The site plan is usually a single drawing of the entire building that shows the addition as the "area of new work." Normally, there are enough changes to the existing

floor plans to make it necessary to show two drawings of each floor—the existing plan and the proposed plan. This requirement changes the organization of a typical set of plans as follows:

As mentioned earlier, two ¼-in.-scale floor plans for most houses can fit on a standard 24-in. by 36-in. sheet. The floor plans for a typical two-story house are normally placed on the same sheet so they can be aligned with each other to simplify drafting and make comparison easier. For a two-story addition, it is more convenient to put both first floors on one sheet, followed by both second floors on another. This way, again, the addition drawing can be aligned with and compared to that of the existing building.

You don't usually need to draw separate as-built elevations or sections, though it might be helpful to

indicate the location of the existing building or framing with a dotted line or arrow (see the drawings on p. 204). The detail drawings that show the connections between the existing structure and the new work must of course have each item labeled. Acceptable abbreviations are (E) for "existing" and (N) for "new." For the most part, the other drawings are similar to those for new construction.

Producing working drawings If you follow the procedure outlined above—first drawing the as-built plans to their final scale, next photo-reducing them for the preliminary design work and then blowing up the designs to trace over—the working drawings are about one-third complete by the time the working-drawing phase begins. The site plans, floor plans and elevations are already drawn

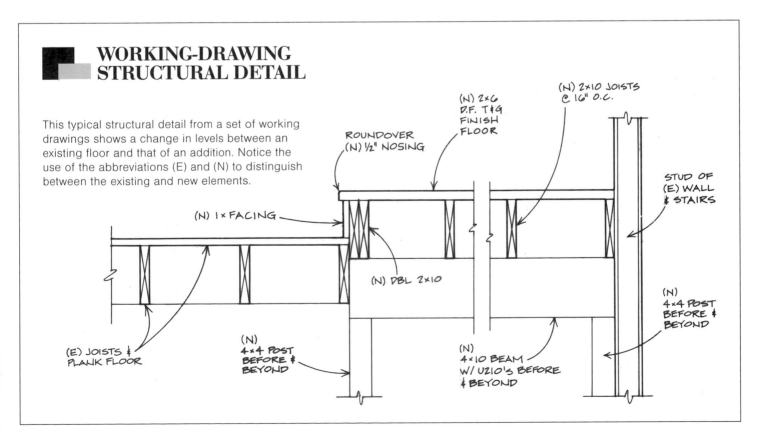

WORKING-DRAWING STRUCTURAL DETAIL

This typical structural detail from a set of working drawings shows a change in levels between an existing floor and that of an addition. Notice the use of the abbreviations (E) and (N) to distinguish between the existing and new elements.

Computer-Aided Design and Drafting (CADD)

Using a computer can greatly facilitate the task of designing an addition, especially producing the working drawings. There are a number of factors to consider, however, before investing in expensive machinery and software with the intention of using them as the primary design tools.

Designing with computers

Advocates of computer-aided design point to the speed with which today's computers and CADD applications can draw lines, write and reposition labels, perform square-footage and materials calculations, incorporate changes in the plans and, perhaps most important, allow the designer to rotate perspective views of the building to create the illusion of a three-dimensional view. In today's construction market, these features are essential to the efficient design of large-scale projects such as office buildings, where a change in the shape, dimensions or labels of a single modular component might have to be duplicated on many stories or could cause entire segments of the building to be redrawn.

On a small-scale project like an addition, however, the speed and efficiency advantages of CADD may be overrated. It takes a great deal of input time to create the as-built design templates. Typically, hand drafting is at least as fast at this stage of the computer's development. While it is true that once the as-builts are created they can be almost instantly duplicated for manipulation, the preliminary design sketching is still a particularly slow process on the computer. Finally, making changes to a single component, as opposed to changes to a modular component in a large building that will be duplicated, often takes as long, if not longer on the computer than by hand.

Another problem is encountered in the printing of the plans. A plotter, or printer, large enough to print on standard 24-in. by 36-in. sheets is a major investment, particularly for a small firm. Though disks with the plans can be sent to blueprinting services for reproduction, the process is awkward, especially if the plans need revision from time to time.

Perhaps the most important problem in using computers in design, though, lies in the interface between computers and people and the way computers force the designer to work. To begin with, computer screens of sufficient size and power to project several images that are large enough to see at one time—such as can be arranged on a design sketchboard—are extremely expensive by the standards of a small design office. Also, the large screens require an enormous amount of computing power, so they have to be driven by a comparably

and partially labeled, and the principal section, foundation and framing plans, which for the most part can be traced using the other drawings as templates, should go quickly.

The details remain to be drawn, and for an addition they are more numerous and laborious than those of a typical house because of all of the connections. (Using a computer can save a lot of time in drawing the details, as explained in the sidebar above.)

When the tracings are finished, they should be checked by someone other than the main draftsperson to make sure that they are complete and free of errors. Then they can go to a blueprint store for reproduction.

Six or eight sets are usually needed initially. Most building departments require two sets—one for the job site and one to keep on file. The designer needs a set, the owners should have a copy, and a few copies will be needed by the primary contractors and subcontractors so they can begin working up estimates while the plans move through city hall.

Remember to mark "Preliminary, not for construction" on all of the prints, except those that are submitted to city hall. After the permit is granted (see p. 170) and the job-site prints are released by the building department, the revisions required by the authorities should be drawn on the tracings, and a final set of working-drawing prints made for everyone on the project.

Engineer's reports

Unusual structures or difficult sites may require that written recommendations from a structural or geotechnical engineer (or both) be attached to the plans. Typically, the designer all but completes the working drawings, leaving off those labels and dimensions that will be specified by the engineer, and then sends copies of the plans (blueprints) to the engineer for review.

expensive computer. Although it is easy to switch back and forth between images on a computer, the effect is not the same as seeing the whole site/floor plan and a series of elevations and other drawings laid out for viewing.

The other interface problem lies in the capacity of the machines for hand sketching. Although electronic sketch pads are available, they cannot yet simulate real sketching well enough to enhance the complex relationship between the eye and the hand that allows for the free flow of ideas. In short, you can draw better with a pencil.

Drafting with computers

Turning from designing to producing the working drawings, however, the computer becomes an indispensable tool, especially for details. First, the problem of scale in printing is overcome when drafting details, because most details fit on the standard 8½-in. by 11-in. sheets handled by typical office printers. The sheets can be easily and cheaply reproduced as "stickybacks" (adhesive-backed transparencies) and pasted onto the standard-format plans. Second, hundreds of architectural details illustrating framing, roof assemblies and so on are available in electronic form on disk. The drawings from these "detail libraries" can be called up by CADD programs and readily modified as the particular design requires.

Computers also help with a variety of repetitive graphic tasks such as writing general notes and titles for reproduction on stickyback.

Other office uses

Computers are indispensable for auxiliary services such as spreadsheet accounting for feasibility and construction estimates (and running the office) and writing reports.

While CADD needs considerable development before it can replace the pencil as the primary design tool for small projects, any serious design or construction office needs to have at least one computer capable of doing some, if not most, of the detail drafting and of performing other office functions.

As time goes by, computers are becoming better and better design tools. As long as the designer understands the current limitations of computers, it makes sense (within reason) to invest in higher-capacity machines with more growth potential.

The engineer "sizes" the structural members and specifies the shear-wall schedule, the strength of the concrete, the types and numbers of metal connectors and other structural requirements. The engineer's recommendations may be marked on the blueprints with a red pen or submitted in a separate report. The blueprints are then returned to the designer, who completes the drafting on the tracings, incorporating all of the engineer's specifications. (There should be no great surprises or changes, since the engineer has been consulted since the beginning on unusual projects—see chapters 6, 7 and 8.) Then the final plans, along with the auxiliary calculations or reports, if any, are submitted to the building department.

Designers who are not trained as engineers need not concern themselves with the details of calculations or other highly technical information. The marks on the blueprints use nomenclature understandable to the carpenter in the field—"6x12 header," "2x10 joists," and so on. They can simply be copied onto the tracings.

Depending on the situation, the building department may require that the structural drawings—the floor plans, sections and structural details—be stamped by the engineer with his or her state registration mark. This way the authorities know that a licensed engineer has reviewed the plans and the specifications are on the prints. The building department's plan checker will review the plans as well, and may occasionally disagree with the engineer's findings or calculations and require revisions.

Energy reports
Some states or jurisdictions require heat-loss and other energy calculations and specifications. In some areas, it is acceptable just to submit the report and follow the recommendations. Other jurisdictions require that the specifications be placed directly on the plans. When the latter is required, the energy consultant normally provides the

designer with an adhesive-backed transparency known as a "sticky-back," which can be attached directly to the tracings. The stickyback, like the engineer's marks on the plans, specifies basic information, written in carpenter's nomenclature, about the thickness of the insulation, the types of windows, and other energy-conserving requirements.

MASTER PLANNING

As mentioned in Chapter 1, it is a good idea to develop some sort of master plan for every remodeling project. Even if there is no plan to build anything other than the current addition, you should consider the potential of every foot of the house and site for the information such a survey might yield. Perhaps you will discover a future project that could significantly increase the property's value for very little money or help realize its ultimate aesthetic potential.

The future project might not even be an extension of the current addition. It might turn out to be a small, intimate garden with a gazebo in one corner of the property. Shouldn't the current addition have a window that catches a glimpse of it?

Where a phased addition project is planned, you can use the list of goals and priorities discussed at the end of Chapter 11 as the basis for creating a master plan. Ideally, the most important goals will be met in the first phase of the project. The list can be rearranged as the design's possibilities are explored during the preliminary design-sketching phase.

The master plan has three purposes: First, to divide the project into phases for reasons of affordability or convenience. Second, to avoid long-range mistakes such as building the addition on the best location for a future swimming pool. Third, to help with the sale of the house if, for whatever reason, the later phases of the plan are not completed.

Would-be buyers may not see the potential for a new wing or recreation room if it is merely described to them by the owners. As most realtors can attest, however, a conceptual drawing, particularly one that shows that the entrances, exits and other major features that have already been built during the first phase of the project align with the future space, will often help make the sale. As another example, it is much easier to convince people of the possibility of building a second story over a recently completed, single-story room addition if the new structure has already been provided with a two-story foundation and has a flat roof that can easily be built over.

The keys to master planning

The first key to effective master planning is to work out the deferred portion of the project in sufficient detail so that the current portion will actually fit with it. Draw the deferred work to scale on the preliminary design drawings (see pp. 200-201) and update the drawings, in outline at least, as the design is developed. Make detailed working drawings for the current project only—leave the future work in outline form.

Issues to consider in master planning include: Will the future extension fit within the design envelope? Will the structural connections be straightforward, or will they require a lot of remodeling of the newly built addition? Can the floor of the present addition be extended at its same level on a sloping site without running into problems at grade? If a new electrical subpanel is installed for the current project, will it have sufficient amperage to serve an adjacent room or spa in the future? If not, now is the time to run the heavier wire.

The second key to master planning is to make sure that when the current project is complete it will stand alone if the next phase is never built. In the example given above, the designer might provide a flat roof over a room addition in anticipation of a future second story. Although this solution could work well if the addition was in the backyard and hard to see from the street, a highly visible flat-roof addition can look out of place alongside a home with a pitched roof, devaluing the building.

The owners may fail to complete the planned second story for a variety of reasons, but chief among them are likely to be financial constraints or the need to relocate. Both could compel the owners to sell the house, and although the additional space provided by the first phase of the project will raise the house's value, the aesthetic debacle of an addition that looks tacked on will lower it—perhaps so much so that building the first phase will not even pay for itself.

So the designer must be aware that it takes more than an initial enthusiasm to realize long-range goals, and design thoughtfully. The goal of master planning is to provide the owners with a completed version of what they can afford now, and save them from having to take steps backward at a later date. It is only through master planning that a variety of basic approaches to each set of program requirements can be considered.

Curiously, master planning is often overlooked on small-scale projects. Home owners seem to perceive that planning is superfluous and expensive, something that only cities should be involved in. Designers, seeking to please their clients, often accept this notion passively.

Nothing could be farther from the truth. Just as a lack of thorough programming can lead to reversals in the design process, a lack of good master planning can lead to much more serious and expensive embarrassments even before the initial phase of the project is complete. This is an instance where the designer or builder should take the lead, and make sure that what's done is what is in the best long-range interest of the owners—especially since the master plan for a residential property is not all that complex and develops naturally along with the preliminary design.

Master-Plan Checklist

This checklist can be used to make sure that the master plan for the building and site is properly organized and documented.

A. Project sequence

☐ Single project?

☐ Phased project?

    1. How many phases? _____

    2. Which elements phased? _____

    3. Which functional and aesthetic goals are fulfilled in each phase? _____

    4. Approximate time frame for completion of each phase ____

☐ Other considerations?

B. Master-plan documents

☐ Master-plan checklist (this list, with copy for owners)

☐ Graphic documents of proposed project phases:

    1. Detail level: ☐ Schematic

                  ☐ Preliminary sketches

                  ☐ Scaled plans and elevations

                  ☐ Working drawings

    2. Documents reproduced for owners? _____

    3. Future construction shown on current working drawings? _____

C. Special design considerations for master plan

☐ Need to improve existing structure or subsystems?

☐ Special provisions on site (e.g., extension of retaining walls)?

☐ Other special considerations?

13
GETTING READY TO BUILD

"The journey well begun is half over," goes an old Chinese saying. Similarly, the addition project that is well designed is half built, but only if the designer has thought carefully about all of the construction issues. The need to consider costs, logistics and the availability of materials while designing has been emphasized throughout this book. If this recommendation is followed, a great deal of the thinking and problem solving that is all too often left to the builder—and begins after the working drawings have been issued—is already done.

Estimating the cost of an addition project, for example, should start with the feasibility consultation (see pp. 14-16) and be reviewed periodically as the design progresses. Although detailed material take-offs and labor analyses must wait until the working drawings are complete, there should be few, if any, surprises if the designer has dealt with the budget conscientiously.

Also, there should be no remodeling surprises—discoveries of hidden pipes, inadequate framing, and so forth. These problems should have been ferreted out during the detailed measuring and evaluation session (see pp. 186-189) and dealt with as part of the design.

All too often, however, such problems are discovered after the working drawings are complete and put out for bid. When the bids are much higher than expected as a result of unforeseen problems, the owners are suddenly confronted with four choices: exceed the budget, sacrifice quality, scale down the project (which means redeveloping the design and redrawing the working drawings) or, last, completely abandon the project after having invested in the design.

The best way to ensure that budget surprises and other unforeseen problems are avoided is to have a builder on the design team. Today's standard practice of having designers who are not involved with construction produce the working drawings and put them out to bid invites the opposite effect—unforeseen problems are likely to cause the estimates or final costs to exceed the budget.

For the job to go smoothly, not only must the addition be well designed, but the construction itself must be carefully planned as well. This chapter addresses the critical question of who will build the addition, including a discussion of the nature of the builder's contract and the builder's relationship with the owners. It also covers estimating for construction, and ends by describing a systematic approach to planning the construction of an addition.

THE RIGHT APPROACH

If they have not already done so, the owners and designer can start to look for a builder once the working drawings are complete. In the traditional scenario, the drawings are sent out to several contractors for competitive bids, and the one who submits the lowest bid gets the work. One of the problems with this approach, however, is that it is based on the mistaken assumption that the construction documents adequately describe the work so that all bids are for the same exact performance.

At best, that is only partly true. The plans are to the finished house what an outline is to a book—a great deal of filling in must take place before the project is complete. To draw plans and write specifications that describe every last detail of the work would be so expensive that there would be hardly any money left to build with. Though much of the design is complete, a lot is left open to interpretation.

The conventional way of dealing with the discrepancies between the drawings and the finished building is to have the plans drawn by an architect and then have the architect watch the contractor to make sure that the work is performed correctly. What constitutes correct performance is, of course, a subjective judgment since even the best of plans leave as many questions as they answer. If this is the arrangement, the architect is in a position to interpret the plans as he or she sees them, and the contractor is also free to reject this interpretation and claim that work is being demanded that was not covered in the bid.

The project, then, starts out with a potential built-in conflict, imposed by convention, between two of the three principal players—the architect and contractor—with the owners most likely to side with the architect if any problems arise. Rather than working as a team to solve the problems, the parties are working at odds while trying to decide who is wrong.

Ironically, the parties may be naturally agreeable people who want to work together, but they have bought into a system that postulates that builders are inclined to do shoddy work, rather than their best, and need constant correction. This type of thinking sets the stage for conflict. It is critical, then, to find a way within the existing legal structure—which does offer certain protections—for people to work together toward the common goal of building the best addition possible.

The right approach can mean that no one loses, everyone wins, and the project comes out well. To find that approach, let's begin by considering who might build the addition, and what relationship they might have with the owners.

Choosing a builder

The owners are responsible for hiring a builder. They may choose to hire a general contractor or a designer/builder or decide to act as the contractors themselves and hire carpenters and other tradespeople to do the actual construction.

General contractors Many, if not most, additions are built by licensed general contractors hired by the owners. A general contractor takes on the whole project, and typically hires subcontractors to do specialized work like electrical wiring. Licensed contractors operate under a set of contracting laws imposed, in most cases, by the state government.

For the owners, the advantage of hiring a licensed general contractor is that the basic terms of the agreement between the contractor and the owners are defined by the contracting laws. As well as stipulating that the contractor will perform the work properly, the laws include a series of mutual protections to ensure, for example, that the contractor maintains a bond, or insurance policy, that protects the owners if the contractor fails to complete the work or damages the property. The contractor is also responsible for paying the workers and deducting their taxes, and for insuring them against bodily harm, so the owners are safe from liability. The laws also specify how the contractor performs other managerial work like hiring and paying subcontractors and procuring and reselling building materials.

The owners reciprocate by paying the contractor and making decisions in a timely fashion so the project can proceed without interruption. Except for making sure that there is money in the account and that the trim, fixtures and paint colors are selected on time, the owners don't have to worry about much, assuming the contractor is competent.

If the owners do not pay the contractor within a reasonable period of time, the contractor may place a lien on the property; that is, obtain a legal document that forces all construction to stop (so the owners can't just dump a contractor who is owed a large sum of money and hire someone else) and makes it impossible for the owner to sell the property without paying the contractor. If either the contractor or the owners fail to perform their obligations, liens and other safeguards should mitigate at least some of the damage.

Although the relationship between the contractor and owners is fairly well defined, the exact nature of their contract is not. The lack of specificity is to allow contracts to be written so the parties can choose between fixed bids, time and materials contracts or any other type of arrangement they wish to enter into (see pp. 217-218). The owners and builder, working as a team, can structure the contract to take advantage of the mutual protections afforded them by law while avoiding some of the pitfalls inherent in the competitive bidding system.

Designer/builders Whereas a typical general contractor only builds the addition, a designer/builder designs and builds it. Many designer/ builders are licensed general contractors, while others are primarily architects or designers who regularly build.

Hiring a designer/builder instead of a general contractor has several advantages for the owners. First, they will get someone who has an investment in making the job look as good as it can (to show off the design) and is responsible for both the concept and the end result. It is often possible to get better work than by the traditional means of hiring designers and builders separately, since a designer/builder is sufficiently familiar with construction techniques to make sure they are accounted for in the design phase.

Second, a great deal of hassle is eliminated by avoiding a repetition of the lengthy process of interviewing, hiring and working with two different parties. Also, there will be no conflict between the designer and the contractor, and less likelihood that the builder will write a change order (addendum to the contract) that adds to the cost every time there is an opportunity for a minor enhancement that is not specified on the plans. Overall, the entire process from feasibility through construction should run more smoothly and efficiently when one individual or firm controls it.

Some people argue that the designer and the builder should be separate individuals so that the designer can protect the owners' interests by watching over the builder. Who will keep an eye on the single individual or firm in charge of the whole process? What if the unsupervised designer/builder buries shoddy construction beneath the walls and floors, hidden from the untrained eyes of the owners, only to surface at a later date, long after the pay checks are cashed?

In reality, it's extremely unlikely that the designer/builder will take advantage of the owners. By the time construction starts, the designer/builder has a long-standing relationship with the owners; the final design is the product of that relationship. The designer/builder, who has had plenty of time to contemplate a variety of means for turning what is, after all, his or her own design into reality, has little motivation to do anything but the best work.

Also, the plans are reviewed by a plan checker, who is usually an engineer, and the work is inspected by building officials (see Chapter 10). While this does not guarantee good work, it at least offers a reasonable assurance that the building codes and a minimum acceptable standard of workmanship are upheld.

All in all, fostering a spirit of mutual understanding and teamwork between the owners and the builder or designer/builder is normally a much better insurance of quality workmanship than adopting a negative and suspicious supervisory attitude aimed at enforcing agreements that are always subject to interpretation.

The owner as contractor In the conventional relationship between the owners and contractor discussed above, the owners write checks and the contractor does everything else. While this is easy for the owners, it is also expensive. Although people usually think of contractors as builders, most of them, in reality, are administrators. The owners pay not only for the labor and materials but also for the contractor's overhead, the administrative services and a profit of 5% to 20% on top of all the other costs.

One way to save money, perhaps enough money to make the project feasible, is for the owners to take over some or all of the administration of the project. In many states, the owners can act as the contractors on their own homes, hiring either licensed or unlicensed people to assist them with the building, as long as they provide accident insurance (worker's compensation) in case anyone is injured on the job.

The administrative duties cannot be undertaken casually, however, especially for a project the size of an addition, because there are numerous potential liabilities and pitfalls. Owners who are serious about acting as their own contractors must be willing to do three things:

First, they must be willing to learn enough about the design and construction process to be able to converse intelligently with the builders and other parties. If the owners order materials, for example, they need to understand not only the professional nomenclature, but also how to make an acceptable substitution of one material for another if the first is unavailable. (Classes are offered in owner contracting in many areas.)

Second, the owners must be willing to make a serious commitment to spend the time needed—on a daily basis throughout the course of the entire project—to meet with the builders and undertake all of the responsibilities that go along with contracting. These responsibilities include arranging for the procurement of materials, negotiating with and supervising subcontractors, arranging for inspections, and many other tasks.

Finally, the owners need to define their responsibilities and those of the builders clearly. Frequently, the owners can undertake only some of the duties of the contractor. For example, they can provide the insurance and help make the big decisions, but they don't have the time to stay in touch with the ever-changing agendas of day-to-day building.

In such cases, the responsibility for keeping the job going usually falls to the head carpenter (as it often does when a contractor runs the job). The owners who have exercised their right to act as the contractor must now accept the concomitant responsibility of treating the head carpenter fairly, and not simply and unexpectedly leave him with contractor's duties while offering him workman's wages.

As with most problems on a construction project, clear communication is the key. The owners and builder should decide who is responsible for what from the outset—preferably by writing it down. If it turns out that the owners' commitments are unmanageable, the problem should be discussed as soon as it becomes obvious.

One problem with having marginally informed owners and a head carpenter who is not a contractor run a project is that there may not be enough know-how to get the job done. The head carpenter can handle day-to-day decisions, but there are times when changes in the plans or other major issues will require the judgment of someone with more experience.

One way for the owner-as-contractor scenario to work, then, is to hire a third party, someone with a thorough knowledge of construction, as a consultant. A logical choice would be the designer, if he or she knows building as well as drawing and has the proper administrative skills. An experienced contractor who is willing to put in a few hours of supervising on the side could be a good choice, too.

Qualified consultants are relatively expensive, but high hourly fees are easily mitigated by the savings to the project and, in total, are cheap compared to the overhead, administration fees and profit paid to a contractor.

Although acting as the contractor means a real commitment of time and energy on the part of the owners, it can be well worth the trouble if the savings are as much as 20% of, say, $150,000. The designer or designer/builder, always acting in the owners' best interest, should explore this possibility with them.

The owner as builder Simple arithmetic shows why owners who have jobs and family responsibilities should not attempt to build projects as large as additions. It takes a crew of two carpenters and a helper, along with two or three subcontractors and their helpers, a minimum of two and usually three to six months to build a typical addition. That's the work of three trained people for an average of four months and three more people, the subcontractors, for another month —about 330 person days of work.

An owner, working during vacation time and on weekends—without any breaks to mow the lawn, visit with friends, watch a game or rest— might be able to work about 110 days a year. The project will already take a minimum of three years to build.

Next, add in the set-up and breakdown time: Professionals spend half of Monday getting the job going and half of Friday winding it down. Owners spend part of Saturday starting up and part of Sunday cleaning up—thus actually work for little more than one day each weekend. The 110 days per year is now reduced to about 60, and the project takes six years.

Now factor in most owners' lack of expertise, equipment and trained help and, being generous, say it will take them only twice as long as the professional to get things done. Now the addition takes 12 years to build. So much for tackling the job alone.

The owner as helper You may have seen signs in automotive garages that read:

My Rates
Basic work	$35/hr.
If you watch	$45/hr.
If you help	$65/hr.

The professional builder in charge of the project should be careful to make sure that well-meaning owners do not interfere with the construction schedule, both for their own sake and that of the owners. If the owners really want to get their hands dirty, that can be arranged, but it should not be on a part of the job that takes a high level of skill or is critical to the schedule. Skilled work can be muffed by an amateur, and the results will reflect badly on the builder. Critical scheduling must not be tampered with, and the builder should agree with the owners that if their share of the work is not progressing satisfactorily, someone can be hired to get it done.

Still, it is a good thing that the owners wish to participate and learn, since they will better appreciate the efforts of the builder and feel as though the house is more "theirs" when the project is finished. As long as their assigned tasks are appropriate for their skill level, and their time is managed as intelligently as any other worker's would be, the owners can be of great help to themselves and the project.

The best fit
Whether the addition is built by a conventional contractor, a designer/ builder or a carpenter working for the owners-as-contractors, one or two individuals, usually one, will be in charge of the day-to-day work and the overall project. This "builder" should be selected according to several criteria, not simply because he or she submits the lowest bid.

First and foremost, the builder should be able to get along with the owners, show sensitivity to their needs, and respond openly and informatively to their questions. The builder's relationship with the owners may turn out to be even more intimate than the designer's. He or she will be at the house every day for several months, and must be able to listen to the owners' concerns without becoming defensive or attempting to snow or bully them.

It is also important for the owners to know how the builder is doing personally. It's all well and good that the builder did a terrific job on someone else's addition last year, but did he lose money on it? Has he recovered from that loss? Does he harbor a grudge about it? Is he in the middle of an ugly divorce? Don't put the builder on the spot— just sit him down for coffee and have a pleasant conversation, as one would with anyone who would be around the house for six months.

Next, the owners should make sure that the builder understands the intent of the design and is enthusiastic about the project. Ask more questions. Now that the builder has had time to study the plans and make estimates, what does he or she like most about the design? Any suggested improvements? Any trepidation about the construction process? Remember, if the builder takes pride in the project rather than treating it as just another job, it will come out better.

It is important, of course, to ask the standard questions about the builder's qualifications for this particular project. Has he or she done others like it, or on a similar scale? Does the builder have the workers, equipment, connections with subcontractors and suppliers needed to perform the work? Check references and talk to former clients. If the builder has a license, check on its status. Have an attorney, the designer or another consultant look over the proposed contract.

Ultimately, however, these are just surface issues. There are lots of builders who are qualified but because of personality reasons, preoccupations or other factors may not be the best fit with the owners or the job. Selecting the right person is the trick, and, if it comes down to one or two candidates, go with the one who everyone involved in the selection process feels the most comfortable with and make a commitment to keep the lines of communication open.

BUILDING CONTRACTS

Like design contracts (see Chapter 11), building contracts describe the project, the obligations of both parties and the financial terms. As with design contracts, they may be written as letters of agreement or printed on standard forms.

Building contracts can vary significantly in their financial arrangements. The three basic arrangements are the *fixed-bid contract,* the *time and materials contract* and the *incentive contract.*

Fixed-bid contracts

A fixed bid is an agreement to perform all the work for a specified amount of money. The price usually includes profit and overhead, as well as administrative, labor and material costs.

The primary advantage of a fixed bid is that the owners know in advance how much they'll have to pay. This reassurance can relieve tension during the project. Having a signed contract for a fixed amount can also make it easier for the owners to obtain loans.

The hidden drawback of fixed bids, however, is that even the most experienced and conscientious builders often estimate incorrectly. After accounting for all the variables, experienced builders usually add a "fudge" factor in case something goes wrong during the construction. If the addition is built for the estimated cost, the owners end up paying this extra amount as a sort of penalty.

Perhaps a more common and certainly a much more serious problem is that of underbidding. The problem lies in the basic nature of the competitive bidding system itself, which pits one builder against another in a dispute over what are perceived to be limited opportunities. For no matter how much the project is actually worth, the builder will always be concerned about losing the job and tempted to bid too low.

A low bid is especially dangerous for those who are most likely to build an addition—small-time builders who have an enormous overhead compared to their typical profit margin. Additions are tricky, and their budgets are often slim pickings. Sadly, someone who is highly motivated to do the work out of love for the project can be even more likely to underbid it just to get the job.

Underbidding is not just a problem for the builder. There is the danger that the builder simply will be unable to complete an underbid project. Not only does the builder lose money and possibly face bankruptcy, but the owners must then hire someone else to finish the job. This adds new start-up costs and potentially expensive delays, which entirely defeat the purpose of choosing a low bid in the first place.

A lawsuit could theoretically recoup some of the owners' losses. But litigation, which tends to drag on and seldom ends satisfactorily for anyone involved—except the lawyers— may cost even more money. Some relief is guaranteed through the contractor's completion bonds, but it seldom covers all of the direct expenses, not to mention the hidden costs in time and energy. If the bid is too low, everyone loses.

Time and materials contracts

A time and materials contract is an agreement whereby the owners pay only for the cost of labor (including administration) and materials. While labor and materials accurately reflect the true, direct cost of the project—and in that sense are a fair price, at least for the owners—a straight time and materials contract offers no assurance that the price will not just keep going up and up.

Time and materials arrangements often start well, but in many cases the good feelings generated by early successes soon dissipate. As the job drags on—and all jobs drag on, particularly from the perspective of the owners, who may only partially understand the building process—the owners naturally try to put pressure on the builders to work faster. The resulting friction usually lowers efficiency, or at least takes the fun out the work.

The greatest danger, however, is that since there is no set ceiling on the cost, the owners may believe that some figure they heard in a conversation months before was an actual estimate, now exceeded, and they have been misled. This can cause trouble, from demands for the builder to work for little or nothing to the ever-looming lawsuit.

Finally, there is no opportunity for the builder to make a profit. If the contract is written to protect the owners by putting a ceiling on the cost, the builder takes all of the risk and burden without compensatory reward.

Incentive contracts

The best way to avoid the problems of the fixed bid or the wide-open time and materials contract is to adopt a modified time and materials arrangement in which the project's cost is estimated as closely as possible, then the builder is given an incentive for beating that cost. The contract also contains a ceiling, usually 10% to 15% higher than the estimated cost, to protect the owners.

The reward for coming in under the estimate is a variable amount of cash, which increases according to the owners' savings. For example, if the work comes out to $7,000 less than the estimate, the reward might be $5,000. The owners save a couple of thousand bucks, and the builder makes a "profit" over and above his or her actual costs. If the savings are only $3,500, the reward might be $2,500, and so on.

If the job costs exactly the same as the estimate, there is no reward. As costs exceed the estimate, the builder is paid for time, materials and justifiable overhead only and does not make a profit. When the ceiling is reached, the job must be completed without further remuneration. (The latter is provided for in typical state contracting laws.)

Thus, up to the value of the estimate, the builder has a positive incentive to work efficiently and keep costs down. The negative incentive built into most contracts from the outset kicks in only when the estimate is exceeded. The estimate itself is based on an open process of discussion between the designer, builder and owners, so there are no surprises.

This approach promotes flexibility. Since the owners and the builder are cooperating in working within a budget, they can make the mutual decision to add or subtract optional features (more expensive tile, for example) at any time. If the feature is added, the estimated overall cost can be raised slightly, so the builder's incentive is not reduced. If the less expensive option is exercised, the builder's incentive remains in place.

Although it has flexibility, the success of an incentive contract depends on making the original estimate as accurately as possible, which is one more benefit this type of contract offers to the owners and everyone else involved.

ESTIMATING

Accurately estimating the cost of a remodel is one of the most difficult parts of the project. The problem does not lie so much in figuring the materials—though it is somewhat difficult to make a complete list at the outset because things change as the job progresses—as in predicting, or actually believing, the amount of labor required. Mistakes in estimating can be the undoing of even the most experienced builder, and the larger and more complex the project, the wider the possible variations.

Conversely, the smaller the overall budget, the more critical the mistakes. One thousand dollars is just 1% of a $100,000 job, but 20% of a $5,000 job. While the arithmetic may seem obvious, it's amazing how quickly a few extra steps can add up to $1,000.

Costs are usually broken down into materials, labor and overhead, while price includes profit as well. (Note that there is a distinction between an estimate and a bid. An estimate is an approximation of a job's cost, while a bid is a written offer to do a job for a fixed amount of money.) Materials are the easiest cost to calculate, and estimating the materials not only gives you some fairly solid figures but also an opportunity to continue developing the job strategy, since the quantities of materials and the order of their arrival on the job site affects the flow of the work.

Take-offs and materials lists

Take-offs are lists of materials made by measuring the plans and calculating, for example, the amount of concrete or framing lumber needed for particular parts of the building (see the sidebar on pp. 220-221). The materials list is derived by adding together a bunch of take-offs and differs from them in that it is consolidated. That is, while the take-offs might specify that you need 60 studs for one wall, 40 for another, and so on, the materials list will simply state the total number of studs needed for the project. The take-offs are used for planning the job and ordering materials for each phase of the work, while the consolidated materials list is used for overall cost estimating and obtaining quantity discounts.

For a typical addition, take-offs and material calculations take one person about two days. It is a good idea to do the take-offs in the order in which the addition will be built. Shoring might come first, for example, or concrete-form materials. This way, the list will be easier to use for estimating labor (see below) and for ordering materials as the job goes along.

Once the take-offs are complete and added together to produce the materials list, the consolidated list is then submitted to one or more suppliers—usually a general lumber store in the case of an addition—for cost quotes. (In most cases, you should order a little more material than is needed to cover waste.)

Virtually all stores give quantity discounts and showing them the full list, rather than buying the materials piecemeal as the job goes along, can represent substantial savings. Between inflation and unanticipated items, material costs may climb by 10%. Many stores will guarantee their quote for several months, if the builder gets all the materials from them as the job goes along. (Some stores will do the take-offs and quote directly from a set of plans. Others have on-line access to their price books. The builder can save a lot of time by taking advantage of these types of services.)

Using quality materials from reliable, well-stocked and well-organized suppliers ultimately saves money. Cut-rate stores that cater to home owners and "week-end warriors" tend to sell nails that bend, lumber that splits and plywood that is out of square. The builder who saves a couple of bucks at the store will no doubt lose even more money fiddling around with funky materials on the job site.

Labor

To estimate labor, begin by listing in order all the tasks that will have to be performed to complete the addition. (It helps to refer to the chronologically organized take-off lists discussed above.) The task lists should be broken down into as many subcategories as possible. For example, it is of little use to call a portion of the job "framing" and guess that it will take "two to three weeks." Framing should be broken down into categories like "mudsills, kneewalls, rim joists, common joists, and blocking." By referring to the take-offs, the builder can assign each category a quantity, such as:

Task #14—Replace 25 lineal feet (L.F.) of 2x4 kneewall with 2x6.
It would be nice if you could simply plug quantities like 25 ft. of kneewall into a database or spreadsheet as one factor in a reliable formula like:

Kneewall: Total time to build = 5 min. per L.F. x number of L.F.
Though some books claim to provide such information, it's a good idea to be skeptical of their data to save embarrassment and money. One problem with this type of formula is that most of the data is based on new construction, where tradespeople can be timed as they perform repetitive tasks in comparable situations. No such opportunity exists in remodeling: Each situation is different, and the performance of each task is hampered by the addition of one, two or even more supplementary tasks.

The builder, therefore, needs to supplement the list of tasks by accounting for the unusual procedures

(text continues on p. 222)

SAMPLE TAKE-OFFS

The drawings and table shown here demonstrate how the quantities of two types of materials (concrete and framing lumber) are derived from measurements of the foundation and floor-framing plan for a small room addition and bedroom expansion.

Concrete take-off

The sectional indicators cutting through the various parts of the main foundation wall each represent a drawing (section 5/1, 5/2, etc.) of a cross section of the wall. The table at right is used to calculate the amount of concrete needed (in cubic yards).

In the section 5/1 drawing, for example, the total area of the cross section is 2 sq. ft. (1.33 + 0.66). Multiplying the 2-sq.-ft. cross section by 1 lin. ft. yields 2 cu. ft. for each lineal foot of foundation. Since the portion of the foundation with the cross section 5/1 is 13 ft. long, it will require 2 x 13 or a total of 26 cu. ft. of concrete altogether.

Figures are derived for each part of the foundation wall, and then added together to produce the subtotal of 132.6 cu. ft. This figure is added to the subtotal for the new concrete slabs to produce a total of 167 cu. ft., which divided by 27 cu. ft. per yd. (3x3x3) equals 6.18 cu. yd.

Lumber take-off

Calculating the amount of lumber needed to build the floor frame is straightforward. All framing members for this addition are pressure-treated 2x8s. The total lineal footage of ledger stock needed is taken from the foundation measurements. The floor joists are all 2x8x12s, and simply have to be counted. Similarly, the blocking can be easily measured and totaled.

CONCRETE: FOUNDATION WALLS

Section	Stem wall	+	Footing	=	Sq. ft.	x	L.F.	=	Total cu. ft.
5/1	1.33		0.66		2		13.0	=	26
5/2	1.33		0.66		2		31.5	=	63
5/3	(existing)		(existing)						
5/4	(existing)		(existing)						
5/5	1.33		0.66		2		4.5	=	9
5/6	1.66		1.00		2.66		13.0	=	34.6
5/7	(existing)		(existing)						
							Subtotal	=	132.6

CONCRETE: SLABS

Thickness	x	Width	x	Length	=	Total cu. ft.
0.33		4.5		12	=	17.8
0.33		4.0		12.5	=	16.5
				Subtotal	=	34.3
				Foundation-walls subtotal	=	132.6
				Total cu. ft.	=	167/27 = 6.18 cu. yd.

FRAMING LUMBER

Item	Size	Count/L.F.	Order (Lengths)	Total quantity (L.F.)
Ledgers	2x8	88 L.F.	2/14s & 4/16s	92
Floor joists (room addition)	2x8	26 pieces	26/12s	312
Floor joists (new bedroom)	2x8	3 pieces	3/14s	42
Blocking (room addition)	2x8	32 L.F.		
Blocking (new bedroom)	2x8	4 L.F.		
Blocking subtotal	=	36 L.F.	3/12s	36
		Total	=	482 L.F.

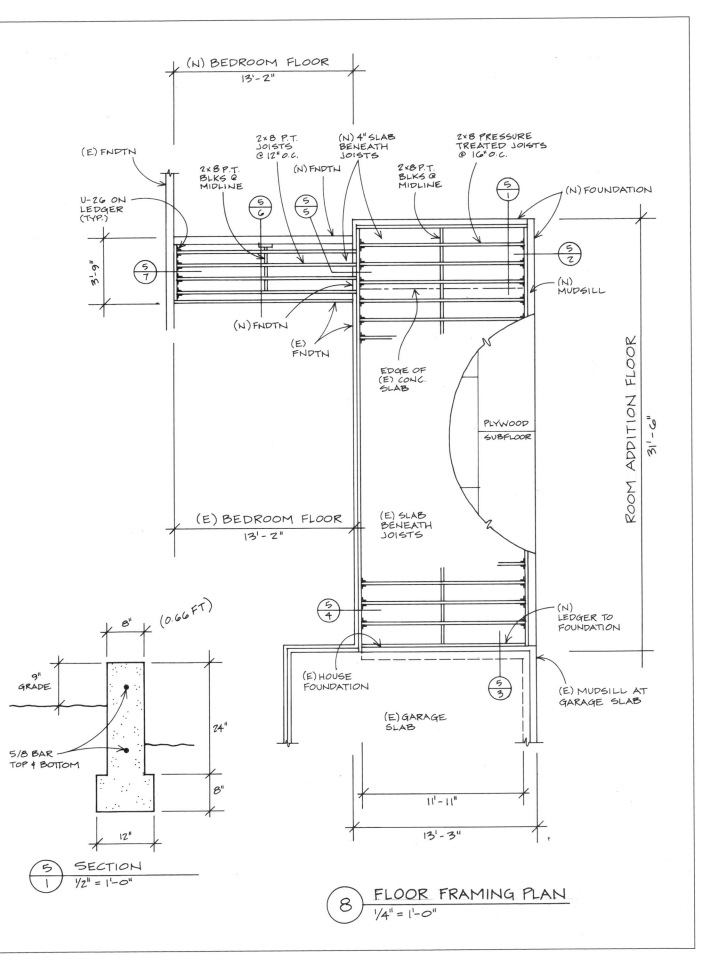

(N) BEDROOM FLOOR
13'-2"

(E) FNDTN

U-26 ON LEDGER (TYP.)

3'-9"

5/7

2×8 P.T. BLKS @ MIDLINE

2×8 P.T. JOISTS @ 12" O.C.

(N) 4" SLAB BENEATH JOISTS

(N) FNDTN

5/6

5/5

(N) FNDTN

(E) FNDTN

2×8 P.T. BLKS @ MIDLINE

2×8 PRESSURE TREATED JOISTS @ 16" O.C.

5/1

(N) FOUNDATION

5/2

(N) MUDSILL

EDGE OF (E) CONC. SLAB

ROOM ADDITION FLOOR
31'-6"

PLYWOOD SUBFLOOR

(E) BEDROOM FLOOR
13'-2"

(E) SLAB BENEATH JOISTS

5/4

(N) LEDGER TO FOUNDATION

(E) HOUSE FOUNDATION

5/3

(E) MUDSILL AT GARAGE SLAB

(E) GARAGE SLAB

11'-11"

13'-3"

8"   (0.66 FT)

9" GRADE

24"

5/8 BAR TOP & BOTTOM

8"

12"

5/1   SECTION
½" = 1'-0"

8   FLOOR FRAMING PLAN
¼" = 1'-0"

associated with each segment of work. For example:

Task #14—Replace 25 lineal feet (L.F.) of 2x4 kneewall with 2x6.
- *Remove existing wires*
- *Remove heat duct*
- *(note, access by crawling only)*

With this done, the builder can establish a base time for each task and add the supplemental tasks to that. If an estimating manual or the builder's own records or experience can be used to determine that it takes about 5 min. per lineal foot to build kneewall, for example, the builder can use that figure as a base. Then the extra steps and conditions that will slow down the work can be factored in:

- *Remove and replace electrical wires, phone cables, etc.: 2 min. per L.F.*
- *Remove heat duct: 1 min. per L.F.*
- *Working on hands and knees and passing materials into crawl space: 4 min. per L.F.*

These factors combined equal 7 min. per ft., which, added to the original 5, makes the task take 12 min. per ft., or almost two-and-a-half times the baseline factor.

At 12 min. per ft., 25 L.F. of kneewall will take 300 min., or five hours, to build. This means the task will span a lunch break, so it will have two start-up periods, one for the initial setup and one after the break to bring out the tools and get going again. Also, the site should be cleaned and the materials rearranged before the next task is started. Realistically, the 25 ft. of kneewall will take six to six-and-a-half hours, or most of a day, to build.

Unfortunately, there is no way to get around applying this type of thorough, systematic thinking to unfamiliar tasks and new projects. Every aspect of the job must be analyzed at this level of detail to make sure that small factors are not overlooked and, cumulatively, do not add up to big costs.

For this reason, it is extremely important for builders to keep construction records. Employees should be asked to make fairly close estimates of the time they spend on each task at the end of each day (before they forget). If this information is gathered and analyzed—a task that is greatly simplified by the use of a computer and an inexpensive spreadsheet program—a solid database, invaluable for estimating, can be assembled in a short time.

Subcontractors

The extensive use of subcontractors' estimates can greatly simplify the builder's work. Subs usually specialize in just one trade, which means that many of their jobs are similar enough so that they can give reliable bids. Each bid means one less part of the project for which the general builder has to provide estimates.

During the actual construction, the subs can be even more valuable. Builders usually have their hands full keeping the job on schedule and dealing with the many unforeseeable problems that arise each week. A good sub—one who starts and finishes on time, cooperates with the main crew, cleans up promptly and does quality work—can give an embattled crew a shot in the arm by infusing positive energy and bringing the project one step closer to completion.

Overhead and operating expenses

The amount of the builder's overhead attributable to a specific project depends on several factors, including the number of projects being built at one time, the size and relative costs of each project and the time spent on the project by non-building employees. While the variables are too complex to consider here, it should be noted that overhead is a part of every job, and even the builder who is working on a shoestring budget must plan for it in order to make money. The average cost of such basic items as operating vehicles, replacing tools and renting a space to keep them, for example, must be added to the cost of materials and labor if the builder is to have enough money to perform well, particularly during the course of a long job.

Frequently overlooked costs are those of getting materials to the site, picking up workers who don't have transportation, conferring with the owners after hours, shopping for fixtures with the owners, waiting to get the permit, waiting for the building inspector, calling the concrete company to find out where the truck is, waiting outside the gates for the dump to open, and so on. Most builders don't keep records of these activities because of the random way in which they occur (and possibly because knowing just how much time they take would be too frightening). Still, they must be accounted for, and it is probably wise to figure that at least 5% of the total labor budget will be spent on these trifling but necessary tasks.

Job-Site Evaluation for Construction

The information on this list is used for planning the job and figuring costs.

1. Access

• What is the primary access to the site? Will access require the removal of fences, tree branches or other obstacles? Is it necessary to use the neighbors' property for access? Can permission be obtained? Is there parking for work vehicles?

• Will the owners provide keys to the house? Are there burglar alarms, tenants, pets or other special access problems?

• Will scaffolds, tall ladders, ramps or other special equipment be required? How will materials be lifted to second stories, passed through tight openings, and so on? Are there difficult stairs or tight corners in corridors that will require alternative routing of large items? Will concrete have to be pumped?

2. Demolition

• What parts of the building should be removed or demolished first? What special tools or equipment are needed? Where can waste materials be piled until they are hauled away? Do they need to be sorted into types (wood, metal, hazardous materials, etc.)? Should a dumpster be rented?

3. Storage

• Where can materials and tools be stored? What about risk of theft? If a garage or other space is to be used, will the owners clean it out? On time?

4. Shoring

• Will portions of the building need shoring? Shoring is not shown on the working drawings—what materials are needed? Can the shoring lumber be re-used for framing?

5. Measurements

• Are the principal measurements on the plans accurate? To what tolerances? Are the dimensions given for existing framing members nominal or net? If they are nominal, what are the actual dimensions?

• Where is the property line? Where is the set-back? How accurate are these lines? Does the addition conform to the set-back? Will a survey be needed?

6. True

• Are the walls plumb? Flush? Floors level? Building square?

• How far off true is the building? Is this reflected or noted on the plans?

7. Power

• Is the existing electrical system adequate to run high-amperage building tools? 220? Grounding? On all circuits or some? GFCI?

• Does the project include an electrical upgrade? If so, can it happen at the beginning of the project, so there is adequate grounded power for tools?

8. Safety

• Are there special hazards that might lead to an accident? Branches near wires? Weak exterior stairs? Low overhangs? Messy areas of the job site? Stored solvents or other fire hazards? Collapsing chimneys or loose bricks?

The final estimate

Once the costs of materials, rentals, labor, subcontractors' wages and applicable overhead have been calculated, the information should be assembled into a final, complete estimate that is used as the basis for writing the contract. If there are still unknowns—the price of doors that the owners are to provide, for example—a maximum allowance can be made for such items. The final estimate should also include one-time costs specific to the job such as the contractor's insurance and completion bonds.

After all the figures are totaled, a safety factor should be added to cover unpredictable problems. Not only do things often go wrong, they seldom go right. It is likely that at least one hour out of each eight-hour day will be spent doing something that couldn't be predicted. That's 12.5% of the time.

The baseline estimate for the contract, then, should be the sum of the labor, materials and other factors plus 10% to 15% of that figure. Since the difference between 10% and 15% may be several thousand dollars, the builder will ultimately have to rely on intuition to decide just how much of a safety factor is needed.

Remember that the incentive contract discussed above adds another 10% to 15% to the baseline estimate as a safety margin. That plus the safety factor added here totals 30% higher than the actual calculated cost. While it might look high on paper, it is often barely enough in reality.

SAMPLE FLOW CHART

This sample flow chart is the first section of a chart used for organizing and sequencing the major operations in building an addition. The chart, which was drawn with an inexpensive program on a computer, is an adaptation of standard flow chart symbols and methods.

By following the chart, the builder knows the order in which the operations should be performed and which auxiliary tasks must accompany each operation. References are given to secondary flow charts (e.g., "Ref. F.C. #2) and to materials take-off lists ("Ref. T.O.L. #2 & #3).

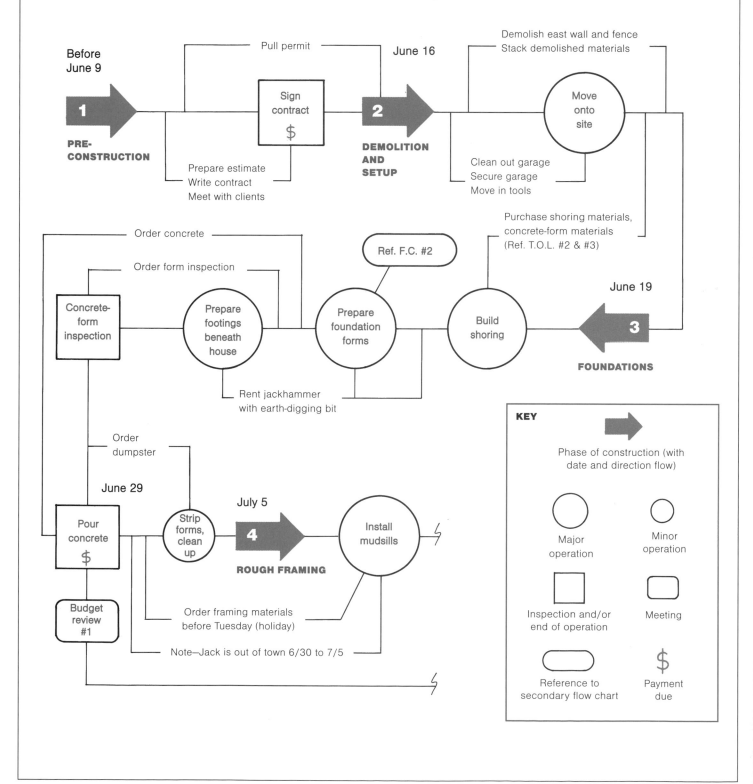

PLANNING THE JOB

The information gathered by estimating the project's costs is highly useful for planning. By now, the builder has listed all of the major tasks and most of the minor tasks and knows which materials and specialized equipment are needed for each stage of the operation. Planning the job requires, first, a visit to the site to determine if there are any special problems or conditions for which the crew must prepare and, second, a session at the office to gather all of the accumulated information into one master construction plan or flow chart.

At the site

The first step in turning blueprints into an addition is to make sure that the plans really work. The builder must check the accuracy of the plans and take notes on job-site factors that will affect the construction strategy (see the sidebar on p. 223). This check is done at the site, with the plans in one hand and a tape measure or level in the other.

As discussed in Chapter 12, it is standard practice for the general notes on the working drawings to include a disclaimer that states that "all measurements must be verified in the field by the builder." This disclaimer should not be interpreted as condoning sloppy design, but rather as anticipating that some dimensions will change during construction.

To save money, for example, the builder might choose to modify the plans and use deeper floor joists spaced farther apart. This type of change is acceptable as long as height restrictions and building-code requirements are met (see

Chapter 10) and the designer confirms that the architecture will not be adversely affected. Naturally all the remaining vertical measurements will change, and it is the builder's responsibility to make the adjustments.

Inaccuracies in the drawings, however, cannot be tolerated because they will cause countless headaches. If the builder discovers problems with the drawings, they should be returned to the designer for correction before construction begins.

In the office

Upon completing the job-site survey, the builder can add the field notes on the site conditions to the take-offs and the list of tasks used for estimating. These can be woven into a master job plan and laid out in graphic form as a flow chart (see the drawing on the facing page).

The flow chart A flow chart gives you several kinds of information at once: the order in which tasks must be performed, the schedule (dates), the relationships between tasks and the alternative paths that may be taken if the main path is blocked because of a logistical breakdown or other factors.

Like the take-offs and labor-estimating task lists, the flow chart should be broken down into as many discrete steps as possible. The job strategy also needs to be flexible, and room should be left on the chart to reflect changes.

While it may take a few hours, or even a day, to consolidate the information from the estimates, field notes and other sources into a flow chart, those hours are probably among the most valuable spent during the entire project. The flow

chart is to the construction process what the blueprints are to the building: Without the chart and the plans, every task will require that the chief carpenter (or possibly the entire crew) stop and figure out what needs to happen next, who will do it, and when and where to get the materials for the next phase. The hours that slip away while such decisions are made on the site far outnumber those spent drawing up the flow chart in the builder's office.

Tracking the job

One of the most important administrative tasks of the builder is to make sure that the job stays on track—essentially that it follows the flow chart. The day-to-day schedule and order of tasks will naturally vary somewhat from the chart. But the big items—completing one major phase of the job before beginning the next, comparing the finances to the progress at the appropriate intervals—must be tracked in order for the job to come to a successful conclusion. Time should be set aside for tracking the job, and the cost of the hours it takes should be part of the labor estimate.

14
TECHNIQUES FOR ADDING ON

Building an addition is something of a construction anomaly in that it is neither remodeling nor new construction, yet it requires skills in both fields as well as a knowledge of problems peculiar to additions. General remodeling and new construction techniques are beyond the scope of this book, though several excellent references are given in the bibliography. The purpose of this final chapter is to focus on the techniques seldom discussed in standard construction texts that are essential for adding one structure to another.

Construction techniques for adding on fall into five major categories: *demolition*, which prepares the existing building for connection to the addition and includes removing roofs and creating openings in walls that will lead to the new space; *protection* of the building once it has been laid open; *shoring*, or temporarily propping up those parts of the building where existing supports will be replaced; *layout*, or establishing baselines and measurements for building the addition; and making *connections* between the existing building and the addition.

Although some of the principles for performing these operations are explained here, there are so many special considerations in building an addition that builders must find a way to solve each problem as it is encountered. That challenge, after all, is what makes building worthwhile for most professionals.

DEMOLITION

If the building is to be remodeled, not just removed, demolition must be done sensitively and intelligently. Too much demolition will require too much replacement, while too little means that work on the addition will have to be stopped so that incomplete tasks can be finished. Structural demolition can endanger the building and workers. Demolition work should be performed, or at least closely supervised, by an experienced remodeling carpenter, not left up to laborers.

For maximum efficiency and minimum damage, demolition for remodeling should proceed in the reverse order of construction. If a window is to be converted to a door, for example, its interior and exterior moldings should be carefully removed first. Then the nails that are holding the jambs, header and sill to the framing can be cut with a reciprocating saw. After the window unit is safely stored, the siding and interior finish below the opening

should be neatly cut along the inside edge of the trimmer or king stud before it is removed. Finally the lower framing should be removed as a unit by cutting the plates where they connect to the trimmer or king stud and prying the sole plate off the subfloor with a bar. Keep all the moldings and trim pieces, because they might come in handy later.

Demolishing roofs

Roofs yield copious quantities of heavy material that must be removed and hauled off at considerable expense. Like most heavy materials, old roofing should be handled as little as possible. Ideally, you should set up a steep plywood chute that will carry the shingles directly into a dumpster or a truck to minimize handling.

Once the roofing and sheathing are removed, you might choose to leave the ridge and a few of the

---

Safety on the Job Site

When people are hurt on the job site, it is almost always because no one has taken the appropriate measures to prevent them from getting hurt. Safety measures usually require very little time and effort, especially compared to the amount of time and effort it takes to shut down the job, pack someone off to the emergency room, have the injured person off work for one or more days and possibly have to find a replacement.

Safety equipment is relatively inexpensive: a couple of nails to keep a ladder from shifting, a 2x4 for a safety rail, a rope to keep someone from falling, some plastic goggles and earplugs, a broom to keep the floor free of debris—none of these are going to break the budget for the job.

Taking the time to use these devices is such a negligible investment, compared to the financial and emotional risks of getting someone injured, that failing to do so goes beyond stupidity.

In recent years we have learned more about safe construction practices, and particularly about hidden dangers like asbestos and other toxic dusts and gases that are already on the site or

contained in new construction materials. References that discuss these substances and other safety concerns are cited in the bibliography. It is our professional responsibility not only to build as sound and safe a building as possible, but also to build it in as safe a manner as possible.

rafters in place, at least temporarily. This skeletal structure can support tarps for weather protection until it is time to install the second-story subfloor or otherwise cover the space below. Leaving rafters every 4 ft. to 6 ft. is adequate to support tarps.

Avoiding pipes and wires

Whenever possible, locate pipes and wires within the walls and ceilings before cutting openings. In walls, pipes usually run vertically from the sub-area to the fixture they serve, but they occasionally take short horizontal jogs. The original wiring usually runs vertically from the attic or sub-area through the stud "bays," or spaces between studs, in which outlets and switches are mounted. Wires also run horizontally from outlet to outlet within a room, about 1 ft. off the floor, and across ceilings to light fixtures. Wires to ceiling lights on lower floors usually run between the second-floor joists directly above the stud bay that houses the switch. Many older houses have been remodeled or had their plumbing or wiring upgraded, however, and there may be wires or pipes in other locations. Always check carefully before cutting into a wall or ceiling.

Turn off the circuit that feeds the wires within a wall before removing the siding and/or interior wall coverings. Once you think you have turned off a circuit at the main service panel or subpanel, test the outlets and switches nearest the wall to be demolished to see if they're still hot. As the saying in the electrical trade goes, "electricians are never killed by electricity—only by assumptions."

Cutting plaster walls

If interior walls are covered with wood lath and plaster, special care must be taken when cutting through them because lath bounces violently when gripped by the teeth of a reciprocating saw. A couple of tricks can save a lot of cracked plaster. First, always use a new (i.e., sharp), fine-toothed blade; a large-toothed blade will simply grab the lath like a hand and shake it, cracking plaster along the entire piece. Second, hold a board firmly against the lath to limit its flexibility. The board will cut down on the overall motion and allow the blade to work through hard knots that might otherwise bounce away from the teeth.

Reuse and recycle

Most building materials can be reused or recycled. Good planning and careful demolition allow you to reuse sound windows and doors in the addition. Old cabinets can be painted and used for storage in a new laundry room or garage, or at least temporarily used by the crew to hold tools and supplies.

Framing lumber that can't be readily reused in the building can be cut down to size for firewood for about the same price that it can be taken to the dump. Even broken-up concrete can be used in low garden walls, as fill for a nonstructural slab or to level yards. Avoid off-site dumping whenever possible.

PROTECTING THE BUILDING

Once demolition begins, the building must be protected against the weather, illegal entrance and damage from the construction itself.

Tarps are the most common form of protection against rain. They work best when sloping, so that water will run off. As mentioned above, the existing roof structure can serve as a set of tent poles for the tarps, or other supports can be rigged up (see the photo on the facing page). When several tarps are needed to cover large spaces, they should be overlapped by at least 2 ft. at the seams. All tarps should be secured against the wind with ropes.

Openings in exterior walls should be covered with plywood. Screw the plywood on from the inside so that it cannot simply be pulled off or pushed in by would-be thieves. Other common-sense security measures include installing temporary lights on motion detectors near openings, locking up tools or removing them from the site and keeping the street side of the job site clean so that it's less obvious that work is being done. It helps, of course, if the owners are staying in the house, but their presence makes it even more important to secure the openings as well as possible.

More buildings are probably damaged by construction itself than by theft or vandalism. Construction damage can be minimized if you take a few simple precautions: nailing plywood running boards across the tops of ceiling joists so that workers don't slip off and step through the ceiling; wrapping the exposed corners of hallways and stairwells with cardboard to protect them against dents; covering floors with kraft paper; cleaning the job site frequently so that dirt and dust are not ground into the floors; and putting away tools and loose lumber so they don't become hazards.

Thoroughly cleaning, organizing and securing the job site takes most crews about an hour a day, and this time should be accounted for when the estimate is prepared.

SHORING

Shoring is temporary structural support used to prop up the building while the permanent supports are being installed (see the drawing on p. 230). Well-designed shoring is substantial enough to keep the house safe and level, but it should use a minimal amount of wood to keep costs down. Although engineers are frequently required to design the structural supports for the building itself, it is usually left to the builder in the field to size the shoring members (even though they may support the building for months at a time).

Shoring walls

To determine the size and number of members needed for a shoring wall, the builder should first find out what's supporting the existing house. The bearing capacity of a typical permanent wall has a safety factor that allows it to carry about two times its actual vertical load. If you make a shoring wall half as strong, then, you are taking a chance. In most cases, providing

A temporary triangular structure can be used to support tarps to protect exposed parts of the building when there is a threat of rain.

about two-thirds of the strength will support the building with a minimal investment.

A permanent kneewall with 2x6s on 16-in. centers and a double top plate, for example, will support most two-story houses. While a shoring wall with 2x6s on 32-in. centers and a single plate would be risky, 24-in. centers with a double plate should work fine in most situations. (If in doubt, call a structural engineer.)

Openings in shoring walls

Shoring walls often need openings large enough to allow wheelbarrows or sheets of plywood to pass through. The beams of the openings can be sized relative to the existing headers that span the build-

ing's windows. Beams supporting a single story can be reduced to about two-thirds of the depth of the headers needed to carry the same load in a permanent installation. For example, a temporary 4x6 can replace a permanent 4x10 with the same span. For a two-story building, however, you should downsize the member by only one increment: A 4x10 can be reduced to a 4x8, but no smaller.

One way to eliminate all doubt about the strength of the shoring (and save money) is to choose members that can be reused in the permanent framing. Since oversized headers are commonly used in standard framing, the shoring headers can be made the same size as the

Shoring for Foundation Replacement

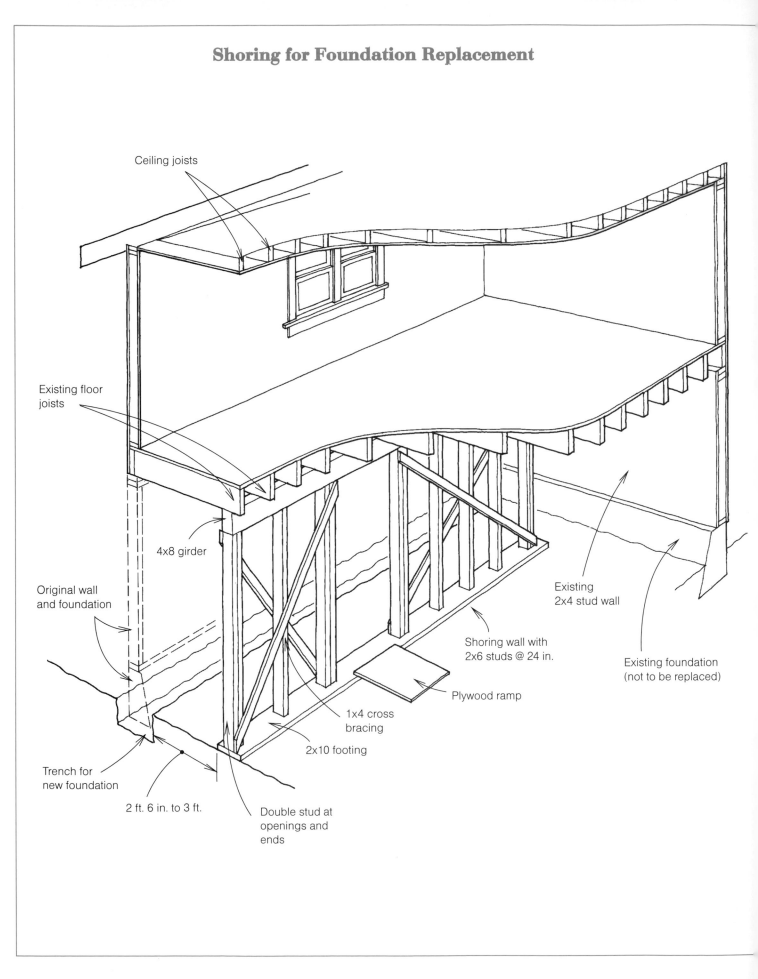

Ceiling joists

Existing floor joists

Original wall and foundation

4x8 girder

Existing 2x4 stud wall

Existing foundation (not to be replaced)

Shoring wall with 2x6 studs @ 24 in.

Plywood ramp

1x4 cross bracing

2x10 footing

Trench for new foundation

2 ft. 6 in. to 3 ft.

Double stud at openings and ends

Part of the original foundation for this one-story house had to be replaced with a stronger foundation to support a second-story addition. Shoring was used to support the house while the foundation and exterior wall were removed.

The shoring wall, supporting just one story, has 2x6 studs at 24 in. on center. It replaced a kneewall with 2x6 studs at 16-in. on center. The 2x10 footing, which spreads out the load to some extent, is continuous so that the two wall segments tend to act more as a single unit. The girder also ties both segments together, as well as acting as a header to span the opening.

Shoring walls should be built 2½ ft. to 3 ft. back from the wall they are replacing, for three reasons: first, to provide enough space between the walls for working and for moving tools and materials in and out; second, to ensure that the shoring is not too close to the edge of a foundation trench, which could collapse; and third, to make sure that the shoring is close enough to the original wall so that it supports the same load, without excessive cantilevering.

To build a shoring wall like the one shown, first toe-nail the girder to the existing floor joists, using temporary 2x6s to support the girder while nailing. Then set the 2x10 footings in place, and cut the double studs to fit so tightly that they have to be tapped into place with a hammer. Secure all connections with double-head nails.

Once the shoring wall is installed, the existing kneewall and foundation can be removed. Before building the new permanent kneewall, measure the house to make sure it is still level and plumb, since relocating its weight from wall to wall may cause it to shift. Once the new foundation and kneewall are complete (not a moment before!), the shoring can be removed to allow the house to settle down onto the new foundation before the second-story load is added. Recheck the house for level and plumb.

headers that will span the largest permanent opening and remnants can be used for smaller windows. (The rule of thumb for permanent headers is that 1 in. of header depth equals 1 ft. of span: A 4x4 spans a 4-ft. opening; since there is no 4x5, a 5-ft. opening would need a 4x6. While this rule is handy for preliminary design, the size of the permanent header should be double-checked by the structural engineer.)

Posts have limited use in platform framing, so shoring posts are best made by nailing studs together temporarily. For ease of disassembly, all shoring should be fastened with double-headed nails.

Horizontal stability of shoring walls is normally provided by 1x cross braces that go all the way from the top to the bottom of the wall and are nailed at each stud (single braces are ineffective because they work in only one direction). If additional horizontal stability is needed (as, for example, in seismic zones), plywood sheets can be nailed over the shoring walls instead.

Building walls in tight spaces

The most efficient way to frame a wall is to build it on the floor and tilt it up. If a shoring wall or a permanent partition wall is installed in an existing room, it must be built shorter than the room height so it can be tilted up. A good trick is to build the wall 1 in. short, tilt it up and then use a piece of continuous 1x (¾-in. net) material as a spacer to fill in the gap between the wall's top plate and the soffit (see the drawings on p. 232). Adding the spacer still leaves a ¼-in. gap, which allows for variations in the soffit.

Shoring walls Shoring walls can be wedged snugly in place by lifting the ¾-in. spacer to the soffit and inserting shim shingles from each side of the wall between it and the plate. The shingles should be located beneath each of the joists above to provide continuous support.

The tightly wedged shingles will hold the wall in place, and it is not necessary to nail into the joists (a few nails tying the shims together will help stabilize the wall during assembly, however). When the shims are pulled out, the wall can be lowered with little damage to the ceiling, other than a possible dent from the ¾-in. spacer in the soft drywall or plaster. Such dents can easily be repaired with extra-fine drywall "topping" compound.

Partition walls Assemble permanent partition walls in the same manner as shoring walls, but drive a long nail through the plate, shim shingles, ¾-in. spacer and ceiling material to anchor the wall to the joists. A ¼-in. gap remains between the continuous ¾-in. spacer and the top plate of the wall, except where the shim shingles are placed, but this has no structural implications for a partition wall.

Bearing walls Bearing walls, on the other hand, must have a direct connection to the joists above, so the ceiling material will have to be removed. Bearing walls need two top plates, which must be securely attached to the framing above and cannot be built as tilt-up walls in existing rooms. The best procedure is to face-nail the first plate to every joist and the second plate to the first plate, thus eliminating the need for shims. After the sole plate is nailed to the floor, the individual studs are cut to fit snugly and toe-nailed into place.

WALLS IN TIGHT SPACES

Because the diagonal measurement of a stud wall is slightly greater than its height, temporary shoring walls and permanent partition walls must be built a little shorter than the ceiling so they can be tilted up.

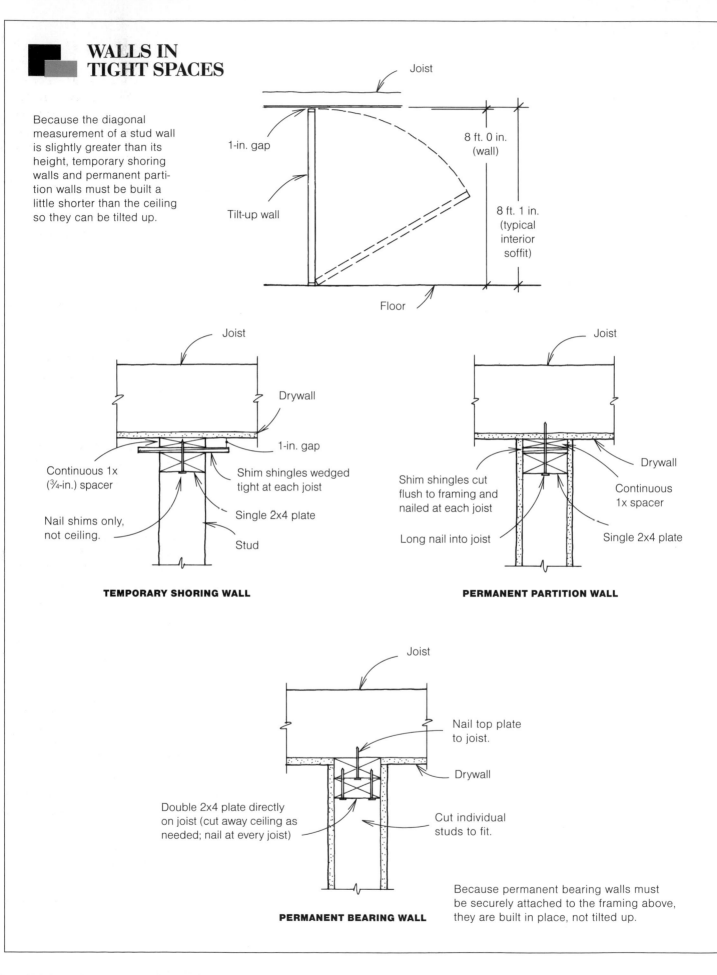

Joist

1-in. gap

Tilt-up wall

8 ft. 0 in. (wall)

8 ft. 1 in. (typical interior soffit)

Floor

Joist

Drywall

1-in. gap

Continuous 1x (¾-in.) spacer

Shim shingles wedged tight at each joist

Single 2x4 plate

Nail shims only, not ceiling.

Stud

TEMPORARY SHORING WALL

Joist

Shim shingles cut flush to framing and nailed at each joist

Long nail into joist

Drywall

Continuous 1x spacer

Single 2x4 plate

PERMANENT PARTITION WALL

Joist

Nail top plate to joist.

Drywall

Double 2x4 plate directly on joist (cut away ceiling as needed; nail at every joist)

Cut individual studs to fit.

PERMANENT BEARING WALL

Because permanent bearing walls must be securely attached to the framing above, they are built in place, not tilted up.

LAYOUT

Measurements for most additions are based on the existing house rather than the surveyed property lines used for new construction. If you are lucky and the house is "true," you can simply align the addition with the existing structure. A true house is the exception, however, not the rule, and for most projects you must make important decisions about measurements early on and then follow them through systematically to the end.

Measuring for true

The building can be measured for true in four ways: for *level* (horizontally), *plumb* (vertically), *flush* (consistency within a plane) and *squareness* (built with 90° corners). A building that is out of true should not be used as the basis for the addition's measurements. They should be taken from baselines established by the builder.

Level and plumb are normally measured with a hand-held spirit (bubble) level. A wall may be tested to see if it is flush by attaching sticks to its corners and stretching a mason's string tautly between them (see the drawing on p. 234). The string should be set equidistant from both corners. The distance to the wall may then be measured at any point along the string. If the distance is consistent, the wall is flush.

It is difficult to determine whether an existing building is square without a formal survey. For an addition project, however, the squareness of the existing building is not as important as that of the addition. (Directions for laying out a square addition based on a flush wall are given below.)

Establishing baselines for the addition

Since few houses are true, it is often up to the builder to establish *baselines,* or straight lines on which all the rest of the measurements are based. Baselines may be established using a builder's level or a transit. It is acceptable to establish lines that do not follow the existing planes of the building (such as the bottom edge of the siding, a floor or a vertical corner). However, all the implications for framing and finishing must be thought through before this decision is made.

For example, if a second story is to be added to a house that drops 3 in. from one side to the other, should the second-story floor frame be shimmed so that it is level? In almost all cases, the answer would be yes because the rest of the second-story framing follows the new floor frame, but there are some important side effects to consider.

If the new line between the stories is demarcated by exterior trim, the trim will be 3 in. narrower on one end than on the other; this will be visible from as far as a block away. If the interior ceiling of the first floor hangs from the new floor frame, it might appear to be way off level, even though it is actually level and it is the room below that is off. The ceiling line is particularly pronounced in kitchens, where upper wall cabinets must look correct to the eye, whether or not they are level. There are a number of ways to compensate for these differences in the design—by gradually stepping down the molding, for example—but they must be thought through in advance so they don't look like an attempt to cover a mistake.

Laying out a square addition based on an existing flush wall is a fairly straightforward procedure. For a rectangle to be square, its diagonals must be equal. Square for large dimensions is normally established by setting up batter boards, since long lines projected from hand-held squares can be significantly inaccurate. In the drawing on p. 234, the boards are set up to establish baselines for a room-addition foundation. If the end wall of the house is flush, it can be used as one baseline for squaring the addition. Attach strings at the same height to nails at the corners. Wrap the strings around the batter board and cross them with a third string, which is placed the same distance from the house as the outer edge of the new foundation.

Once the strings are in place, adjust them back and forth until the diagonals are equal and the distance between the house and the third string is correct all along the line. Then use a level or a plumb bob to project lines on the ground directly below the strings. If the strings have to be moved, the batter boards can remain in place so they can be strung again whenever it is necessary to check the foundation forms for square.

CONNECTING THE HOUSE AND THE ADDITION

One of the main differences between adding on and simply remodeling a house is that a number of special problems are encountered at the transition between the new and existing spaces. Some of the problems are minor and can be solved cosmetically—for example,

LAYING OUT A ROOM-ADDITION FOUNDATION

MEASURING FOR TRUE
To test a wall for flush, use a mason's string stretched between sticks at the corners. Check for level and plumb using a carpenter's level. Check for square, by measuring diagonals.

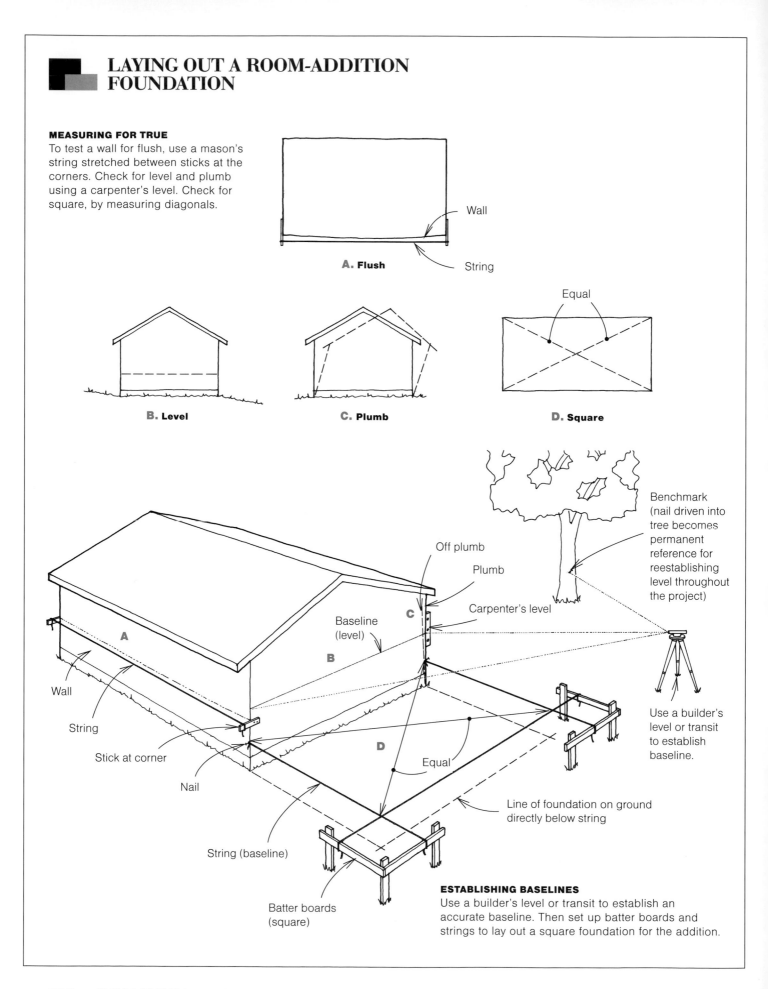

Wall

String

A. Flush

B. Level

C. Plumb

Equal

D. Square

Off plumb

Plumb

Baseline (level)

Carpenter's level

C

B

A

Wall

String

Stick at corner

Nail

D

Equal

String (baseline)

Batter boards (square)

Benchmark (nail driven into tree becomes permanent reference for reestablishing level throughout the project)

Use a builder's level or transit to establish baseline.

Line of foundation on ground directly below string

ESTABLISHING BASELINES
Use a builder's level or transit to establish an accurate baseline. Then set up batter boards and strings to lay out a square foundation for the addition.

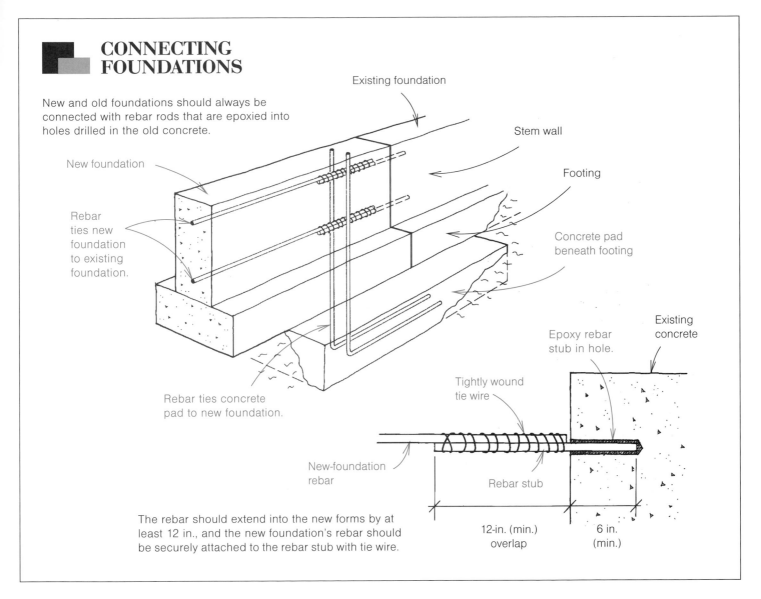

CONNECTING FOUNDATIONS

New and old foundations should always be connected with rebar rods that are epoxied into holes drilled in the old concrete.

Existing foundation

Stem wall

New foundation

Footing

Rebar ties new foundation to existing foundation.

Concrete pad beneath footing

Rebar ties concrete pad to new foundation.

Epoxy rebar stub in hole.

Existing concrete

Tightly wound tie wire

New-foundation rebar

Rebar stub

The rebar should extend into the new forms by at least 12 in., and the new foundation's rebar should be securely attached to the rebar stub with tie wire.

12-in. (min.) overlap

6 in. (min.)

compensating for the difference in the thickness of the walls and variations in the color and texture of the finishes. Other problems are important structural differences, since the new and existing structures often respond differently to the soil and loading conditions.

Connecting new and old foundations

Connections between new and old foundations require particular attention. The two foundations should always be connected with rebar (see the drawing above). In the best applications, at least two, 6-in. (minimum) deep holes are drilled in the existing concrete, and rebar stubs that extend out 12 in. or more are epoxied in place. These same stubs are wired to the new rebar in the forms, so there is a degree of continuity. The surface of the old concrete should be thoroughly cleaned before the pour, and precoated with an adhesive designed to strengthen the connection.

To install the rebar into the existing foundation, drill the holes with a carbide-tipped masonry bit. Wear safety goggles and work gloves and make sure you have a firm grip on the drill. A drill that is powerful enough to penetrate the hardened concrete develops high torque and can break wrists or fingers if it hits an obstacle like a piece of rebar or a rock hidden beneath the surface.

Use a drinking straw or piece of plastic tubing to blow the dust out of the hole before the epoxy is applied. The epoxy may be mixed by hand and stuffed into the hole, but many builders prefer to use glass capsules that are filled with an

CONNECTING FRAMES

Because of the difference in dimensions between the rough or partially surfaced lumber in older houses and today's surfaced pieces, care must be taken to align the floor, wall and ceiling frames correctly when building a room addition. (In this drawing, existing elements are labeled in black; new elements are labeled in blue.)

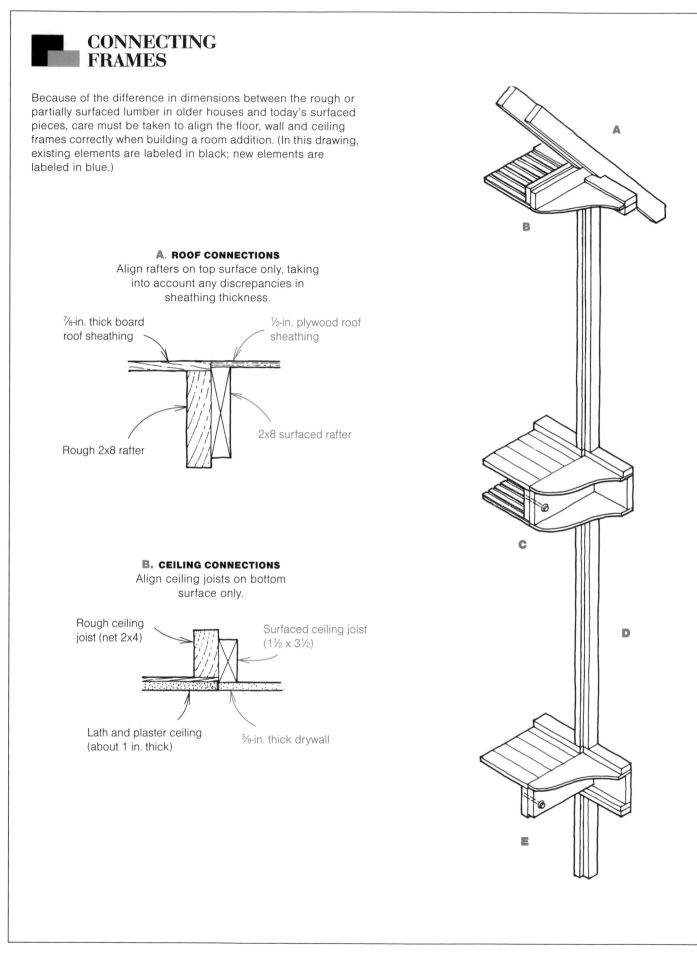

A. ROOF CONNECTIONS
Align rafters on top surface only, taking into account any discrepancies in sheathing thickness.

⅞-in. thick board roof sheathing

½-in. plywood roof sheathing

Rough 2x8 rafter

2x8 surfaced rafter

B. CEILING CONNECTIONS
Align ceiling joists on bottom surface only.

Rough ceiling joist (net 2x4)

Surfaced ceiling joist (1½ x 3½)

Lath and plaster ceiling (about 1 in. thick)

⅝-in. thick drywall

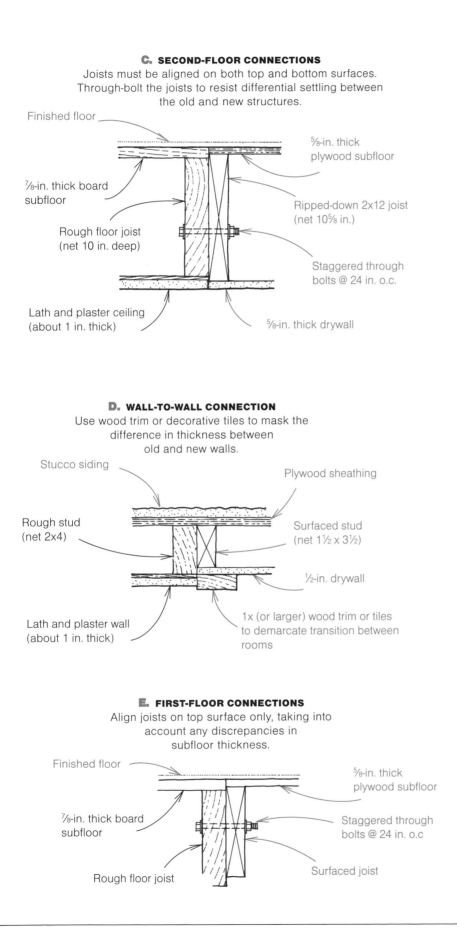

C. SECOND-FLOOR CONNECTIONS

Joists must be aligned on both top and bottom surfaces. Through-bolt the joists to resist differential settling between the old and new structures.

Finished floor

7/8-in. thick board subfloor

Rough floor joist (net 10 in. deep)

Lath and plaster ceiling (about 1 in. thick)

5/8-in. thick plywood subfloor

Ripped-down 2x12 joist (net 10 5/8 in.)

Staggered through bolts @ 24 in. o.c.

5/8-in. thick drywall

D. WALL-TO-WALL CONNECTION

Use wood trim or decorative tiles to mask the difference in thickness between old and new walls.

Stucco siding

Rough stud (net 2x4)

Lath and plaster wall (about 1 in. thick)

Plywood sheathing

Surfaced stud (net 1 1/2 x 3 1/2)

1/2-in. drywall

1x (or larger) wood trim or tiles to demarcate transition between rooms

E. FIRST-FLOOR CONNECTIONS

Align joists on top surface only, taking into account any discrepancies in subfloor thickness.

Finished floor

7/8-in. thick board subfloor

Rough floor joist

5/8-in. thick plywood subfloor

Staggered through bolts @ 24 in. o.c

Surfaced joist

epoxy and resin mix. The capsules are placed in the hole, and the rebar is driven in with a hammer, crushing the glass and mixing the epoxy and resin. For positive mixing, turn the bar with a pipe wrench as many times as is specified in the epoxy manufacturer's instructions.

Underpinning the connection

Because of varying loads and soil conditions, the addition is likely to settle at a different rate from the house. One way to help compensate for differential settling is to underpin part of the old foundation with an extended piece of the new one, so that they act together.

Extend the new foundation trench beneath the existing footing, usually for about 2 ft., depending on the engineer's specifications. (Don't extend the trench too far because the load on the cantilevered foundation might crack it.) Use rebar to tie the extended concrete pad to the main foundation (see the drawing on p. 235).

Connecting new and old frames

Because of the ease of building with the platform-framing system, the builder of an addition to a balloon-framed house should convert to platform framing for the addition. Converting to platform framing is relatively easy for a second story. Once the spacers that clear the first-story ceiling joists are in place, the platform and walls can be built as they are in new construction. The plywood sheathing spans the joint between the old and new frames, and is usually sufficient to tie the structure together, though additional metal ties may be necessary (see Chapter 8).

Attaching a room addition to a balloon or an older platform frame can be more problematic, however (see the drawings on pp. 236-237). Because of the dimensional differences between old and new lumber, the joists and studs must be aligned carefully so that the existing and original walls, ceilings and floors are in the same plane. Perfectly matching the walls or floors, however, is too costly in most cases since it would require the installation of a furring strip on each stud, ripping down oversized wood, or some other labor-intensive, wasteful technique.

One way to design around the problem is to avoid lining up the new and old walls by having the wall jog in or out at the transition to the addition. There may not be enough space on the lot to jog outward, however, and jogging inward can constrict the addition. Alternatively, the transition can be given a special interior treatment like pilasters and a low header, a built-up arch or even tiles that are approximately as thick as the difference between the walls. Exterior treatments can include installing solid-wood stops for stucco or shingles.

Transitions at the first-floor frame over a crawl space or undeveloped basement are easier because the bottoms of the new and old joists, which seldom have the same depth, need not align. The transition should be shown in detail on the working drawings, however, since there are numerous opportunities for mistakes when matching the new plywood subfloor, usually ⅝ in. thick, with the existing ¾-in. or ⅞-in. board subfloor, and then matching the new flooring to the old.

Second-floor transitions are more difficult because both the floors and ceilings must be aligned and the joists are often different sizes. One trick is to drop a header over the entry to the new space, making a clean break between the new and old ceilings and allowing them to be different heights. If the ceiling between the two spaces must be continuous, it might be possible to use thicker second-story subflooring, first-floor ceiling drywall, or both, to compensate for small differences in joist size.

When this is not possible, the best solution is to buy joists deeper than needed and rip them down to match the existing joists—for example, use new, ripped down 2x12s to match existing rough 2x10s. Shimming entire floor frames should not be undertaken since it is time-consuming and potentially inaccurate and unstable.

Ceiling joists can be fudged at their tops, and rafters in attics do not need to align precisely at their bottoms. Vaulted ceilings with exposed soffits do need precise alignment, however, and should be treated like second-story floor frames.

Waterproofing and roof alignment

Waterproofing at the transition between the existing building and the addition is critical since even small leaks can eventually cause structural problems. A few common-sense measures are given here, but the real secret to waterproofing is to understand that water—which can find its way into the tiniest of holes and even be absorbed upward beneath the flashing—must be kept moving, down and away from the building.

New roofs to old buildings A new roof may join the building by abutting the wall or the existing roof.

If roofs are connected at the same level, in most cases it is best to recover both roofs, since it is very difficult to make a waterproof seam between the new and existing roof coverings. Seek the advice of a professional roofer before choosing this design.

Waterproofing is easier when the new roof butts into an existing wall. The connection between the roof and the wall must be flashed, with the flashing extending under the siding to ensure a waterproof joint (see the drawings on the facing page). It is not good enough to bend some flashing up onto the siding and caulk it or paste it up with roofing tar. It will leak in the not very distant future.

Connecting a roof to a wood-sided or wood-shingled wall is fairly easy. The siding is removed or cut back, and the flashing is installed and covered again. Removing and replacing stucco, however, is time-consuming. A good trick is to cut an upwardly angled slot in the siding with a circular saw fitted with a carborundum blade. The flashing can then be slipped into the slot and caulked, without the need to tear up the siding.

If the option exists, the designer should set one roof below the extended eave of the other. This way, the joint will be somewhat protected from the weather. (But make sure to leave enough room to apply shingles and flashing.)

SPECIALISTS AND TEAMWORK

There are more exceptions than rules to the remodeling aspects of building an addition. The best means of shimming walls, matching plaster and paint, applying moldings, repairing salvageable windows, and moving or bypassing wires changes from project to project and as our collective knowledge of building techniques grows. Each year dozens, if not hundreds, of new products and tools are introduced, and even the best-informed builder cannot keep track of them all.

There is a temptation for the general builder to tackle everything from foundation forms to faux finishes. This way of working is, in fact, highly inefficient. It requires the builder to own an amazing variety of tools and master enough skills for several lifetimes. The principal skill needed to guide a project to successful completion, however, is often overlooked in a builder's training. It is the skill of leading the construction team.

To lead the team successfully requires an overview of the many steps needed to build an addition—provided in part by this book and in part by experience—as well as the judgment to know when to delegate responsibilities and the communication skills to make sure that everyone has the information to do his or her job correctly.

In the final analysis, it is neither the ability to draw or design, measure boards or operate machinery but the ability to communicate that is the most important skill in the designer or builder's repertoire. Speaking to, listening to and reaching a clear understanding with everyone from the owners to the structural engineer to the ditch digger is the ultimate key to success in designing and building an addition.

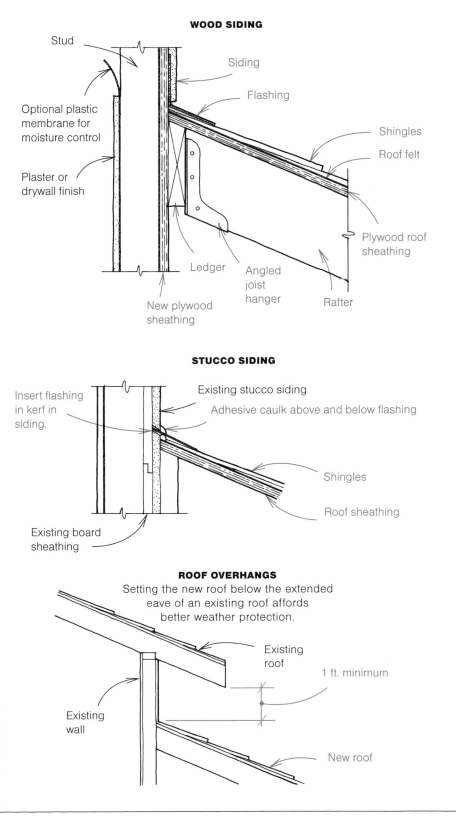

CONNECTING ROOFS TO WALLS

The joint at the connection between a roof and a wall must be flashed; the flashing must go underneath the siding, not on top of it.

WOOD SIDING

Stud

Siding

Flashing

Optional plastic membrane for moisture control

Shingles

Roof felt

Plaster or drywall finish

Plywood roof sheathing

Ledger

Angled joist hanger

Rafter

New plywood sheathing

STUCCO SIDING

Insert flashing in kerf in siding.

Existing stucco siding

Adhesive caulk above and below flashing

Shingles

Roof sheathing

Existing board sheathing

ROOF OVERHANGS
Setting the new roof below the extended eave of an existing roof affords better weather protection.

Existing roof

1 ft. minimum

Existing wall

New roof

APPENDIX I
EXISTING CONDITIONS CHECKLIST FOR REMODELING AND ADDITION PROJECTS

The following checklist was developed for evaluating the existing site and building for feasibility assessment and preliminary design. It is intended to serve both as a written record of the site inspection and as a reminder of the many items and issues that must be accounted for when assessing a project's feasibility. The background material needed to understand the list is covered in chapters 6 through 10.

While most of the list focuses on the physical condition of the site and building, the first part covers wider issues that affect all the sites in the area, such as zoning and the local climate. Some of the first items should be filled in even before the designer reaches the site, so that time is not wasted evaluating projects that are not feasible because of zoning restrictions or other reasons.

For the most part, the remainder of the list is concerned with physical rather than aesthetic aspects of design—for example, the condition of the windows rather than their style or the amount of light they let in. A checklist of architectural features and other design parameters can be found in Appendix III (Master Design-Parameters Checklist) on pp. 251-253.

Existing Conditions Checklist for Remodeling and Addition Projects

Project title

_____

Address

_____

Evaluation by _____ Date ___ / ___ / ___

1. DESCRIPTION OF PROPOSED PROJECT

a. Type of project _____

b. Number of rooms/spaces to be modified or added _____

c. Total square footage _____

   Square footage of special spaces (kitchen, etc.) _____

d. Probable addition type:

   Room addition _____

   Second story _____

   Combination _____

e. Notes or comments _____

2. PLANNING AND ZONING ISSUES

a. Zone type (R-1, etc.) _____

b. Proposed use OK? _____

c. Design-envelope requirements:

   1. Setbacks: Front _____ Sides _____ Rear _____ Other _____

   2. Height restrictions (and method of determining height) _____

   _____

   3. Allowed lot coverage (%) _____

   4. Does existing building conform? _____

   5. Means of measurement (to fence or walk, survey, etc.) _____

   6. Other _____

d. Design-review requirements? _____

e. Building moratoriums? _____

f. Other _____

3. BUILDING CODE ISSUES

a. Applicable codes: UBC _____ Other ICBO codes _____ NEC _____

   Special state or federal regulations _____ Local or other codes _____

b. Existing code violations or obviously unsafe conditions? _____

4. REGION AND LOCAL AREA

a. Regional type (mountain, coastline, etc.) _____

b. Special regional or historical design requirements _____

c. Regional hazards and conditions:

   Hurricanes, tornadoes _____

   Flooding from rain _____

   Drifting snow storms _____

   Earthquake hazard _____

   Fires (in UWIZ) _____

   Other _____

d. Local area hazards and conditions:

   Flood zone _____

   Landslide zone _____

   Special seismic studies or liquefaction zone _____

   Environmental studies _____

   Fire vulnerability _____

   Other _____

5. CLIMATE

a. Area climate: Subtropical _____ Desert _____ Cool or hot arid _____

   Lowland temperate _____ Alpine temperate _____ Coastal (fog) _____

   Subarctic _____ Other _____

b. Microclimate: North slope _____ South slope _____ Other sun, wind or

   local climate conditions _____

c. Ground heave from frost? _____ Excessive rain? _____

   Snow load? _____ Other? _____

d. Existing building appropriate for climate? _____

6. SITE CONDITIONS

a. Description:

   Slope: Steep _____ Medium _____ Slight _____ Flat _____

   Retaining walls _____

   Vegetation _____

   Notes _____

b. Soil problems:

   Uncompacted soil: Naturally loose soil _____ Landfill _____

   Sumps, leach fields, old wells _____ Other _____

   Landslide evidence: Cracks in walks, drives, foundation or building ___

   Failing retaining walls _____ Top or bottom of steep hill _____

   Other _____

   Expansive soil _____

   Other _____

c. Drainage problems:

   Site erosion _____

   Standing water or dried ponds _____

   Foundation cracks or efflorescence _____

   Cracked mud in crawl space _____

d. Special site problems:

   Underground oil tanks _____ Other conditions _____

7. DRAINAGE SYSTEM

a. Site drainage _____

b. Foundation drainage _____

c. Gutters and leaders _____

d. Sump pump and pipes _____

e. Other _____

8. FOUNDATIONS

a. Approximate age _____

b. Type:

   Piers: Wood _____ Masonry _____ Concrete _____

   Continuous perimeter: Brick or stone _____ Concrete (battered or

   inverted-T) _____

c. Dimensions (inches):

   Stem wall _____ (w) _____ (h)

   Footing _____ (w) _____ (h) _____ (depth below grade) _____

d. Reinforced? _____

e. Problems: Crumbling _____ Cracks _____ Rotation _____ Other _____

f. Notes _____

9. SUB-AREA

a. Seismic resistance: Anchor bolts _____ Shear wall _____

   Shear clips _____ Other _____

b. Structural pests _____ Termite report? _____

c. Ventilation _____

d. Other conditions _____

10. FRAMING

a. Type: Balloon _____ Platform _____ Other _____

b. Lumber:

   Type: Rough _____ S2E _____ S4S _____

   Net dimensions (inches):

   Studs _____ x _____ Floor joists _____ x _____ Ceiling joists _____ x

   _____ Rafters _____ x _____ Others _____ x _____

c. Condition: Sagging floors _____ Unsupported joists _____

   Tilting walls _____ Sagging rafters _____ Other _____

11. SHEATHING AND SIDING

a. Sheathing:

   Type:

   Board: Horizontal _____ Diagonal _____

   Plywood or OSB _____ (thickness and nailing schedule) _____

   Other _____

   Condition _____

b. Siding:

   Type:

   Board _____ (style: lap, rustic, etc.) _____

   Wood shingle _____

   Stucco _____

   Other _____

   Condition _____

c. Paint or finish:

   Type (note lead hazards) _____

   Color scheme _____

   Condition _____

12. WINDOWS AND DOORS

a. Windows:

   Type: Wood _____ Metal _____ Other _____

   Condition _____

b. Doors: Condition _____

13. ROOF

a. Type: Composition shingle _____ Roll _____ Wood shingle or shake _____

   Slate or tile _____ Other _____

b. Approximate age _____

c. Condition _____

d. Number of layers _____

e. Notes _____

14. PORCHES, DECKS AND STAIRS

a. Type of construction: Wood _____ Concrete _____ Other _____

b. Location (relative to project) _____

c. Condition (dryrot, weak railings, etc.) _____

15. INTERIOR SPACES

a. Living, dining, bedrooms, halls:

   Floors: Type _____ Condition _____

   Walls and ceilings _____

   Doors and windows _____

b. Kitchen:

   Surfaces (floors, etc.) _____

   Cabinets _____

   Fixtures (stove, etc.) _____

   Notes _____

c. Baths:

   Surfaces (floors, etc.) _____

   Tile _____

   Fixtures _____

d. Other _____

16. ATTIC AND INSULATION

a. Attic:

   Framing problems _____

   Ventilation _____

   Piping, duct or electrical problems _____

   Notes _____

b. Insulation:

   Type: Fiberglass batt _____ Blown-in _____ Other _____

   R-value _____

17. ELECTRICAL SYSTEM

a. Service: Wires _____ Volts _____ Amps _____

b. Main panel:

   Breakers _____ Fuses _____ (type) _____

   Main shutoff rating (amps) _____

Number of circuits _____

Notes _____

c. Internal wiring:

Type: Knob and tube _____ 2-wire (ungrounded) Romex _____

3-wire Romex _____ Other _____

d. Subpanel(s):

Fuses _____ Breakers _____

Capacity _____

Location _____

e. Fixtures:

Outlets grounded _____ GFCI _____ Lights working _____

Notes _____

f. Conditions and hazards:

Extension cords _____ Exposed wires _____ Poor connections _____

Overloaded fuses _____ Other _____

18. PLUMBING SYSTEM

a. Water supply:

Public _____ Private _____

Street shutoff _____

b. Main supply pipe:

Type (copper, etc.) _____

Capacity (size) _____

Condition _____

House shutoff _____

c. Secondary supply pipes:

Type (copper, etc.) _____

Capacity (size) _____

Condition _____

d. Drains:

Main drain (size and condition) _____

Secondary drains (size and condition) _____

e. Vents:

Number and capacity _____

Location _____

f. Water heater:

Type (gas, etc.) _____ Age _____

Capacity _____ Condition _____

g. Fixtures (toilets, sinks, etc.):

Number and location _____

Condition _____

h. Notes _____

19. HEATING SYSTEM

a. Heater:

Energy: Gas _____ Oil _____ Electric _____ Other _____

Type: Central _____ (gravity _____ forced air _____) Floor _____

Wall _____ Baseboard _____ Radiant floor _____ Other _____

Number of units and location _____

Capacity (Btus/hr.) _____

Condition _____

Can plenum be modified? _____

Asbestos? _____

b. Notes _____

20. OTHER SYSTEMS AND CONDITIONS

a. Special systems (burglar alarm, etc.):

Type _____

Capacity to serve addition or expand _____

Parts and service available _____

b. Health and safety considerations:

Asbestos in walls, ceilings, siding, etc. _____

Radon or other hazardous materials _____

Safe stairs _____

Adequate fire egress _____

Will addition block egress? _____

Other _____

NOTES:

_____

_____

_____

_____

_____

_____

_____

_____

_____

_____

_____

_____

_____

APPENDIX II
SAMPLE RESIDENTIAL PLAN CHECKLIST

This checklist is used by the plan checkers of the City of Berkeley, California, to make sure that the addition plans contain all the necessary information and conform to all applicable codes and zoning ordinances.

The checklist is made available to designers, builders and the general public. It, or a similar checklist provided by another city or the International Conference of Building Officials (ICBO), can be used as the basis for your own code and ordinance compliance checklist. Study the checklist before drawing the plans, and then refer to it before submitting them to make sure that your plans are complete.

RESIDENTIAL PLAN CORRECTIONS

PROPERTY ADDRESS	PROJECT DESCRIPTION			PLAN CHECK #
ARCH./ENGR./DRAFTSPERSON	ADDRESS			PHONE NUMBER
PROPERTY OWNER	ADDRESS			PHONE NUMBER
APPLICANT	ADDRESS			PHONE NUMBER
RES. & GAR. (ATTACHED/DETACHED)	NO. OF STORIES	FLOOR AREAS	STATED VALUATION	EXP. SOIL Y/N

BEFORE APPROVAL FOR CODE COMPLIANCE OR ISSUANCE OF A BUILDING PERMIT, THE PLANS AND APPLICATION FOR THIS CONSTRUCTION REQUIRE THE INFORMATION, REVISIONS AND CORRECTIONS INDICATED BY THE CIRCLED ITEMS BELOW. THE APPROVAL OF PLANS AND SPECIFICATIONS DOES NOT PERMIT THE VIOLATIONS OF ANY SECTION OF THE BUILDING CODE, OR OTHER COUNTY ORDINANCE OR STATE LAW.

NOTE: Numbers in parentheses refer to code sections of the 1991 editions of the Building Code (B.C.), (T=Table), Plumbing Code (P.C.), Mechanical Code (M.C.) and 1990 Electrical Code (E.C.).

INSTRUCTIONS

A. Corrections with circled item numbers apply to this plan check.

B. To the right of the circled corrections please indicate the sheet number and detail or note number on the plans where the corrections are made. Resubmit marked original set of plans and ( ) corrected sets of plans, calculations and this correction sheet. Separate sheet for response may be used.

APPLICATION

	SQ. FT.	UNIT $	$ VALUE
LIVING			
GARAGE			
DECK			
OTHER			

1. Valuation is low. It should be $_____.
   Correct the application and pay a supplemental check fee of $_____ prior to resubmittal. [304(c)]

2. Separate permit(s) is/are required for accessory building, swimming pool, retaining wall, demolition. [301(a)]

REFERRALS

3. Approval is required by the _____. [303(a)]

4. Fire Department approval is required. [303(a)]

5. A geological report/soil report is required. [2905(c)]

6. Approval from Department of Public Works Engineering Division is required. Incorporate all requirements into plan. [303(a)]

7. Approval from Department of Public Works Traffic Division is required. Incorporate all requirements into plan. [303(a)]

8. Rough grading approval is required before building permit will be issued. [BC 7003A]

ZONING DIVISION

9. Approval from the Zoning Division is required prior to issuance of building permit. [303(a)] Incorporate all requirements into plans.

PLAN/SITE REQUIREMENTS

10. The address of the building and the name and address of the owner(s) and person(s) preparing the plans are required on the first sheet of the plans. [302(b) (d)]

11. A complete plot plan showing:
    Lot dimensions/yard setbacks/street name(s)/north arrow/existing building to remain/distance between buildings/_____ is required. [302(d)]

12. Delete notes and details that do not apply to this project. [302(d)]

13. Indicate detail and section references as to their appropriate location on plan views. [302(d)]

14. Provide existing and proposed contours/spot elevations to indicate general site slope and drainage pattern. [302(d)]

15. Grading permit may be/is required. (Plans and permit for grading may be processed and issued separately from and prior to this building permit.) [302(a)] A grading permit is required for the following:
    a. All cuts exceeding three (3) feet in depth except footings, basements and retaining walls.
    b. All fills:
       1. Intended to support structures not included in this building permit.
       2. That obstruct or divert a natural drainage course.
       3. On natural slopes exceeding 5:1 (H:V).
       4. Whose depth exceeds three (3) feet at its deepest point and when under the supervision of a licensed soils engineer or geologist.
    See also item No. 5. [302(b) & 7003(a) and (b) Appendix]

16. Specify finish floor elevation of first floor. [302(d)]

FIRE ZONE REQUIREMENTS

17. The following are required for buildings located in Fire Zone 2. [Berkeley Building Code 1603]

    a. Roofs shall be "Fire Retardant" Class A minimum. Provide a complete description of roofing assembly.

    b. Exterior siding shall be as for any exterior portion of a one-hour rated wall assembly.

    c. Decks, balconies and exterior stairs located on a slope of 15% or greater shall be constructed of heavy timber, one-hour or non-combustible construction.

    d. Spark arresters shall be provided on all chimneys.

    e. Overhangs extending more than 10 in. from exterior walls should be of one-hour fire resistive or of heavy timber construction.

    f. Vents are prohibited on any side of structure facing a slope down and away from the structure. Eave vents shall not be continuous strip and shall have features to inhibit intrusion of fire.

18. A minimum of a Class C roofing assembly is required unless in hillside district where Class A roofing assembly is required.

BUILDING SITING

19. Walls closer than three (3) feet to property lines shall be of one-hour fire-rated construction, have no openings, and shall have 30 in. parapets when the building floor area exceeds 1,000 square feet on any floor. [504(b), T 5-A and 1710(a)]

20. Detached garage/carport walls less than three (3) feet from property line shall have one-hour exterior protection with no openings. [504(b) & T 5-A]

21. Buildings adjacent to ascending or descending slopes shall be set back according to the requirements of 2907(d) & 7011.

22. Projections including eaves, roof overhangs, balconies, decks, etc., shall be of one-hour fire resistive construction, heavy timber or of non-combustible material if they project into the three (3) foot setback area from the property line. [1711] No projections allowed within two (2) feet of the property line. [504(b)]

23. Eaves over required windows shall be not less than thirty (30) in. from the side and rear property lines. [504(a) & 1711]

24. Exterior stairways are not permitted closer than three (3) feet to property line. [3306(m)]

ROOF COVER

25. For roof covering specify:

    a. Manufacturer and type of built-up roofing assembly.

    b. Roof slope(s) of all areas on the roof plan.

    c. Type/manufacturer and ICBO/UL number of shingle/tile roof. [302(c)(d)]

26. Roof slope is not adequate for _____ type of roof cover specified. [3203 & T 32-B]

27. The minimum slope for a built-up roof with gravel surfacing and type III asphalt is 1/2 in. per foot. [3203 & T 32-G]

28. Show size/locations of the roof/deck drains and overflows on plans. [3207]

29. Specify minimum 1/4 in. per foot slope for drainage or design to support accumulated water. [2305(f), 3207(a) & 2511 (d)6]

30. Specify approved weatherproof walking surface material at decks and balconies. [2516(c)11]

DESIGN REQUIREMENTS

31. Provide complete floor plans, including existing. Designate existing and proposed use of all rooms on plans.

32. Walls and floors separating dwelling units within the building shall not be of less than 1-hour fire-resistive construction. [1202(b)] Provide a reference detail for the 1-hour wall and floor/ceiling assembly. Note all the particulars of the assemblies.

32A. Specify sound insulation with an STC rating of at least 50. [3501(a)]

33. Habitable rooms other than kitchens shall contain at least 70 sq. ft. floor area. [1207(b)] Appears to be deficient in _____.

34. No habitable room (other than a kitchen) shall be less than seven (7) feet in any dimension. [1207(c)]

35. Show on plans that ceiling height for habitable rooms is a minimum of seven (7) feet six (6) inches. [1207(a)]

36. Show on plans that ceiling height for laundry rooms, hallways, corridors and bathrooms is a minimum of seven (7) feet. [1207(a)]

37. Verify that new addition does not block natural light, ventilation and egress of adjoining habitable rooms. [1204 & 1205]

38. Window areas of habitable rooms shall be at least 1/10 of the room floor area with a minimum of ten (10) square feet. Appears to be deficient in _____. [1205(b)]

39. At least 1/2 of the common wall between _____ shall be open and have an unobstructed opening area of not less than 25 sq. ft. or 1/10 of the floor area of the interior room, whichever is greater, if light and ventilation are being supplied from an adjacent room. [1205(a)]

40. Porch over required windows at _____ shall have a minimum clear height of seven (7) feet with longer side at least 65% open and unobstructed. [1205(a)ex.1]

41. Openable window area of habitable rooms shall be 1/20 of the room floor area with a minimum of five (5) square feet. [1205(c)]

42. In lieu of openable windows for habitable rooms, a mechanical ventilating system capable of providing two (2) air changes per hour (with 1/5 of air supply from the outside) shall be provided. Show size of unit and location of registers. [1205(c)]

43. In bathrooms, laundry rooms, water closet compartments and similar nonhabitable rooms, 1/20 of room floor area is required to be openable with a minimum of 1.5 square feet. Appears to be deficient in

    _____.

44. Provide mechanical ventilation capable of providing five (5) air changes per hour in bathrooms, water closet compartments, laundry rooms and similar rooms if required openable windows are not provided. (Ductless fans are not acceptable in rooms containing tubs or showers.) [1205(c)]

45. Dimension on the plans the thirty (30) in. clear width for water closet compartment and 24 in. clearance in front of water closet for _____ bathroom. [511(a)]

46. Wall covering shall be cement plaster, tile or approved equal to a

height of 70 in. above drain at showers or tub with showers. Materials other than structural elements to be moisture resistant. Glass enclosure doors and panels shall be labeled Category II. Swing door outward. Net area of shower receptor shall be not less than 1,024 sq. in. of floor area, and encompass 30 in. diameter circle. [510(b), 5406(a), 5407, Std. T-54 & UPC 909]

47. In _____ bedroom, provide one openable escape window meeting all of the following: a net clear openable area of not less than 5.7 sq. ft., a minimum clear 24 in. height and 20 in. clear width, and a sill height not over 44 in. above the floor. [1204]

48. Show location(s) of smoke detector(s) in each sleeping room, at a point centrally located in the corridor or area giving access to each sleeping area, in close proximity to the stairway on the upper level, on each story and in the basement. Detectors shall sound an alarm audible in all sleeping areas of the dwelling unit. [1210(a)] In new construction required smoke detector(s) shall be hard wired to 110V with a battery backup.

49. Show location of 22x30 in. attic access with 30 in. minimum headroom. [3205(a)]

50. Provide full height cross section through _____ showing framing, interior/exterior sheathing, plate heights, insulation, foundation, finish grade, etc. [302(d)]

51. Show how dwelling is provided with comfort heating facilities capable of maintaining a room temperature of 70°F at a point three (3) feet above the floor in all habitable rooms. [1212]

52. Specify locations of all doors and windows requiring safety glazing.

EXITS AND STAIRS

53. One exit door shall be not less than 3 ft. wide and 6 ft. 8 in. in height so mounted that the clear width of exitway is not less than 32 in. [3304(f)]

54. Landings at doors shall have a length measured in the direction of travel of not less than 36 in. [3304(j)]

55. A door may swing over landing that is not more than 1 in. below threshold. [3304(i)]

56. Occupants on floors above the second story shall have access to two separate exits. (Exception: floor or occupied roof area less than 500 sq. ft. may have one exit). [3303(a)]

57. Provide section and details of interior/exterior stairway showing:
    a. Maximum rise of 8 in. and minimum run (tread) of 9 in. [3306(c) ex.1]
    b. Minimum width of 36 in. [3306(b)]
    c. Minimum headroom of 6 ft. 8 in. [3306(o)]
    d. framing (stringer) size, bracing, connections, footings.
    e. Enclosed usable space under stairway requires one-hour construction on enclosed side. [3306(m)]

58. Delete diagonal riser at landing unless width of run at narrow end is at least 6 in. [3306(d)]

59. Spiral stairway shall not serve as required exit for area exceeding 400 sq. ft. [3306(f)]

60. Submit shop drawings for spiral stairway showing compliance. [3306(f)]

61. Provide spiral stairway column base connection/footing detail. [302(d)]

62. Provide connection detail of handrail on open side of stair adequate to support a load of 200 lb. applied in any direction at any point on the rail. [2308(a), T 23-B footnote 10, 3306(i.1)2G.1 CCR]

62A. Provide guardrail construction detail capable of resisting a 20 plf load applied perpendicular to the top of the rail. [2308(a), T 23-B]

63. Handrails shall satisfy the following:
    a. Provide continuous handrail for stairways with 4 or more risers. [3306(i)ex.3]
    b. The top of handrails shall be 34 to 38 in. above the nosing of treads and landings. [3606(i)]
    c. Intermediate balusters on open side(s) shall be spaced so that a sphere 4 in. in diameter cannot pass through. [1712(a)]
    d. Return handrail to newel post or wall. [3306(i)]
    e. Handgrip surface 1-1/2 in. to 2 in. in cross section, smooth, 1-1/2 in. clearance from the wall.

64. Provide 36 in. min. high protective guardrail for decks, porches, balconies, raised floors (more than 30 in. above grade or floor below) and open side(s) of stairs and landings. Openings between balusters/rails shall be such that a sphere 4 in. in diameter cannot pass through. [1712(a)]

VENTILATION

65. Show on plans attic ventilation type, size and location. The required ventilation area ratio is 1/150 of attic area or 1/300 of attic area if at least 1/2 of the vent area is provided by ventilators located in the upper portion of the space to be ventilated at least 3 ft. above eave vents with balance of the required ventilation provided by eave or cornice vents. Openings to have 1/4 in. corrosion-resistant metal mesh covering. [3205(c)]

66. Show underfloor ventilation opening size and locations equal to 1 sq. ft. for each 150 sq. ft. of underfloor area. Openings shall be as close to corners as practical and shall provide cross ventilation along the length of at least two opposite sides. Openings shall have at least 1/4 in. corrosion-resistant metal mesh covering. [2516(c)6]

67. Provide and detail 2 in. air space between wood-framed wall and planter box. Exterior wall sheathing shall extend down to sill. Flash top of air space. [2516(c)7]

GARAGE AND CARPORT

68. The following are required for attached garage/carport:
    a. Specify make-up of one-hour fire-resistive construction on the garage side for walls, ceilings, posts and beams of garage adjacent to or supporting the dwelling. [503(d) & T 5-B] (Does not apply to one-story carport.)
    b. Self-closing, tight-fitting, solid-wood 1-3/8 in. thick door at openings to dwelling. [503(d)ex.3]
    c. Delete openings from garage into room used for sleeping. [1104]
    d. Door may swing into the garage if floor or landing in the garage is not more than 1 in. lower than the door threshold. [3304(i)]
    e. A 3-1/2 in. concrete or asphalt floor. [1105 & 2623]
    f. A garage/carport floor system adequate to support a wheel load of 2000 lb. [2304(c)]

VENEER/FIREPLACE

69. Specify/detail masonry veneer material, thickness, backing, anchorage, footings and support over openings. [Chapter 30]

70. For fireplace/chimney specify the following:

    a. Chimney shall extend 2 ft. above roof/wall within 10 ft. [3703(c) & T 37-B]

    b. Anchor chimney to floor and roof/ceiling joists and reinforce masonry chimney. [3704(c)]

    c. Spark arrester required in Fire Zone 4. [3703(h)]

    d. Hearth extension beyond opening.

71. For factory built metal fireplace specify:

    a. Manufacturer, model and ICBO/UL number. [3705(a)]

    b. Installation and use shall be in accordance with their listing. [3705(a)]

CONSTRUCTION MATERIALS

72. Specify grade and species of framing lumber, treated mudsills, type and grade of plywood, design strength of concrete and glued-laminated timber, ASTM designation of structural steel shapes and masonry units, mix of mortar and grout. [302(d)]

FRAMING

ROOF/CEILING:

73. Provide roof framing plan, specify the size, spacing and direction of rafters. [302(c)] For plywood roof diaphragm, specify thickness, grade, panel span rating, nailing schedule, panel layout pattern.

74. The _____ x _____ rafters at _____ o.c. over _____ exceed the allowable span for _____ grade. [T 25-U-R]

75. Ridge boards and valley and hip members shall be not less in depth than the cut end of the rafter. It shall be designed as a vertical load-bearing member when roof slope is less than 3 in. in 12 in. [2517(h) 1 & 3]

76. Roof purlins shall not be smaller than the rafters they support. The max. span for 2x4/2x6 in. roof purlin(s) is 4/6 ft., but in no case shall the purlin be smaller than the supported rafter. For purlin supports, provide struts not smaller than 2x4 in. with an unbraced length not over 8 ft. and not flatter than 45° from the horizontal to bearing walls or partitions. [2517(h)6]

77. Provide designed ridge beams (4x min.) for open beam vaulted ceilings when ceiling joists or rafter ties are not provided. [2517(h)]

78. Provide manufactured roof truss profiles (wet signed by engineer, layout plan and calculations from truss manufacturer. [302(d)]

79. Provide ceiling framing plan showing ceiling joist size, spacing, direction and span on plans. [302(d)]

80. The _____ x _____ ceiling joists at _____ o.c. over _____ exceed the allowable span for _____ grade. [T 25 U-J-6]

81. Rafter ties spaced 4 ft. max. on centers are required immediately above ceiling joists which are not parallel to the rafters. [2517(h)5]

82. Show blocking at ends of rafters and trusses at exterior walls, and at supports of floor joists. [2517(d)3 & 2517(h)7]

83. Show draft separation for attic areas between units in a duplex. 2516(f)4, ii]

WALLS:

84. Specify the header size at door, window and other openings over 4 ft. wide in bearing walls. [2517(g)5]

85. The _____ x _____ header at _____ exceeds the allowable span for _____ grade.

86. Detail required for header support at the corner window(s) _____. [302(d)]

87. Studs in bearing walls are limited to 10 ft. in height unless an approved design is submitted. [2517(g)1]

88. Note or detail lateral support for the top of interior non-bearing walls when manufactured trusses are used. [2517(g)2]

89. Studs supporting two floors, roof and ceiling shall be 3x4 or 2x6 at 16 in. on center. [2517(g) T 25-R-3]

90. Note the use of full-length studs (balloon framing) on exterior walls of rooms with vaulted ceiling. [2517(g)]

91. Bracing of exterior/main interior walls shall conform with methods and locations as specified. [2517(g)3]

FLOORS:

92. Provide floor framing plan showing size, spacing and direction of floor joists. [302(c)]

93. Doubled joists are required under parallel bearing partitions. [2517(d)5]

94. The _____ x _____ floor joists at _____ on center over _____ _____ exceed the allowable span for _____ grade. [T 25-U-J-1]

95. The _____ x _____ floor girder/beam under _____ exceeds the allowable span for _____ grade. [2517(c)]

96. For plywood floor diaphragm, specify thickness, grade, T&G edges, panel span rating, nailing schedule and panel layout pattern. [302(d)]

97. Bearing partitions, perpendicular to joists, shall not be offset from supporting girders, beams, walls or partitions more than the depth of the joists. [2517(d)5]

FOUNDATION

98. The foundation plan does not comply with the soil report recommendation for this project. Please review the report and modify design, notes and details as required to show compliance with _____. [2904(b)]

99. The soils report requires foundation excavations to be reviewed by soils engineer. Note on the foundation plan (prior to requesting a Building Division foundation inspection, the soils engineer shall inspect and approve the foundation excavations). [2905(a)]

100. Soil bearing pressure is limited to 1000 lb. per sq. ft. unless soils report recommends otherwise. [2906 & T-29-B]

101. Call out minimum thickness of 3-1/2 in. thick concrete (floor slab on grade), reinforcement and moisture barrier, if any, on foundation plan. [2623 & 2902]

102. Call out foundation bolt size and spacing on foundation plan. [2907(f)]

103. Specify size, spacing, ICBO number and manufacturer of power-driven pins. (Not permitted on perimeter footings). [306(l)]

104. If required by structural calculations, show size, location and embedment length of hold-down anchors on foundation plan. [3212-f] Note

on plan that hold-down hardware shall be secured in place prior to foundation inspection. [2303(a)]

105. Detail (and reference location on foundation plan) typical foundation sections for: perimeter walls, interior beating walls, depressed slabs, foundation common to dwelling and garage, garage entrance, spread and/or post pads. [302(d)]

106. Foundation sections (12 in., 15 in., 18 in.) wide, (6 in., 8 in., 10 in.) thick, and (12 in., 18 in., 24 in.) depth below natural grade surface or certified fill grade are required. [T 29-A]

107. Provide detail for stepped footings when slope of top and/or bottom of footing exceeds one in ten. [2907(c)]

108. Show minimum 18 in. clearance from grade to bottom of floor joists and minimum 12 in. clearance to bottom of girders. [2516(c)2]

109. Specify that foundation sills shall be pressure treated, or foundation-grade redwood. [2516(c)3]

110. Foundation cripple walls shall be framed and sheathed per [Sec. 2517(g)4]. Specify stud size if wall is over 4 ft. high.

111. Provide a weep screed for stucco at the foundation plate line a minimum of 4 in. above grade. [4706(e)]

112. Show location of underfloor access crawl hole (18 in. x 24 in.). [2516(c)2]

STRUCTURAL

113. Light frame construction of unusual shape, size or split-level shall be designed to resist lateral forces. Submit design for lateral forces. [2517(a)]

114. Exterior/interior walls shall be effectively braced using one of the methods provided in section 2517(g) and table 25-V, or provide an engineered bracing system with supporting structural calculations. [302(b)]

115. Framing using structural steel shapes, reinforced concrete (except conventional footings and slab on grade), structural masonry, etc., require the plans and calculations to be signed and sealed by architect or civil/structural engineer. [302(b)]

116. Cross-reference all calculations for joists, beams, shear walls, etc., to framing/floor plans. [302(d)]

117. The _____ is inadequate to resist lateral forces/uplift wind pressure. Show roof/floor diaphragm nailing, wall bracing, shear connections, tie down hardware and hold-down anchors. Submit lateral design. [2337(a)]

118. Submit structural calculations/design details for _____ _____. [302(d)]

119. Detail the shear transit connections which transfer lateral forces from horizontal diaphragms through intermediate elements and shear walls to the foundation. [302(d)]

120. Specify on the framing plans the shear wall material, thickness, size and spacing of fasteners and sole plate nailing. Call out anchor bolt spacing on foundation plan. [302(d)]

121. Detail how the interior shear walls are connected to the roof diaphragm. [302(d)]

122. Provide drag strut at _____. Detail the strut and top plate connection. [302(d)]

123. Design and details are required for retaining walls over 4 ft. high or with surcharge. Engineer's signature required if wall is surcharged or over 5 ft. high. [301(b)5 & 2308(b)]

MECHANICAL/ELECTRICAL/PLUMBING

124. Show location of forced-air unit/return air grill/water heater on floor plan. [MC 302(c)] Specify source of combustion air for mechanical appliances. [MC 601-607]

125. A circulating air supply opening or duct of 2 sq. in. per 1000 BTU is required for the forced-air furnace(s). Show on plans. [MC 707(a)]

126. Clothes dryer located in an area that is habitable or containing other fuel-burning appliances shall be exhausted to the outside. Exhaust duct length is limited to 14 ft. with 2 elbows. [MC 1903(b)]

127. Show location of the attic furnace and 30x30 in. scuttle on the plans. [MC 708]

128. Show how heat-producing appliances (water heater/dryer/furnace) in garage will be protected from automobile damage (wheel blocks are not sufficient). Elements of appliances which create a glow, spark or flame shall be located a minimum of 18 in. above garage floor. [MC 508]

129. For open-top broiler/barbecue unit, show details of mechanical exhaust system (hood, duct and one-hour shaft), when penetrating ceiling or floor. [MC 1902]

130. Indicate the location and capacity of the electrical service panel.

131. Where the electrical service is located in/on the attached garage and a furred garage wall is the method to run the non-metallic sheathed cables to the residence through the fire wall, provide a detail showing how the penetration will be fire-stopped. [EC 300-21]

132. Specify the locations of all electrical switches, receptacles and lighting fixtures on the plans and identify fluorescent and GFI-protected lighting fixtures/receptacles.

ENERGY CONSERVATION

133. Submit two (2) sets of T24 Energy Compliance documents for review. CR-IR & MF-IR forms shall be printed on the plans for future field references. The residence(s) shall conform to the State energy standards. [California Code of Regulation, title 24, Part 6-101]

134. Add Berkeley "Residential Energy Conservation Ordinance" (RECO) measures to plans. [Berkeley City Ordinance 6009-N.S.]

_____
_____
_____
_____
_____

RETURN THIS SHEET AND REVISED PLANS AND SPECIFICATIONS WHEN CORRECTIONS HAVE BEEN MADE

CHECKED BY: PHONE: DATE

RECHECKED BY: PHONE: DATE

APPENDIX III
MASTER DESIGN-
PARAMETERS CHECKLIST

Design parameters consist of program elements, or the requirements and objectives for the design, and design determiners, or the physical, architectural, legal and budgetary factors that influence the design.

This master list can be used to summarize and coordinate all the design-parameter information that must be assembled before the schematic and preliminary design work begins. Information from the book's other lists and questionnaires

covering design parameters—in some cases the entire document—can be used to complete some of the items listed here. (See the discussion under "Design Parameters" on pp. 181-183.)

I. PROGRAM REQUIREMENTS AND OBJECTIVES

A. THE OWNERS' REQUIREMENTS AND OBJECTIVES

  1. Functional requirements:

    a. Type of space(s) needed (eating, sleeping, entertainment, relaxing, work, storage, etc.) _____

    b. Size and number of space(s) needed _____

    c. Special features (wheelchair access, etc.) _____

  2. Architectural and stylistic preferences:

    a. Sources of owners' vision:

      Natural world _____

      Remembered spaces _____

      Buildings _____

      Books, magazines _____

      Composite _____

      Other _____

    b. Design sense:

      Formal or informal _____

      Open or closed spaces _____

      Conservative or progressive _____

      Rigid or flexible _____

      Simple or complex _____

      Other _____

    c. Style and color preferences:

      Particular architectural style (Modern, Post-Modern, Colonial, Ranch, etc.) _____

      Preferred color scheme(s) _____

    d. Compatible with current house? _____

    e. Other _____

  3. Requirements during construction:

    a. Preferred construction schedule _____ Moratorium on special dates, days? _____

    b. Health conditions:

      Dust-free environment _____

      Sleeping hours _____

      Wheelchair access _____

      Other _____

    c. Home-office conditions:

      Quiet hours _____

      Separate phone _____

      Electrical disruption warning for computer user _____

      Other _____

    d. Privacy conditions: Bathroom for workers _____ Other _____

  4. Other information _____

    (Add information from feasibility questionnaire, "Learning about the Owners" [p. 8])

B. THE DESIGNER'S REQUIREMENTS AND OBJECTIVES

  1. Project compatibility:

    a. Does the project fit the designer's:

      Skills _____

      Schedule _____

      Monetary requirements _____

      Sense of aesthetics _____

      Career goals _____ ?

    b. Other compatibility issues _____

  2. Client compatibility:

    a. Good rapport _____ Open, easy exchange of information _____

      Frankness _____ Emotional connection _____

    b. Common vision _____

    c. Other considerations (including elusive feelings and doubts)

      _____

  3. Personal goals for the project:

    a. Design challenges _____

    b. Opportunities to try new ideas _____

    c. Aesthetic and architectural standards _____

    d. Other goals _____

II. DESIGN DETERMINERS

A. GENERIC DESIGN DETERMINERS (requirements that would apply to any building)

  1. Shelter:

    a. Climate control: Energy efficiency _____ Bioregionally appropriate design? _____

    b. Safety: Code compliance _____ Additional safety issues and factors (e.g., smoke detectors, baby monitor, animal control, swimming-pool fence, special hazards) _____

    c. Healthy environment:

      Sanitation _____

      Non-toxic building materials _____

      Noise and pollution control _____

      Natural light _____

      Healthy interior/exterior integration _____

      Interior harmony (balance of contrasting elements like private vs. common spaces, small vs. large paces, bright-active-noisy vs. dim-serene-quiet spaces) _____

      Special considerations _____

    d. Security:

      Fences _____

      Burglar alarm _____

      Securing rear entrances, windows _____

      Other _____

2. Appropriate architecture (see also "Architectural factors" below):
   a. Integration with site, existing building(s) _____
   b. Neighborhood compatibility _____
   c. Sense of hearth and home _____
   d. Other architectural considerations _____
3. Ease of construction:
   a. Appropriate technology _____ Unusual equipment _____
      Unusual methods _____
   b. Accessible materials _____ Special orders _____
      Remote sources _____
   c. Manageable construction logistics _____ (Sensitive) site _____
      Obstacles _____
4. Affordability (see also chart on pp. 14-15 and "Budget factors" below):
   a. Design to meet budget: Appropriate size _____ Quality of construction and finishing details (A, B or C, see Chapter 1) _____
   b. Budget compliance (cost-control methods)
      i. Contract: Fixed bid _____ Cost plus contract _____
         Incentive contract _____
   c. Safety nets
      i. Contract allows deletion of lower priorities if budget is exceeded _____
      ii. Contract includes: Completion bonds _____ Mediation clause _____
      iii. Contract specifies relationship with subcontractors, etc. _____
      iv. Assurance of sufficient funding for project: Existing cash _____ Loan based on equity or other collateral _____ Private money sources _____ Other _____ Backup plan for funding deficit _____

B. PROJECT DESIGN DETERMINERS (characteristics of the particular site and building)
   1. Physical factors (site and soil, structural and subsystem considerations: Add information from Appendix I, "Existing Conditions Checklist"):
   2. Architectural factors:
      a. Space and layout
         i. Problems with current floor/yard plan, window arrangements, etc. (can these be easily corrected or eliminated when building the addition?) _____
         ii. Likely areas for transition to addition _____
         iii. Areas of lot to be used or conserved (priorities) _____

      b. Architecture and style
         i. Analysis of existing style and means of blending with it _____
         _____
         ii. Does the building need: More articulation _____ Brighter colors _____ Surface treatment _____ ?
         iii. Does the building suggest a particular treatment? _____
      c. Coordination of landscaping with addition design _____
      d. Other considerations _____
   3. Legal factors (planning and zoning regulations, building codes, etc.: Add information from Appendix I, "Existing Conditions Checklist"):
   4. Budget factors (see also chart on pp. 14-15):
      a. Method of cost calculation:
         Square footage _____
         Other means _____
         Predicted degree of accuracy _____
      b. Amortized cost/value of project _____ (include terms of loans, etc.) _____
      c. Special considerations _____

NOTES:

_____
_____
_____
_____
_____
_____
_____
_____
_____
_____
_____
_____
_____
_____
_____
_____
_____
_____
_____

APPENDIX IV
SIZING JOISTS AND RAFTERS FROM THE CODE BOOK

The allowable spans for floor joists, ceiling joists and rafters are easily determined by using the span tables found in the Uniform Building Code (UBC) or the abridged "Dwelling Construction under the Uniform Building Code" books.

Designers or builders simply need to know what species and grade of lumber is used for framing in their part of the country. (Just call the local lumber store and find out what they sell as their basic framing lumber and what grades it's available in.)

Then, using Table 25-A in the UBC (1991 edition), look up the lumber by species, find its grade and determine its "modulus of elasticity." (Don't be concerned about the meaning of the term, just the number associated with it.) Douglas fir, for example, is logged in the Pacific Northwest and is the most commonly used framing lumber on the Pacific Coast and in many of the Western states. In Table 25-A, Douglas fir (northern, 2x5 and wider) is assigned four grades:

GRADE	ROUGH TRANSLATION OF GRADE	MODULUS OF ELASTICITY
No. 1 and Appearance	Finished grade (kiln-dried and knot-free). Used for furniture, beams that show, etc.	1.8
No. 2, Dense	Select structural (usually kiln-dried; small, tight knots). In most species will cover greater spans than #2. Can be used for furniture or beams that show (usually stained).	1.7
No. 2	Construction grade (air-dried). Used for framing.	1.7
No. 3	Lower construction grade (green). Used for temporary work, some framing.	1.5

So the modulus of elasticity of northern, 2x5 or wider, #2 Douglas fir is 1.7. With this information, you can determine the correct sizes and spacing of joists for any span.

To size floor joists, for example, turn to Table 25-U-J-1 (UBC, 1991), Allowable Spans for Floor Joists—40 lb. per sq. ft. live load. ("Live load" means the weight of the floor system itself, the "dead load," plus the expected load, or "design load," of people and furnishings that sit on the floor; 40 lb. per sq. ft. is the standard live load for residences.) Look under the modulus

of elasticity heading on the top of the table and find 1.7. If the span happens to be 15 ft. 11 in., look down the 1.7 column and find the number that is equal to or greater than 15 ft. 11 in.

JOIST SIZE	(INCHES) SPACING	MODULUS OF ELASTICITY				
		1.5	1.6	1.7	1.8	1.9
2x8	12.0			14-5		
	16.0			13-1		
	24.0			11-5		
2x10	12.0			18-5		
	16.0			**16-9**		
	24.0			14-7		
2x12	12.0			22-5		
	16.0			20-4		
	24.0			17-9		

This simplified version of the UBC table shows that 2x10 joists installed 16 in. on center will make the span, whereas 2x8s, for example, even spaced as closely as 12 in., will not. In most circumstances, the designer or builder would simply specify "2x10s @ 16 in. o.c."

However, there are times when other allowable spans might serve better. It could be cheaper, for example, to use 2x12s on 24-in. centers. To figure this out, the designer would have to calculate the total amount of wood for both sizes, then price them at the lumber store.

Price may not be the only consideration. A disadvantage of wide, 24-in. spacings is that the plywood subfloors tend to get bouncy. There may also be requirements for extra-stiff floors in a workout room or where pianos or waterbeds might go. (40 lb. live-load floors will handle these loads, but the owners may want stiffer floors.)

So each design will have to be thought through. In most cases, however, the joist size that can make the span at 16 in. on center will be the optimum choice.

Note. The tables shown here are modified versions of the UBC tables, to be used as examples only. For real work, use tables from the applicable current codes.

BIBLIOGRAPHY

ARCHITECTURE AND DESIGN

Ching, Francis D.K. 1979. *Architecture: Form, Space and Order*. New York: Van Nostrand Reinhold. 394 pp.

A masterpiece. Ching explains the basics of architecture using hundreds of drawings of essential concepts, and hundreds more drawings of those concepts put into practice in outstanding homes and buildings from around the world. Articulation of form, defining and organizing spaces, scale, proportion, circulation and ordering principles are clearly explained.

Ching, Francis D.K., and Cassandra Adams. 1991. *Building Construction Illustrated*, 2nd ed. New York: Van Nostrand Reinhold. 400 pp.

An excellent general reference. Ching's unique graphic approach clearly illustrates all the major systems of a building. Also includes sections on site work and materials.

Ching, Francis D.K., and Dale E. Miller. 1983. *Home Renovation*. New York: Van Nostrand Reinhold. 337 pp.

Beginning with planning and design, this information-packed manual explains how to improve existing space, convert unused space and add onto a house through hundreds of drawings and corresponding text.

McAlester, Virginia and Lee. 1984. *A Field Guide to American Houses*. New York: Alfred A. Knopf. 524 pp.

Clearly organized by period, style and detail, this convenient guide identifies hundreds of house types from native American dwellings to those in the "neo-eclectic" style. Useful for the addition designer who wishes to achieve stylistic continuity with the existing house.

Ramsey, Charles George, and Harold Reeve Sleeper. 1994. *Architectural Graphic Standards*, 9th ed. New York: John Wiley and Sons. 918 pp.

This standard design reference is a must for every professional designer. Graphic format provides essential information about ergonomics, dimensions and clearances of furnishings, and every aspect of sitework, solar orientation, climate design and building construction. Earlier editions remain useful.

Roberts, Rex. 1964. *Your Engineered House*. New York: Evans and Co. 237 pp.

Explains the correct location of rooms for climate design, along with some basic engineering, weatherproofing and construction techniques.

Thallon, Rob. 1991. *Graphic Guide to Frame Construction: Details for Builders and Designers*. Newtown, Conn.: The Taunton Press. 225 pp.

Hundreds of detailed drawings of foundations, floors, walls, roofs and stairs fill this no-nonsense, how-to-put-it-together book.

Energy-efficient design

Anderson, Bruce (Ed.). 1990. *Solar Building Architecture*. Cambridge, Mass.: MIT Press. 368 pp.

Collected technical articles address nitty-gritty solar-design issues.

Anderson, Bruce, and Michael Riordan. 1976. *The Solar Home Book: Heating, Cooling and Designing with the Sun*. Harrisville, N.H.: Cheshire Books. 298 pp.

A thorough, readily understandable introduction to designing solar houses and retrofitting existing houses for better solar performance.

Anderson, Bruce, and Malcolm Wells. 1994. *Passive Solar Energy: The Homeowner's Guide to Natural Heating and Cooling*. Amherst, N.H.: Brick House Publishing Co. 168 pp.

Recognized experts in solar design and alternative construction, architects Anderson and Wells pool their knowledge in this readable primer.

Energy-Efficient Houses (Great Houses series). 1993. Newtown, Conn.: The Taunton Press. 158 pp.

Informative case studies from *Fine Homebuilding* magazine (full color).

Watson, Donald, and Kenneth Labs. 1983. *Climatic Design*. New York: McGraw Hill. 280 pp.

Chock-full of design information in an easily understandable, graphic format, this comprehensive volume contains all the principles and practices for designing energy-efficient homes based on local climate.

Wright, David. 1984. *Natural Solar Architecture*, 3rd ed. New York: Van Nostrand Reinhold. 272 pp.

One of America's premier solar-home designers explains how it's done in this colorfully illustrated manual.

Structural engineering

Schwartz, Max. 1993. *Basic Engineering for Builders*. Carlsbad, Calif.: Craftsman Book Co. 383 pp.

An excellent introduction for anyone who wants to understand structural-engineering principles without having to pursue a degree in the subject.

Western Wood Products Association. 1991. *Western Lumber Grading Rules*. Portland, Oreg.: Western Wood Products Assoc. 238 pp. (Also available: supplementary color pamphlets showing lumber grains and finish products.)

Pocket manual with periodic supplements useful for determining lumber strength by grade. Includes information grade marks, moisture content of lumber and glued products.

Wilson, Forest. 1983. *Structure: The Essence of Architecture*. New York: Van Nostrand Reinhold. 128 pp.

This short, popular introduction explains structural considerations in building design to the layperson.

Wilson, Forest, and Henry J. Cowan. 1981. *Structural Systems*. New York: Van Nostrand Reinhold. 256 pp.

A highly readable and entertaining introduction to the principles of structural engineering. Optional mathematical exercises supplement the text.

Earthquakes

Demoscole, Toni. 1995. *Earthquake: Home Safe Home* (video cassette). San Mateo, Calif.: KCSM TV.

To promote public safety, the service organization Rotary International retained structural engineer and teacher Demoscole to produce this seismic retrofitting guide based on his class for home owners at the Building Education Center of Berkeley, Calif. Video shows how to install anchor bolts, shear wall, etc.

Yanev, Peter I. 1991. *Peace of Mind in Earthquake Country*. San Francisco: Chronicle Books. 218 pp.

An excellent introduction to the causes and effects of earthquakes and how to protect houses against them. Useful for the layperson and professional builder alike.

Architectural graphics and drafting

Ching, Francis D.K. 1975. *Architectural Graphics*. New York: Van Nostrand Reinhold. 128 pp.

A good introduction to architectural sketching, drafting, perspective and rendering by a master architectural draftsman. Explains tools, techniques and theory.

Leseau, Paul. 1980. *Graphic Problem Solving for Architects and Designers*, 2nd ed. New York: Van Nostrand Reinhold. 144 pp.

Focuses on using graphic techniques to solve a variety of problems within and outside of architecture. Discusses flow charts and touches on computer graphics.

Leseau, Paul. 1980. *Graphic Thinking for Architects and Designers*. New York: Van Nostrand Reinhold. 211 pp.

Explains drawing basics, the nature of schematics and their use in architectural design. An excellent primer on the tools needed for translating program information into graphic format and, ultimately, successful designs.

Stitt, Fred A. 1990. *Architect's Detail Library*. New York: Van Nostrand Reinhold. 608 pp. (Also available on disk from Guidelines Publications, Orinda, Calif.)

Hundreds of standard construction details with notes and dimensions.

Wakita, Samua A., and Richard, M. Linde. 1984. *The Professional Practice of Architectural Working Drawings*, 2nd student ed. New York: John Wiley and Sons. 649 pp.

More than comprehensive enough for residential and small-scale projects, the student edition of this standard text is a welcome addition to any design library.

GENERAL CONSTRUCTION, RENOVATION, REMODELING

Campbell, Robert, and N.H. Mager. 1965. *How to Work with Tools and Wood*. New York: Pocket Books. 448 pp.

Originally published by Stanley Tool Company, this handy little manual is crammed full of carpentry techniques and hints useful to any builder or remodeler.

Dietz, G.H. 1991. *Dwelling House Construction*, 5th ed. Cambridge, Mass: MIT Press. 440 pp.

A classic in its field, this 1946 architecture text is still in print because it does such an excellent job of explaining the entire process of building a house from the foundations through the roof. Section on framing is particularly useful. Clearly and profusely illustrated.

Fine Homebuilding on Frame Carpentry. 1990. Newtown, Conn.: The Taunton Press. 128 pp.

Reprinted articles from *Fine Homebuilding* magazine full of useful information.

Fine Homebuilding on Remodeling. 1993. Newtown, Conn.: The Taunton Press. 128 pp.

Selected articles from *Fine Homebuilding* magazine reprinted in full color.

Kohl, Leonard. 1991. *Carpentry*, 2nd ed. Homewood, Ill.: American Technical Publishers. 720 pp.

In the opinion of many, the best general text in the field.

Litchfield, Michael W. 1991. *Renovation: A Complete Guide,* 2nd ed. Englewood Cliffs, N.J.: Prentice Hall. 566 pp.

An excellent general survey by the founding editor of *Fine Homebuilding* magazine. Discusses most topics in sufficient detail for practical application. Covers materials and tools as well as renovation techniques.

Love, T.W. 1976. *Construction Manual: Rough Carpentry.* Carlsbad, Calif.: Craftsman Book Co. 285 pp.

An excellent intermediate-level manual. Formulas and tables explain how to size beams, girders and other structural members for preliminary design.

Nash, George. 1992. *Renovating Old Houses.* Newtown, Conn.: The Taunton Press. 344 pp.

The definitive book for renovators who want to bring an old house back to life without destroying its spirit.

Roskind, Robert. 1984. *Building Your Own House.* Berkeley, Calif.: Ten Speed Press. 436 pp.

Step-by-step carpentry procedures for the novice builder. Clear drawings and photos throughout. Particularly useful for building room additions or the post-platform work on second stories.

Layout

Jackson, W.P. 1979. *Building Layouts.* Carlsbad, Calif.: Craftsman Book Co. 238 pp.

Covers basic site and grading layout, foundations, frames, stairs and more.

Foundations

Brown, Robert Wade. 1992. *Foundation Behavior and Repair: Residential and Light Commercial,* 2nd ed. New York: McGraw-Hill. 271 pp.

An excellent, somewhat technical guide to evaluating foundations and the underlying causes of their problems, including soil conditions.

International Conference of Building Officials. 1992. *Concrete Manual,* rev. ed. Whittier, Calif.: ICBO. 352 pp.

This thorough, informative book on the properties and composition of concrete, form work, placement, reinforcement, and so forth is a first-rate introduction to the topic. Used to train building inspectors and other officials.

Plumbing and electrical

Hemp, Peter. 1994. *Installing and Repairing Plumbing Fixtures.* Newtown, Conn.: The Taunton Press. 183 pp.

Covers all standard residential plumbing fixtures and appliances, with a useful section on troubleshooting plumbing problems.

Hemp, Peter. 1994. *Plumbing a House.* Newtown, Conn.: The Taunton Press. 215 pp.

A comprehensive guide to designing, installing and repairing plumbing systems in new construction and remodels.

Massey, Howard C. 1994. *Basic Plumbing with Illustrations*, 2nd ed. Carlsbad, Calif.: Craftsman Book Co. 381 pp.

An excellent reference with all the information needed by the nonspecialist for designing a residential plumbing system.

Richter, H.P., and W.C. Schwan. 1992. *Wiring Simplified,* 37th ed. Minneapolis: Park Publishing. 175 pp.

This classic, based on the National Electrical Code, has guided generations of beginning electricians and builders through the mazes of wiring and codes.

Williams, T. Jeff. 1982. *Basic Wiring Techniques.* San Francisco: Ortho Books. 96 pp.

A good, quick overview of household electrical systems is provided in this well-illustrated manual.

Safety

American National Standards Institute. 1968. *Practice for Occupational and Educational Eye and Face Protection* (ANSI Z87.1-1992). New York.

American National Standards Institute. 1969. *Practices for Respiratory Protection* (ANSI Z88.2-1969). New York.

Occupational Safety and Health Association. 1992. *All about OSHA* (OSHA 2056). Washington, D.C.

Occupational Safety and Health Association. 1992. *Construction Industry Digest* (OSHA 2202). Washington, D.C.

Underground construction

Carmody, John, and Raymond Sterling. 1985. *Earth Sheltered Housing Design,* 2nd ed. New York: Van Nostrand Reinhold. 350 pp.

One of several publications sponsored by the Underground Space Center of the University of Minnesota. Covers siting, energy, structural design and waterproofing, and presents numerous case studies of underground housing. Rich in technical information and construction detail—useful to anyone considering adding a basement.

Wells, Malcolm. 1991. *How to Build an Underground House.* Brewster, Mass.: Malcolm Wells. 96 pp.

Useful information on the design, natural lighting, ventilation, waterproofing and other aspects of underground construction for those who are considering adding a basement.

FEASIBILITY ASSESSMENT

Becker, Norman. 1993. *The Complete Book of Home Inspection,* 2nd ed. Blue Ridge Summit, Pa.: TAB Books (McGraw-Hill). 264 pp.

Useful information for initial feasibility and subsequent detailed assessment of the existing house's structure and subsystems. The author is a mechanical engineer and the founder of the American Society of Home Inspectors.

Liederman, Dan and Paul Hoffman. 1989. *Renovating Your Home for Maximum Profit.* Roseville, Calif.: Prima Publishing. 390 pp.

A thorough discussion of what pays and what doesn't in home renovation—useful for feasibility assessment.

Pearman, Donald V. 1988. *The Termite Report: A Guide for Homeowners and Home Buyers on Structural Pest Control.* Alameda, Calif.: Pear Publishing. 139 pp.

A long-needed and welcome addition to carpentry literature, this easy-to-read book explains structural pests and their control. Essential information for assessing the existing structure.

Estimating

Jackson, W.P. 1987. *Carpentry Estimating.* Carlsbad, Calif.: Craftsman Book Co. 320 pp.

A useful guide to take-off techniques and materials estimating.

Means, R.S. 1995. *Means Square Foot Cost Data.* Kingston, Mass.: R.S. Means Co. 442 pp.

Although the figures must be adjusted to reflect remodeling costs and the local economy, this handy, up-to-date reference for calculating the cost of new construction by the square foot provides valuable feasibility information. Updated annually.

Walker's Remodeling Estimator's Book for the Professional Remodeling Contractor. 1987. Lesie, Ill: Frank R. Walker Co. 334 pp.

Thorough, basic cost-estimating manual for feasibility, design and construction phases of an addition project.

BUILDING CODES

Dwelling Construction under the Uniform Building Code. 1994. Whittier, Calif.: International Conference of Building Officials. 105 pp.

A handy, abbreviated version of the full code book covers residential work only. Essential for efficient design of houses or additions. (An abbreviated version of the Uniform Mechanical Code is also available.)

Hageman, Jack M. 1992. *Contractor's Guide to the Building Code,* 3rd ed. Carlsbad, Calif.: Craftsman Book Co. 526 pp.

Explains the UBC and the reasons behind the requirements.

Kardon, Redwood. 1995. *Code Check: A Field Guide to Building a Safe House.* Newtown, Conn.: The Taunton Press. 32 pp.

Flip-book listing the 600 most common building-code violations.

National Electrical Code. 1993. Quincy, Mass.: National Fire Protection Association. 917 pp.

Standard electrical reference adopted by most municipalities.

Uniform Building Code (3 vols.). 1994. Whittier, Calif.: International Conference of Building Officials.

The most widely adopted model code in the United States. Volume 1 contains administrative, fire- and life-safety and field-inspection provisions; Volume 2 includes structural-engineering design provisions; and Volume 3 contains material, testing and installation standards. (Also available: the Uniform Mechanical Code and Uniform Plumbing Code.)

INDEX

CREDITS

EDITOR PETER CHAPMAN

DESIGNER/LAYOUT ARTIST HENRY ROTH

ILLUSTRATOR VINCE BABAK

PHOTOGRAPHER PHILIP WENZ (*except as noted on p. 263*)

ART ASSISTANTS AMY BERNARD, LYNNE PHILLIPS

TYPEFACE STONE SERIF

PAPER WARREN PATINA, 70 LB., NEUTRAL pH

PRINTER QUEBECOR PRINTING/KINGSPORT, KINGSPORT, TENNESSEE